AF686922

Law of Contract in Uganda

David J. Bakibinga

Fountain Publishers

Fountain Publishers
P.O. Box 488
Kampala

© David J. Bakibinga 2001
First published 2001

All rights reserved. No part of this publication may be reproduced or transmitted, in any form or by any means, electronic, mechanical, photocopying, recording or otherwise or stored in any retrieval system of any nature without the written permission ot the publisher.

ISBN 9970 02 245 8

Cataloguing-in-publication Data

Bakibinga J. David
Law of Contract in Uganda – Kampala: Fountain Publishers, 2001
196 p. 25 cm
Includes index

ISBN 9970 02 245 8
1. Laws – Uganda 2. Company law – Uganda 3. Commercial laws – Uganda
346.02'096761

DEDICATION

To the memory of my maternal grandfather
Dyonansi Ndizairayo

TABLE OF CONTENTS

TABLE OF CASES

C

D

E

F

G

H

I

J

K

L

M

P

R

S

T

U

V

W

Y

Z

TABLE OF STATUTES

UNITED STATES LEGISLATION

OTHER KENYA LEGISLATION

PREFACE

This book is yet another attempt at filling a gap in Ugandan legal literature. While acknowledging pioneering works in this area, it has to be admitted that such works were geared towards a comparative treatment of the East African legal position on the law of contract. They did not focus purely on the Ugandan position. In this respect, therefore, the present work could be said to be unique. Apart from that, the existing literature in this area is dated having been produced about two decades ago. This work updates the legal position and takes into account the peculiar position of Uganda having, by virtue of Judicature Act, 1967, discarded use of "statutes of general application in force in England on 11 August, 1902." This approach has been confirmed by the Supreme Court in *Uganda Motors Ltd. V. Wavah Holdings Ltd.* The obvious implication of having to rely on the common law where there is a statutory *lucanae* in the law poses an enormous challenge to our law courts.

Given the common law origin of our law inevitable reference has been made to cases decided in common law countries particulary from Kenya, Tanzania, Nigeria and the United Kingdom.

The book starts with an introduction which examines the history of contract and law applicable in Uganda. Thereafter the ingredients of forming the contract are considered in the form of offer, acceptance, consideration, contractual intention and capacity. Subsequently is treatment of the form and terms of a contract, an analysis which takes into account developments in England especially in relation to exemption clauses and fundamental breach. Vitiating elements of a contract, namely mistake, misrepresentation, duress, undue influence and illegality are then examined. It should be noted here that the treatment of these factors is more expansive than can be found in existing East African legal literature. Next is an analysis of the concept of privity which is extended to agency and assignment. It is perhaps in relation to the requirements for valid assignment that one is likely to encounter difficulties arising from the exit of English "statutes of application". Reference has, therefore, been made to the U.K. Judicature Act, 1873 by way of comparison and anticipation of the development of the law from a statutory perspective. The last chapters deal with discharge of the contract and remedies for breach of contract.

In preparing this book I have drawn on my experience of teaching the subject and other related subjects of about twenty years. Additionally, a number of persons have assisted in the endeavour. In particular I wish to mention my wife, Florence Tibagonzeka, who typeset the substantive chapters, table of statutes and index; Mrs Florence Kasule who worked on a rather involved table of cases; Ms Joyce Musoke and Godfrey Kyedza both of whom assisted with miscellaneous aspects of production. Finally, I hereby express my appreciation to my wife, daughters, Matama and Babirye and son, Mutekanga who had to put up with long hours of silence, inconvenience and unpredictable moods in the process of gestation of this work.

David J. Bakibinga
Professor of Commercial Law
Makerere University
December 2000

1
INTRODUCTION

The notion of Contract is prevalent mainly in what are termed market economies. This is based on the idea that individuals are free to regulate their rights and duties through mutual agreement. It follows that the principle of freedom of contract is important in market economies and democratic societies as contrasted with totalitarian or ancient societies.

1. Historical development of modern law of contract

(a) Brief examination of contract in ancient docieties

It was observed by Sir Henry Maine[1] that in primitive societies an individual had no right to create for himself rights. If there were such a right then only few rights were created by him. This also applied to duties.

The rules to which an individual was subject stemmed firstly from the station or status into which he was born and secondly from the imperative commands addressed to him by the chief or head of the household to which he belonged. Consequently such a system left very little room for contract.

It is notable that Maine's explanation refers to "contract" as a legal institution in a primitive society. It does not refer to agreement as a social institution. The distinction is important in that while agreement as a social institution was prevalent in ancient societies, "contract" as a legally enforceable agreement was not typical of such societies. In this regard it is rationalized[2] that ancient society was dominated by formalism and fiction. Consequently the only enforceable agreement was a "Contract under seal".

The modern law of contract (which developed much later than that of property), evolved and developed in the Courts after the Norman conquest in Britain. After the Norman conquest, but before the development of the action of *assumpsit* there were two recognized forms of action for enforcing rights: (i) Action of Debt and (ii) Action by writ of Covenant. We shall briefly examine each in turn.

(i) Action of debt

This was available to a plaintiff who alleged that a defendant had promised a sum of money or quantity of goods or chattels. However, in the fourteenth Century debt action was only used for recovery of money while detinue was used for recovery of specific chattels. Debt action was based on the idea that the defendant was wrongfully detaining money which belonged to the plaintiff. Furthermore, it applied to situations where a contractual connection was remote e.g. enforcing repayment of a loan; recovering price of goods supplied; rents from a lease and (feudal) customary dues. Nevertheless three types of debt actions are identifiable. First, the debt on record which was an action for payment of a sum of money ordered to be paid by court as entered in its record. Second debt on obligation which was based on a sealed document. Third, a debt

---

1 Maine, H. *Ancient Law* See also generally Cheshire Fifoot and Furmston's *Law of Contract* (Butterworths' 12th Ed 1991), Chapter 1.

2 Achike, O. *Nigerian Law of Contract* (1981), p.4

contract which was difficult to prove but was proved by trial by battle or compurgation (where the debtor, helped by 12 compurgators or 12 respectable neighbours testified that they believed that the money was not owed.)

(ii) Action on covenant

The action on covenant is traceable to the thirteenth century. It was used in cases involving movables and immovables. The action was based on the fact that an undertaking by a party to be charged had been given or performed in a particular form which the law recognized and protected. The form constituted the contract. Such undertaking was normally evidenced by a seal. However, if the plaintiff's action was for a definite and fixed sum, the proper remedy was an action by debt.

The nature of debt in relation to informal agreements where neither party had fulfilled his undertaking proved unsatisfactory. Consequently, a new action developed.

(b) Development of assumpsit[3]

The action of assumpsit was aimed at enforcing informal promises. It developed from the action on trespass (a tortious remedy.)

The action on trespass was a remedy available to a plaintiff for direct injury to his person or property. Later, this action was used to enforce actions which were not direct or physical. It then became *Trespass on the Case.* At the outset, this action was used to recover damages from the defendant for his wrongful act which had occasioned harm to the plaintiff. Consequently, in the early stages this was an action for MISFEASANCE (wrong) of the defendant though in fact constituting trespass. For instance, if the defendant left a piece of log lying in an unlighted road and the plaintiff's lorry crashed on it, the action was one of case. The defendant was said to be liable for carelessness, but not on any promise. Thus in the *Humber Ferryman Case*, a defendant received the plaintiff's horse and undertook to transport it across the river in his boat. He negligently overloaded the boat, which overturned and the horse drowned. It was held that the defendant, was liable for the value of the horse on ground of carelessness. In a case like this the plaintiff would allege that the defendant received the horse and "undertook" or "assumed" or "promised" to carry it safely. this was the basis of the special action on the case called ASSUMPSIT. In other words, the debtor "undertook" or "promised".

(iii) Nonfeasance

As long as the plaintiff's action rested on wrongful act as distinguished from the defendant's breach of promise "action of case in assumpsit" was not contractual but delictual (tortious). In this regard, the case in the original form was only available for misfeasance i.e. where a promised act had been improperly done and not for non-feasance, i.e. where the defendant had completely failed to act. However later in the sixteenth century, the King's Bench allowed assumpsit to lie for non-feasance. In the same century, the action of assumpsit was extended to cover a situation where debt should have been the proper action. This was based on the reasoning that if a debtor, after incurring debt made a new promise to pay it, action of assumpsit could lie as an alternative to the action on debt. This was known as *Indebitus assumpsit.*

Contrary to the view of the Court of Common Pleas that an assumpsit action could only lie when a debtor made a later promise to pay it, the King's Bench was prepared to extend the action to a situation where a debtor had not made any later promise to pay. Thus in *Slade's Case*[4], Slade instituted assumpsit against a debtor who had assumed and promised to pay him the sum of sixteen pounds being a debt incurred by the defendant for corn and wheat sold by the plaintiff to the latter. There was no later promise to pay the debt apart from the actual bargain itself. The defendant's Counsel contended that the proper action was debt and not assumpsit. It was held

---

[3] Cheshire & Fifoot's *Law of Contract, supra* n.1. pp.4-6.

[4] (1602) 4 Co. Rep.91a, Yelv 21, Moore KB 433,667. See also[1971] Camb. L.J.51.

that although action on debt could be maintained, assumpsit could be opted for by the plaintiff. Second, that every executory contract imports in itself an assumpsit.

(c) Consideration

The concept of consideration appears to have been recognized towards the end of the Sixteenth Century. Basically it meant that where the plaintiff brought an action for assumpsit for misfeasance, it was necessary to show that he had suffered damage (i.e. consideration). If the action was for non-feasance, the plaintiff had to show payment of consideration. However, contracts under seal were not required to be supported by consideration. Their mere form and ceremonies accompanying them ensured enforceability.

2. The Law of contract in Uganda

(a) Received law

The Law of Contract in Uganda is largely based on English principles of the law of contract. Thus Section 3 of the Contract Act[5] provides that "subject to any written law for ;the time being in force, ... the common law of England relating to contracts as modified by:

(a) the doctrines of equity;
(b) the public general statutes in force in England on 11 August 1902
(c) the Acts of Parliament of the United Kingdom mentioned in the Schedule to the Act shall extend and apply to Uganda." This has been modified by the Judicature Statute, 1996 which deleted reference to statutes of general application.[6a]

It has been argued[7] that the reception date of 11th August applies only to the third subheading i.e. referring to English Statutes. This is in turn subject to local circumstances[8].

It follows that when examining the law of contract in Uganda it is necessary to primarily examine English rules of contract and the effects, if any, of modifications of such rules by native law, custom or statute.

Related to the issue of reception date and application of English law is the issue of precedent. Precedent "is a system by which earlier decisions of the Courts are followed in later cases where the facts are similar. Furthermore, a court is only bound to follow an earlier judgment if the decisions came from a higher court or in some cases a Court on the same level"[9]. In Uganda's context, the decisions of the Supreme Court of Uganda and its predecessor Courts of Appeal must be followed by the lower Courts. However, the Supreme Court is itself not bound by its own previous decisions and is, therefore, free to overrule an earlier case if it feels that the earlier decision no longer provides a suitable precedent.

Another aspect which requires examination is the relationship between English precedents and Ugandan law.[10] This is significant in the light of Section 3(3) of the Judicature Act, 1967 which provides thus:

---

5 Cap 75 Laws of Uganda Vol. II

6a S.3 16(2)(b). See also *Uganda Motors Ltd. v. Wavah Holdings Ltd.* Civil Appeal No. 19/91 (Supreme Court).

7 Hodgin, R.W. *Law of contract In East Africa* (1975) p.3

8 Judicature Act No. 11 of 1967, Section 3(3)

9 Sawyer & Hiller, *the Doctrine of Precedent in the Court of Appeal for East Africa* (T.P.H. 1971). See also Hodgin, supra p.4

10 See further Elias, "Colonial Courts and the Doctrine of Judicial Precedent" 18 Mod L.R.356; Allott, "The Authority of English decisions in Colonial Courts (1957) *J.A.L.*23; Allott, *Essays of African Law;* Allott, "Judicial Precedent In Africa Revisited" (1968) *J.A.L.*1; Seidman, "Reception of English Law" 1969 *E.A.L.R.*47.

> The applied law, the common law and the doctrines of equity shall be in force only so far as the circumstances of Uganda and of its peoples permit, and subject to such qualifications as circumstances may render necessary.

Commenting on a similar provision in the Kenyan Order, in Council Denning L. J. (as he then was) thus stated:[11]

> This wise provision should, I think, be liberally construed. It is a recognition that the common law cannot be applied in a foreign land without considerable qualification. Just as with an English Oak so with the Common Law. You cannot transplant it to the African continent and expect it to retain the tough character which it has in England. It will flourish indeed but it needs careful tending. So with the Common Law. It has many principles of manifest justice and good sense which can be applied with advantage to people of every race and colour all the world over: but it has also many refinements, subtleties and technicalities which are not suited to other folk. These offshoots must be cut away. In these far off lands the people must have a law which they understand and which they will respect. The common law cannot fulfil this role except with considerable qualifications. The task of making these qualifications is entrusted to the judges of these lands. It is a great task. I trust that they will not fail therein.

It has been observed[12] that initially the courts, in pursuance of Denning L.J.'s dictum declined to follow the English rules on charters or letters patent preferring a more informal agreement as sufficient. However, subsequently there were few efforts to "adopt a more liberal construction with respect to 'refinements, subtleties and technicalities' of the English Common law." The result was that before Independence the courts tended to feel more tied to English precedents and precedents from the East African Court of Appeal, although subsequently earlier decisions could be departed from on ground that they were given *per incuriam* i.e. in ignorance of an earlier decision or in conflict with an earlier decision.[13]

The inflexibility on following English precedents was relaxed once the Court of Appeal for East Africa became independent. Thus *Bhatt v. Luxmichand*[14], Crabbe J. A. stated:

> ... there is no authority of any Court binding on this Court in view of the present constitutional developments in the former East African Territories over which the Court has jurisdiction.[15]

Furthermore in *Rashid Moledina and Co. (Mombasa) Ltd v. Hoima Ginners Ltd.*[16] Newbold P. thus stated:

> It is clear that this Court is not bound by any English decisions whether given before or after independence. Nevertheless this Court would pay due regard to the decision of any Commonwealth court where a similar system of law to that appertaining in East Africa exists and will, of course, pay special regard to the decisions of the English courts, especially where those decisions enunciate the common law or equity or interpret statutes of general application or statutes which have been substantially copied in East Africa.

11 Nyali v. A-G [1955] 1 All E.R.646

12 Hodgin, *supra* n.7 p.6

13 See *Kiriri Cotton Co. Ltd. v. Dewani* [1958] E.A.239

14 [1964] E.A. 414

15 *ibid.* p.436

16 [1967] E.A.645. See also *Dodhia v. National Grindlays Bank Ltd.* [1970] E.A. 195; *Mayers v. Akira Ranch Ltd.*[1972] E.A. 347.

(b) Customary law

Section 16(2) (b) ii of the Judicature Statute, 1996 provides that the High Court shall exercise its jurisdiction in conformity *inter alia* with "any established and current custom or usage." In Section 17 is indicated that nobody should be deprived of any benefits of any existing custom unless such is repugnant to natural justice, equity and good conscience or is directly or by necessary implication in conflict with any written law.

The import of those provisions is that customary contract law maybe applied subject to the qualifications in terms of repugnancy and compatibility with the written law. It has been argued[17] these qualifications have the effect of "introducing the whole body of English contract law and consequently all customary contract law is therefore 'inconsistent with (a) written law'".

Thus in *Wambwa v. Okumu*,[18] a dispute arose as to the custody of a four year old illegitimate girl. The African Court had applied Bagishu Customary law and custody was awarded to the father on payment by him of cattle valued at Shs.200/= to the other party. Part of the grounds of appeal was the point that the Guardianship of Infants Act[19] allows the Court to be guided by what the Court feels to be in the best interests of the child. In this case, the Court felt that the mother was in the best position to care for a young female child. It was possible to refuse to follow customary law because that law was inconsistent with the Act.[20]

Another illustration is provided by the Nigerian Case, *Labinjoh v. Aboke*[21]. In that case, an 18 year old girl living with her parents was sued for the price of goods sold and delivered to her. In the Lagos Magistrate's Court, she opposed the action arguing that she was protected by the Infants Relief Act (IRA), 1874 of the United Kingdom. The Police Magistrate held that the Infants Relief Act 1874 was a statute of general application and was in force in Nigeria by virtue of Section 14 of the Supreme Court Ordinance 1914. As a result the contract on which the plaintiff based his claim was, under Section 1 of the Act (1874) void and the claim was dismissed. The plaintiff appealed to the Divisional Court on the ground that the Magistrate was wrong in holding that the IRA, 1874 applied between a native and a native. The Divisional Court held that the IRA , 1874 was a statute of general application but the age of infancy in England was not the same as that in Lagos. Under Customary law, the age of majority was puberty. Consequently the defendant was liable under IRA 1874. The defendant appealed to the full court which remitted the case back to the Police Magistrate to ascertain whether there was any native law and custom applicable on the matter. In this respect Combe C. J. observed firstly that transactions between natives which are not covered by Ordinance or subsidiary legislation may be governed by either native law and custom or English law. Second, when a dispute arising from such transactions comes before the Court, the Court has to determine whether English law or native law and custom should govern the matter before the Court. Third, that the general rule was that if there is a native law and custom applicable to the matter in dispute and such law is not repugnant to natural justice, equity and good conscience or incompatible with any local ordinance and if it does not appear that it was intended by the parties that the obligations under the transactions should be regulated by English law, the matter in controversy shall be determined in accordance with native law and custom.

It is finally notable that Magistrates Courts are empowered to apply customary contract law subject to the qualifications of repugnancy and incompatibility with any written law.[22]

---

17 Hodgin, *supra* n.7 p.10
18 [1970] E.A. 578. See also Hodgin, *ibid.*
19 Cap. 144, S.17 (Kenya)
20 See further, Cotran, "Custody of Children Under Customary Law" 4 E.A. L.J. 153.
21 (1924) 5 NLR 33
22 Magistrates Courts Act 1970, Section 9. The wording is similar to Judicature Statute, 1996, S.17.

2
FORMATION OF CONTRACT

1. Consent

In order for a Contract to come into existence, there must be mutual consent between the contracting parties.

In other words the parties must be *ad idem,* or a meeting of minds of the contracting partiesThe Consent should be outwardly manifested or shown i.e. it should be express.[23] In *Ansah v. Amalgamated Banket Areas Ltd.*[24] the plaintiff had bought from a previous occupier a house on the land for Thirty pounds and improved it. He brought an action against the respondents asking for an injunction to prevent the respondents from demolishing the house or alternatively that he misunderstood the terms of the written agreement. It was held that the plaintiff could not rely on the agreement, the terms of which he had repudiated. The Court further observed[25] that if an agreement is void for being misunderstood, then there is no agreement between the parties who are never *ad idem*.

Apart from an express agreement, the agreement or part of it maybe inferred from (i) the conduct of the parties or (ii) from general or local customs governing such bargains or (iii) from a recognised course of dealing between the parties. In *Jupiter General Insurance Company v. Kasanda Cotton Co.*[26], A insured his cash in transit with B & Co. The premium depended on the amount of cash insured. As it was not possible for A to guess the amount when the policy was taken out, the premium was paid at the end of each year. When A made a claim against B and Co., they argued that there was no valid policy because no premium had been paid and there was no way at that date of knowing how much it would finally be. The Court of Appeal rejected that defence. This was the way the two parties had done business in the past without complaint. Consequently, the contract would be worked out the same way as it had been in earlier years. Furthermore in *Ghulum Kadir v. British Overseas Engineering Co. (E.A) Ltd.*[27], A agreed to buy steel bars from B. The order stated that the price was subject to fluctuation and increase in freight and insurance rates. The price went up 7% and A agreed to this. It later went up another 4% and A's agent confirmed the order. A later repudiated the order claiming that the contract was too uncertain in its terms. The Court decided that A knew that the market was in an uncertain state and the use of the phrase "subject to fluctuation" showed that he was willing to absorb any increases that might legitimately arise. Consequently, there was a valid contract.

---

23 *Norwich Union Fire Insurance Society v. Price*[1943] A.C. 455; *Smith v. Mansi* [1963] 1 W.L.R. 26, *Upton v. Powell* [1942] 1 All E.R.220

24 (1938) W.A.C.A 81. See also *Scammell and Nephew Ltd. v. Ouston* [1941] All E.R.14

25 *ibid* per Yates J.

26 1966 (1) A.L.R. Comm 292

27 [1957] E.A. 131. See also Hodgin, *supra*, p.24.

2. Offer

(a) Nature of offer

It is evident from the discussion above that consent is critical to the formation of a contract. However, consent must of necessity be preceded by an offer from one of the parties. Offer is an expression of readiness to contract on terms specified by the offer or, which, if accepted will give rise to a binding contract. The offer may be in writing, by conduct or words.

Thus in *Carlill v. Carbolic Smoke Ball Co.*[28a], the defendants advertised an offer of One hundred pounds to any user of their Carbolic smoke ball who caught influenza after using it in accordance with certain conditions. They also stated that they had deposited the sum of One thousand pounds with a bank to show their sincerity in the matter. Relying on the advertisement, the plaintiff bought a smoke ball which she used as directed in the advertisement. Nevertheless, she caught flu. She sued the defendants for One hundred pounds. The defendants argued firstly that there was no offer but a mere statement of intention - a mere puff. Second, that even if there was an offer it could not be binding upon them since it was not made to a particular person. Third, that there was no communication of acceptance. It was held firstly that from the language of the advertisement, there was a definite offer. Second, this was an offer which was made to anyone who performed the conditions in the advertisement. Third, the actual performance of the condition constituted the acceptance.

Furthermore, in *Otis Elevator Co. v. Singh & Ors*[29], the defendants were a firm of building contractors erecting a building which required a lift. The plaintiffs tendered for erection of the lift and addressed it to the architects. The defendants replied to the tender (when it came into their hands), accepting a quotation of Shs.85,700/= for the supply and erection of the lift. Owing to increase in customs duty, the plaintiffs had to pay more than anticipated for materials and parts used in the erection of the lift. They sought to recover this additional expense under a clause in the agreement, which provided for variation in price depending on Customs duties and other charges. The defendants denied liability on two grounds. First, that no contract existed between the plaintiffs and the defendants. Second that if any contract existed between the two parties, it did not contain the variation clause pleaded. It was held that the letter written by the plaintiffs in reply to the quotation addressed to the architects amounted to an offer to accept the quotation. The offer was accepted by the plaintiffs by their conduct in performing the works and also confirmed by the subsequent payment of the full amount quoted as contract price. Furthermore, that the variation Clause formed part of the contract and entitled the plaintiffs to recover an additional amount of Shs.15,244/=.

(b) Distinction between offer and invitation to treat

A major characteristic of an offer is that it must be such that if accepted, it will result in a contract. For instance, a situation where the buyer "offers" to buy a house leaving it to the seller to fix the price is not an offer but an *invitation to treat* or invitation for offers. Such a phenomenon does not give rise to any contractual reaction.

Thus in *Grainger v. Gough*[30] it was observed that the issue of catalogue containing descriptions of goods for sale at specified prices is not in itself an offer. It is an invitation to treat. It may, however, lead to an offer, when a potential buyer orders any of the goods in the catalogue and the order is accepted by the seller.[31]

28a [1893] 1 Q.B. 256

29 [1967] E.A. 78.

30 [1896] A.C.325.

31 *Spenser v. Harding* (1870) L.R. 5 C.P.561

Furthermore, in *Mayanja-Nkangi v. National Housing Corporation*[32] ,the plaintiff, who was an advocate and member of Parliament, between May 1962 and November, 1964 claimed that on 10 June, 1964, he had received a letter from the Minister of Housing and Labour which offered the recipients the opportunity of hire-purchasing a house in Kampala. Pursuant to that letter, the plaintiff met the Permanent Secretary in that Ministry who showed him a document roughly outlining the main points of the terms of agreed purchase and an initial payment of 20% of the purchase price and the period of payment to be over 15 or 20 years at the option of the purchaser.

In September 1964, the plaintiff met the Minister and a purchase price of Five thousand pounds was arranged. The plaintiff then sent a cheque of One thousand pounds and was given a receipt by National Housing Corporation (NHC).

By statutory instrument, the Minister of Housing and Labour ordered the transfer to NHC of several government properties then vested in Uganda Land Commission (ULC). However, actual transfer was not effected until 1st April, 1965. The house paid for by the plaintiff was among these.

The plaintiff claimed that following payment of 20% of the purchase price, a valid contract was made and he sought specific performance. The defendant corporation argued that there was no binding contract between the parties since at the time of the contract the registered proprietor of the house and land was U.L.C. and the Minister had no authority to enter into any contract in respect of that property.

It was held firstly that the initial letter from the Minister of Housing and Labour was an invitation to treat. Second, there was no contract as the transaction relied upon by the plaintiff was still in the course of negotiation and that no concluded contract was made between the parties.

It is significant that display of articles in shop windows with prices attached is not an offer to a person who produces the required sum of money.[33] In *Fisher v. Bell*[34], the respondent, a shopkeeper, displayed in his shop window a knife with a price attached. He was charged with offering a flick knife contrary to Section 1(1) of the Restriction of Offensive Weapons Act, 1959. The issue was whether display of a knife constituted an offer for sale within the Act. It was held that the display of a knife was merely an invitation to treat and shopkeeper not liable.

Another aspect which touches on whether an offer exists relates to auction sales. An advertisement of auction to sell certain goods is not an offer to hold the auction nor an offer to sell the goods. Thus in *Harris v. Nickerson*[35], the plaintiff travelled to an advertised place of an auction sale. However, he found that the sale had been cancelled. He sued for damages arising from his transport to the venue. It was held that he could not succeed as the advertisement was an invitation to treat. Furthermore, when an auctioneer invites bid, this is not an offer, but an invitation to treat.[36] Each bid constitutes an offer which may be accepted by the auctioneer at the fall of the hammer or in any customary manner.

(c) Communication of offer

The general rule is that an offer becomes effective once it is communicated to the offeree. Thus in *Fitch v. Snedakar*[37], $200 reward was offered for the arrest of a criminal. The plaintiff, who was

32 [1972] 1 U.L.R.37. See also *Katalemwa Traders v. Attorney General*(1992) VI K.A.L.R 32-39; *Kabaseke Stores Co. Ltd. v. Attorney General* (1990-91) II KALR 70-74. *Bweya Steel Works Ltd. v. N.I.C.* [1985] HCB 58-61; *Afro Traders & Farmers (U) Ltd v. Gailey & Roberts* [1983] HCB 48.

33 *Timothy v. Simpson* (1834) 6 C & P 499

34 [1960] 3 All E.R. 731. See also *Pharmaceutical Society of Great Britain v. Boots Cash Chemists (Southern) Ltd.*[1952] 2 All E.R. 459; *Afro Traders & Farmers (U) Ltd. v. Gailey & Roberts* [1983] HCB 48.

35 (1873) L.R. 8 Q.B. 286

36 C.f. *Warlow v. Harrison* (1859) 1 E & E on auction "without reserve" which is subsequently subjected to a reserve price.

37 (1868) 38 NY 248. See also *R. V. Clarke* (1927) 40 CLR 227; Cheshire & Fifoot's *Law of Contract supra n.*p.55

unaware of the reward apprehended the criminal and later claimed the reward. The claim failed and the Court held that a person can only act as an offer if he is aware of the offer. In this regard, where an offer is posted, it is deemed to have been made at the place and time of posting. It can therefore, only be accepted after the time of posting.

(d) Termination of offer

There are four main ways through which an offer can be terminated, namely by revocation, rejection, lapse of time and death of either of the parties. Each will be examined in turn.

(i) Revocation

The general rule is that an offer may be revoked at any time before it is accepted[38]. This is unaffected by the fact that an offeror has indicated a period within which the offer should be accepted or rejected. Thus in *Routledge v. Grant*[39], Grant offered to buy R's house. He gave 6 weeks within which R should respond. Grant then withdrew the offer before the end of the 6 weeks. It was held that the defendant was entitled to withdraw his offer even before the 6 weeks had passed, if the offer had not been accepted.

It is notable that an offer becomes irrevocable as soon as the offeree starts to comply with the conditions for its performance.

Needless to say a revocation of offer must be communicated to the offeree. Where notice is given orally by the offeror, communication is effected when the offeree hears it for instance on telephone. Where the notice is given by letter, the offeree must *actually* receive the letter of revocation. In this respect it matters not whether he reads the letter or not. Receipt is sufficient for purposes of revocation.

Thus in *Bryne v. Van Tienhoven*[40], on 1st October, the defendant posted a letter in Cardiff to Bryne in New York offering to sell him goods. The plaintiff received the letter on 11 October and the same day accepted the offer by telegram and a letter written on 15 October. However, on 8th October, the defendant had posted a letter revoking the offer. The plaintiff argued that the offer was accepted by means of the letters. The defendant contended that the offer had been withdrawn before acceptance. It was held that the attempted revocation was inoperative until the receipt of the letter on 20th October.

Notice of revocation may be gathered from a third party and would be effective to revoke the offer. Thus in *Dickinson v. Dodds*[41], the defendant offered to sell a house to the plaintiff and promised to leave the offer open for a given time. Before the expiration of the offer and before acceptance by the plaintiff, the defendant sold it to a third party. The plaintiff was informed of the sale by another person. Notwithstanding, within the period of the offer, he delivered a letter of acceptance to the defendant. It was held that there was no contract because the plaintiff could not accept following the defendant's unwillingness to sell to him.

(ii) Rejection

The rejection of an offer terminates the offer. Rejection is effective from the time it is actually communicated to the offeror. Rejection may take two forms i.e. express rejection or through a counter offer by the offeree which has the effect of destroying the offer. Thus in *Hyde v. Wrench*[42], the defendant on 6 June offered to sell an estate to the plaintiff for One thousand pounds. On 8

---

38 *Financings Ltd. v. Stimson* [1962] 1 W.L.R. 1184.

39 (1828) 4 Bing. 653

40 (1880) C.P.D. 344

41 (1876) 2 Ch.D. 463

42 (1840) 3 Beav.334; See also *Brogden v. Metropolitan Rly Co.* (1877) 2 App.Cas. 666; *Otis Elevator Co. v. Singh* [1967] E.A. 78

June, in reply, the plaintiff made an offer of Nine hundred and fifty pounds, which was refused by the defendant on 27 June. Finally, on 29 June, the plaintiff wrote that he was prepared to pay One thousand pounds. It was held that no contract existed. By his letter of 8 June, the plaintiff had rejected the original offer and was no longer able to revive it by changing his mind and tendering a subsequent acceptance.

Furthermore, in *Khaled v.Athanas Bros (Aden) Ltd*[43], A was a majority shareholder in a private company and offered to buy B's minority shareholding. Various offers were made and finally B accepted Forty thousand British Pounds. A formal document was drawn up for B's signature but B objected to the payment provisions and withheld his signature until alterations were made. These were finally made, B signed and then A purported to revoke his offer. It was held that when B demanded the alterations to the formal agreement, this amounted to a counter offer. But as A continued with his side of the contract, he had obviously agreed to forego the right to call the matter to a close. As the negotiations had gone on for over a year with the initiatives being taken by both sides, it could not be said that the offer lapsed. Finally, A's purported revocation was invalid since it came after B had signed the agreement.

(iii) Lapse of time

Where an offer has been made for a limited time, it terminates at the expiration of the specified time. Where there is no time limit on the offer, it expires after a reasonable time depending on the circumstances. Thus in *Ramsgate Victoria Hotel Co. v. Montefiore*[44], the defendant applied in June for shares in the plaintiff company and had paid a deposit into the company's bank. He heard nothing more until the end of November, when he was informed that the shares had been allotted to him and that he should pay the balance due upon them. It was held that his refusal to take them up was justified. His offer should have been accepted, if at all, within a reasonable time, and the interval between June and November was excessive. Further in *East African Industries Ltd v. Powysland Ltd.*[45], the plaintiffs advertised for tenders on 10th August to supply grains. The defendants made an offer on 16th August. Acceptance of this offer was communicated on 25th September. The defendants then refused to supply the grain alleging that the delay was unreasonable and therefore their offer lapsed. The Court accepted this and stated:

> When ... it is taken into consideration that the commodity to be supplied was one in which the market fluctuates considerably from day to day it is clear that a reasonable time lapsed sufficient to revoke the proposal.

Additionally in *Virji Kimji v. Clutterbuck*[46], A ordered timber from B. There was no reply from the offeree but four and a half months later, B sent the consignment of timber. A, successfully alleged that such a delay amounted to a lapse of time whereby his original offer was revoked.

(iv) Death of either of the parties

The death of the offeree terminates the offer since an offer is personal to the offeree.[47] Similarly, the death of the offeror terminates the offer if the offeree is aware of it,[48] although this has been doubted and the view proffered that death does not generally operate as a revocation but only in exceptional cases[49] such as the offer containing an element personal to the offeror e.g. as an author.[50]

---

43 [1968] E.A. 31

44 (1866) L.R. 1 Exch.109. See also the American Case *Loring v. City of Boston* 7 Metcalf 409 (1844) and Cheshire & Fifoot *supra* p.62 and *Khaled & Ors v. Athanas Bros (Aden) Ibid.*

45 5 E.A.L.R.121. See also Hodgin *supra* p.28

46 6 E.A.L.R. 56; Hodgin *ibid.* p.29

47 *Reynolds v. Atheston* (1921) 125 L.T. 690, 695-696 per Warrington L. J. See also *Re Irvine* [1928] 3 DLR 268.

48 *Dickinson v. Dodds* (1876) 2 Ch.D. 463, 475

49 *Brodbury v. Morgan* (1862) 1 H & C. 249

50 Cheshire & Fifoot, *supra* p.63

3. Acceptance

(a) Nature

Acceptance converts the offer into a contract and is basically an indication to enter into and be bound by the contract. Acceptance can be in writing, oral or inferred from conduct.

In *Felthouse v. Bindley*,[51] the plaintiff offered, in a letter, to buy his nephew's horse for Thirty Pounds and 15 Shillings. He said "if I hear no more about him, I consider the horse is mine at Thirty pounds, fifteen Shillings." The nephew did not reply the letter but told the defendant, an auctioneer, not to auction the horse, since it was already sold. However, the auctioneer sold the horse by mistake. It was held that since the nephew had not in words or acts indicated acceptance of the plaintiff's offer, there was no contract of sale and the horse remained the property of the nephew. Consequently, the plaintiff could not succeed.

In order for acceptance to be effective, it must be absolute and unqualified. Thus in *Jones v. Daniel*,[52] A wrote to B offering to buy property for One thousand, four hundred and fifty pounds. B's solicitor, while accepting the offer added "we enclose contract for your signature." The Contract contained some terms which had not appeared in the offer. It was held that there was no contract.

Furthermore, so long as the parties are *ad idem* (meeting of the minds) as to the major object of the contract, the introduction of meaningless phrases in the Contract will not vitiate it. Thus in *Nicolene Ltd. v. Simmonds*[53] the plaintiff offered to buy from the defendant goods on terms and conditions set out in an enclosed order. The defendant wrote a letter accepting the offer. His letter contained *inter alia* the words:

> assume that we are in agreement that the usual conditions of acceptance apply

There was no "usual conditions" operating between the parties. In an action for non-delivery of the goods agreed upon, the defendant argued that he did not accept the plaintiff's offer and that his letter was only a qualified and invalid acceptance. The Court of Appeal observed that since there were no such usual conditions to which the defendant referred, the clause was meaningless and severable from the defendant's letter. Consequently, the defendant's letter amounted to an unqualified acceptance.

(b) Counter offer

Related to acceptance, if the offeree's acceptance amounts to a counter-offer, no contract arises. In effect a counter-offer amounts to rejection of the offer.[54] In *Hart v. Mills*[55], the defendant ordered four dozen bottles of wine but the plaintiff sent him 8 dozens. The defendant took only 13 bottles and sent back the rest. The plaintiff sued claiming the price of the original 4 dozens ordered by the defendant. It was held that the defendant was liable only for the 13 bottles he kept and was at liberty to reject the whole as a counter-offer.

At this stage it is necessary to distinguish a counter offer from a request for information. A mere request for information does not affect the offer. Thus in *Simpson v. Hughes*[56] B offered to sell land to A but did not indicate the time for completion of the sale. A accepted the offer and then inquired from B when the transfer would be completed. B contended that the inquiry modified the offer. It was held that the inquiry did not affect the valid acceptance of the offer.

---

51 (1862) 11 C.B.N.869; See also *Jetha Petrol Station v. Lalani* [1958] E.A.455.
52 [1894] 2 Ch.332
53 [1953] 1 All E.R. 822. See also *Nwangwu v. Nzekwu* [1957] F.S.C.36 (Nigeria)
54 *Hyde v. Wrench, supra* n. 42
55 (1846) 15 L.J. Ex.200
56 (1897) L. J. Ch.334. See also *Stevenson v. Mclean* (1880) 5 Q.B.D. 346.

For acceptance to be effective, it must be unconditional. Where an agreement is subject to a formal contract being drawn up, the view is held that if the formal contract is a way of reducing to writing what has been agreed upon, the agreement is effective. Thus in *Branca v. Cabaro*[57], a vendor agreed to sell the lease and goodwill of a mushroom farm on the terms of a written document which was declared to be "provisional agreement until a fully legalised agreement, drawn up by a solicitor and embodying all the conditions herewith stated, is signed." It was held that by using the word "provisional", the parties had intended the document to be an agreement binding from the outset though subsequently to be replaced by a more formal contract. However, if the condition is that an agreement is not effective until a formal contract has been drawn up, then it is not effective.[58]

(c) Communication of acceptance

For acceptance to be effective it must be notified to the offeror. Thus in *Powell v. Lee*[59], the plaintiff applied for an appointment as Headmaster of a school run by the defendants. The defendants approved his appointment. One of them, without authority told the plaintiff of the decision to appoint him. The defendants later changed their minds on the appointment. It is notable that the acceptance was not communicated to the offeree by the defendant or his authorised agent. It was held that there was no acceptance.

Formal acceptance may be waived as in a situation where performance of the conditions of the offer is deemed to be acceptance.[60] Furthermore, the offeror may indicate the mode of acceptance. For instance, it may be indicated that acceptance is effective only if it is made in a manner prescribed. Thus in *Entores v. Miles For East Corpn*[61] the plaintiffs were a London Company and the defendants were an American Corporation with agents in Amsterdam. Both the plaintiffs in London and the defendants' agents in Amsterdam had equipment known as "Telex Service" whereby messages could be despatched by a teleprinter operated like a typewriter in one country and almost instantaneously received and typed in another. By this instrument, the plaintiffs made an offer to the defendants' agents to buy goods from them, and the latter accepted the offer. The plaintiffs then alleged that the defendants had broken their contract and wished to serve a writ upon them. this they could do although the defendants were an American corporation with no branch in England, provided that the contract was made in England.

The defendants contended that they had accepted the offer in Holland and that the contract had, therefore, been made in that country. It was held that the parties were in the same position as if they had negotiated in each other's presence or over the telephone. There was, therefore, no binding acceptance until it had been received by the plaintiffs and this took place in London and that a writ could, therefore, be issued.

(d) Acceptance through the post

Where the post is used as a means of acceptance, then acceptance is effected the moment it is posted. Thus in *Henthorn v. Fraser*[62], the plaintiff, who lived at B visited the defendant in L on 7 July and received an offer to sell certain houses for Seven hundred and fifty British Pounds between 12 noon and 1.00p.m. on 8 July, the defendant wrote to the plaintiff withdrawing the offer. However, on the same day at 3.50 p.m., the plaintiff posted a letter accepting the offer. This was received on 9 July. At 5.00p.m. on 8th July the plaintiff received a letter of revocation of the offer.

---

57 [1947] K.B.854; [1947] 2 All E.R.101

58 *Winn v. Bull* (1877) 7 Ch.D.29

59 (1908) 99 LT 284. See also *Rabophone Facilities v. Blank* [1966] 3 All E.R. 128

60 *Carbolic Smoke Ball Case* [1893] 1 Q.B.256, 269-270 per Bowen, L.J.

61 [1955] 2Q.B.327. [1955] 2 All E.R.493. See also *Brinkibon Case* [1983] 2 AC 34 [1982]1 All E.R. 293 H.L.

62 [1892] 2 Ch.33. For other scenarios affecting the postal rule see Hodgin, *supra*, pp.34-36. See also *Byrne v. Van Tienhoven* (1880) 5 CPD 344, 348; *Adam v. Lindsell* (1818) 1 B & Ald 681.

It was held that as the parties lived in a far off place, acceptance by post was presumed to have been contemplated by them. In consequence the contract was completed at 3.50p.m. on 8 July when the letter of acceptance was posted. It followed that the defendant's letter of revocation was too late and, therefore, ineffective.

The rule applies even where the letter of acceptance is delayed or is lost.[63]

---

[63] *Household Fire and Carriage Insurance Co. v. Grant* (1879) 4 E.D.216.

3
CONSIDERATION

1. Definition

Consideration has been traditionally defined as giving something of value. In other words, it is either some detriment to the promisee in the sense that he may give value or some benefit to the promisor in the sense that he may receive value.[64] Detriment to the promisee is sufficient even though the promisor has not benefitted. Additionally, the benefit and detriment may be factual or legal. It is factual where the consideration consists of a benefit or detriment actually obtained or suffered. It is legal where there is performance of an act which is not already legally due from the promisee.

The traditional definition has been criticised for being unsatisfactory because it is improper to talk of benefit and detriment when both parties expect to and actually do benefit from the contract. Consequently, another definition has been suggested. Consideration is taken to be the price for which a promise is bought[65] and is preferred by some writers as being "easier to understand and corresponds... to the normal exchange of promises and emphasises the commercial character of the English contract."[66]

However, other writers regard this definition as vague since it does not indicate whether consideration exists on a given set of facts.[67] On the other hand, there is the view that consideration is the reason for enforcement of promises, that reason being the justice of the case.[68] However, this approach is criticised on the ground that "justice" is always debatable " so that the suggested definition provides no basis for formulating a coherent legal doctrine ". Professor Treitel concludes[69] that the traditional definition is more consistent.

2. Rules governing consideration

(a) Consideration need not be adequate

Although courts will not enforce a promise, unless some value has been given for it, they do not in most cases inquire into the adequacy of such value or whether the agreement is unfair or harsh. Thus in *Haig v. Brooks*[70], the plaintiff, in consideration for the defendant's promise to pay for certain bills, surrendered to him a document which was purported to be a guarantee. The plaintiff sued on the promise. The defendant argued that since the document contravened the Statute of Frauds, 1677, it was unenforceable, being a worthless document. It was held that the "worthless" document was valuable consideration and its adequacy could not be inquired into. Similarly in

---

64 *Currie v. Misa* (1875) L.R. 10 Ex.153, 162

65 *Pollock on Contracts*(13th Edn.) p.133. See also *Dunlop v. Selfridge* [1915] A.C. 847, 855.

66 Cheshire and Fifoot, *Law of Contract supra* p.73.

67 Treitel, G. H. *Law of Contract* (8th Edn. 1991) p.66.

68 Atiyah, *Consideration in Contracts: A Fundamental Restatement* Canberra 1971, p.60

69 Treitel, supra n.4 p.66

70 (1840) 10 A & E 309

Patel Brothers v. Hasmani[71]. A owed B Shs.27,000 =. A's father agreed to pay B Shs.18,000/= if B did not sue A. A cheque was given but later A's father claimed that B had done nothing, given no consideration for the cheque. It was held that forebearance to sue was on B's part good consideration for the cheque. Also in *Thomas v. Thomas*[72], the plaintiff's deceased husband expressed desire that the plaintiff should be entitled to make use of his house if she survived him on payment of One Pound per year. The plaintiff sued the husband's executors for breach of this agreement. It was held that although the husband's wishes were not sufficient consideration, the payment of one pound per annum by the widow was good consideration for the husband's promise.

The rationale for the rule is that courts will not inquire into adequacy of consideration on the premise that it would not interfere in bargains actually made by the parties to the contract. Furthermore, in situations, where contracts result into excessive profits or excessive prices are charged, it has been suggested that the courts are not well equipped to develop a system of price control. The approach of the courts was summerised by Lord Denning in *Lloyd's Bank v. Bundy*[73] when he stated that "no bargain will be upset which is the result of the ordinary interplay of forces."

Although, the general rule that adequacy of consideration should not be a ground for impeaching a contract is recognised, in equity the courts have sometimes refused specific performance of a contract or set it aside or even reopened it by varying its terms on the ground that adequate value has not been given to a party needing special protection.[74] Equity also declined to aid a "volunteer" i.e. a person who has given no substantial consideration but could nevertheless enforce a promise at law because it was made in a deed or supported by nominal consideration.[75]

(b) Consideration must not be past

If A presents a car to B and a year later, B promises to pay Five Hundred British Pounds, there is no consideration for B's promise as A did not give B the car in return for it. This is so because there was a lapse of time between an act and the promise said to have been in return for it. In this instance the consideration is regarded as past consideration and, therefore, bad.[76] If therefore, a thing is guaranteed after it has been sold, there is no consideration for the guarantee. Thus in *Roscorla v. Thomas*[77], the defendant sold a horse to the plaintiff, but afterwards the defendant in consideration for the previous sale promised the plaintiff that "the horse was sound and free from vice. The Plaintiff sued for breach of warranty when he found the horse was vicious. It was held that the sale did not constitute an implied warranty that the sale was free from vice. The warranty given by the defendant was subsequent and independent of the sale and was therefore, unenforceable since the consideration was past and bad in law. This approach may be contrasted with the position in the East African Case *Motor Mart & Exchange Ltd. v. Gandhiv Anor.*[78] In this case, the first defendant entered into a hire purchase agreement on 11 July, 1960 with the plaintiffs in respect of a motor vehicle and on 20 July, 1960, the second defendant guaranteed due performance of the agreement by the first defendant. The first defendant, having defaulted, the plaintiffs first

71 19 E.A.C.A. 170

72 (1842) 2 Q.B.851.

73 [1975] Q.B. 326, 336

74 *Tennent v. Tennent's Trustees* (1870) L.R. 2Sc & Div.6,9

75 *Jefferys v. Jefferys* (1841) Cr & Ph.138. See also Treitel, *supra* n.4 p.73. See also *Eastern Province Bus Co. Ltd. v. Hadi Jamal* (1953) 20 E.A.C.A. 102; *Zainab Gulab v. Kulsum Khalek* [1961] E.A.487.

76 *Dent v. Bennett* (1839) 4 My & Cr 269; *Eastwood v. Kenyon* (1840) 11 A & E 438.

77 (1847) 2 Q.B.234

78 [1963] E.A.657. See also *Jetha Petrol Station v. Lalani* [1958] E.A. 455.

terminated the agreement and demanded return of the vehicle and later sued the defendant for instalments in arrears; return of the vehicle and its value and damages. The second defendant contended that since the guarantee was given after the execution of the hire purchase agreement, there was no consideration and that the car was not hired to the first defendant at the second defendant's request. It was held that the vehicle was hired to the first defendant at the request of the second defendant. Second, that the expression, "had done" in Section 2(d) of the Indian Contract Act connotes something done before the vehicle was supplied to the first defendant. Accordingly, although the guarantee was executed after the hire purchase agreement, there was good consideration for the guarantee.

(c) Relaxation of the rule

The rule about past consideration has been relaxed by providing that an act done before a promise can be considered if three conditions are satisfied. First, the act must be done at the request of the promisor. Second, it must have been understood that payment would be made. Third, payment, if it had been promised, must have been legally recoverable.

Thus in *Lampleigh v. Brathwait*[79], Brathwait killed M. He asked the plaintiff to use his good offices to obtain a pardon from the King, which the plaintiff did. In so doing the plaintiff incurred expenses and the defendant later promised to pay him One Hundred British Pounds for expenses and exertion. The defendant failed to pay the money and the plaintiff sued in *assumpsit*. It was held that the plaintiff was entitled to recover the One Hundred pounds.

Furthermore, in *Re Casey's Patents, Stewart v. Casey,*[80], "owners of patent rights wrote to the plaintiff and promised in consideration of your services as the practical manager in working both patents, we hereby agree to give you one third share of the patents."

The plaintiff sued on this agreement. The defendant argued that the consideration was past and therefore, bad. However, the court held in favour of the plaintiff for three reasons. First the services were rendered at the defendant's request. Second, the services were ultimately paid for. Third, the plaintiff was entitled to recover payment under the promise and if the amount was not stated, he could recover on *quantum meruit*.

In a recent Privy Council Case, *Pao On v. Lau Yiu Long*, Lord Scarman stated thus:[81]

> "An act done before the giving of a promise to make a payment or to confer some benefit can sometimes be consideration for the promise. The act must have been done at the promisor's request, the parties must have understood that the act was to be remunerated further by a payment or the conferment of some other benefit, and payment, or the conferment of a benefit must have been legally enforceable had it been promised in advance."

Another exceptional limitation to the rule is Section 27(1) of the Bills of Exchange Act[82] where it is provided that valuable consideration for a bill of exchange may take two forms. First, any consideration sufficient to support a simple contract and second an antecedent debt or liability. Consequently, past consideration in this instance must relate to negotiable instruments.[83]

A further exception is to apply the trust concept by saying that a contract between two parties should be read as creating a trust in favour of the third party. While not allowing him to enforce the contract *perse*, it permits him to enforce the trust in equity.[84]. However, this attempt to import into contract the trust concept has been disapproved.[85]

---

79 (1615) Hobart 105;. See also *Kennedy v. Brown* (1863) 13 CB (NS) 677 per Earle, C.J.
80 [1892] 1 Ch.104
81 [1980] A.C.614, 629, [1979] 3 All E.R.65, 74.
82 Cap 76 Laws of Uganda (1964 Edn.)
83 *Tapply v. Sheather* (1862) L.T.398; *Oliver v. Davis* [1949] 2 All E.R. 353; *Currie v. Misa* (1875) L.R. 10 Ex 153.
84 See *Sat Dev. Sharma v. The Home Insurance Company of New York* [1966] E.A.8. For more discussion, see Chap.11 *infra*.
85 *Ibid* relying on *Re Schebsman* [1944] Ch.83

Another exception to the rule is where a third party has been accorded statutory rights to sue on the contract to which he is not a party.[86] Thus in *Kayanja v. New India Assurance Company Ltd.*[87] the appellant was injured in a road accident by a car owned and insured by X but driven at the time by Y. The insurance policy purported to cover any authorised driver. The appellant was awarded Shs.87,000/= (Eighty-seven Thousand Shillings) damages and claimed that sum from the insurance company. While appreciating that the appellant had no common law right to maintain an action and was, therefore, a stranger to the policy and could not sue thereon,[88] the Court of Appeal allowed the appeal on the basis of the statutory requirements.[89]

(c) Consideration must move from the promisee

A person can only enforce a promise, if he himself has provided consideration for it.[90] He cannot sue if consideration for the promise moved from a third party.

Thus in *Dunlop v. Selfridge*,[91] the defendants bought tyres from Dew Company. The tyres were manufactured and sold to Dew Company by the plaintiffs under an agreement which required Dew Co to impose on all its buyers an undertaking not to sell below list prices. In consideration for Dew Co.'s undertaking, the plaintiffs gave them a discount on the price. However, the defendants in full knowledge of the imposition sold the tyres below list prices. The plaintiff sued for breach of contract. It was held that the action could not be sustained because the plaintiffs had not furnished any consideration to Selfridge i.e. consideration had not moved from Dunlop to Selfridge.

This approach should be contrasted with the view that while consideration must move from the promisee, it need not move to the promisor.[92] For instance, consideration may be provided by a promisee giving up a job[93] or tenancy of a house[94] although the promisor does not directly benefit.

(d) Consideration must be of some value

An act, omission or promise will only amount to consideration if the law recognises that it has some economic value. In this regard, something can be of value even if the value cannot be determined.[95] However, "natural affection of itself is not sufficient consideration. Similarly, sentimental motives for promising do not constitute consideration".[96]

The following issues arise from an assessment of the value of consideration.

(i) Whether a promise to pay less than amount owed is sufficient consideration

In *Pinnel's Case*,[97] it was stated *obiter* that payment of a lesser sum on an earlier day than the day on which the debt was due, if accepted by the plaintiff in full satisfaction of a greater amount would be sufficient to relieve the defendant from further liability. Furthermore, in *Sibre v. Tripp*[98] the plaintiff sued the defendant for a debt of One Thousand British Pounds but the debt was settled on condition that the defendant would give the plaintiff promissory notes in Three Hundred pounds in full satisfaction. This was accepted by the Court.

---

86 Motor Vehicle Insurance (Third Party Risks) Statute No.11 of 1988 as amended by Statute No.5 of 1991.

87 [1968] E.A. 295.

88 Following *Halal Shipping Co. v. Securities Bremmer* [1965] E.A. 690.

89 Following *New Great Insurance Co. of India v. Cross* [1966] E.A. 90.

90 *Barber v. Fox* (1682) 2 Wms Saurd 134

91 [1915] A.C. 847 H.L.(E); *Tweddle v. Atkinson* (1861) 1 B & S 393.

92 *Re Wyvern Developments Ltd.* [1974] 1 W.L.R. 1097.

93 *Jones v. Padavatton* [1969] 1 W.L.R.628

94 *Tonner v. Tanner* [1975] 1 W.L.R.1346 c.f. *Horrocks v. Forray* [1976] 1 W.L.R. 230. See also *Official Receiver v. United Stores Ltd & Ors.*[1962] E.A.180; *Jetha Petrol Station v. Lalani* [1958] E.A.455.

95 *Bret v. J.S.* (1600) Cro Eliz.756

96 *Thomas v. Thomas* (1842) 2 Q.B.851; *White v. Bluett*(1853) 23 L.J. Ex.36. See also *Bweya Steel Works Ltd*

97 (1602) Co. Rep. 117. See also *E.A. Plans Ltd. v. Smith* [1974] HCB 97

98 (1846) 15 M & W 23

The essence of the rule is that a debt of Shs.10,000/= can be extinguished by a cheque of Shs.4,000/= or other payment in full satisfaction on an earlier date at the request of the creditor. This is based on the principle that the court does not inquire into the adequacy of consideration.[99]

(ii) Whether performance of an existing contractual duty amounts To Consideration

Where a promisee only performs a duty which he is under an obligation to perform, this does not amount to consideration. Thus in *Stilk v. Myrick*[100], two seamen while on a voyage deserted the ship. The captain promised to pay the crew if they would handle the ship to its destination. One of the seamen sued for his extra wages. It was held that he could not succeed because he had not furnished consideration.

(iii) Whether promise to perform existing contractual duty to a third party amounts to consideration

A promise to perform to a third party is sufficient consideration provided the promisee thereby benefits and the promisor suffers detriment. Thus in *Shadwell v. Shadwell*,[101] an uncle wrote to his nephew, the plaintiff promising him One Hundred and fifty pounds per annum on his marriage. The plaintiff was already engaged to be married to X. They later got married. The plaintiff sued the executors of his uncle on the deceased's promise. It was argued by the defendant that since the plaintiff was bound already to get married, there was no consideration for the uncle's promise. It was held that he could succeed because the promise was one which only became binding if and when marriage took place.

(iv) Whether a promise to perform existing public duty amounts to consideration

A promise to perform or the performance of an existing legal duty does not amount to consideration. Thus in *Collins v. Godefroy*[102], the plaintiff was ordered to appear before a court. The defendant promised to pay him if he appeared in Court. The plaintiff sued the defendant on the promise. It was held that the action could not succeed because the plaintiff did not furnish any consideration for the promise. He was only doing what the law required him to do.

However, a promise which exceeds one's legal obligation amounts to consideration. Thus in *England v. Davidson*,[103] the defendant promised to give a reward to anyone who would give information leading to the conviction of a criminal. A Police Constable gave the required information. The Constable sued the defendant. The defendant argued that since the constable was only doing his legal duty, he could not recover on the promise. Second that such a promise was contrary to public policy. It was held that the Constable's service was outside the scope of his duties and amounted to sufficient consideration.

(v) Whether a promise by a third party to pay a lesser amount constitutes consideration

Part payment by a third party if accepted by a creditor in full settlement, will extinguish a creditor's claim for the balance. Thus in *Welby v. Drake*,[104] the defendant, who was the son of the third party owed the plaintiff Nine British Pounds. The father paid a lesser sum to the plaintiff, who accepted the same. Later the plaintiff sued the defendant for the balance. it was held that he could not succeed as the sum advanced by the father constituted sufficient discharge.[105]

---

99 *Haigh v. Brooks* (1839) 10 A & E 309, 334. c.f. *Central London Property Trust Ltd. v. High Trees House* [1947] K.B.130; *Combe v. Combe* [1951] 1 All E.R. 767.

100 (1809) 1 Camp 317. See also *Pao On v. Lau Yiu Long* [1980] A.C. 614, 633 *Sybron Corp v. Rochem Ltd* [1984] Ch.112.

101 (1860) 3 L.T.628. See also *The Eurymedon* [1975] A.C.154; *The New York Star* [1981] 1 W.L.R.138

102 (1831) 1 B & Ad.950 c.f. *Willis v. Peckham* (1820) 1 Br & B 515; *Thoresen Car Ferries Ltd v. Wey mouth Portland B.C* [1977] 2 Lloyds' Rep 614, 619.

103 (1840) 11 Ald & E. 850. See also *Ward v. Byham* [1956] 2 All E.R.318; *Glasbrook Bros. Ltd. v. Glamorgan C.C.* [1925] A.C. 270; *Harris v. Sheffield United F. C. Ltd.* [1988] Q.B.77.

104 (1825) 1 C & P 557.

105 See also *Hirachand Punamchand v. Temple* [1911] 2KB 330.

3. Equitable or promissory estoppel

The doctrine of estoppel is relevant, in the context of consideration to those situations where a party to a legal relationship promises, by words or conduct to the other party that he is willing to alter the basis of the relationship and the other party alters his position because of that assurance. The promisor cannot then go back on his word without giving the other party a reasonable time to reorganise himself. Thus in *Combe v. Combe*[106], a wife brought divorce proceedings and obtained a decree *nisi* against her husband. The husband then promised to allow her One Hundred British Pounds per annum free of tax as permanent maintenance. The wife had not applied to the Divorce Court for maintenance and the forebearance was not at the husband's request. The decree was later made absolute. The husband never made the annual payments and the wife sued the husband on his promise to make them. Judgment was given to the wife. The court was of the view that the principle in the *High Trees Case*[107] enabled the wife to succeed since the husband had made an unequivocal promise to pay the annuity intending the wife to act upon it and she had in fact so acted. this was independent of the requirement of consideration which was inapplicable. However, the Court of Appeal in England overruled this decision and clarified the position thus:[108]

> The principle in the *High Trees Case* does not create new causes of action where none existed before. It only prevents a party from insisting upon his strict legal rights, when it would be unjust to allow him to enforce them, having regard to the dealings which have taken place between the parties.

Furthermore, it was explained[109] that since the principle never stands alone as giving a cause of action in itself, it can never do away with the necessity for consideration when that is an essential part of the cause of action. In so doing the Court of Appeal emphasized that the principle of promissory estoppel is "used as a shield and not a sword".

In the *High Trees Case*[110] itself in September 1939, the plaintiffs leased a block of flats to the defendants at a ground rent of Two Thousand, Five Hundred British Pounds per annum. In January 1940, the plaintiffs agreed in writing to reduce the rent to One thousand, Two Hundred and fifty British Pounds because of war conditions which had caused many vacancies in the flats. No express time limit was set for the reduction. From 1940 to 1945, the defendants paid the reduced rent. In 1945, the flats were again full and the receiver of the plaintiff company then claimed the full rent both retrospectively and for the future. He tested the claim by suing for rent at the original rate for the last two quarters of 1945. It was held that the agreement of January 1940 was intended as a temporary expedient only and had ceased to operate early in 1949. Rent originally fixed by the contract was, therefore, payable and the plaintiffs were entitled to judgment. However, if the plaintiffs had sued for arrears for the period 1940-1945, the agreement made in 1940 would have operated to defeat the claim. Denning J. (as he then was) agreed that there was no consideration for the plaintiff's promise to reduce rent. Consequently, if the defendants had sued upon that promise, they would have failed and therefore, estoppel applied. He explained that under this doctrine, if one person makes to another a clear and unambiguous representation of fact intending that other to act on it, if the representation turns out to be untrue, and if, that other acts upon it to his prejudice the representor is "estopped" from denying its truth.[111] The equitable principle

---

106 [1951] 1 All E.R. 767.

107 *Central London Property Trust Ltd. v. High Trees House* [1947] K.B. 130.

108 [1951] 2 K.B. 215 per Denning, L.J. (as he then was).

109 *ibid* [1951] All E.R. 767, 769-770 per Asquith L.J. See further *Tool Manufacturing Co. Ltd. v. Tungsten Electric Company Ltd.* [1955] 2 All E.R. 657.

110 *supra* n.44. See also *RatRatansi v. Israel* (1953) 20 E.A.C.A. 127.

111 Following *Hughes v. Metropolitan Rail Co.* (1877) 2 App. Cas.439.

was explained to be similar to the doctrine of estoppel in that it expands it to include promises as well as statements of fact and is known as *promissory estoppel* as distinguished from an estoppel founded upon a misrepresentation of fact. It may also be described as *quasi estoppel.* This estoppel covered the promise of the landlords in the *High Trees Case.* They were, therefore, estopped from going back on the promise to reduce rent during the war.

The *High Trees Case* principle has been applied in East Africa. Thus in *Century Automobiles Ltd. v. Biemer,*[112] A leased premises to B, allowing a three months termination period on either side. B wanted to convert one of the buildings but did not want to risk incurring expenses only to find that A might exercise his right of termination. A promised, however, that there was no chance of doing this for three to four years. B therefore carried out One Thousand and Eight Hundred pounds worth of alterations. Eight months later A gave his three months' notice. It was held that A was estopped from doing this. The Court observed that[113] the doctrine of equitable estoppel applied to Kenya and that three elements for its application were required. First that there must be a clear and unequivocal representation. Second, there should be an intention that the representation should be acted upon and finally that there should be action on the representation in the belief of its truth.

In line with the observation in the *Combe Case*[114] that the principle of promissory estoppel can only be used as a defence against the plaintiff who is trying to renege on his original promise, and cannot be used offensively, there has been East African authority to this effect. Thus in *Malji Jetha v. Commissioner of Income Tax*[115] the plaintiff sought declaration that the Commissioner of Income tax be prevented from enforcing his legal right to collect taxes on the ground that he had given the plaintiff an oral undertaking that he would examine fresh accounts before deciding on the amount owed. The plaintiff's claim was dismissed on the ground that he was seeking not to protect a legal right conferred upon him but to defend himself against the exercise of a right conferred by law upon the defendant.

Furthermore, in the Nigerian case, *Ajayi v. R.T. Briscoe (Nig) Ltd.*[116] the defendant appellant contracted with the plaintiffs respondents for hire purchase of 11 lorries. The plaintiffs agreed to recover the instalments due under the contract and obtained judgment. The defendant appealed to the Federal Supreme Court of Nigeria and for the first time pleaded promissory estoppel. He alleged that the plaintiffs had voluntarily promised to suspend the payment of instalments until certain conditions had been fulfilled and that this promise had not been kept. The appeal was dismissed on the grounds firstly that the appellant had not proved failure to fulfil the conditions and secondly that he had not altered his position in reliance upon the promise. However, the Privy Council fully accepted the doctrine of promissory estoppel and would have applied it if the evidence so warranted. The Privy Council further stated that promissory estoppel was subject to three qualifications. First the other party must have altered his position. Second, that the promisor can resile from his promise on giving reasonable notice, which need not be a formal notice, giving the promise a reasonable opportunity of resuming his position. Third, the promise only becomes final and irrevocable if the promisee cannot resume his position.

---

112 [1965] E.A. 304 C.A. (E.A.)

113 Following *Nurdin Bandali v. Lombank Tanganyika Ltd.* [1963] E.A. 304 C.A. See also Evidence Act, Section 113 (Uganda) Morris, *Law of Evidence in East Africa*, pp. 160-169. See further *Commissioner of Lands v. Hussein* [1968] E.A. 585; *Runda Coffee Estate Ltd. v. Ujagar Singh* [1966] E.A. 564.

114 *Supra* n.99

115 [1967] E.A. 50

116 [1964] 3 All E.R. 556. P.C. See also *W.J. Allan & Co. Ltd. v. El Nasr Export and Import Co.* [1972] 2 Q.B.189, 213, [1972] 2 All E.R., 127, 140 per Lord Denning, M.R.

4
CONTRACTUAL INTENTION

(a) Intention and relation to binding contract

In *Brooker v. Palmer,*[1] Lord Greene M.R. stated thus:[2]

> The law does not impute intention to enter into legal relationships where the circumstances and the conduct of the parties negate any intention of any kind

1. Inducements

It follows from the above statement that statements which form the basis of a contract must contemplate legal consequences. Consequently, a statement which is made to induce a contract such as a mere puff or words uttered in conversation but which are not seriously meant will not be binding even if the other party acts on them. Thus in *Weeks v. Tybald*[3], the defendant "affirmed and published that he would give One Hundred Pounds to him that should marry his daughter with his consent." The plaintiff married the defendant's daughter with his consent and sued on the promise. It was held that "it is not reasonable that the defendant should be bound by such general words spoken to excite suitors."

(b) Statements inducing a contract

It is further significant that a statement which is made to induce a person to enter into a contract may be "a mere representation" and sometimes a term of a contract. The distinction between the two depends on the intention with which the statement is made. This is to be gathered from the contract if it exists. However, sometimes the very existence of the contract depends on the intention itself. This may happen where the statement inducing the contract cannot take effect as one of the terms of the contract, but only as a collateral contract. Thus in *Heilbut, Symons & Co. v. Buckleton*[4], the plaintiff said to the defendant's manager that he understood that the defendants will be bringing out a rubber company. The manager replied that they were. On the strength of this statement, the plaintiff applied for and was allotted shares in the company. The company turned out not to be a rubber company. The plaintiff claimed damages alleging that the defendant had warranted that it was a rubber company. It was held that the claim could not succeed as what the defendant's manager said was not intended to have contractual effect.

---

1 [1942] 2 All E.R. 674

2 *ibid* p.677

3 (1605) Noy 11

4 [1913] A.C.30. See also *I.B.A. v. E.M.I. Electronics Ltd.* (1980) 14 Build L.R.1 c.f. Atiyah, *The Rise and Fall of Freedom of Contract* p.772.

2. Commercial arrangements

Situations where intention to be legally bound is negatived

The intention to be legally bound may be negatived by an express provision in the agreement.

(i) Honour clauses

In *Rose & Frank Co. v. J.R. Crompton & Bros. Ltd.*[5] an agency agreement provided: "This arrangement is not entered into, nor is this memorandum written as a formal legai agreement and shall not be subject to legal jurisdiction in the Law of Courts, but is only a definite expression and record of the purpose and intention of the parties concerned to which they each honourably pledge themselves..." It was held that the agreement was not a legally binding contract as it was not intended to have this effect. Similarly in *United African Co. Ltd. v. Johnson*[6] the plaintiff engaged the defendant as their produce clerk under a written agreement. The agreement provided that the clerk was to be responsible for shrinkages, as may be made by the company as an act of grace. The defendant argued that under the agreement he was entitled to an allowance for shrinkage. It was held that the clause did not give the defendant any right to an allowance for shrinkage.

In *Jones v. Vernons Pools Ltd.*,[7] the plaintiff pleaded that he had won a football pool dividend, but that his coupon which he posted to the defendants was lost by them. The plaintiff's suit was based on the coupon but the defendants prayed in defence the honour clause which prevented legal meaning being attached to the sending and acceptance of coupons as "transaction binding in honor only." It was held tat the claim could not succeed as the "honour clause" prevented action in a court of law.

(ii) Agreements subject to contract

Agreements for sale of land or other real property are usually made "subject to contract." The effect of such words is to negative contractual intention so that the parties are not normally bound until formal contracts have been exchanged.[8]

(iii) "Ex Gratia" compromise

In *Edwards v. Skyways Ltd.*[9] employers promised a dismissed employee an "ex gratia payment." It was held that the words "ex gratia" did not negative contractual intention but only mean that the employers did not admit any pre-existing liability to make the payment.

3. Social and domestic arrangements

Many social arrangements do not amount to contracts because they are not intended to be legally binding. For instance, accepting an invitation to dinner does not give rise to a contract. Similarly, providing residential accommodation for close friend does not amount to a contract as it is an act which is done without any intention to enter into legal relations.[10]

---

5 [1925] A.C. 445; [1923] 2 K.B. 261

6 (1935) 12 N.L.R. 38. See also *S.A. Buko v. Nigerian Pools Co. Ltd.* 1966 (2) A.L.R. Comm.200 where the court refrained from pronouncing on the effect of an "honour clause". See also the discussion thereof in Hodgin, *Law of Contract in East Africa* (1975) pp.63-64.

7 [1938] 2 All E.R. 626

8 See *Rose & Frank Co. Case* [1923] 2K.B. 261, 294

9 [1964] 1 W.L.R. 349

10 *Heslop v. Burns* [1974] 1 W.L.R. 1241; *Horrocks v. Forray* [1976] 1 W.L.R. 349

Furthermore, many domestic arrangements are not intended to be legally binding. Thus in *Balfour v. Balfour*,[11] a husband who worked in Ceylon promised to pay an allowance of Thirty British Pounds to his wife who had to stay in England on medical grounds. The wife's attempt to enforce the promise failed on two grounds. First she had not provided any consideration. Second, the parties did not intend the arrangement to be legally binding. The point was that most domestic arrangements between husband and wife are not contracts. In the words of Atkin L. J.[12] (as he then was):

> These agreements or many of them, do not result in contracts at all ... even though there may be what as between other parties would constitute consideration for the agreement. They are not contracts because the parties did not intend that they should be attended by legal consequences.... Agreements such as these are outside the realm of contracts altogether.

It is notable, though, that it is quite possible for a husband to enter into a binding contract with his wife. For instance a husband can be his wife's tenant,[13] and binding separation agreements are often made when husband and wife agree to live apart.[14] In *Synge v. Synge*[15], before his marriage, a man promised his future wife to leave her a house if she married him. It was held that she could enforce the promise even if it was made informally and in affectionate terms.

Related to domestic arrangements is the proposition that a promise to pay a child an allowance during study is not a Contract, although it may become one if it is part of the bargain to the child to enter into some particular course of study.[16] However, there is no contract where a mother agrees to nurse her child who has fallen ill or been injured even though this involves her giving up work in order to do so.[17]

Nevertheless, where adult members of a family (other than husband and wife) share a common household, the financial terms on which they do so may be intended to have a contractual effect. Thus in *Parker v. Clark*[18], a young couple were induced to sell their house and move in with their elderly relations on the latter's promise to leave a share of the proposed joint home. After some misunderstandings the young couple left the home sued for breach of contract. The defendants argued that their promise was not legally binding. It was held that the contract was binding because the young couple would not have left their house on the faith of merely a social arrangement.

4. Other Cases

(a) Agreements which give wide discretion

A discretionary promise may be too vague to constitute consideration for the other party's promise and therefore unenforceable. Thus in *Taylor v. Brewer*,[19] the plaintiff agreed to do work for a Committee who resolved that he should receive "such remuneration... as should be deemed right." The plaintiff's claim for a reasonable remuneration for work done failed. It was said that the promise to pay was "merely an engagement in honour."[20]

---

11 [1919] 2 K.B. 571

12 *Ibid* p.578. See also *Eliza Morris v. John Monrovia* (1930) W.A.C.A.70

13 *Pearce v. Merriman* [1904] 1 K.B. 80 c.f. *Hardwick v. Johnson* [1961] 1 W.L.R. 921; *Morris v. Tarrant* [1971] 2 Q.B.143.

14 *Merrit v. Merrit* [1970] 1 W.L.R.1121

15 [1894] 1 Q.B. 466. See also *Shadwell v. Shadwell* (1860) 9 C.B. NS 159 and *supra* Chapter 3.

16 *Jones v. Padavatton* [1969] 1 W.L.R.328, 333.

17 Treitel, *op.cit.* p.152

18 [1960] 1 W.L.R. 286

19 (1813) 1 M & S 290. See also *Esso Petroleum Ltd. v.Commissioners of Customs & Excise* [1976] 1 All E.R.117

20 *Ibid.* p.291

(b) Collective agreements

Agreements as to rates of wages and conditions of work are usually reached after collective bargaining between trade unions and employers or associations of employers. Terms of such contracts may be incorporated in individual service contracts and thus become legally binding on the parties to those contracts. The general common law view is that collective agreements between trade unions and employers are not intended to be legally binding.[21] In Britain the Trade Union and Labour Relations Act 1974 goes further to provide [22] that a collective agreement is "conclusively presumed not to have been intended by the parties to be a legally enforceable contract" unless it is in writing and expressly provides the contrary.

---

21 See *Ford Motor Co. v. A.E.F.* [1969] 1 W.L.R. 339

22 S. 18, (1), (2). *See also The Universe Sentinel*[1983] A.C.366, 380; *The Rosso* (1982) 2 Lloyd's Rep. 120

5
CONTRACTUAL CAPACITY

1. Infants or minors

Under Ugandan Law , a minor is a person who has not reached the age of majority i.e. eighteen (18) years[23]. In other jurisdictions, it has been held [24] that under native law and custom the age of majority is the age of puberty.

Contracts made by a minor may be (i) binding during minority; (ii) voidable; (iii) void or (iv) unenforceable against the minor both during and after minority.

(a) Binding contracts

An infant is bound under the common law for two types of contract *viz* contracts for necessaries and contracts of an educational character beneficial to him.

(i) Necessaries

Apart from things which are necessary for human existence such as bread, food and clothes, necessaries include items which are reasonably necessary for the infant having regard to his station in life.[25] Consequently, a watch, transistor radio or motor-cycle may be considered necessaries given the station in life of the infant. The onus of proving that goods are necessaries lies on the person supplying them. In *Ryder v. Wombwell*[26], the son of a deceased baronet bought jewelled cuff links for Twelve British Pounds and Ten Shillings each and an antique goblet to give to a friend. It was held that the goods were not necessaries.

Where the necessaries are goods, the infant will only be liable if four conditions are satisfied. The goods must be (i) suitable to his condition in life; (ii) necessary to his requirements at the time of sale; (iii) necessary to his requirements at the time of delivery.[27] (iv) goods which he was not supplied at the time of sale and delivery. Thus in *Nash v. Inman*[28], a tailor sued an infant, who was a Cambridge Undergraduate for the price of clothes including eleven (11) waistcoats. The action failed because the tailor had not adduced evidence to show that the clothes were suitable to the condition in the life of the infant and (ii) that the infant was not adequately supplied with the clothes.

Furthermore, a minor is not liable if he already had an adequate supply, even though the supplier did not know this.[29]

---

23 Contracts Act Cap. 75 Laws of Uganda (1964 Edn.) S.3(2) See also *Kimera v. Jiwani* [1971] U.L.R. 194. Compare with S.9(1) Family Law Reform Act, 1969 (U.K.); Age of Majority Act, 1974 (Kenya); Age of Majority Act, Cap 431 (Supp 1969) (Tanzania). See also Sawyerr "Contractual Capacity of Minors and the Conflict of Law In East Africa "1 E.A.L.R. (1968).

24 *Labinjoh v. Abake* (1924) 5 N.L.R.33 (Nigeria)

25 *Peter v. Fleming* (1840) 6 M & W 42; Sale of Goods Act Cap. 79, S.2.

26 (1868) L.R. 4 Ex.32

27 Sale of Goods Act, Cap. 79, S.4

28 [1908] 2 K.B. 1.

29 *Barnes v. Toye* (1884) 13 Q.B.D. 410; *Johnstone v. Marks* (1887) 19 Q.B.D. 509.

If the conditions necessary for the minor to be liable are satisfied, then he must pay a reasonable price for the goods.[30] However, this will apply to a situation where the necessaries have been "sold and delivered" to the infant. In other words, the contract must have been executed. An infant will not be liable on an executory contract. Three reasons are given for this proposition. First, the infant's liability springs from the fact that he has been supplied with goods and not because he has contracted.[31] Second, under Section 4 of the Sale of Goods Act, a minor is only liable for a reasonable price and not the contract price. This means that there is no consensual contract.[32] Third, Section 4 of the Sale of Goods Act provides that an infant will be liable for necessaries which are "sold and delivered" to him. The definition does not seem to apply to goods which are sold but are not delivered to the infant. This approach contrasts with the decision in *Roberts v. Gray*,[33] where an infant was held liable on an executory contract. The case was explained on the ground that the contract in question was educational in nature for the infant's benefit. However, Professor Treitel has suggested that[34] if an infant is liable on an executory beneficial contract, there is no reason why he should not be liable on an executory contract for necessaries.

Furthermore, at Common law, a person who spends money in buying necessaries for a minor is entitled to recover it from him[35], although a loan *perse* to an infant cannot be recovered at law. However at equity a lender to a minor can recover such part of the loan as was actually used by the minor to discharge his liability for the necessaries supplied to him.[36]

(ii) Educational contracts for a minor's benefit

It is not every contract for the benefit of the minor which binds him. However, contracts for his education, service or apprenticeship or for enabling him to earn his living (except trading contracts) are binding unless they are contrary to his interests. Thus in *Doyle v. White City Stadium Ltd.*,[37] D a minor was a professional boxer. He made a contract to fight for Three Thousand British Pounds, win, draw or lose subject to the rules of the British Boxing Board of Control. These rules stated that a boxer who was disqualified would not be paid. D was disqualified for hitting below the belt. He sued for Three Thousand British Pounds. It was held that since the contract was for his benefit in encouraging professional boxing, the infant was bound by it even if in this instance it operated against him. Similarly in *Chaplin v. Leslie Frewin (Publishers) Ltd.*[38], an infant contracted to give a firm of publishers the exclusive right to publish his memoirs. The Court of Appeal held by a majority that this was a contract which could bind the infant since it was for his benefit. It would enable him to "make a start as an author."

Furthermore an infant is bound by a service contract which is for his benefit even though some of the clauses in the contract are to his disadvantage. Thus in *Clements v. L & N.W. Ry*[39], an infant porter agreed to join an insurance scheme to which his employers contributed and to give up any claim for personal injury under the Employers' Liability Act 1880. His rights under the Scheme were more beneficial than those under the Act. It was held that the contract was on the whole beneficial and the infant was bound by it. However, a minor is not bound by a contract which is

---

30 Sale of Goods Act, Cap 79, S.4.

31 *Nash v. Inman*, *supra* n.6, p.8. per Fletcher-Moulton L.J. c.f. Buckley L.J. who stated that a minor can contract for necessaries.

32 *Pontypridd Union v. Drew* [1927] 1 K.B. 214, 220

33 [1913] 1 K.B. 520, 530

34 Treitel, *Law of Contract* (8th Edn. 1991), p.485

35 *Ellis v. Ellis* (1689) Comb. 482; *Earle v. Earle* (1712) 10 Mod. 67.

36 *Marlow v. Pitifield* (1719) 1 P. Wms 558; *Re National Permanent Benefit Building Society* (1869) L. R. 5Ch. App. 309, 313.

37 [1935] 1 K.B. 110

38 [1966] Ch. 71, 85, 95

39 [1894] 2 Q.B. 482

on the whole harsh and oppressive. Thus in De *Francesco v. Barnum*[40], a girl was apprenticed for stage dancing by a deed provided as follows: that (i) she should be entirely at the disposal of the dancing master; (ii) she should get no pay unless he actually employed her, which he was not bound to do; (iii) he could send her abroad; (iv) he could put an end to the contract if, after fair trial he found her unsuitable; (v) she should not accept any professional engagement with the defendant without the master's consent. It was held that the master could not sue the defendant for inducing a breach of the deed because it was unreasonably harsh and invalid.

Finally trading contracts entered into by a minor however beneficial to him are not binding on him.[41]

(b) Voidable contracts

In four situations an infant's contract is voidable i.e., it binds both parties, but the infant can escape liability by repudiating before majority or within a reasonable time thereafter. However, the other party cannot repudiate.

(i) Contracts concerning land

An infant lessee is liable for rent unless he repudiates the tenancy contract.[42] An infant who agrees to buy land is similarly bound unless he repudiates[43]. The same principle applies where a minor agrees to sell land.[44]

(ii) Shares in companies

An infant who agrees to subscribe for shares or buys shares which are not fully paid in a company is liable for calls on them unless he repudiates.[45] Where he repudiates, he ceases to be liable and can have his name removed from the company's register.[46] However, if the minor buys shares from a previous owner and fails to repudiate liability for calls on them, the Company cannot generally avoid the transaction and so make the transferror liable for the calls.[47] Nevertheless, if the Company is wound up while the buyer is still a minor, the liquidator can exercise the minor's right of repudiation for him and so make the transferor again liable on the calls.[48]

(iii) Partnership

A minor can become a partner and is to an extent bound by the partnership agreement. However, he cannot be sued on the agreement during his infancy by persons who give credit to the firm or be made liable for its losses.[49] However he is liable if after he attains majority. Additionally, he is not entitled to any share of the profits or assets of the partnership until its liabilities have been paid off.[50]

(iv) Marriage settlements

A marriage settlement binds a minor unless he repudiates.[51]

(c) Void contracts

Section 1 of the Infants Relief Act, 1874, which previously applied in Uganda[52] provides that all contracts whether by specialty or simple contract entered into by minors.

---

40 (1889) 43 Ch.d. 165; (1890) 45 Ch.D. 430

41 *Mercantile Union Guarantee Corporation v. Ball* [1893] A.C. 360

42 *Keteley's* Case (1613) 1 Bromnl 120

43 *Thurstan v. Notts* [1902] 1 Ch.1; *Orakpo v. Manson Investments Ltd.* [1978] A.C. 95, 106, 113

44 *Slator v. Trimble* (1861) 14 Ir. C.L.R. 342

45 *Dublin v. Wicklow Ry v. Black* (1852) 8 Ex.181

46 *Ibid.*; See also *Steinberg v. Scala (Leeds) Ltd.*[1923] 2 Ch.452

47 *Lumsden's Case* (1868) L.R. 4 Ch.App 31; *Gooch's Case* (1872) L.R. 8 Ch. App. 266

48 *Capper's Case* (1868) L.R. 3 Ch. App 458

49 *Goode v. Harrison* (1821) 5 B & Ald. 147, 157. *Lovell v. Beauchamp P* [1894] A.C. 607.

50

51 *Duncan v. Dixon* (1890) 44 Ch.D.211; *Edwards v. Carter* [1893] A.C. 360; [1892] 2 Ch.278.

(i) for the repayment of money lent or to be lent;
(ii) for goods supplied or to be supplied (other than contracts for necessaries;
(iii) all accounts stated with minors are absolutely void.
In *Coutts & Co. v. Brown-Lecky*[53], B an infant had an overdraft with the bank. X and Y guaranteed it. The bank sued X and Y for payment. It was held that as the loan by the bank to B was void, X and Y could not be held liable.

Even if a minor has induced a void contract by misrepresenting that he was of full age, he cannot be sued on that contract.[54]

Under Section 2 of the Infants Relief Act, 1874, contracts falling under that act cannot be ratified by the minor after he comes of age.[55]

The issue arises as to whether the infant can recover or benefit under a void contract. Four situations can be considered.

(i) Benefit to infant under void contract for sale of goods
If the infant benefits under a void contract for the sale of goods, he cannot retain the goods and recover the money he has paid for them. Thus in *Valentini v. Canali*,[56] the infant plaintiff agreed to take a lease of the defendant's house and to pay One Hundred and Two British Pounds for furniture in it. After paying Sixty-eight pounds on account and using the furniture for some months, he repudiated and sued to recover back the Sixty-eight British Pounds. The claim failed because he could not recover money paid for something he had used.

(ii) Money paid by infant under void contract
Money paid by an infant under a void contract can be recovered by him only if there has been total failure of consideration. Thus in *Steinberg v. Scala (Leeds) Ltd.*[57], S an infant agreed to take Five Hundred British Pounds 1 shares in a company and paid 10s on each share. She received no dividend on the shares. While still a minor, she repudiated the contract and brought an action (i) to recover the money she had paid; (ii) for a declaration that she was not liable for future calls. It was held firstly that as the shares had some market value she could not recover money already paid out but secondly she was not liable on future calls on the shares.

(iii) Delivery by infant of goods under void contract
If an infant delivers goods under a void contract he cannot get them back unless there is total failure of consideration. Thus in *Pearce v. Brain*[58], an infant plaintiff exchanged his motor-cycle for the defendant's car. Four days later, the car broke down due to a defect. The plaintiff's claim to recover the motor-cycle in return for the damaged car failed.

(iv) Fraudulent conversion of goods by an infant
If an infant fraudulently obtains goods but not money, he may be ordered by the Court to return the goods which are in his possession and have not been paid for.[59]

2. Corporations

A company or corporation is a distinct entity separate and set apart from members or shareholders of the company, although it is an artificial person created by law.[60] A Corporation may be (i) a

52 See Judicature Act 1967, S.3(2)(b); Hodgin, *supra* p. 67. See also Betting & Loans (Infants) Act, 1892 (U.K.).
53 [1947] K.B. 104
54 *R Leslie v. Sheill* [1914] 3 K.B. 607.
55 See also *Smith v. King* [1892] 2 Q.B. 543
56 (1889) 24 Q.B.D. 166
57 [1923] 2 Ch.452.
58 [1929] 2 K.B. 310, following *Valentini v. Canali, supra* n.56
59 *Stocks v. Wilson* [1913] 2 K.B. 235. See also Minors Contracts Act, 1987 (U.K.); S.3 under which a minor could be held liable to restore certain benefits received by him under a contract which did not bind him.
60 *Salomon v. Salomon* [1897] A.C. 22. See also Bakibinga, *Company Law In Uganda* (1993) Chap.2.

company registered under the Companies Act, Cap.85 or (ii) a corporation formed by a special act or statute of parliament such as the Uganda Revenue Authority Statute No.6 of 1991.

The capacity of a corporation is limited in two main ways. First by natural possibility and second by legal possibility.

(a) Natural possibility

Since the company is an artificial entity, it can only contract through agents, usually its officers or directors.[61] It cannot enter into contracts of a personal nature such as being treasurer of a friendly society[62] or act as a solicitor, medical doctor or accountant.

(b) Legal possibility

Certain restrictions may be imposed on the powers of a corporation on its formation by the statute creating it. As far as statutory corporations are concerned the doctrine of *ultra vires* applies to them. Under that doctrine, a company can only engage in those activities which are contained in its objects in the memorandum of association. Any act which is outside those objects is beyond its powers.[63]

(c) Forms of contracts concluded by corporations

At common law contracts concluded by corporations had to be made under seal. However, this principle has been superseded by the Companies Act[64] which allows a company through its agents to contract in the same way as a natural person.

3. Unincorporated bodies

Unincorporated bodies such as clubs[65] can contract through agents who are normally the executive committee or other designated persons.

4. Mental patients

A mental patient or lunatic has been described[66] as "a person of unsound mind means an idiot or a person suffering from mental derangement".

A contract with a mental patient is valid except in 2 cases.

(a) Where the disability is known to the other party

If the other party to a contract with a mental patient knows of the patient's disability, the contract is voidable at the patient's option.[67] The burden of proof is on the patient to show that the disability prevented him from understanding the particular transaction[68] and the other party knew this. However, it would appear, that the patient becomes bound by the contract if he ratifies it after he is cured.[69]

---

61 See Bakibinga *ibid.* Chapter 12 especially pp.230 - 232.

62 *Re West of England & South Wales District Bank* (1879) 11 Ch.D.768.

63 *Ashbury Rly Carriage Co. v. Riche* (1875) L.R. 7 H.L.653. See also Bakibinga *ibid.* pp.48 - 64.

64 See Article 80 Table A and Bakibinga *ibid.* pp.191 - 200, 231.

65 See Bakibinga *supra* n.60 pp.25-30.

66 Mental Treatment Act Cap.270, Section 2.

67 *Imperial Loan Co. v. Stone* [1892] 1 Q.B. 599

68 *Re: K* [1988] Ch.310

69 *Birkin v. Wing* (1890) 63 L.T. 80.

(b) Where the mental patient's property is subject to the court's control
An attempt by a mental patient to dispose of the property subject to Court's control is not binding on him since control over the property lies with Court.[70] However, the transaction binds the other party if the Court approves of it.[71]

(c) Necessaries

Where necessaries are sold and delivered to a mental patient, he must pay a reasonable price therefor.[72]

5. Drunkards

Contracts made by persons who are so drunk at the time as not to understand what they were doing are voidable at the option of the person who was drunk provided that the other person knew of this condition.[73] The burden of proof of drunkenness lies on the drunkard. A contract made by a drunkard can be ratified or affirmed when he is sober.[74] A drunkard is also liable to pay a reasonable price for necessaries supplied to him in same way as a mental patient and minor.[75]

---

70 *Re Walker* [1905] 1 Ch.160; *Re Marshall* [1920] 1 Ch.284
71 c.f. *Baldwyn v. Smith* [1900] 1 Ch.588
72 Sale of Goods Act, Cap 79, Section 4. See also *Re Beavan* [1912] 1 Ch.196.
73 *Gore v. Gibson* (1843) 13 M & W 623
74 *Mathews v. Baxter* (1873) L.R. 8 Ex.132
75 Sale of Goods Act, Cap 79, S.4.

6
FORM AND TERMS OF A CONTRACT

1. Form

(a) General rule

The law may require that a contract shall be made in a certain form and that this should follow a certain manner including the marking or recording of the contract. In modern legal systems such formal requirements generally consist of writing, sometimes with additional requirements e.g. those of a deed or of authentication by a notary.[76]

The requirement for a contract to fulfil a certain form may be necessary for a number of reasons.[77] First it promotes certainty as it is usually relatively easy to tell whether the required form has been used. In addition a requirement of writing simplifies the problem of ascertaining the contents of the agreement. Second, form has a cautionary effect in that a person may hesitate longer before executing a deed than he would before making an oral promise. Third, form has a protective function in that it is used to protect the weaker party to a contractual relationship by ensuring that he is provided with a written record of the terms of the contract. For instance, an employee must be informed in writing of the terms of his employment[78] and a contract of sale of goods of the value of Shs.200/= and above must be in writing.[79] The second and third purposes of form are also shown by elaborate formal requirements that protect a hirer under certain hire-purchase agreements in other jurisdictions.[80] Finally, form may serve a "channelling" purpose that is the use of a certain form may help to distinguish one type of transaction from another.

On the other hand, form is disadvantageous in the sense that it may be time-consuming and clumsy and that it is a source of technical pitfalls.[81] It has been observed[82] that "even the relatively simple requirement of writing is open to these objections and has therefore been regarded as inconvenient from a commercial point of view". Consequently the general rule is that contracts can be made informally.[83]

(b) Statutory exceptions

To the general rule mentioned above are a number of exceptions many of which depend on statutes which deal with specific types of contracts. Some of these contracts must be made by deed, some must be in writing and others must be evidenced by a note or memorandum in writing. A few illustrations are given here.

---

76 Treitel, *Law of Contract* (8th Edn., 1991) p.161

77 *Ibid.* pp. 161-162

78 Employment Decree 1975 Section 10.

79 Sale of Goods Act, Cap. 79, S.6. See also *Kabaseke Stores Company Ltd. v. Attorney General* (1990-1991) II KALR 70.

80 E.g. Consumer Credit (Agreements) Regulations made under Consumer Credit Act, 1974, S.60 (U.K.). Hire Purchase Acts of Kenya and Tanzania.

81 See *Kabaseke Case supra.* n.79

82 Treitel, *supra* n.76, p.162

83 *Beckham v. Drake* (1841)9 M & W79, 92. See also Hodgin, *Law of Contract In East Africa* (1975, Rep. 1982)p.18.

(i) Contracts which must be in writing

In the Registration of Titles Act[84] is set out the exact form that transfers of land and leases must take. Other types of contract which must be in writing include bills of exchange, promissory notes[85] and bills of sale.[86]

The effect of non-compliance with the requirement of writing is illustrated by the case of *Pandit v. Sekatawa*[87]. In that case, the plaintiff advocate sued to recover professional fees from the defendant whom he had represented in a court action. The defendant argued that their contract was not in writing as required by the Advocates' Rules 1950.[88] The argument was accepted by the Court and rationalised by Udo Udoma C.J. (as he then was) thus:

> It is patently obvious that the terms of the ... provision (S.10) there is no valid agreement before this court capable of creating any legally enforceable right in favour of the plaintiff, the agreement testified to not having been made in writing nor signed by the first defendant or any of the defendants, sought to be charged.

The Court further explained that observance of the requirement of writing was necessary to prevent advocates appearing without instructions nd later attempting to enforce their claims for professional fees.[89]

A bill of sale is void unless it is in writing in the Statutory form.[90] Similarly a bill of exchange will be invalid if it is not in writing.[91] A transfer of land which does not comply with the Registration of Titles Act is void.[92]

(b) Contracts which must be evidenced in writing

Some statutes do not require contracts to be made in writing, but only to be evidenced by a written document.

(i) Contracts of Guarantee

Section 4(1) of the Contract Act[93] provides that

> No suit shall be brought whereby to charge the defendant upon any special promise to answer for the debt, default or miscarriage of another person unless the agreement ... or since memorandum or note thereof, is in writing and signed by the party to be charged therewith or some other person thereunto by him lawfully authorised.

The provision has been interpreted to apply whether the liability guaranteed is contractual or tortious.[94] However, it applies where a third person promises the creditors to pay the debt. It does not apply where the third party's promise is to the debtor.[95] The provision applies to a guarantee but not to an indemnity. A guarantee is a promise to pay another's debt if he fails to pay. An indemnity is a promise to indemnify the creditor against loss arising out of the principal contract.[96]

84 Cap 205, Section 91 and seventh schedule.

85 Bills of Exchange Act, Cap 76 (Laws of Uganda 1964 Edn.,) Ss. 3(1), 17(2).

86 Bills of Sale Act Cap.77 read together with Bills of Sale Acts, 1878 and 1882 (U.K.)

87 1964(2) A.L.R. Comm.25

88 See now Regulation 1 of Advocates (Professional Conduct) Regulations, 1977 which appears not to impose the condition of writing.

89 See also Hodgin, *supra n.83* p.14.

90 Bills of Sale Act 1878 (Amendment) Act, 1882 and Cap.77.

91 Bills of Exchange Act, Cap 76, S.3(2). See also S.17(2)(a) thereof.

92 Registration of Titles Act Cap 205, Ss. 91, 94 and 139

93 Cap 75 (Laws of Uganda 1964 Edn.)

94 *Kirkham v. Marter* (1819) 2 B & Ald. 613

95 *Eastwood v. Kenyon* (1840) 11 A & E 438

In the case of a guarantee the liability of the principal is primary and that of the guarantor only secondary. It follows that if the principal debtor is not liable, the guarantor is not liable either. In contrast, a promise to indemnify creates primary liability which arises even though the promisee has no enforceable rights under the principal contract.[97]

Furthermore Section 4(1) only applies to a guarantee which stands alone and not to one which is part of a larger transaction.[98] Similarly a guarantee given by a *del credere* agent is not covered by the provision. It is notable that such an agent guarantees the solvency of the third party between whom and his principal makes a contract, i.e. he promises the principal to pay if the third party does not. This is in line with the main object of a *del credere* agency which is to enable the principal to sell and the agent to earn his commission.[99]

Additionally, a guarantee is not covered by the provision, if it is given to protect some proprietary interest of the guarantor. Thus A may buy goods from B which are held by C as security for a debt owed by B to C. If A induces C to deliver the goods to him by promising to pay B's debt in case B does not pay it, A's promise is not covered by the provision.[100] The reason for this is that the main object of A's promise is to protect his own property and not to guarantee B's debt.

(ii) Contracts of sale of goods

A contract for the sale of goods where the purchase price exceeds Shs.200/= must be evidenced in writing.[101]

(iii) Type of evidence required

Contracts falling within Section 4 of the Contract Act must be evidenced by a signed note or memorandum in writing. However, the exact nature of the evidence required is not specified by the Act. Nevertheless some rules have been laid down by parliament and the Courts. First, the memorandum should identify the parties by naming or identifying them[102] and also state the capacity in which they contract.[103] The memorandum could sufficiently describe the parties without actually naming them.[104] Second, the memorandum of guarantee need not state the consideration for the guarantee.[105] Third the memorandum must contain the material [106] terms of the contract. If it only states some of the terms, the parties will be "distinctly at issue as to what the contract was and the very object of the [provision] was to prevent parol evidence being gone into to elucidate that which the parties failed to make distinct by reducing it into writing."[107] Fourth, the memorandum must be signed by the party to be charged or by his agent lawfully authorised to sign for him. The requirement of signature has been liberally interpreted. Thus a party need not sign his full name: initials suffice.[108] In addition, the signature may be printed [109] and may be in any part of the document, not necessarily at the bottom.[110] Fifth, the memorandum

---

96 *Birkmyr v. Darnell* (1704) 1 Salk 27; *Argo Caribbean Group v. Lewis* [1976] 2 Lloyd's Rep.289. See also Treitel, *supra* n.76 p.166.

97 *Yeoman Credit Ltd. v. Latter* [1961] 1 W.L.R. 828; [1961] 2 All E.R. 281; [1962] 2 Q.B.508.

98 *Sutton & Co. v. Grey* [1894] 1 Q.B. 285; Treitel, *supra* n.76, p.166.

99 *Couturier v. Hastie* (1852) 8 Ex. 40, 56. See also *infra* Chap.12

100 *Fitzgerald v. Drressler* (1859) 7 C.B. (N.S.) 374 interpreting Section of the *Statute of Frauds 1677* U.K. which is *pari materia*, see also Treitel *supra* n.76.

101 Sale of Goods Act, Cap 79, S.6 *Kabaseke Case*, supra n.79.

102 *Williams v. Jordan* (1877) 6 Ch.D. 517

103 *Dewar v. Mintoft* [1912] 2 K.B. 373

104 *Carr v. Lynch* [1900] 1 Ch. 613; See also *Leslie and Anderson (Nairobi) Ltd. v. Kassam Jivraj & Co. Ltd.* 17 E.A.C.A. 84

105 Mercantile Law Amendment Act 1856, S.3 (U.K.)

106 *Hawkins v. Price* [1947] Ch.645 c.f. *Beckett v. Nurse* [1948] 1 K,B. 535 *Tweddle v. Henderson* [1975] 1 W.L.R. 1496; [1975] 2 All E.R. 1096.

107 *Caddick v. Skidmore* (1857) 2 D & J 52, 56.

108 *Hill v. Hill* [1947] Ch.231, 240

109 *Schneider v. Norris* (1814) 2 M & S 286

need not be prepared for the purpose of satisfying the statutory requirements of written evidence. A writing which comes into existence before an action is brought[111] on the contract will suffice so long as it acknowledges or recognises the existence of the contract[112]. Finally, where no single document fully records the transaction, it may be possible to produce a sufficient memorandum by joining together two or more documents[113]. This is possible where one document expressly or impliedly refers to another transaction. Consequently, if that transaction is also recorded in a document, and that document was in existence when the first was signed,[114] the two documents can be joined.[115] Joinder is also possible through an intermediate document. Thus in one case,[116] three telexes were involved.

(iv) Effect of non nompliance

Failure to comply with the requirements above does not make the contract void but only unenforceable[117]. While the contract can be made orally, it can only be enforced by action if a note or memorandum of it exists signed by the party against whom enforcement is sought. Since the contract is not void, money paid or property transferred under it cannot be recovered back merely because the contract is not evidenced in writing.[118]

Section 4 of the Contract Act could cause hardship to a party who had wholly or partly performed a contract which was unenforceable for want of written evidence. To meet this hardship Equity developed the doctrine of part performance, under which the party who had rendered such performance could enforce the contract inspite of the lack of proper note or memorandum.[119] The doctrine of part performance "was in the past restricted to contracts which were specifically enforceable in Equity, or perhaps (more narrowly) to contracts for the disposition of interests in land".[120] Consequently, contracts of guarantee were, by necessary implication, not covered by the doctrine and the normal remedy against a guarantor would be a common law action for the amount which he had promised and not a claim for specific performance. However, the possibility of the doctrine being applied to contracts of guarantee has not been ruled out in Britain[121] since it "is conceivable that a contract of guarantee might in exceptional circumstances be specifically enforceable."[122] Consequently, acts done by the creditor in reliance on the guarantee could be regarded as sufficient part performance. However, Professor Treitel concludes that such a possibility is remote and that it "is highly unlikely that the doctrine will be applied to contracts of guarantee."[123]

The doctrine of part performance has been considered in East Africa. Thus in *Credit Finance Corporation Ltd. v. Ali Mwakasanga*[124] ,A took a lorry on hire purchase, signed his part of the contract and paid a deposit. Later the finance company denied that there was a valid contract on the grounds that they had not signed. The Court of Appeal held that A's behaviour was a sufficient act of part performance and consequently the contract was enforceable.

---

110 *Evans v. Hoare* [1892] 1 Q.B. 593

111 *Lucas v. Dixon* (1889) 22 Q.B.D. 357; *Farr, Smith & Co. v. Messers* [1928] 1 K.B. 397; *Kanti Printing Works v.Tanga District Council* Civil Appeal No.18 of 1970 C.A.

112 *Tweddle v. Henderson, supra* n.106.

113 Treitel, *supra* n.76, 169

114 *Re Danish Bacon Co. Ltd. v. Staff Pension Fund* [1971] 1 W.L.R. 248.

115 *Long v. Millar* (1879) 4 C.P.D. 450

116 *The Anemone* [1987] 1 Lloyd's Rep 547

117 *Elias v. George Saliely & Co. (Barbados) Ltd.* [1983] 1 A.C. 646, 650 c.f. *Carrington v. Roots* (1837) 2 M & W 248, 255, 257.

118 *Thomas v. Brown* (1876) 1 Q.B.D. 714; Treitel, *supra* n.76 pp.890 - 891; *Low v. Fry* (1935) 152 L.T. 585.

119 Treitel, *supra* n.76 pp.170 - 171; Hodgin, *supra* pp.16-17.

120 Treitel, *ibid.* p.170 relying on *Britain v. Rossiter* (1879) 11 Q.B.D. 123; *Mc Manus v. Cooke* (1887) 35 Ch.D. 681.

121 *The Anemone* [1987] 1 Lloyd's Rep. 546, 557.

122 Treitel *supra* n.76 p.170. See also *Beswick v. Beswick* [1968] A.C. 58.

123 *Ibid* p.171

2. Terms of a contract

(a) Nature

Undertakings or promises which are contained in the contract are known as the terms of the contract. They should be distinguished from *representations* which are made before the contract is entered into and which are not intended to form part of the contract.

Parties to a contract normally state the terms of the contract. These are known as *express terms*. However, if a term is not expressly stated, it is known as an *implied term*, either because the parties so intended or applies by operation of law, or by custom or usage.

Each of these terms will be considered in turn.

(b) Express terms

Where a contract is made orally, the terms of the contract can be proved by oral evidence normally by the person claiming that there is a contract. Once this is established, a further question can arise as to the meaning of the words used. In answering this question, the Court applies the objective test of agreement. Under that test a party cannot enforce the contract in the sense which he gave to the words if the sense differs from one which the other party reasonably gave them.[125]

Where the contract is in writing, its terms can be ascertained by means of documentary evidence. Where these are clear, a court must give effect to the terms. It is not the duty of the Court to rewrite an expressly stated contract for the parties.[126] However, if the written contract is ambiguous then the court may construe it in order to clear up the ambiguity. This may involve looking at a number of documents.

Joinder of documents

The terms of a contract may be contained in more than one document. One of these may expressly refer to another e.g. where a contract is made subject to standard terms settled by a trade association. Those terms are then incorporated by reference into the contract; if there are several editions of the standard terms, the contract is *prima facie* taken to refer to the most recent edition.[127] It may also incorporate amendments validly made by the association.[128]

Alternatively, a contract may be contained in several documents even though one does not expressly refer to the other. For instance a series of dealings may take place under a "master Contract", a formal document being executed each time an individual contract is made. All these contracts may be subject to the master contract even though they do not refer to it.[129]

The parol evidence rule

The parol evidence rule is to the effect that evidence cannot be admitted (or that even if admitted, it cannot be used) to add to, vary or contradict a written instrument.[130] In relation to contracts "the

---

124 [1959] E.A. 79 C.A. following *Brogden v. Metropolitan Railway C.*(1877) 2 App. Cas.666. See also *Mukisa Biscuit Manufacturing Co. Ltd. v. West End Distributors* [1970] E.A. 469 C.A. where it was stated that a Contract is less likely to be found void for uncertainty if executed or partly executed.

125 *Eyre v. Measday* [1986] 1 All E.R. 488; *Thake v. Maurice* [1986] Q.B. 644, see also Grubb [1986] C.L.J. 197.

126 *Davies v. Davies* (1887) Ch.D. 359. See also *Stephen Mabosi v. Uganda Revenue Authority* High Court Civil Suit No.699 of 1993 dealing with the issue of variation of a seizure notice.

127 *Smith v. South Wales Switchgear Ltd.* [1978] 1 W.L.R.165 [1978] 1 All E.R. 18.

128 *Shearson Lehman Hulton Inc. v. Moclaine Watson & Co.* [1989] 2 Lloyd's Rep 570, 589; [1990] 3 All E.R. 723. See also *Adamastos Shipping Co. v. Anglo Sexon Petroleum Co.* [1959 A.C. 133; *The Oceanic Amity* [1984] 2 All E.R. 140.

129 Treitel, *supra* n.76 p.176. See also *Panorama Developments (Guildford) Ltd. v. Fidelis Furnishing Fabrics Ltd.* [1971] 2 Q.B.711.

130 *Jacobs v. Batavia & General plantations Trust Ltd.* [1924] 1 Ch.287, 295; For a recent exposition, see *Rabin v. Gerson Berger Association Ltd.* [1986] 1 W.L.R. 526, 531, 537. Section 90 Evidence Act, Cap 43 (Uganda).

rule means that, where a contract has been reduced to writing, neither party can rely on evidence of terms alleged to have been agreed, which is extrinsic document, i.e. not contained in it."[131]. Although the rule is generally stated as applying to *parol* evidence, it applies just as much to other forms of extrinsic evidence.[132] However, if a contractual document incorporates another document by reference, evidence of the second document is admissible although the rule prevents a party from relying on evidence that is extrinsic to both documents.[133]

The rationale for the rule is the promotion of certainty by holding that parties who have reduced a contract to writing should be bound by the writing alone.[134]

Where, however, there is a dispute as to what was actually said at the time of contracting, evidence extrinsic to the document may be admitted in a number of exceptional instances[135] which are considered here.

(i) Validity

Additional evidence will be admitted by Court to show whether a contract is valid. Consequently, evidence will be admitted to show that a contract is tainted or vitiated by misrepresentation, fraud, mistake, incapacity, lack of consideration, establishment of the defence of *non est factum* or that the document was not intended to have legal effect.[136] In *East African Power & Lighting Co. Ltd. v. Dandora Black Trap Quarries Ltd.*[137], the plaintiff sued the defendant on a minimum consumption agreement for the supply of electricity under which the defendant undertook to pay a minimum charge of Shs.12,840 per annum for a period of 46 months from 1st January 1965. The defendant made part payment of the sum and the plaintiff demanded the balance. The defendant admitted the agreement but claimed that it was void and unenforceable because it (i) lacked consideration and (ii) was illegal as contravening the Electric Power Act. It was held that although Section 97 of the Kenya Evidence Act[138] prohibited the giving of secondary evidence of the terms of a written contract, a recital in regard to the agreement, though not a term of the contract, may be referred to in order to resolve the ambiguity. The recital referred to the defendant's request for construction works and an undertaking by the plaintiff to carry out the works. Consequently, it was permissible for the defendant to produce evidence to show that no works were carried out and he was entitled to adduce evidence as to the absence of consideration. However, on the evidence, the plaintiff had shown that there was good consideration.

Oral Evidence will also be admitted to show how a contract came to be executed.[139]

(ii) Additional terms

Evidence may be adduced to show that there are other additional terms and conditions attached to the contract.[140] In *Roshan v. Singh*[141], A, a subcontractor, under a written agreement agreed with B to carry out certain excavation and filling work at Shs.15/= per 100 cubic feet. Later A's copy of the agreement was amended by the substitution of the figure 17 for 15 and the alteration was signed by B. This issue arose as to the admissibility in evidence of the alteration. It was held

---

131 Treitel, *supra*, p.176; *Choitram v. Lazar* [1959] E.A.157

132 *Mabosi v. U.R.A. supra* n.126

133 *Jacobs v. Batavia supra* n.130; *Gailey & Roberts v. Salem* [1962] E.A.376.

134 *Rabin v. Gerson Berger Association Ltd. supra* n.130 pp.534, 537

135 Evidence Act, Cap.43, S.91.

136 *Ibid.* S.91(a); *Campbell Discount Co. v. Gall* [1961] 1 Q.B.431; *Roe v. R. A. Naylor*(1918) 87 L.J. K.B. 958, 964; *Cheleta Coffee Plantations Ltd. v. Mehisen* [1966] E.A.203; *Orion Inc. C. PLC v. Sphere Drake Ins PLC*[1990] 1 Lloyd's Rep. 465.

137 [1967] E.A. 728. Chanan Singh J.

138 equivalent to S.90 Evidence Act (Uganda)

139 *Bilous v. Bilous* [1957] E.A. 96.

140 Evidence Act, s.91 (b), (f)

141 [1959] E.A. 717

that by a subsequent Oral agreement the written agreement had been extended to apply to a new task and at the same time an alteration was made in the rate of payment recorded in the written agreement. Accordingly, evidence under proviso 6 of Section 92 of the Indian Evidence Act.[142] was admissible to show how the language of the altered instrument related to existing facts.

In *Jos Hansen & Soehne v. Jetha Ltd.*, [143] the plaintiff, a decree holder applied for the recording of an adjustment of a decree and for its execution against three alleged sureties. The application was opposed by the sureties on the ground that they had not completed the contract of guarantee and that the application was time-barred. The document relied upon as a contract of guarantee was a letter addressed to the plaintiff, the introductory part of which began " We the undersigned". At the foot of the letter were the signatures of 3 alleged sureties and an empty space for a fourth signature. It was held that the letter was silent upon the question whether the signatures of the four sureties was a condition of the guarantee. Consequently, oral evidence was admissible under the proviso to Section 92 of the Indian Evidence Act, 1872.[144] Furthermore, the oral statement of the sureties that their signatures alone were sufficient security was not a subsequent modification of the guarantee but was a collateral oral term.

(iii) Application of usage or custom

Extrinsic evidence can be admitted to show that a contract is subject to any usage or custom not inconsistent with the express terms of the contract.[145] In *Palgrave, Brown & Son Ltd. v. S. S. Turid (Owners)*[146], a charterparty provided that the expenses of discharging the Cargo should be borne by the charterer "as customary". A custom that the expenses should be borne by the ship owner was held to be inconsistent with the charterparty.

(iv) Operation of the contract

Extrinsic evidence can be used to show that a contract has ceased to operate or is not yet in operation.[147] Evidence is also admissible to show that a written contract has been varied or rescinded.[148]

(v) Aid to construction

Extrinsic evidence can be admitted to enable the court to construe or interpret the contract where it is ambiguous.[149] In *Visram v. Bhatt & Ors*[150], the plaintiffs let out to the defendant an undefined area within one of two plots by the plaintiffs measuring 525ft x 325ft for quarrying purposes at a monthly rent. The defendants agreed to fence the area but did not do so. The plaintiff sued for damages for trespass and wrongful quarrying and succeeded. The judge relied on oral evidence defining the area let. On appeal, the defendants argued that oral evidence was wrongly admitted to explain a plain ambiguity under Section 99 of the Evidence Act of Kenya.[151] The plaintiffs argued that the oral evidence was properly admitted under Section 102[152] of the Evidence Act of Kenya as extrinsic evidence to resolve an ambiguity as to the application of the lease in its context. It was held that where the words in a lease are clear in themselves and it is only by

---

142 equivalent to Evidence Act, S.91(f)

143 [1959] E.A.563

144 equivalent to Evidence Act, S.91 (Uganda)

145 Evidence Act, S.91 (e); *Humfrey v. Dale* (1857) 7 E & B 266, 275

146 [1922] 1 A.C. 397

147 *Pym v. Campbell* (1856) 6 E. & B. 370; Evidence Act, S.91(c)

148 *Morris v. Baron & Co.* [1918] AC.1; Evidence Act S.91(d)

149 Evidence Act, S.91 (f); *Bank of New Zealand v. Simpson* [1900] A.C. at p.189 *Roshan v. Singh* [1959] E.A. 717;

150 [1965] E.A. 789

151 Equivalent to S.92 Evidence Act (Uganda)

152 See Evidence Act, S.91(f)

extrinsic evidence that the ambiguity is shown to exist, extrinsic evidence to resolve the ambiguity is admissible under Section 102 of the Evidence Act (Kenya). Consequently, oral evidence of the area leased was properly admitted.

(vi) Identification of subject matter

Extrinsic evidence is admissible to identify the subject-matter of a contract. For instance if the contract refers to "your milk", it may be necessary to show that this means not only milk produced by the plaintiff, but also milk produced on a neighbouring farm[153] and to define the exact area of land conveyed where the conveyance fails to make this clear.[154] In addition such evidence will also be admissible to define the extent of the party's obligations under a contract e.g. to show that a contract to pump oil out of a stranded tanker only obliged the party rendering the service to take away so much oil as to avert the risk of pollution.[155] Where a lease contains a covenant to repair evidence can be given as to the character of the premises in order to determine the extent of the obligation imposed by the covenant.[156] Evidence is also admissible to show whether a guarantee relates to one debt only or is a continuing one[157] and to which of a number of transactions a guarantee relates.[158]

(vii) Proof of collateral agreement

Oral evidence can be admitted to prove the existence of a collateral agreement.[159] Thus in *Mann. v.Nunn*[160] , the plaintiff orally agreed to take a lease of the defendant's premises if the defendant would first do certain repairs. A written agreement was later executed, but did not refer to the defendant's promise to do the repairs. It was stated that "the parol agreement neither alters nor adds to the written one but is an independent agreement.[161] In *Jos Hansen & Soehne v. Jetha Ltd.*,[162] it was held that the oral statement of sureties that their signatures alone were sufficient security was not a subsequent modification of the guarantee but was a collateral oral term. Furthermore, in *Ishakiya v. Jusub,*[163] the plaintiff sued for unpaid rent. He relied on a written agreement dated 29 March, 1955 in so far as letting was concerned and pleaded a subsequent oral agreement as regards the amount of rent to be paid. The defendant argued that by virtue of Section 91 of the Evidence Act of Uganda, the subsequent oral agreement could not be proved. It was held that an agreement for a lease need not by law be in writing for purposes of proviso (d) to Section 91 of the Evidence Act. Second, that the tenancy agreement was an agreement for lease and in the circumstances there was nothing in law to prevent the parties, before the rent was paid, from agreeing by another agreement that the rent should be a fixed sum. Finally, the evidence of the subsequent parol agreement was admissible.

(c) Implied terms

There are three categories of implied terms. First are terms which are implied in fact. These are terms which are not expressly set out in the contract but which the parties must have intended to include. Second, are terms implied in law, i.e. terms imported by operation of law although the parties may not have intended to include them. Third are terms which are implied by custom.

---

153 *Macdonald v. Longbottom* (1859) 1 E & E 977.
154 *Scarfe v. Adams* [1981] 1 All E.R. 843
155 *The Pacific Colocotronis* [1982] 2 Lloyd's Rep 40. Treitel *supra* p.183
156 *Burges v. Wickham (1863) 3 B & S 669, 698*
157 *Heffield v. Meadows (1869) L.R. 4 C.P. 595*
158 *Perry Lease Ltd. v. Imeear Ltd. [1988] 1 W.L.R. 463*
159 *Evidence Act, S.91 (e), (d)*
160 *(1874) 30 L.T. 526*
161 *Ibid.*, p.527
162 *supra* n.143 and text thereof.
163 [1965] E.A. 241

(i) Terms implied in fact

The principle upon which a Court would act in implying a term of fact was stated by Mackinon L. J. thus:[164]

> Prima facie that which in any contract is left to be applied and need not be expressed is something so obvious that it goes without saying; so that, if while the parties were making their bargain, an officious bystander were to suggest some express provision for it in the agreement, they would testily suppress him with a common 'of course.

The implication must be obvious and necessary to give the transaction such business efficacy as the parties must have intended. Thus in *Luxor (Eastbourne) Ltd. v. Cooper*,[165] the defendant employed an estate agent to sell two Cinemas and promised to pay him a commission "on completion of sale." Before the agent effected the sale, the defendant sold the Cinemas himself. It was held that no term could be implied to the effect that the defendant should not except for good cause refuse to sell to a person introduced by the agent since it was not clear that both parties would have agreed to such a term.

The courts are reluctant to imply a term especially where the parties have entered into a carefully drafted written contract containing detailed terms agreed between them. Thus in *Shell U.K. Ltd. v. Lastock Garages Ltd.*[166], a written contract provided that Shell should supply petrol and oil to the defendant garage company which in turn undertook to buy such goods solely from Shell. During a price war, Shell reduced the price of petrol to neighbouring garages so that the defendant could only trade at a loss. The Court of Appeal rejected the agreement that a term should be implied in the contract that Shell would not "abnormally discriminate" against the defendant. The Court reasoned firstly that the proposed implication would not have been agreed to by Shell. Second, the implication was too vague. Conversely in *Mukisa Biscuit Manufacturing Company Ltd. v. West End Distributors*[167], it was held *inter alia* that as reasonable terms will be implied in respect of remuneration and termination and for carrying out the intention of the parties, the test of reasonableness will be invoked to cure uncertainty in other respects where the parties intended to enter into a legally binding agreement.

In the *Moorcock*[168], a case which has been applied in East Africa, A agreed that B should use their jetty to unload his ship. At low tide, the ship grounded on the river bed and was damaged. The court held that A was liable implying into the contract that the area should be reasonably safe for such use to which A knew it was to be put.

(ii) Terms implied in law

The law sometimes implies certain obligations in a contract. For instance in a contract of employment, an employee impliedly undertakes that he is reasonably skilled and that he will faithfully serve his employer and not to act against the employer's interests and that he will indemnify his employer against all liabilities incurred by the employer as a result of his wrongful acts. The employer will on the other hand impliedly undertake that he will not require the employee to do any unlawful act and that he will provide safe premises.[169]

---

164 *Shirlaw v. Southern Foundries* [1939] 2 K.B. 206, 227. affd. [1940] A.C. 701 [1939] 2 All E.R. 113, 124.

165 [1941] A.C. 108, 137. See also *Campling Bros & Vanderwal Ltd. v. United Air Service Ltd.* 19 E.A.C.A.155; Note J.A.L. 223 (1962); *Hassanali Issa & Co. v. Jeraj Produce Shop* [1967] E.A. 555.

166 [1976] 1 W.L.R. 1187; [1977] 1 All E.R. 481. See also *Damodar Jinabhai & Co. Ltd. v. Eustace Sisal Estates Ltd.* [1967] E.A. 153; 1966 (2) A.L.R. Comm.514; *Otis Elevator Co. v. Singh & Ors.* [1967] E.A. 78 1966 (2) A.L.R. Comm. 337. *Rhodes v. Forwood* (1876) 1 App. Cas 256.

167 [1970] E.A. 469 C.A.; *Osman v. Ngoni-Matengo Co-op. Marketing Union* [1962] E.A. 1.

168 [1886-89] All E.R. Rep. 530; (1889) 14 P.D. 64; Cheshire & Fifoot, *supra*, pp.143 - 44.

169 *Hivac v. Park Royal Scientific Instruments Ltd.* [1946] Ch. 169; *Wessex Diaries v. Smith* [1935] 2 K.B. 80; *Lister v. Romford Ice & Cold Storage Co. Ltd.* [1957] A.C. 555; *Gregory v. Ford* [1951] 1 All E.R. 121

As far as Uganda is concerned, the most significant terms implied by law are those in respect of contracts for the sale of goods which are governed by Sections 14 to 17 of the Sale of Goods Act.[170]

Terms condition as to title of seller

Section 14 provides that unless circumstances show a different intention, there is implied on the part of the seller, (i) a condition that he has the right to sell; (ii) a warranty for quiet possession and enjoyment of the goods by the buyer; (iii) a warranty that the goods are free from any third party charge or encumbrance.[171] In *Ali Kassam Virani Ltd v. United Africa Co. (Tanganyika) Ltd.*[172], goods were delivered to and paid for by the buyer. However, the coffee was later confiscated by the police. The respondents asked for refund of the price but the appellant refused. They sued and obtained judgment for the price. In the meantime the managing director of the appellant company was convicted of receiving stolen coffee. It was held that the appellant were in breach of warranty for quiet possession and enjoyment by the respondent as buyers arising from the confiscation of the goods by the police.

Similarly in *Lakhamshi Bros Ltd. v. R. Raja & Sons*,[173] the appellant Company bought from the respondent 44 Cases of boot polish of which they sold 12. The remaining 32 were seized by the been disturbed by the police together with the evidence of the respondent's knowledge that their title was liable to challenge established *prima facie* a breach of warranty for quiet possession of the goods which the respondents had failed to rebut.

Implied condition as to description

Section 15 provides that where there is a contract of sale of goods by description, there is an implied condition that the goods correspond with the description, and if the sale is by sample and description, it is not sufficient that the bulk of the goods correspond with the sample if they do not correspond with the description.

In *Nurmohamed Nurjii & Ors. v. Dattu*,[174] the buyer at an auction bought a quantity of "black pepper." He later attempted to repudiate the contract on the grounds that the bulk did not match the description given. The Court of Appeal disallowed the buyer's argument holding that the leading case of *Wallis v. Pratt*[175] was distinguishable in that a totally different article had been delivered in that case. Here the goods matched the description used and understood by the spice dealers, even though botanically speaking, the description given was not correct.[176]

Implied condition as to quality or fitness of goods

Section 16(a) provides that unless a different intention appears from the contract between the parties, there is an implied condition that the goods sold are fit for the particular purpose. However, for Section 16(a) to apply the buyer must make known to the seller the purpose for which he required the goods[177] and it is clear that the buyer relies on the seller's skill or judgment. Additionally, the article sold must be an article normally supplied by that seller in the course of his business.

---

170 Cap. 79

171 See also the Nigerian Case *Akoshile v. Ogidan* 19 NLR 87

172 [1958] E.A. 204 C.A.

173 [1966] E.A. 178; 1966(1) A.L.R. Comm 245.

174 22 E.A.C.A. 294. See also Hodgin, *supra* p.81.

175 [1910] 2 K.B. 1003; *Varley v. Whipps* [1900] 1 Q.B.513; *Re Moore & Co.*[1921] All E.R. 466

176 See further *Juthalal Velji v. Jivra* 16 E.A.C.A.75

177 *Ashington Piggeries v. C. Hill* [1971] 1 All E.R. 847 [1972] A.C.441

In *Norman v. Overseas Mortor Transport (Tanganyika) Ltd.*,[178] a car was delivered to the appellant by the respondent under an agreement which provided that liability in respect thereof ends when the car is delivered in a roadworthy condition. The car was delivered in England for use in East Africa. The material defect was due to modifications for tropical use not being effected. The appellant sued the respondent and claimed damages for delivery of a defective car. He was unsuccessful at first instance and appealed. It was held on appeal that the appellant must have been held to have treated any breach of condition arising from the defects other than overheating as a breach of warranty under Section 13 and since the defects were all remedied, and he continued to use the car, he could not rely on them to repudiate the contract. Second, it was held that overheating of the car was due to failure to effect modifications which it is usual to effect when, and not before the car is brought to the tropics. Consequently, it could not be said that the car was not in a roadworthy condition when delivered.

In *Massey Harris & Co. v. Miller*[179], Section 16 was applied to a hire-purchase transaction on grounds that the transaction was similar to a transaction of sale. Section 16(b) provides that where goods are bought by description from a seller who deals in goods of that description, there is an implied condition that the goods shall be of merchantable quality provided that, if the buyer has examined the goods, there shall be no implied condition as regards defects which such examination ought to have revealed. In *Doola Singh & Sons v. The Uganda foundry & Machinery Works*,[180] the defendants sold a saw bench to the plaintiffs. After it had been installed and had worked for five minutes, it ceased. The reason was that it had been carelessly assembled by the seller and wrong components had been used. It was held that the seller was liable as there was no opportunity of examination by the appellants which would have revealed defects therein.

Implied condition as to sale by sample

There is an implied condition that if a contract of sale is by sample, then the bulk of the goods must correspond with the sample in quality. In addition, the buyer must be given an opportunity to compare the bulk with the sample. It is also implied that the goods shall be free from any defect rendering them unmerchantable which would not be apparent on reasonable examination of the sample.[181]

In *Jafferrali Abdulla v. Janmohammed's Ltd.*[182], the buyer bought 22 cases of plates at the time of bidding and said "This is a sample of the plates". The buyer successfully bid for the plates only to discover later that many of them were broken. It was held that this constituted a sale by sample and the buyer had not been given a reasonable opportunity of comparing bulk with sample. The Court dismissed an attempt to rely on an exclusion clause in the handbill of the auction on the grounds that the auctioneer knew that many plates were damaged and could not therefore seek protection from that clause.

Doubtful Cases

Sometimes it is not clear whether a term is implied in fact or law. Thus in *The Moorcock*[183] the defendants owned a wharf and made a contract to allow the plaintiffs to unload their ship at the wharf. The ship was damaged by settling at low water on a ridge of hard ground. It was held that the defendants were liable for this damage as they were in breach of an implied term that they would take reasonable care to see that the berth was safe. The case is regarded as the leading authority on terms implied in fact, but some passages in the judgment refer to terms implied in law.

---

178 [1959] E.A. 131 C.A.

179 [1959] E.A. 431 C.A.

180 12 E.A.C.A. 33. See also *Godley v. Perry* [1960] All E.R. 36

181 Sale of Goods Act, Cap.79. S.17.

182 18 E.A.C.A. 21 Hodgin *supra* p.84

183 (1889) 14 P.D. 64.

Lord Esher M.R. said that it must be implied that the defendants had "undertaken to see that the bottom of the river is reasonably fit for the purpose ..."[184] On the other hand, Bower, L.J. stated:[185]

> An implied warranty, or, as it is called a *Covenant in law* ...is in all cases founded on the presumed intention of the parties *and upon reason*... In business transactions such as this what the law desires to effect by implication is to give business efficacy to the transaction as ;must have been intended at all events by both parties who are businessmen.

Concerning this quotation, Professor Treitel has thus commented:[186]

> *The Moorcock* therefore seems to illustrate the process of implication in law rather than that of implication in fact. It differs from the category of terms implied in law... in that the implication relates to a particular transaction rather than to a group of contracts; it resembles that category, however, in that the implication is based on objective criteria of reasonableness.

The Moorcock has been followed in Uganda. Thus in *Lulume v. Coffee Marketing Board*,[187] the plaintiff was employed by the defendant as a labour/welfare officer. He was dismissed by payment to him of 3 months salary in lieu of notice and was required to leave the house provided for him 7 days thereafter. He sued for damages for wrongful dismissal. He argued that having been a member of the defendant's pension scheme, it was an implied condition of the contract that he was a permanent member of the defendant's staff and could not be dismissed and the three months' notice was inadequate. It was held that no stipulation could be implied in a contract unless upon the evidence, it must be taken to have been mutually intended and necessary to give business efficacy to the document.[188] Second that membership of the pension scheme did not imply immunity from dismissal.

3. Terms implied by custom

Any contract, whether written or not may be deemed to incorporate any relevant custom of the market, trade or locality in which it is made unless the custom is inconsistent with the express terms or with the nature of the contract. In cases of such inconsistency the custom is said to be "unreasonable" and only binds a party if he knew it.[189] It follows that a custom which is "reasonable" binds both parties whether they knew of it or not.[190]

Terms may also be implied by trade usage. Thus in *British Crane Hire Corpn. Ltd. v. Ipswich Plant Hire Ltd.*,[191] the owner of a crane hired it out to a contractor, who was also engaged in the same business. It was held that the hirer was bound by the owner's usual terms though these were not actually communicated at the time of the contract. Furthermore, in *Fleury and King v. Mohamed Walli & Co. & Juma Hemani*[192], X ordered 1,000 dozen handkerchiefs. These were delivered in batches of 30. X claimed that he was entitled to a reduction in the price because in Zanzibar there was a trade custom that they be delivered in twelves. The Court was willing to imply such a term.

---

184 *Ibid.* p.67

185 *Ibid.* p.68. Emphasis supplied

186 Treitel, *supra* p.194.

187 [1970] E.A. 155 c.f. *Osman v. Ngoni Matengo Co-op. Marketing Union* [1962] E.A. 1 P.C.

188 following The ***Moorcock*** *supra* n.183

189 Treitel, *supra* p.194

190 *Reynolds v. Smith* (1893) 9 T.L.R. 494

191 [1975] Q.B. 303

192 1 Z.L.R. 17; Hodgin *Law of Contract In East Africa* p.90 For guideline on when a trade usage would be implied in a contract in East Africa. See *Shah v. Standard Bank Ltd.* 1967(1) A.L.R. Comm. 209.

4. Exemption clauses

Many contracts are made in a standard form that is their terms are set out in printed forms which are used for all contracts of the same kind. Such terms are usually settled by a trade association for use of its members for contracting with each other or with members of the outside public. There are cases where forms are provided by statute.[193]

The main purpose[194] of these standard forms is to save time in three main respects. First, the work for instance of insurers, bankers and carriers would be complicated if all the terms of every contract had to be freshly settled for each transaction. Second, they are aimed at allocating contractual risks. Thus by putting certain risks on one party, they can be used to determine in advance who is to bear the expense of insuring against those risks.[195] Third, they assist a contracting party to quote differential rates based on services offered and risks undertaken by him. A main shortcoming though of standard form contracts is that they may be used to exploit and abuse the superior bargaining power of one party in contracts between suppliers of goods and services and private consumers. In this context, a supplier could use a standard form to exclude or limit liability which he would otherwise be subject and this would lead to hardship on the part of the inferior party.

(i) Incorporation of exemption clause into a contract

A party to a contract who wishes to rely on a clause excluding or limiting his liability must show that it was incorporated in the contract and that as a matter of construction, it covers the loss or damage which has been suffered. Even where he shows these aspects, the clause may be held to be invalid or inoperative.

An exemption clause can be incorporated in the contract by signature, notice or course of dealing.

Signature

A person signing a contractual document is bound by its terms, even though he has not read them. Thus in *L'Estrange v. Graucob Ltd.*[196], the proprietress of a cafe bought can automatic cigarette vending machine. She signed, but did not read a Sales agreement which contained an exemption clause in regrettably small print. It was held that she was bound by this clause with the result that she could not rely on defects in the machine as a defence to a claim for part of the price or as entitling her to damages.

Notice

Where the exclusion clause is set out or referred to in a document which is simply handled by one party to another or displayed where the contract is made, it will only be incorporated in the contract if reasonable notice of its existence has been given to the party adversely affected by it. Thus in *Dar-es-Salaam Motor Transport Co. v. Mehta*[197], the appellant, a transport company failed to deliver to the respondents a parcel of cloth which had been consigned by them. The words, "All parcels accepted and carried subject to the conditions of carriage," appeared on the consignment note issued by the appellant. Under the conditions of carriage which appeared on the notice boards in their premises, the appellants reserved to themselves an unfettered discretion to refuse to carry any goods for any reason, whatsoever. They also purported, by notice, to

---

193 E.g. Companies Act, Cap.85 Table A providing for Articles of Association

194 See generally Treitel, *op.cit. supra* pp.196 - 197.

195 See e.g. *The Maratha Envoy* [1978] A.C. 1,8; *Photo Production Ltd. v. Securicor Transporot Ltd.* [1980] A.C.827, 843, 851.

196 [1934] 2 K.B. 394.

197 [1970] E.A. 596 C.A. See also *Mugumuza v. Agip Petrol Station* [1975] H.C.B. 288, *United Garments Industries v. NOTCO* [1977] H.C.B. 128.

exempt themselves from liability for any loss, injury or delay in respect of any goods. There was no evidence that the parcels had ever been refused and although the receipt given referred to conditions of carriage, it did not say where these were to be found. It was held that the conditions exempting the appellants from liability were not sufficiently brought to the attention of the respondents or their agents to make them part of the contract.

Whether such notice has been given depends on three main factors viz. the nature of the document the degree of notice and time of notice.

Nature of the document

An exemption clause is not incorporated in the contract, if it is set out or referred to in a document which is not intended to have contractual force. Thus in *Chapelton v. Barry UDC*[198], the plaintiff hired a deck chair from the defendants for 3 hours. He paid 2 pence and was given a ticket which he did not read. It was held that the defendants were not protected by an exemption clause printed on the ticket as it was a mere voucher or receipt. It did not purport to set out the conditions on which the plaintiff had hired the chair but only to show how long he had hired it and that he had paid a fee. Similarly in the East African Case, *B.A.T. Kenya Ltd. v. Express Transport*[199], the defendant contracted to carry a "Packer" machine for the plaintiff. In the course of carriage, the machine fell and was damaged. The plaintiff sued the defendant for damages. The issue arose at the trial as to whether the phrase all goods at owner's risk" which appeared on the defendant's letter heads and on the drivers' instruction briefing form, excluded any liability. It was held that the phrase "all goods at owner's risk" was not brought home to the mind of the plaintiff's officials and was ineffective to exempt the defendants from liability. Second, it was held that the document containing the purported exception of liability by virtue of the phrase was ineffective.

However, a document would be regarded as contractual if the party to whom it was handed knows that it was intended to have that effect or if it was delivered to him in such circumstances as to give him reasonable notice of the fact that it contained conditions.[200] Furthermore, simply because a document is described as a receipt will not prevent it from having contractual effect.[201]

Degree of notice

A party relying on the exemption clause need not show that he has actually brought it to the notice of the other party but only that he took reasonable steps to do so. Thus in *Parker v. S.E. Ry*,[202] the railway company tried to rely on an exemption clause which was printed on the back of a cloakroom ticket issued on the deposit of luggage and also displayed on the walls of the cloakroom. The trial Court put to the jury the question whether the plaintiff (who had not actually read the ticket or the displayed notice) ought in the exercise of reasonable caution to have read the conditions. A verdict was delivered in the plaintiff's favour. On appeal, the Court of Appeal ordered a new trial on ground that the trial court had applied the wrong test by looking at the situation from the plaintiff's view. The correct approach was to look at the situation from the defendant's point of view and ask whether they had done "what was reasonably sufficient to give the plaintiff notice of the conditions."

The issue as to whether adequate notice has been given in turn depends on two factors viz. steps to give notice and nature of the exclusion clause.

---

198 [1940] 1 K.B. 532

199 [1968] E.A. 171 following *Curtis v. Chemical Cleaning & Dyeing Co. Ltd.* [1951] 1 All E.R. 631. See also *Gailey & Roberts Ltd. v. Salum* [1962] E.A. 376 C.A.

200 *Harling v. Eddy* [1951] 2 K.B. 739, 746; *The Polyduke* [1978] 1 Lloyd's Rep 211.

201 *Watkins v. Rymill* (1883) 10 Q.B.D. 178.

202 (1877) 2 C.P.D. 416. See also *Dar - es- Salaam Motor Transport Case, supra* n.197 and text thereof;
V.W. *Nehru v. Commissioner of Transport* [1962] E.A. 300; *Edher Ahmed v. GM of E.A.R. & H. Administration* [1965] E.A. 141.

203 [1930] 1 K.B. 41. See also *Nehru & Edher Ahmed Cases Ibid.*

Steps to give notice

Where notice is contained in a contractual document (e.g. passenger ticket), it is usually sufficient for the exclusion clause to be prominently set out or referred to on the face of the document. Thus in *Thompson v. L & M L& S Ry.*[203] the plaintiff asked her niece to buy a railway excursion ticket for her. The ticket, which cost 2s 7d. had on its face the words, "see back" and on the back was a statement that it was issued subject to the conditions set out in the company's timetable which could be bought for 6d. These conditions included an exemption clause. The plaintiff could not read the words on the ticket as she was illiterate. The jury found that the defendants had not taken reasonable steps to bring the conditions to the plaintiff's notice. The Court of Appeal held that there was no evidence to support this finding as the notice was clear and as the ticket was a common form document. Consequently, the exemption clause was incorporated in the contract. This case illustrates the principle that a clause can be incorporated by reference.[204] The illiteracy of the plaintiff was treated as immaterial. However, the position could be different where the person relying on the clause knows or should know of the other party's disability.[205]

Examples of situations where an exemption clause would not be incorporated are where there are no words on the face of the document drawing attention to it;[206] where the words are made illegible by a date stamp;[207] where the exemption clause is hidden in a mass of advertisements.[208]

Nature of the exclusion clause

The more unusual or unexpected a particular term is, the higher will be the degree of notice required to incorporate it. Where the clause is of such nature that the party adversely affected would not normally expect it, then the other party will not be able to incorporate it by simply handing over or displaying a document containing the clause. He should go further and "make it conspicuous" [209] or take steps to draw attention to it.[210]

Time of notice

An exemption clause is only incorporated into the contract if notice of it is given before or at the time of contracting. In *Olley v. Marlborough Court*,[211] the plaintiff booked a room in the defendant's hotel. She later saw a notice in the hotel bedroom exempting the defendants from liability for articles lost or stolen unless handed to management for safe custody. It was held that the contract was made at the reception desk when the defendants agreed to accept the plaintiff as a guest. Since the notice was seen by the plaintiff later, it was not incorporated in the contract.

Course of dealing

Where there has been a long consistent course of dealings on terms incorporating an exemption clause, then the clause may apply to a particular transaction even though in relation to it the usual steps to incorporate the clause have not been taken.[212] However, the clause will be inapplicable if the transaction in question was not part of a consistent course of dealings.[213]

---

204 *Smith v. South Wales Switchgears Ltd.* [1978] 1 W.L.R. 165.

205 *Richardson, Spence & Co. v. Rowntree* [1894] AC 217

206 *Richardson case, ibid. Henderson v. Stevenson* (1875) L.R.2 S.C. & Div. 470.

207 *Sugar v. London, Midland & Scottish Ry.* [1941] 1 All E.R. 172.

208 *Stephen v. International Steering Car Co. Ltd.* [1903] 19 TLR 620.

209 *Crooks v. Allen* (1870) 5 Q.B.D. 38, 40.

210 *Lewis Ralph Dodd v. Chandrakant Nandha* [1971] E.A. 58. See also *J. Spurling Bradshaw* [1956] 1 W.L.R. 461, 466; 2 All E.R. 121, per Denning L.J. and Hoggett 33 M.L.R. 518.

211 [1949] 1 K.B. 332; *B.A.T. Kenya Ltd. v. Express Transport* [1968] E.A. 171, *Dodd v. Nandha Case ibid. Dar-es-Salaam Motor Transport Case supra* n.197 *Mugumuza v. Agip Petrol Station* [1975] HCB 288.

212 *Hardwick Game Farm v. Suffolk Agricultural etc. Assoc.* [1969] 2 AC.31, 90, 104, 113, 130.

213 Treitel, *op.cit. supra* p.201

(ii) Construction

Contra Proferentum rule

Exemption clauses are strictly construed against the parties who rely on them. For instance, a provision that a seller gives "no warranty express or implied" will not protect him from liability for breach of condition.[214] In *Omer Saleh Audalih v. Besse & Co. (Aden) Ltd.*,[215] it was held that the exemption clause in issue contemplated warranties implied by the Sale of Goods Ordinance and in construing it *contra-profer entem*, it did not exonerate respondents for breach of an implied condition if such condition arose under the Ordinance.

In addition, a clause protecting a seller from a breach of implied conditions and warranties does not protect him from breach of an express term of the contract.[216] Similarly, a provision in a hire purchase agreement that "no warranty, condition, or description or representation is given", will not exclude liability for breach of a collateral undertaking previously given.[217] In *Gailey & Roberts v. Salum*[218] it was held that the respondent had agreed to buy a "certain tractor" duly repaired and put in running condition and nothing less. Where the first agreement and the hire purchase agreement were in conflict, the written words of the first agreement overrode the printed words of a standard form excluding liability.

(iii) Fundamental breach

Courts are reluctant to allow a contracting party to rely on an exemption clause where he has committed a breach of contract which is considered particularly serious. Previously, effect was given to this judicial policy through two techniques. First the exemption clause was construed narrowly so that it did not exclude liability for serious breach which had occurred. Second, was the approach that the breach of some previous breach amounted to repudiation of the contract which the innocent party could accept and by doing so he put an end to the contract (including the exemption clause) except for the purpose of claiming damages. In view of this approach, certain various breaches prevented a party from relying on an exemption clause however drafted. At one stage this rule had attained the status of substantive law.[219] However, in 1966, the British House of Lords reverted to the view that the rule was one of construction only. It left open the possibility that it may remain a rule of substance in certain phases of its operation. The House of Lords did not overrule cases decided under the former substantive doctrine but explained them as illustrations of the rule of construction.[220]

Breach of fundamental terms

Certain terms of the contract are regarded as fundamental. It is assumed that exemption clauses do not on their true construction apply where such terms have been broken. This idea is normally applied to contracts for the supply of goods. The effect is that a person who supplies something essentially different from that which he contracted to supply will not be protected by an exemption clause. For instance a person who contracted to sell peas would supply something "essentially different "if he delivered beans.[221]

---

214 *Wallis, Son & Wells v. Pratt & Haynes* [1911] A.C. 394.

215 [1960] E.A. 907 C.A.

216 *Andrew Bros v. Singer* [1934] 1 K.B. 17.

217 *Webster v. Higgins* [1948] 2 All E.R. 127

218 [1962] E.A. 376 C.A. See also *Chatrisha & Co. Ltd. v. Puranchand L& Sons* [1959] E.A. 746; *Kenya Trading Corp. v. Algermene Bank Nederland N.V.* Civil Case 1034 of 1971 Kenya. Hodgin *supra* p.103.

219 *Karsales (Harrow) Ltd. v. Willis* [1956] 2 All E.R. 866

220 *Suisse Atlantique Societe d'Armement Maritime S.A. v. Rotterdamischo* [1967] 1 A.C. 361.

221 *Charter v. Hopkins* (1838) 4 M & W 399, 404

In *Pinnock Bros v. Lewis & Peat Ltd.*,[222] copra cake was sold "not warranted free from defect", However, it was so adulterated by castor beans as to poison the cattle to which it was fed. It was held that where "a substance quite different from that contracted for has been delivered, that clause has no application as such a difference of substance cannot be said to be a "defect". In *Nichole v. Godts*,[223] the defendant sold "foreign refined rape oil warranted only equal to sample". It was held that the phrase referred only to the quality of the goods and not to their description. Consequently, the seller could not rely on it where the goods were not "foreign refined rape oil". In *Smeaton Hanscomb & Co. v. Sassoon I Seaty & Co.*,[224] it was held that a seller of "mahogany logs" could not rely on an exemption clause if he delivered pine logs. In *Karsales (Harrow) Ltd. v. Wallis* [225], it was held that the seller of a new car would be in breach of a fundamental term if he delivered one that was second hand. In this case, the actual decision was based on the idea that the supplier could not, as a matter of substantive law exclude liability for defects of this very serious kind. However, using the reasoning in the *Suisse Atlantique Case*[226] this type of case is explained on the ground that the exemption clause in it did not as a matter of construction apply to breaches of fundamental terms.

In the East African Case of *Gailey & Roberts Ltd. v. Salum*[227] the respondent had agreed to buy a tractor "duly repaired and put in running condition." However, upon taking delivery, the tractor broke down before reaching his farm. After repair, it reached the farm and broke down again. It was held that since the respondent had agreed to buy a certain tractor and nothing else, where the original agreement and hire purchase agreement were in conflict, the written words of the first agreement overrode the printed words of a standard form which contained an exclusion clause in regard to the road-worthiness of the vehicle.

It has been suggested that a fundamental term is narrower than a condition" [228] of the contract. Thus if a seller of "mahogany logs equal to sample" delivered logs of inferior quality he would commit a breach of condition.[229] but not a breach of a fundamental term. Similarly a supplier of a motor vehicle which corresponds with the contractual description does not commit a breach of a fundamental term simply because he breaks an implied undertaking as to fitness of the vehicle for the purpose for which it was supplied.[230]

Deviation and Analogous Cases

The benefit of an exemption clause is lost by a ship owner who has, without justification [231] deviated or departed from the agreed or usual route.[232] It is also lost by a warehouseman who has stored goods in a place other than that agreed. In *Produce Marketing Board v. Uganda Railways Corporation*[233], the defendants agreed to carry and clear the plaintiff's gunny bags from Mombasa to 5th street Industrial Area, Kampala respectively. The goods were instead delivered to a 7th Street railway siding. The first defendant contended that they were protected from liability by an exemption clause contained in the Tariff Book which provided that they were not liable for any loss or damage occasioned by deviation, misdelivery etc. except upon proof of wilful misconduct

222 [1923] 1 K.B. 690

223 (1854) 10 Ex. 191

224 [1953] 1 WLR 1468, 1470;

225 [1956] 1 WLR 936, 955; [1956] 2 All E.R. 866

226 *supra* n.220

227 [1962] E.A. 376 C.A.

228 *Smeaton Hanscomb & Co. Ltd v. Sassoon I Setty & Co. (No.1)* [1953] 1 W.L.R. 1468, 1470.

229 Treitel, *supra* p.208; Sale of Goods Act, Cap 79, S.17

230 *Astley Industrial Trust v. Grimeley* [1963] 1 W.L.R. 584; *Omer Saleh Audalih v. Besse & Co.* [1960] E.A. 907

231 *Kish v. Taylor* [1912] A.C. 604, 617. N.B. deviation may be justified for the purpose of saving life or property at sea. See Carriage of Goods by Sea Act 1971 (U.K.)

232 *Joseph Thorley Ltd. v. Orchis Ss. Co. Ltd.* [1907] 1 KB 660

233 [1992] III KALR 36.

by its employees. It was held that the exemption clause did not apply in this instance where loss was occasioned by misdelivery or deviation by its employees. Consequently the first defendant was guilty of a fundamental breach of contract.[234]

The benefit of an exemption clause will also be lost by a bailee such as a clearer or carrier who parts with possession of goods entrusted to him in the course of unauthorised subcontracting.[235] However, such a person will not lose the benefit of an exemption clause merely because he has broken some other term. For instance, the Shipowner may still be protected although he may have broken his undertaking to supply a seaworthy vehicle.[236] The reason for the distinction is that the terms as to the route and as to the place where the goods are to be stored are fundamental, while other terms are not.[237] The importance of the term as to the route is explained on the ground that the owner of the goods may only be covered by insurance when the goods are on the agreed route.[238] Consequently, as soon as the ship departs from that route, the courts hold the carrier liable as if he were an insurer.

In terms of construction, similar to supply of goods cases, it is necessary first to construe the contract as a whole in order to determine which obligations are imposed by the fundamental term. Thus in deviation cases, the court will for this purpose consider the agreed or usual route, if any,[239] as well as the liberty to deviate given by the contract of carriage, although such liberties are strictly interpreted[240]

In a warehouseman's contract, the first question is just where did he undertake to store the goods? In *Gibard v. G.E. Ry*[241], a contract to store a bicycle left at the defendant's cloakroom was interpreted as one to store in any convenient place nearby. Consequently an exclusion clause was held to apply when the bicycle was stolen even though it had been stored in the hall and not the cloakroom. In contrast, in *Davies v. Collins,*[242] the defendants accepted the plaintiff's uniform for cleaning and had it cleaned by a subcontractor, who lost it. An exemption clause which started with the words "whilst every care is taken ..." was held not to protect the defendants as they could not take care of the uniform while it was in the hands of a sub-contractor.

Differences Between Supply of Goods and Deviation Cases

In sale of goods cases the effect of the breach is that the victim does not get the substance of what he bargained for. However, in deviation cases, courts are not concerned with the *effect* of the breach. Departure from the agreed route, however irrelevant, deprives the shopowner of the benefit of the exemption clause.[243] In *Joseph Thorley Ltd. v. Orchiss Co. Ltd.,*[244] a cargo of beans was damaged through being mixed with poisonous earth. The carrier lost the benefit of his exemption clause because he had deviated, though the deviation did not cause the loss. In *James Morrison & Co. v. Shaw Savill & Albion Co. Ltd.,*[245] a shipowner lost the benefit of an exemption clause even though the ship might just as probably have been sunk on the proper route.

---

234 See also *Woolf v. Collis Removal Services* [1948] 1 K.B. 11, 15.

235 *Davies v. Collins* [1945] 1 All.E.R. 247

236 *Kish v. Taylor* [1912] A.C. 604

237 Treitel, *supra,* p.210

238 *Hain SS v. Tate & Lyle Ltd.* (1936) 41 Com Cas 350, 354

239 *Frenkel v. Mac Andrews & Co. Ltd.* [1929] A.C. 545

240 See *Glynn v. Margetson* [1893] A.C. 351

241 [1921] 2 K.B. 426

242 [1945 1 All E.R. 247

243 *Suisse Atlantique Case* [1967] 1 A.C. 361, 423

244 [1907] 1 K.B. 6604

245 [1916] 2 K.B. 783.

Similarity between supply of goods and deviation cases

In both supply of goods and deviation cases the **manner** or **form** in which the breach is committed is irrelevant. In supply of goods cases this is assumed. In deviation cases so long as the carrier's act is voluntary, it does not matter that the deviation was innocent. Thus in *L & N.W. Ry. v. Nelson*[246], the label came off a van load of theatrical properties and its contents were despatched to wrong destinations by a station master. Despite the fact that he had acted under an honest mistake, the railway company lost the protection of its exemption clause.

(iv) Consequence of breach

Breach sale and hire purchase cases

The consequences of fundamental breach are illustrated by reference to sale and hire purchase cases in which the supplier's breach consists in supplying goods which are not fit for the particular purpose for which the customer requires them. It is significant that the mere fact that a supplier is in breach of an implied undertaking as to fitness does not put him in breach of a *fundamental breach* if the defect is so serious as to make the thing practically useless for the customer's purposes[247]

(v) Contracts for execution of works

Contract for execution of works include those for installation of machinery or of an air conditioning system on another's premises. Where the work is defective and as a result the premises are destroyed, there will be a fundamental breach[248].

(vi) Rule of Construction

Over the years, the courts particularly in Britain had developed 2 rules relating to fundamental breach. First, that by a rule of law no excluding or limiting term may operate to protect a party who is in fundamental breach of his contract.[249] Second, that the question is not one of substantive law but depends upon the construction of the individual contract.[250] The rule of law approach applied whether or not it defeated the intention of the parties. However, the rule of construction is said to exist to give effect to that intention. Before 1964 in Britain, the courts preferred the first approach. However in 1964 in the case of *U.G.S. Finance Ltd. v. National Mortgage Bank of Greece S.A.*, [251] the second approach was preferred. Pearson L. J. indicated that the issue of fundamental breach is a rule of construction that normally an exception or exclusion clause or similar provision in a contract should be construed as not applying to a situation created by a fundamental breach of the contract. This is not an independent rule of law imposed by the Court on the parties in disregard of their contractual intention. It is a rule of construction based on the presumed intention of the parties. This approach was adopted three years later by the *Suisse Atlantique Case* [252a]. In that case, the plaintiffs owned a ship which in December 1956, they chartered to the defendants for the carriage of coal from United States to Europe. The charter was to remain in force for 2 years' consecutive voyages. The defendants agreed to load and discharge

---

246 [1922] A.C. 263. See also *Produce Marketing Board v. Uganda Railways Corporation* Civil Suit No.8 of 1990 (Byamugisha J) [1992] III KALR 36

247 *Yeoman Credit Ltd. v. Apps* [1962] 2 Q.B. 508; *Gailey & Roberts v. Salum* [1962] E.A. 376 C.A.

248 *Harbutt's "Plasticine" Ltd. v. Wayne Tank & Pump Co. Ltd.* [1970] 1 Q.B.447 [1970] 1 All E.R.255

249 *Karsales (Harrow) Ltd. v. Wallis* [1956] 2 All E.R. 866; *Yeoman Credit Ltd. v. Apps* [1962] 2 Q.B. 508; *Harbutt's "Plasticine" Case ibid. Gailey & Roberts v. Salum* [1962] E.A. 376 C.A. *Produce Marketing Board v. Uganda Railways Corporation supra* n.246

250 *Swisse Atlantique Case* [1967] 1 A.C. 361; *Photo Production Ltd. v. Securicor Transport Ltd* [1980] A.C. 827; [1980] 1 All E.R. 556; Nicol and Rawlings 43 MLR 567.

251 [1964] 1 Lloyd's Rep 446, 453

252a *Supra* n.243

cargoes at specified rates and if there was any delay they were to pay US $1,000 per day as demurrage. In September, 1957, the plaintiff claimed that they were entitled to treat the contract as repudiated by the defendant's delays in loading and discharging cargoes. The defendants rejected this contention. In October 1957, the parties agreed (without prejudice to their dispute) to continue with the contract. The defendants later made 8 round voyages. The plaintiffs claimed all the money which they had lost through the delays. The defendants argued that the claim must be limited to the agreed demurrage for the actual days in question. The plaintiffs replied that the delays were such as to entitle them to treat the contract as repudiated. Consequently, the demurrage clause did not apply and they could recover their full loss. All the courts up to the House of Lords held that the plaintiffs must fail on the ground that since the parties had chosen to affirm the contract, the demurrage clause applied.

In the House of Lords, it was argued that the defendants were guilty of a fundamental breach of contract which prevented them from relying on "a limiting term." It was a statement of agreed damages in the event of delay. Consequently, it was not necessary for the Court to discuss the meaning and effect of fundamental breach. By way of *obiter* the House of Lords approved the approach of Pearson L.J. in the *U.G.S. Finance Case* [253] and said that the rules to be applied in respect of fundamental breach should be regarded as rules of construction and not rules of law. This approach has been reaffirmed in *Photo Production Ltd v. Securicor Transport Ltd.*[254] where a security firm which had been engaged to safeguard a factory was protected by an exemption clause even though the firm's breach resulted into total destruction of the factory by fire. Lord Wilberforce thus stated on the application of an exclusion clause[255]

> I have no second thoughts as to the main proposition that the question whether, and to what extent, an exclusion clause is to be applied to a fundamental breach, or a breach of a fundamental term or indeed to any breach of contract is a matter of construction of the contract.

It remains to add that in Uganda the first approach to the effect that it is a rule of law that no excluding term will protect a party who is in fundamental breach of his contract[256] applies. The Courts have yet to adopt the "rule of construction " approach prevailing in Britain.

---

253 *Ibid.* See also Cheshire & Fifoot *Law of Contract (12th Edn.) supra* pp. 176 - 177

254 *Supra* n.250

255 See also Cheshire & Fifoot, *Law of Contract, supra* n.253, p.178 Treitel, supra pp.216, 221.

256 See *supra* n.249 and case cited therein. See also Hodgin, *Law of Contract In East Africa*, p.107.

7
MISTAKE

The mere fact that one of the parties to a contract acted under a mistake does not generally as a rule affect the validity of the contract.[257] However, mistake will invalidate a contract on the ground that if one of the parties is mistaken as to the terms of the contract, then there is no consent that is the parties are not *consensus ad idem;* there is no agreement.[258] Consequently, mistake may operate to negative or in some cases nullify consent. Mistake *negatives* consent where it prevents the parties from reaching agreement e.g. because they intend to contract about different things. It *nullifies* consent where the parties reach an agreement which is based on a fundamental mistaken assumption e.g. if a contract is made to paint a portrait of someone who, unknown to either party, has just died.[259] At law the effect of mistake is to make a contract void.[260]

An attempt is now made to examine the two instances where mistake may either negative or nullify consent before looking at the effect of equity on mistake and documents which are mistakenly signed.

1. Mistake nullifying consent

It has been suggested that consent may be nullified if both parties make a fundamental mistake of fact as distinguished from that of law.[261] There are five main types of mistake which nullify consent which we shall consider.

(a) Mistake as to existence of the subject matter of the contract

Consent will be nullified if both parties are mistaken as to the existence of the subject matter. Thus in *Galloway v. Galloway,*[262] a separation deed between a man and a woman who mistakenly thought that they were married to each other was held void because it sought to deal with a marriage which did not exist.

In *Couturier v. Hastie*[263], there was a contract for the sale of Salonica Indian Corn f.o.b. an U.K. port. Before the time of the sale, the cargo had, unknown to B & S become overheated and sold at Tunis to prevent further deterioration. S argued firstly that B was nevertheless liable to pay the price. Second, that what B had bought was an interest in a maritime adventure or such rights as S had under the shipping documents against which payment was to be made. The British House of Lords rejected the arguments and held that B was not liable. The Court indicated[264] that the

---

257 *Solle v. Butcher* [1949] 2 All E.R. 1107, 1119, per Lord Denning.

258 *Bell v. Lever Bros Ltd.*[1932] A.C. 161, 217

259 Treitel, GH *Law of Contract* (International Student Edition 8th Edn. 1991) p.249.

260 *Associated Japanese Bank (International) Ltd. v. Credit du Nord S.A.* [1989] 1 W.L.R. 255, 268; [1988] 3 All E.R.902. Treitel 104 LQR 501.

261 Treitel, *supra* n.259, p.249. For a recent analysis see Smith "Contracts Mistake, Frustration and Implied Terms" (1994) 110 L.Q.R. 400.

262 [1914] 30 T.L.R. 531

263 (1856) 5 H.L.C. 673. See also the Nigerian Case, *Abraham v. Chief Oluwa* (1944) 17 N.L.R. 123

contract showed that what the parties contemplated was that there was an existing something to be sold and bought. The contract was for the sale of existing goods not for the sale goods or documents representing the goods.

This approach has statutory backing in Section 8 and 9 of the Sale of Goods Act[265] which provide:

> 8. "Where there is a contract for the sale of specific goods and the goods without the knowledge of the seller have perished at the time when the contract is made, the contract is void;
>
> 9. Where there is an agreement to sell specific goods, and subsequently the goods, without any fault on the part of the seller or buyer, perish before the risk passes to the buyer, the agreement is thereby avoided."

Section 8 of the Sale of Goods Act was applied in *Leslie and Anderson Ltd. v. Vallabhas Kalidas & Co. Ltd.*[266] In that case the respondents were allotted four bales of gunny bags by the Mengo Pool sometime in July. On 1st August the controller instructed the appellants to send the consignments. On 9th August, they sent the way bill and on the 19th, the respondents paid the price. The goods had been destroyed by fire while in transit. The Court held that the contract was not effective until the 19th August, this being the first date on which the buyers had learnt the identity of the sellers. The contract was, therefore, void under Section 8 because the goods had been destroyed before the date on which the contract came into being.

(b) Mistake as to identity of the subject matter

Such a mistake will occur where one party to the contract intends to deal with one thing and the other party with a different one. In this instance consent is *negatived* but not *nullified*. However, consent would be nullified if both parties thought they were dealing with one thing when they are in fact dealing with another.[267] Thus in *Raffles v. Wichelhaus*[268] E agreed to buy from F a cargo of cotton to arrive "ex Peerless from Bombay. There were two ships called Peerless sailing from Bombay, one sailing in October and the other in December. E meant the earlier one, while F meant the later one. It was held that there was no contract.

(c) Mistake as to possibility of performing the contract

Consent is nullified if both parties believe the contract is capable of being performed when this is not the case. There are 3 types of impossibility.

(i) Physical impossibility

This is illustrated by *Sheikh Bros Ltd. v. Ochsner*[269] where a contract was made for the exploitation of sisal growing on land belonging to A. The contract provided that B was to cut and process the sisal and to deliver the average of 50 tons of sisal fibre per month to A. It was held that the contract was void because the land was not capable of producing 50 tons of fibre per month. Put another way, the contract was void for mutual mistake.

---

264 per Lord Cranworth, L.C. at p.681

265 Cap. 79

266 17 E.A.C.A. 30

267 Treitel, *supra* n.259, p.250. c.f. *Diamond v. British Columbia Thoroughbred Breeders Society* (1966) 52 D.L.R. (2d) 146 where two horses at an auction were confused by the auctioneer *and* by the bidders; but the court held that the difference was one of quality only.

268 (1864) 2 H & C. 906

269 [1957 A.C. 136; [1957] E.A.86 PC. Contrary to the view by Cheshire and Fifoot, *Law of Contract (12 Edn. 1991)*,p.238, Prof. Treitel says (at p.250) the case cannot be dismissed as turning solely on the interpretation of the Indian Contract Act since the Privy Council expressly applied the principles in *Bell v. Lever Bros Ltd.* [1932] A.C.161 a British House of Lords decision. See also Hodgin, *Law of Contract In East Africa* (1975) p.139.

(ii) Legal impossibility

A contract may be void if it provides that something shall be done, which as a matter of law cannot be done. Thus in *Cooper v. Phibbs*[270], a person took a lease of land, which unknown to either party, already belonged to him. It was held that the lease ought to be set aside.

Related to this is that a contract involving the commission of a crime is illegal. A contract may also be illegal even if both parties believe it to be lawful. The parties are then under a mutual mistake as to the legal possibility of performing it.

(iii) Commercial impossibility

This is illustrated by *Griffith v. Brymer,*[271] where a contract made for the hire of a room overlooking the route of King Edward VII's coronation procession was held void because unknown to the parties, the procession had already been cancelled when the contract was made. Professor Treitel has noted in this regard[272] that "performance may have been physically and legally possible but commercially sterile". Arguably there was also mutual mistake as to the *quality* of the subject matter, a subject to which we now turn.

(d) Mistake as to quality of thing contracted for

Where the subject matter of a contract lacks quality which it is believed to have, the first question is whether quality forms part of the contractual description of the thing.[273] If it does then the person giving the description is in breach of contract and liable to the usual remedies for breach.

Thus in *Gompertz v. Bartlett*[274], the plaintiff bought from the defendant an unstamped bill of exchange as a foreign bill. As such it was an inland bill and, therefore void for lack of stamp. It was held that the plaintiff was entitled to recover money he paid on the bill on the ground that the article did not conform with the description of what was sold.

If there is no contractual misdescription, mistake as to quality is said to have no effect. Thus in *Scott v. Littledale*[275] a contract for the sale of tea was held valid in law despite a mistake as to its quality and hence its value.

The rule that mistake as to quality will not invalidate a contract applies especially where goods are sold under a well-known trade name. Thus in *Harrison & Jones v. Burten & Lancaster,*[276] a contract for the sale of " 'Sree' brand Calcutta Kapok" was held valid in spite of the fact that unknown to both parties, it was impure and therefore of no use to B. Furthermore, in *Kennedy v. Panama Royal Mail Co.*[277] the plaintiff applied for shares in a company on the faith of an untrue statement that it had secured a contract to carry mail for the New Zealand Government. The plaintiff received an allotment of shares and the resulting contract between him and the company was held valid.

The law on mistake as to quality of the subject matter contracted is now settled in what is regarded as the leading case in this area, *Bell v. Lever Bros Ltd.*[278] In that case, Bell and Snelling (B & S) agreed with Lever Bros to serve for 5 years as Chairman and Vice Chairman of a company controlled by Lever Bros. Before the end of this period, Lever Bros. wished to terminate the service contracts. For this purpose, they made compensation agreements by which Bell Bros, then discovered that Bell and Snelling had committed breaches of duty which would have justified

---

270 (1867) L.R. 2 H.L. 149, 169, 173; *Bell v. Lever Bros Ltd. ibid.* p.218 per Lords Atkin and Wright.

271 (1903) 19 TLR 434

272 Treitel, *supra* n.259, p.251

273 *Ibid.*

274 (1853) 2 E & B 849.

275 (1858) 8 E & B 815

276 [1953] 1 Q.B. 646; [1953] 1 All E.R. 903

277 (1867) L.R. 2 Q.B. 580

their summary dismissal without compensation. It was found that B & S had at the time of the compensation agreements forgotten about their breaches of duty. Consequently, they were not guilty of fraudulent concealment. The issue, however, remained as to whether Lever Bros could recover back the Fifty Thousand British Pounds on ground that the compensation agreements were void for mistake. They had made the compensation agreements in the belief that the service contracts were valid, when in fact they were voidable. They had paid Fifty thousand pounds for getting rid of B & S, when they might have got rid of them for nothing. Both Wright J at first instance and a unanimous Court of Appeal held that the compensation agreements were void as Lever Bros made a fundamental mistake. The House of Lords by a narrow majority reversed the decision and held that the mistake related only to the quality of the service agreements which were not fundamental. This case has been the subject of controversy[279] and appears not to have been followed in East Africa.[280]

However, in rationalising *Bell v. Lever Bros Case*, Professor Treitel has stated that [281] if parties are basically agreed as to what they are contacting for then there can be no fundamental mistake.

(e) Mistake as to quantity

Mistake as to quantity may also invalidate a contract at law. Thus in *Cox v. Prentice*[282], a silver bar was sold under a mistake as to its weight. The buyer (who was the party prejudiced by the mistake) obtained judgment for the difference in value between the weight of the bar as it was, and as it was believed to be. In *Bell v. Lever Bros*[283], Lord Atkin stated that "an agreement to take an assignment of a lease for five years is not the same thing as to take an assignment of a lease for three years, still less a term of a few months."

2. Mistake negative consent

Mistake will negative consent where the parties are so much at cross-purposes that they do not reach agreement. Examples are first where one party is mistaken as to the identity of the other. Second, where one party intends to deal with one thing and the other a different one. Third where a party intends to deal on one set of terms and other on a different set of terms.

A mistake as to the other party or subject-matter is not effective unless it is fundamental i.e. goes to the root of the contract. It is this requirement which links the cases about to be considered with those in which consent is nullified.

It is also worth noting that the mere existence of mistake does not make a contract void. The Mistake must also induce the contract and also be operative.

An attempt is made to consider these aspects in more detail.

(a) Mistake as to the person contracted with

(i) Fundamental mistake

Consent is negatived if one party is mistaken as to the *identity* of the other person. In *Cundy v. Lindsay*,[284] the plaintiffs received an order for handkerchiefs from a dishonest person, Blenkarn,

---

278 [1932] A.C. 161. For discussion thereof, see Cheshire & Fifoot, *supra* n.269, pp.236 - 238; Treitel, *supra* n.259 pp.252 - 255; Hodgin, *supra* n.269, pp.137 - 139. See also *Solle v. Butcher* [1950] 1 K.B. 671; [1949] 2 All E.R. 1107; *Leaf v. International Galleries* [1950] 2 K.B.86; 1 All E.R. 693; *Malembo v. Bugaga Kwegatta* [1981] HCB 21

279 *Ibid.* See further *Harlington & Leinster Enterprises Ltd v. Christopher Hill Fine Art Ltd.*[1990] 1 All E.R.694

280 *Sheikh Bros v. Ochsner, supra* n.269

281 Treitel *Law of Contract (5th Edn.)* pp.202 - 204.

282 (1815) 3 M & S 344

283 *supra* n.278, at p.223

284 (1878) 3 App Cas c.f. *Baillies Case* (1898) 1 Ch. 110

who gave his address as 37, Wood Street, Cheapside. He signed his name to make it look like Blenkiron & Co., a respectable firm known by reputation to the plaintiffs and carrying on business at 123 Wood Street. The plaintiffs sent the goods to "Blenkiron & Co., 37 Wood Street", where Blenkarn took possession of them. He did not pay for the goods. He sold them to the defendants. It was held that there was no contract between Blenkarn and the plaintiffs as the plaintiffs did not intend to deal with him but with someone else. Therefore, no property in the goods passed to Blenkarn, who could not pass any to the defendants. Therefore, the defendants were liable for conversion.

(ii) Face to face transactions

The difficulty of determining whether a mistake is one of attribute[285] or of identity is compounded where the parties who are alleged to have contracted have met face to face. Thus in *Phillips v. Brooks Ltd.*[286], a rogue called North, entered the plaintiff's shop and asked to see pearls and rings. He selected *inter alia* a ring worth Four hundred and Fifty British Pounds, produced a cheque book, claimed to be Sir George Bullough (wealthy man known to the plaintiff) and gave Sir George's address. The plaintiff checked the address in the directory and then allowed North to take away the ring in exchange for the cheque which was dishonoured. North later pledged the ring with the defendant. The plaintiff claimed that there was never any contract between him and North and North did not have title which he could pass to the defendant. It was held that the defendant had good title to the ring because the contract between the jeweller and North was good. This was because the plaintiff's mistake was one of identity and the jeweller intended to contract with a person he saw in the shop.

A similar result is evident in *Lewis v. Averay,* [287] where the plaintiff advertised a car for sale. He was visited by a rogue who claimed to be a well-known actor called Richard Greene. By this pretence, he induced the plaintiff to sell the car to him on credit and let him take it away in exchange for a cheque which was dishonoured. The plaintiff claimed the car from the plaintiff who had bought it in good faith from the rogue. It was held that the plaintiff could not succeed as the contract between the plaintiff and the rogue was not void for mistake because the presumption that the plaintiff intended to contract with the person before him was not rebutted,[288] and his mistake was not one of identity but as to the credit worthiness of the other party.[289]

However, a mistake as to identity where there are face to face transactions is possible where[290] firstly A induces B to deal with him by pretending to act as agent for C, while in fact intending to contract on his own behalf.[291] Second, a mistake about a person who was present could also be one of identity where he had adopted a physical disguise for example where A induced B to deal with him by disguising himself as C and C was personally known to B, so that B thought A was C. Third the situation presented in *Ingram v. Little* [292] where the plaintiffs advertised their car for sale and been visited by a rogue who falsely claimed to be "PGM Hutchinson of Stanstead House, Stansted Road, Caterham." They agreed to sell the car to him on credit, but only after one of them had checked in a telephone directory that there was a person of that name living at that address. The rogue sold the car to the defendants from whom the plaintiffs claimed it when the rogue's

---

285 See *King Norton Metal Co. Ltd. v. Edridge, Merrett & Co. Ltd.* (1897) 14 T.L.R. 98 where the contract was upheld since the mistake was as to attribute in the form of credit worthiness of the other party.

286 [1919] 2 K.B. 243. See also *Mamujee Bros Ltd. v. Awadh* [1969] E.A. 520

287 [1972] 1 Q.B. 198; [1971] 3 All E.R. 907

288 [1972] 1 Q.B. at pp.208, 209

289 *Ibid.* p.209

290 Treitel, *supra* n.259 p.264

291 *Hardman v. Booth* (1863) 1 H & C 803

292 [1961] 1 Q.B. 31; [1960] 3 All E.R. 332. See also Hall [1961] C.L.J. 86.

cheque was dishonoured. A majority of the English Court of Appeal upheld the claim on the ground that the plaintiffs had intended to deal with the Hutchinson of Stanstead House and not with the person before them as such. Although the decision was doubted in *Lewis v. Averay*[293], it can be supported on its special facts. "i.e. on the ground that the plaintiffs had refused to clinch the deal until they had consulted the telephone directory."[294]

(iii) Distinction between mistake as to identity and as to attribute

The case of *Ingram v. Little*[295] indicates the difficulty of saying exactly what mistake has been made. However, in other cases it may be clear what mistake has been made but there may be a dispute as to whether it should be described as one of *identity or attribute.* Thus in *Lake v. Simmons*,[296] a woman known as Esme Ellison told the plaintiff that she was married to Van de Borgh (with whom she was actually living as a mistress) and that he wanted to give her a necklace which he wished to see on approval. The plaintiff let her take the necklace and entered it in his book as being out on approval to Van de Borgh. Esme Ellison absconded with the necklace. It was held that the plaintiff did not entrust the necklace to her as "customer" within the terms of the insurance policy. Lord Haldane said that there was no contract since there was no *consensus*. The plaintiff "thought he was dealing with a different person, the wife of Van der Borgh ... He never intended to contract with the woman in question."[297] The attribute of a wife here was important for a valid contract. It has been suggested[298] that if a person may be identified by reference to one of his/her attributes, if a mistake is made as to that attribute, then there is a mistake of identity.

In the Kenyan case, *Mamujee Bros Ltd. v. Awadh*,[299] the rogue forged a delivery note in the name of a limited company and presented to X who handed over the goods. The rogue then sold the goods to Y. If X could prove that identity was crucial to them when making the contract then the agreement was void and they could retake the goods from Y. If they could not prove this then the contract was merely voidable. The Court decided that X thought he was dealing with the rogue only as an employee of the company named in the delivery note. The contract was, therefore, void. It was held that Y, the innocent buyer must return the goods to X and try to seek compensation from the rogue.

(b) Mistake as to identity subject matter

This has been discussed under Mistake nullifying consent.[300]

(c) Mistake as to the terms of the contract

Consent is negatived if parties intend to contract on different terms, e.g. if X intends to buy for Shs.45,000/= when Y intends to sell for Twenty Pounds[301] or if A intends to sell rabbit skins at a fixed price when B intends to buy at the same price per pound when there are 3 pieces to the pound[302]

It is significant that mistake as to the terms of the contract in order to negative consent need not be fundamental.[303]

293 *supra* n.287
294 Treitel, *supra* n.259 p.265 relying on Phillimore L.J [1972] 1 Q.B. 198 at p.208.
295 *supra* n.292
296 [1927] A.C. 487 H.L.
297 *Ibid.* p.500
298 Treitel, *supra* n.294, pp.265 -
299 [1969] E.A. 520. See also Hodgin *supra* n.83 pp.141- 142
300 See *supra* notes 267 to 268 and text thereof.
301 *Woodhouse A.C. Israel Cocoal Ltd v. Nigerian Produce Marketing Co.* [1972] A.C.741, 768; *Felthouse v. Bindley* (1862) 11 C.B(NS) 869; (1874) L.R. 9 Q.B.446
302 *Hartog v. Colin & Shields* [1939] 3 All E.R. 566
303 *Smith v. Hughes* (1871) L.R. 6 Q.B. 597

(d) The requirement that mistake must induce the contract

A mistake will only negative consent if it induced the mistaken party to enter into the contract. Thus in *Boulton v. Jones*[304], the plaintiff had just bought the shop of Brocklehurst when the defendant sent his servant to the shop with an order addressed to Brocklehurst for a quantity of hose pipe. The plaintiff supplied the goods thinking that the defendant did not care from whom he received the goods. The defendant was apparently satisfied and used them. He had clearly made a fundamental mistake in that he thought he was dealing with Brocklehurst when he dealt with Boulton. the mistake was significant because Brocklehurst owed money to the defendant who had intended to set off this debt against the price of the goods. It was, therefore, important to him to contract with Brocklehurst rather than Boulton. It was held that there was no contract and the defendant was not liable for the price of goods.

(e) The requirement that mistake must be operative

A mistake which negatives consent is operative in three instances.

(i) Ambiguity

Where there is ambiguity as in the case of *Raffles v. Wichelhaus*[305]. Here a reasonable person could not have known which cargo the parties intended to deal with.

(ii) Mistake known to the other party

This is illustrated by three cases already considered.[306]

(iii) Mistake negligently induced

If X's mistake is negligently induced by Y, then X can treat the contract as void. However, it does not follow that Y can do so. Thus in *Scriven v. Hindley & Co.*,[307]the defendant at an auction bid for two lots believing that both lots were of hemp whereas only one of them was of hemp. The mistake was caused by the misleading nature of the catalogue and the conduct of one of the seller's servants. It was, therefore, operative.

3. Mistake in equity

The common law of mistake can work hardship in three main instances. First a contract may be held valid because of the narrow definition of mistake. As a result, a person may be compelled to pay for what he does not want[308] or something that is virtually worthless.[309] Second, a contract may be held valid despite the existence of a fundamental mistake because of the principle that the mistake must be operative. As a result, a mistaken party can suffer hardship by being bound to a contract which he did not intend to conclude.[310]

In these two situations the common law emphasized the needs of commercial certainty at the expense of justice in individual cases. Third, an innocent third party may suffer hardship where the contract is *void* at common law.

Equity has, therefore, intervened to mitigate the above hardships.[311] As regards the first type of hardship, equity gives relief for certain types of mistake which the common law disregards and also provides flexible remedies. For instance, at common law, there was no power of apportionment

---

304 (1857) 2 H & N 564

305 *supra* n.268 and text thereof. See also *Felthouse v. Bindley supra* n.301.

306 *Cundy v. Lindsay*, supra n.284; *Boulton v. Jones, supra* n.304 and *Smith v. Hughes supra* n.303.

307 [1913] 3 K.B. 564

308 *Smith v. Hughes* (1871) L.R. 6 Q.B. 597

309 *Bell v. Lever Bros., supra* n.278

310 Treitel, *supra* n.259, p.275

311 See Treitel *supra* n.259 p.275

of loss so that the whole loss resulting from a mistake is borne by one party even though both are innocent. At equity, the loss can be apportioned between the two contracting parties. Concerning the second situation equity's intervention is limited to refusal to order specific performance. As regards the third situation, equity provides no relief from hardship to third parties that can arise when the contract is void at law.

However, it has been observed[312] that equity's more liberal treatment of mistake sacrifices the requirements of certainty emphasised by the common law.

An attempt is now made to discuss the types of mistake at equity.

(a) Mistake of fact

(i) Non-fundamental mistake

Equity may give relief to a person who has made a mistake which is not fundamental in the narrow common law sense. Examples are where a purchaser buys from a vendor who has no title,[313] where a purchaser who buys property subject to a charge although he believes it to be free from charge.[314] Additionally, equity would give relief to a vendor who sells property to which he has a greater right than he thinks he has. Thus in *Colyer v. Clay*[315], a person sold his reversionary interest in certain property. He believed it to be a half-share. He was in fact entitled to the whole property and equity provided relief from the mistake.

(ii) Mistake as to value

Equity will in some cases intervene where mistake is merely as to the value of thing sold. Thus in *Re Garnett*,[316] a testator left half his estate to his sister and the other half to be shared equally between his nieces who lived with the sister. The nieces later released their shares to the sister for a consideration of Ten thousand, Five hundred British Pounds. It was held that the release should be set aside because they were worth nearly twice that sum. Nevertheless where the contract price has been fixed by valuation of a third party, equity will not intervene just because the valuation is too high.[317]

(iii) Mistake as to expectation

Equity will only grant relief for a mistake as to existing facts at the date of the contract. It does not give relief as to mistake related to the expectation of parties. Thus in *Amalgamated Investment & Property Co. v. John Walker*,[318] a contract was made for the sale of a London warehouse which the purchaser and to the vendor's knowledge intended to redevelop. Before the date of the contract, a government official had decided that the warehouse ought to be included in the list of buildings of special architectural or historic interest. The actual listing took place after the conclusion of the contract. The effect of the listing was to make it harder to get permission to redevelop. It the permission was refused, this would reduce the value of the property by 1.5m pounds below the contract price of One Million, Seven Hundred and Ten Thousand pounds. It was held that equity could not intervene (whether by rescission or refusal of specific performance) because this was a mistake as to the expectation of the parties.

(b) Mistake of law

(i) Private right and pure mistake of law

Equity can give relief in respect of a pure mistake of law (e.g. misconstruction of a legal document

---

312 *Ibid.*

313 *Hitchcock v. Giddings* (1817) 4 Price 135

314 *Manser v. Back* (1848) 6 Hare 433; *Torrance v. Bolton* (1872) L.R. 8 Ch. App.118

315 (1843) 7 Beav. 188; see also *Cooper v. Phibbs* (1867) L.R. 2 H.L. 149

316 (1885) 31 Ch.D. 1

317 *Campbell v. Edwards* [1976] 1 W.L.R. 403

318 [1977] 1 W.L.R. 164; [1976] 3 All E.R. 509

such as a will or settlement[319] or mistake as to age at which a person can marry or make a will or contractual capacity of a person under disability.[320] Thus in *Allcard v. Walker*[321], a married woman executed a settlement containing a covenant to settle after-acquired property. Under the then existing law, a married woman could not bind herself by such a covenant. In later divorce proceedings, she agreed to an order varying the settlement mistakenly believing that the settlement and the covenant were valid. It was held that the order could be set aside. However subsequently in *Solle v. Butcher*[322] the English Court of Appeal assumed that such a relief could not be given for a pure mistake of law.

(ii) Mistake as to construction

Equity like law will give relief where there is a mistake as to private rights arising out of misconstruction of relevant documents.[323]

(c) Mistaken inferences

Inferences may be drawn from physical circumstances. In such a situation, if there is a mistake as to the inference, equity can provide relief. Thus in *Solle v. Butcher*[324], a flat was extensively altered and then let. Both landlord and tenant thought mistakenly that as a result of the alterations the flat had changed its "identity" so that it was no longer subject to the Rent Acts. Although the English Court of Appeal variously described mistake as one of fact as to private rights or of law,[325] it has been suggested[326] that this is best described as a mistake of secondary fact i.e. inference to be drawn from the primary facts of the alteration. The Court provided equitable relief in respect of the mistaken inferences.

(d) Forms of equitable relief

These include refusal to order specific performance,[327] rescission[328] and rectification[329] and dealt with elsewhere under equitable remedies.[330]

4. Documents mistakenly signed

(a) The general rule and its development

The general rule is that a person is bound by his signature to a document whether he reads it or understands it or not. However by the end of the Sixteenth century an exception to this rule was established. Thus in *Thoroughgood's Case*[331], it was held that if a person who could not read executed a deed after it had been incorrectly read over to him, he was not bound by it. He could plead *non est factum*: it is not my deed. Since the Sixteenth century the doctrine was extended in that it was no longer confined to persons who are unable to read. The reason for the extension

---

319 e.g. *Cooper v. Phibbs* (1877) L.R. 2 H.L. 149
320 Treitel, *supra* n.259, p.277
321 [1896] 2 Ch. 369
322 [1950] 1 K.B. 671; [1949] 2 All E.R. 1107. See *infra* n.324 and text thereof.
323 *Cooper v. Phibbs supra* n.270 and text thereof.
324 *supra* n.322
325 [1950] 1 K.B. 671 pp.685, 693, 705 per Jenkins L. J. dissenting.
326 Treitel *supra* n.259 p.279
327 e.g. *Malins v. Freeman* (1837) 2 Keen 25; *Tamplin v. James* (1879) 15 Ch.D. 215; *Baskomb v. Beckwith* (1869) L.R. 8 Eq.100
328 *Solle v. Butcher supra* n.324; *Cooper v. Phibbs, supra* n.319
329 *Custodian of Enemy Properties v. Reaney* (1922) 1 T.L.R.425; Hodgin *supra* n.269 p.146 - 147 *Singer Sewing Machine Co. v. Khalil Iz Eldin* Vol.11 S.L.R.7
330 Chap.15
331 (1584) 2 Co. Rep. 9a.

was the insistence on the requirement of *consensus ad idem* in contract. Thus in *Foster v. Mackinnon* [332], it was explained that a person who signed a document without being aware of its nature was not bound because "the mind of the signer did not accompany the signature." However it has been said[333] if too wide a scope were given to this argument it could lead to much uncertainty in commercial affairs and would cut across the objective principle that mistake must be operative. Second, it would be inconsistent with the general common law requirement that a mistake must be a fundamental one if it is to negative consent.[334]

It is significant that where the mistake of the signer is known to the other contracting party, the objective principle will not operate in the latter's favour.[335]

(b) Scope of the doctrine of non-est factum

Owing to criticism of the doctrine of *non-est factum* ,its scope is restricted by three rules.

(i) Persons to hom plea available

The extension of the doctrine in the Nineteenth century has been described as "one of the less happy developments in our law"[336] and it was suggested in the same case that the doctrine should not apply in favour of persons of full age and capacity.[337] However, this narrow view of the doctrine was rejected by the House of Lords. Lord Reid thus stated that the doctrine may apply to:[338]

> those who are permanently or temporarily unable through no fault of their own to have without explanation any real understanding of the purport of a particular document, whether that be from defective education,l illness or innate incapacity.

To these must be added persons who have been tricked into signing the document[339]. Consequently, the doctrine may apply not only to the blind and the illiterate, but also to those who are senile, of very low intelligence or unable to read English, but would not protect literate persons of full capacity.[340]

This approach has been applied in East Africa. Thus in *The Director, Jinah's Company Ltd. v. Francis Owino* [341], A pleaded *non-est factum* in relation to a document that he had signed that was in English when in fact he could not read. It was held that he was bound by his signature and it was stressed that in order not to be bound it was necessary for him to show that he executed the deed under a substantial mistake as to its contents and that the mistake was induced by machinations of some person.

(ii) Serious mistake required

In order to restrict the scope of the doctrine, the courts insist that *non est factum* could only be pleaded where the mistake of the signer was a particularly serious one.[342] Previously they gave effect to this policy by drawing a distinction between the "character"[343] of a document and its

---

332 (1869) L.R. 4 C.P. 704, 711

333 Treitel, *supra* n.259, p.291

334 See discussion *supra*.

335 *Cundy v. Lindsay supra* n.284

336 *Gallie v. Lee* [1969] Ch.17, 43 per Salmon L J. (C.A.)

337 *Ibid.* pp.36 - 37

338 [1971] A.C. 1004, at p.1016

339 *Ibid.* p.1025

340 *Ibid.* pp.1016, 1025

341 Civ. App. 22 - D- 67 (Tanzania). See also Hodgin, *supra* n.269, pp.144 - 145.

342 *Ibid.*

343 *Foster v. Mackinnon* (1869) L.R.C.P. 704 (bill of exchange endorsed in the belief that it was a guarantee: plea upheld)

344 *Howatson v. Webbs* [1907] 1 Ch.537 affd [1908] 1 Ch.1 (mortgage of land executed in belief that it was a conveyance: plea rejected).

345 *supra* n.336

"contents"[344] However, in *Gallie v. Lee*[345], the British House of Lords rejected this distinction as unworkable[346] and postulated the requirement that the difference between the document as it was and as it was believed to be must be radical or substantial or fundamental.[347] This means that the seriousness of the mistake is to be judged by the "difference in practical result" rather than by "difference in legal character."[348] The facts of the case were that a widow of 98 wanted to help her nephew, Parkin, to raise money on the security of her leasehold house, provided that she would continue to live there rent free for the rest of her life. Parkin did not want to raise the loan in his own name or to become owner of the house as he feared that this would enable his wife (from whom he was separated) to enforce her claim for maintenance against him. He, therefore, arranged that an intermediary called Lee should raise the money on a mortgage of the house. As a first step in this scheme, a document was prepared which was in fact an assignment on sale of the lease to Lee of Three Thousand British Pounds. The widow did not read this document as her glasses were broken. However, she signed it after being told by Lee that it was a deed of gift to Parkin (who witnessed the document). Lee raised money by mortgaging the house to a building society but did not pay either Parkin or the widow. It was held that the doctrine of *non est factum* did not apply as the widow's mistake was not sufficiently serious. She believed that the document would enable her to raise money on the security of the house and the document was in fact designed to achieve this aim though by a different process from that contemplated by her.[349]

This case has been applied in Uganda. In *Kakande v. Nsimbi*[350], the plaintiff sued the defendant for specific performance (i.e. transfer of land which he had bought from the defendant) and for general damages for breach of contract of sale. The defendant co-owner of a piece of land sold part of the land to the plaintiff through his agent. The sale agreement was drawn up in the English language and by the defendant's advocate and was signed by both parties with the advocate as witness. Later the plaintiff approached the defendant for the latter's signature on a mutation form to enable the plaintiff survey and register into his name the piece of land he bought. The defendant repudiated the contract alleging that he had only leased a piece of land for 10 years to the plaintiff but did not sell it despite the contents of the agreement which he said he signed without the advocate translating it to him in Luganda, the only language he understood. He also claimed to have been blind and hard-working at the material time. It was also argued for the defendant that the sale agreement was null and void under Section 4 of the Illiterates Protection Act (Cap 73), as the advocate never certified on the agreement that he had in fact translated the same to the defendant who had understood it. It was held that the plea of *non est factum* is not available if the signature of a document was brought about by the negligence of the signer in failing to take precautions which ought to have been taken. The defendant should have insisted that the document be read over to him. In this case, it was proved that the Sale agreement was translated to the defendant in Luganda by his advocate before he signed it. Second, Section 4 of the Illiterates Protection Act does not make it mandatory for verification of documents written for illiterates. The Section simply creates a rebuttable presumption that the document was read over to the illiterate in a language he understands. It is for the illiterate to rebut the presumption which the defendant had failed to do.

(iii) Mistake as to identity

Consent may be negatived so as to prevent the formation of a contract where A deals with B in the mistaken belief that B is C.[351] However, if a person signs a document expressed to be in favour of B, he cannot plead *non est factum* simply because he thought the party named was C. In *Gallie v.*

---

346 See *Muskham Finance Ltd. v. Howard* [1963] 1 Q.B. 904 and *Howatson v. Webb supra* n.344

347 [1971] A.C. at pp.1017, 1019, 1021, 1026,1034

348 *Ibid.* p.1017

349 c.f. *Mercantile Credit Ltd. v. Hamblin* [1965] 2 Q.B. 242 *Avon Finance Co. v. Bridger* [1985] 2 All E.R. 281

350 [1984] H.C.B. 37

351 *Cundy v. Lindsay, supra* n.284; *Lake v. Simmons, supra* n.296.

Lee (supra), the doctrine did not apply even though the plaintiff thought she was making a gift to Parkin when in fact she was making a conveyance to Lee. Consequently, the basis of the rule is that the mistaken party can discover the mistake by reading the document.[352]

(iv) Ignorance

The plea of *non-est factum* is not available to a person who signs a document in the belief that it is "only a form" without any exact idea as to its nature.[353] Thus in *Gillman v. Gillman,*[354] a wife, shortly before her husband left her, signed a document which was in fact a separation deed. She did not know this when she signed. She also did not have any definite idea of what it was she was signing. It was held that she was bound by the deed.

(v) Mistake as to capacity

The defence of *non-est factum* is open to a person who signs a document under a mistaken belief as to the capacity in which he signs. Thus in *Lewis v. Clay*[355], the defendant was induced to sign 2 promissory notes by the fraudulent representation that his signature was required as a witness and that the documents were of a private nature. The plea of *non est factum* succeeded even though the defendant could not say precisely what type of document he thought he had signed.

(vi) Carelessness

Carelessness of the signer excludes the doctrine of *non-est factum*. In *Gallie v. Lee (supra)* the second ground for decision in the case was that the widow could only rely on the doctrine of *non est factum* as she had been careless in signing the document without reading it.[356] In the same way a person cannot invoke the doctrine if he signs a document containing blanks which are later filled in otherwise than in accordance with his instructions.[357]

(c) The significance of illiteracy

Since most African Societies are predominantly illiterate, the capacity of illiterates to contract is of considerable interest. Related to this are problems arising from inability to comprehend written documents invariably giving rise to mistake. It is notable, though, that no contractual incapacity is attached to any person by being illiterate. However, it is also recognised that illiteracy is a misfortune and not a privilege.

There are statutory provisions designed to protect illiterates from being taken advantage of when they sign contractual documents which they had no intention to bind them.[358] In *UAC of Nigeria Ltd v. Edems*[359], it was indicated that the object of the Illiterate Protection Act was to protect an illiterate person from possible fraud.

The Illiterates Protection Act defines [360] an "illiterate" as "in relation to any document, a person who is unable to read and understand the script or language in which the document is written or printed as the case maybe".

There are cases where a person may be able to sign his name but not be able to understand the nature and effect of the legal document. The issue then arises as to whether such a person is illiterate. It has been held in Nigeria that the person would be regarded as an illiterate if he is unable to comprehend or understand the effect of the document.[361] This approach is in line with

---

352 Treitel, *supra* n.259, p.293; *Kakande v. Nsimbi, supra* n. 350.

353 *Hunter v. Walters* (1871) L.R. 7 Ch. App 75

354 (1946) 174 L.T. 272

355 (1897) 67 L.J.Q.B. 224

356 See also *Kakande v. Nsimbi, supra* n.95

357 *United Dominions Trust Ltd. v. Western* [1976] Q.B. 513 [1975] 3 All E.R. 1017; Marston [1976] C.L.J. 218.

358 See Illiterates Protection Act, Cap 73 (IPA)

359 1958 N.R.N.L.R. 33

360 Section 2

361 *S.C.O.A. Zaria v. Okon* 1960 N.N.L.R. 35, 38 per Quashie Idun Ag F. J.

the statutory provision[362] which provides for verification by a person, writing on behalf of the illiterate, of the signature of the illiterate. In *U.A.C. of Nigeria v. Edems*[363], the plaintiffs claimed against he first defendant as principal debtor, the sum of Three Hundred and Two British Pounds being the balance owing on a ground account for the season 1956 - 57 and from Ajayi, the second defendant, the sum of Three Hundred British Pounds as bondor of the first defendant. The first defendant admitted liability. The second defendant resisted the claim on the ground that the bond on which the plaintiffs relied did not comply with the Illiterates Protection Ordinance. This was so because the attestation clause did not contain a statement that the bond was read over and explained to the second defendant before he thumbprinted it. There was also no endorsement thereon of the name and address of the writer as required by Section 3 of the Illiterates Protection Ordinance.[364] The Court dismissed the claim against the second defendant on the ground that the fact that the second defendant thumb printed the bond was *prima facie* evidence that he was illiterate. Secondly that the aim of the Illiterates Protection legislation was to protect an illiterate person from possible fraud. Consequently, strict compliance with it by the writer of the document is mandatory. Non compliance renders the document a nullity. In contrast in *Kakande v. Nsimbi* [365], it was held that Section 4 of the Illiterates Protection Act does not make it mandatory for verification of documents written for illiterates. The section simply creates a rebuttable presumption that the document was read over to the illiterate in a language he understands. It is for the illiterate to rebut the presumption which the defendant failed to do. With due respect this is a misconstruction of Section 4 which uses the term *shall* in relation to the steps to be taken to verify documents written for illiterates.

It has also been suggested[366] that compliance with the provisions of the Illiterates Protection legislation must be at the time of executing the document and not afterwards.

---

362 I.P.A. Cap 73, Section 3

363 1958 N.R.L.R. 33

364 equivalent to Section 4 IPA Cap 73 (Uganda)

365 *supra* n.350

366 Achike, O. *Nigerian Law of Contract* pp. 134 - 5; c.f. Bate J. in *Kantoma v. Peter Zochonis* 1964 NNLR 54

8
MISREPRESENTATION

1. Introduction

A person may be able to claim relief if he is induced to enter into a contract by a misleading statement. To claim the relief, the representee should show that the representation was such as the law recognises as giving rise to liability. However, this excludes "mere puffs" and certain statements of law or opinion or as to the future. A number of conditions giving rise to liability must be satisfied. First, the representation must be unambiguous and material. Second it must have been relied upon by the representee. If these requirements are satisfied, the representee may be able to claim damages or rescind the contract or to do both.

There are reliefs available to the representee. First is the common law right to damages where the representation is fraudulent. Second, where the representation is negligent, there is a common law and in some jurisdictions[367] a statutory right to damages. Third, where the representation is wholly innocent there is no right to damages, but the court may in its *discretion* award damages in lieu of rescission. Fourth, the representee can rescind the contract whether the representation is fraudulent, negligent or wholly innocent.

2. Meaning of "representation"

The general rule is that no relief for misrepresentation will be given unless it is a statement of *existing fact*. Relief will, therefore not be available in the following cases.

(a) Mere puffs

There are statements which are so vague that they have no effect at law or equity.[368] Thus in *Dimmock v. Hallet*[369], land was described as "fertile and improvable". This was held to be mere sales talk of which there was no relief. This should be distinguished from precise claims, e.g. that use of carbolic smoke ball will give immunity to influenza or that the coffee offered is the best in the world.[370]

(b) Statement of fact and of opinion or belief

Some statements of opinion are regarded as mere puffs. Others, though more precise are not assertions of fact but only statements of opinion or belief. In *Anderson v. Pacific Fire & Marine Insurance Co.*[371], a statement that an anchorage was safe was held to be a mere statement of opinion. Similarly a statement that land would support 2,000 sheep was also judged to be a statement of opinion.[372] In both cases, the party making the statement had to the knowledge of the

367 Britain : The Misrepresentation Act, 1967

368 Treitel *Law of Contract* (8th Edn. 1991) p. 296

369 (1866) L.R. 2 Ch. App. 21.

370 *Carlill v. Carbolic Smoke Ball Co.* [1893]

371 (1872) L.R. 7 CP 65

372 *Bissett v. Wilkinson* [1977] A.C. 177

other party no personal knowledge of the facts on which it was based. Consequently, it was understood that he could only state his belief. However, if the statement is made by a person who has or professes to have special knowledge or skill relating to its subject matter, the statement is taken to be one of fact.[373]

A statement may, in terms be one of opinion or belief but by implication involve a statement of fact. Consequently, it is a misrepresentation of fact for a person to say that he holds an opinion, which he does not hold such as representing a picture to be by a particular artist when he thinks it is a copy.[374]

(c) Representations as to the future

A representation as to the future does not give rise to a cause of action unless it is binding as a contract.

A person who promises to do something may be making a statement as to his future conduct. If so he does not misrepresent a fact if he fails to do what he said he would do. However, he may also be making a statement as to his present intention. If so, he does not misrepresent a fact, if he fails to do what he said he would do. However, he may also be making a statement as to his present intention. If so, he does misrepresent a fact, if when he made the statement he had no such intention. Courts tend to interpret such statements in the second sense in order to protect the interests of persons deceived by them. In *Edgington v. Fitzmaurice*,[375] the plaintiff was induced to lend money to a company by representations made by the directors that the money would be used to improve the company's buildings and to expand its business. In fact the directors intended to use the money to pay off the company's existing debts. It was held that the directors were liable in deceit. Bowen L. J. thus stated:[376]

> There must be a mis-statement of an existing fact; but the state of a man's mind is as much a fact as the state of his digestion. It is true that it is very difficult to prove what the state of man's mind at a particular time is, but if it can be ascertained it is as much a fact as anything else. A misrepresentation as to the state of man's mind is therefore, a mis-statement of fact.

A statement of belief may also amount to a misrepresentation of fact if it involves an implied assertion that the representor has reasonable grounds for his opinion or belief. A statement of intention may also be coupled with an express statement of existing fact. Consequently, a statement by A that he *had* sold maize and *would* pay over the proceeds to B is a misrepresentation of fact if it is wholly untrue.[377]

(d) Statements of fact and law

At common law, there is no civil remedy for a misrepresentation of law as distinguished from one of fact. Similarly, in equity a money claim cannot be based on a misrepresentation of law.[378] It is also assumed that misrepresentation law is not even a ground for rescission in equity,[379] although this has been doubted. In this regard it has been said that *wilful* misrepresentation is a ground for

---

373 *Esso Petroleum Co. Ltd. v. Mardon* [1976] Q.B. 801; [1976] 2 All E.R. 5; *Box v. Midland Bank Ltd.* [1979] 2 Lloyds Rep 391.

374 *Jendwine v. Slade* (1797) 2 Esp. 571, 573; *Brown v. Raphael* [1958] Ch. 636, 641; [1958] 2 All E.R. 79

375 (1885) 29 Ch.D. 459

376 *Ibid.* p. 482.

377 *Babcock v. Lawson* (1880) 5 Q.B.D. 284

378 *Rashdall v. Ford* (1866) L.R. 2 Eq. 750; *Beattie v. Ebury* (1872) L.R. 7 Ch. App.777; *Eaglesfield v. Londonderry* (1876) 4 Ch.D. 693

379 *Wauton v. Coppard* [1899] 1 Ch.92; *Mackenzie v. Royal Bank of Canada* [1934] A.C. 468. However in both cases the representation was held to be one of fact.

equitable relief[380], although it is suggested [381] that *negligent* misrepresentation of law gives rise to relief at equity.

The distinction between a misrepresentation of law and one of fact may be illustrated as follows.

(i) Powers of companies

An issue arises as to whether a misrepresentation by a director of a company as to its powers is one of law or fact. Thus in *Beattie v. Ebury*,[382] directors represented that they had power under a private Act incorporating the company to issue new preference shares ranking *pari passu* with an existing issue. It was held that this was a representation of law. However, in *Cherry v. Colonial Bank of Australasia*[383], directors who had power to borrow with consent of shareholders borrowed without such consent. It was held that they had impliedly made a representation of fact that they had obtained the shareholder's consent.

(ii) Effect of a document

A representation as to the meaning of a document whose contents are known is one of law. However, a representation as to what those contents are is one of fact. In *Wauton v. Coppard*[384] a prospective buyer of land knew it was subject to a *restrictive covenant* which he was asked to see. It was not shown to him, but was told that there was nothing in the covenant which would prevent him from running a preparatory school on the land. It was held that this was a representation of fact as it concerned the contents and not the meaning of the contract.

(iii) Effect of a statute

A representation as to the meaning of a statute or act of parliament is one of law. This also applied generally to representation as to its contents. However in *West London Commercial Bank v. Kitson*[385], a director of a company represented that they had authority to accept bills on behalf of the company. Under the private Acts incorporating it, the company had no power to accept or authorise anyone to accept bills. It was held that the representation was one of fact as it related to the contents of a private act.

(iv) Applicability of a rule of law

A statement that a statute or a rule of common law applies to a known state of facts may be one of fact or law depending on the circumstances. Thus in *Territorial & Auxilliary Forces Association v. Nichols*[386], a statement was made that the Rent Acts applied to a house which was known to be in occupation of the Crown (government). It was held that this was a misrepresentation of law since it involved the erroneous proposition of law that the Rent Acts bound the Crown. In contrast in *Solle v. Butcher*,[387] a statement was made that the Rent Acts did not apply to a house because its identity was wrongly thought to have been changed by work done to it. It was held that this was a misrepresentation of fact. It is suggested [388] that the proposition of law involved in the statement that the Rent Acts did not apply where the identity of the house had changed was accurate. The only misrepresentation was one of fact that is as to the change of identity.

---

380 *West London Commercial Bank v. Kitson* (1884) 13 Q.B.D. 360, 362 - 363.

381 Treitel, *supra* n.368pp.298, 300; *Andre' & Cie S. A. v. Ets Michel Blank & Fils* [1979] 2 Lloyds Rep. 427.

382 (1872) L.R. 7 Ch.App.777

383 (1869) L.R. 3 P.C. 24

384 [1899] 1 Ch.92

385 (1884) 13 Q.B.D.360. The distinction between a private and public Act is now doubted in view of the Interpretation Act.

386 [1949] 1 K.B. 35

387 [1950] 1 K.B. 671

388 Treitel, *supra* n.368 p.299

(v) Private rights

A representation as to private rights such as pledging of shares to a particular person[389] the holding of a patent in a certain invention[390] or that a particular product embodies somebody's invention[391] are representations of fact.

(vi) Representation of foreign law

Foreign law is a matter of fact.[392] Consequently, representation of foreign law is regarded as one of fact.[393]

3. General conditions of liability

A representation only gives rise to remedies if it is unambiguous, material and a representee has relied on it.

(a) Ambiguity

Where the statement made is ambiguous and the person to whom it is made misunderstands it, the representor is not liable if his interpretation is the correct one and that of the representee wrong.[394] The representor will also not be liable for fraud if the court decides that the representee's interpretation is correct.[395] However, if the representor makes an ambiguous statement intending it in a sense that is to his knowledge untrue and the statement is understood in that sense by the representee, he will be guilty of fraud.[396]

(b) Material

A misrepresentation generally has no effect unless it is material. In other words, it must be one that would affect the judgment of a reasonable man in deciding whether, or on what terms, to enter into the contract. Alternatively, it must be one that would induce him to enter into the contract without making such inquiries as he would otherwise make.[397] Thus in a contract of insurance it is material that the subject matter has been grossly overvalued[398] or that the previous proposal for insuring it has been declined.[399] Similarly, in a contract for a loan of money, it is material that the lender is a notoriously ruthless money lender.[400] Additionally, in a sale by auction of a house, it is material who owns the house as it is to a certain extent a guarantee as to the character of sale.[401] A misrepresentation may also be material although the representor in good faith thinks that it is not material.[402]

There are two major exceptions to the requirement of materiality. First, a person who has successfully perpetrated a fraud cannot claim that the representation he used was material.[403] Second, every representation, however unimportant, is material if the contract expressly so provides.

---

389 *Mackenzie v. Royal Bank of Canada* [1934] A.C. 468

390 *Begbie v. Phosphate Sewage Co. Ltd.* (1875) L.R. 10 Q.B. 491

391 *Lyle Mellor v. Lewis* [1956] 1 W.L.R. 29

392 Dicey & Morris *The Conflict of Laws (11th Edn.)* Rule 18

393 *Andre & Cie S.A. v. Ets Michel Blank & Fils* [1979] 2 Lloyds Rep. 427, 431, 432.

394 *McInerny v. Lloyds Bank* [1974] 1 Lloyds Rep 246, 254.

395 *Akerhielm v. De Mare* [1959] A.C. 789; [1959] E.A. 476; *Gross v. Lewis Hillmark Ltd.* [1970] Ch.445

396 *The Siboen & The Sibotre* [1976] 1 Lloyds Rep. 293, 318

397 *Dimmock v. Hallett* (1866) L.R. 2 Ch. App.21

398 *Ionides v. Pender* (1874) L.R. 9 Q.B.531

399 *Locker & Woolf Ltd. v. W. Australian Insurance Co. Ltd.* [1936] 1 K.B. 408.

400 *Gordon v. Street* [1899] 2 Q.B. 641

401 *Whurr v. Davenish* (1904) 20 T.L.R. 385

402 *Joel v. Law Union & Crown Insurance Co.* [1908] 2 K.B. 863,883

403 *Smith v. Kay* (1859) 7 H.L.C. 750

Thus if a policy of insurance provides (as is usual) that the statements by the assured in the proposal form shall be the basis of the contract or are warranted to be true such statements are material[404] regardless of their inherent unimportance.

(c) Reliance

A person to whom a misrepresentation is made must show that he relied upon it. Consequently he cannot rescind or claim damages for misrepresentation if the representation has not come to his notice.[405] or if he knows the truth or relies on his own information[406] or if he takes the risk of the representation turning out to be true.

4. Damages of misrepresentation

(a) Fraud

At common law, a person suffering loss as a result of acting in reliance on a fraudulent statement can recover damages in an action for deceit. This is possible whether or not he rescinds the contract as well.[407] However, he cannot pursue both remedies if this leads to his recovering double for the same loss.[408]

In *Derry v. Peek*,[409] the British House of Lords decided that a statement is only fraudulent if made (i) with knowledge of its falsity; or (ii) without belief in its truth; or (iii) recklessly, not caring whether it is true or false. Fraud is a serious charge which must be specifically proved.[410]

A statement may be fraudulent although made without bad motive and without intention to cause loss. Thus in *Polhill v. Walter*, [411] an agent purported to accept a bill of exchange on behalf of his principal knowing that he had no authority to do so but believing that his principal would ratify. It was held that he was liable in deceit. In contrast in *Angus v. Clifford*,[412] the directors of a company which had bought a gold mine issued a prospectus containing extracts from an engineer's report said to have been "prepared for the directors." It had in fact been prepared for the sellers of the mine. The directors knew of this but were held not liable for fraud as they did not at the time of issuing the prospectus appreciate the importance of the words "prepared for the directors." It thus appears that a person is not guilty of fraud if he knows that his statement is false but does not appreciate its materiality or relevance.

Some East African cases have considered these principles. Thus in *Friedman v. Njoro Industries Ltd.*[413] ,the injured party was able to show that the defendant had been fraudulent when he said that a rival had already offered a higher price for the shares, thereby inducing him to buy the shares. Similarly, in *Windt v. Parrot*[414], it was held that since the plaintiff made a material, although an innocent misrepresentation to the defendant of the company's financial position at a given date, the defendant was entitled to repudiate the contract.

(b) Negligence at common law

A misrepresentation is negligent if it is made carelessly in breach of a duty owed by the representor

404 *London Assurance v. Mansel* (1879) 11 Ch.D.363, 368
405 *Exp. Biggs* (1859) 28 L.J. Ch.50
406 *Jennings v. Broughton* (1854) 5 D.M & G 126
407 *Newbigging v. Adam* (1886) 34 Ch.D. 582, 592
408 *Archer v. Brown* [1985] Q.B. 401, 415, [1984] 2 All E.R. 267
409 (1889) 14 App. Cas. 337
410 *Wallingford v. Mutual Society* (1880) 5 App Cas.685
411 (1832) 3 B & Ad 114
412 [1891] 2 Ch.449
413 21 E.A.C.A. 172
414 [1976] H.C.B. 28 (Allen, J.)

to the representee to take reasonable care that the representation is accurate. It was previously thought that such a duty only arises out of a pre-existing contract between the representor and the representee or where the relationship between them was "fiduciary".[415] However this narrow view was rejected in the landmark decision of *Hedley Byrne & Co. Ltd. v. Heller & Partners Ltd.*[416] In that case, the plaintiffs suffered loss as a result of giving credit to a firm called Easipower Ltd. They had been induced to give credit by a reference carelessly given by Easipower's bank who knew of the purpose for which the reference was required. It was held that the bank was not liable because the reference was given "without responsibility". However, the British House of Lords stated *obiter* that if there was no disclaimer, the bank would have owed some duty to the plaintiffs.

The principle in the *Hedley Byrne Case* has been applied in East Africa. Thus in *Winther v. Arbon Langrish & Southern Ltd.*,[417] the defendant insurance broker failed to renew an accident insurance when the wife of the policy holder called at their office to ask their advice as to what was needed to be done in relation to the insured's policies. The husband was killed and the wife successfully sued the brokers for negligence. Similarly in *Kirima Estates (U) Ltd v. Korde,*[418] the plaintiff company relied entirely on the advice and opinion of the defendant, an advocate as to the value as security of certain property in lending Shs.60,000/= upon a mortgage which required the principal sum to be repaid in February, 1959. The mortgagor did not pay the principal sum. In 1961, after an action had brought no bids at all, the plaintiff company on the defendant's advice, took over the property and sold it for Shs.45,000/=. It then sued the defendant alleging negligence and claiming from him the loss sustained. It alleged that the property was never adequate security for the Shs.960,000/= lent as the property was not worth Shs.120,000/= as the defendant had represented. Consequently, the defendant was negligent in his duty as advocate in advising as to the value of the property having failed to get the property valued by a surveyor and to make local inquiries as to the value of the property or as to the value of similar properties in the locality. The defendant denied liability and argued that he was under no duty to get the property valued by a surveyor or estate agent. The main issue, therefore, was whether the defendant was under a duty to get the property valued. It was held that defendant was perfunctory and reckless in stating the value of the property to be Shs.120,000/= as he had no reasonable ground upon which to base his valuation. Consequently, he was not only negligent in the discharge of his duty to his client but had also committed a breach of that duty.

The principle in the *Hedley Byrne* case is a clear departure from the common law position that a duty of care only arises if there is a "special" relationship between the parties. The case suggests that a duty of care will generally arise where there is a professional relationship even though it is not contractual. For this purpose immunity from liability for negligence in the conduct of litigation on the part of barristers and solicitors is unaffected by this principle.[419] The duty is, therefore, owed by accountants, surveyors, valuers,[420] analysts etc. even to persons other than their immediate clients who rely on their statements provided that such reliance was anticipated or should reasonably have been foreseen.

A common feature of such cases is that the person making the statement does so in exercise of some professional skill. The absence of this factor was held to negative liability in *Mutual Life & Citizen's Insurance Co. Ltd. v. Evatt.*[421] In that case, the company carelessly gave misleading

---

415 *Nocton v. Ashburton* [1914] A.C. 932

416 [1964] A.C 932; [1963] 2 All E.R. 575 H.L.

417 [1966] E.A. 292 (Harris J.)

418 [1963] E.A. 637 (Udo Udoma C. J.) relying on the *Hedley Byrne case* and *William Abercombie Shaw v. Frederick Chater Jack* (1932) 14K.L.R.1 (P.C.)

419 *Rondel v. Worsley* [1969] 1 A.C. 191 read together with *Somasundram v. Melchior & Co.* [1988] 1 W.L.R.1394

420 *Yianni v. Edwin Evans & Sons* [1982] Q.B. 438; *Smith v. Eric S. Bush* [1990] 1 A.C. 831

421 [1971] A.C. 793; [1971] 1 All E.R. 150. See also 87 L.Q.R. 147; Rickford, 34 M.L.R. 328

information about an associated company to a prospective investor in the latter company., As a result the investor suffered loss. It was held by the Privy Council by a majority that the first company was not liable in negligence as it was not and did not purport to be engaged in the business of giving skilled advice on investments. The majority of the Law Lords regarded this as an essential ingredient of liability. However, there is support for the view that so long as the representor knows (or should know) that the representee will rely on his advice and also purports to have some special skill or competence, he may be held liable even though he is not in the business of giving advice. Thus in *Esso Petroleum Co. v. Mardon*[422], a tenant was induced to take a lease of a petrol station from an oil company by a statement by an experienced salesman on the company's behalf as to the future turnover of the premises. It was held that the company was under a duty of care at common law. It was clear that the tenant had relied on the salesman's superior knowledge and experience. Similarly in *Anderson & Sons Ltd. v. Rhodes (Liverpool) Ltd.*[423], a commission agent made a representation to a seller of potatoes about the solvency of his principal, the buyer. It was held that the agent owed a duty of care to the seller.

The above cases should be distinguished from commercial relationships in which each party consciously relies on his own skill and judgment[424] or where it is reasonable for the representor to assume that the representee will be advised by his own experts.[425] In such cases there would be no duty of care at common law.

(c) Contractual statements

The misrepresentation so far considered is one which induces the representee to enter into the contract but does not actually form part of the contract or otherwise acquire contractual force. Where the misrepresentation does have contractual force, the representee is entitled to recover damages for breach of contract. He may also be entitled to rescind the contract for breach or for misrepresentation. The right to damages here is different from the right to damages for misrepresentation inducing a contract in two ways. First, it is independent of fraud or negligence. Second, it is governed by different rules as to assessment of damages for remoteness.

A contractual statement may either be a term of the main contract or a collateral contract.

(i) Terms of the main contract

A descriptive statement may be actually written into the contract itself. However, if the contract expressly provides that a statement is not to be regarded as a term, effect will be given to such provision by the Court. Nevertheless, a statement is treated as a contractual term if it is expressed to be the basis of the contract.[426] Apart from such express provisions, the issue as to whether the statement is a term or mere representation is one of construction to be determined by the Court.[427] There are certain guiding principles in this regard.

Verification

A Statement is not regarded as a term of the contract if the person making it expressly asks the other party to verify or check its truth. Thus in *Ecay v. Godfrey*,[428] the seller of a boat said that it was sound but advised the buyer to have it surveyed. Such advice negatived any intention to warrant the soundness of the boat. A statement is also not regarded as a term of the contract if circumstances are such that the person to whom it is made would normally be expected to verify it.

422 [1976] Q.B.801. See also *Howard Marine & Dredging Co. Ltd. v. A. Ogden & sons (Excavations) Ltd.* [1978] Q.B. 574, 591, 600 per Lord Denning.

423 [1967] 2 All E.R. 850

424 *Oleificio Zucchi S. A. v. Northern Sales Ltd.* [1965] 2 Lloyd's Rep. 496.

425 *McInerny v. Lloyds Bank Ltd.* [1974] 1 Lloyd's Rep 246

426 e.g. *London Assurance v. Mansel* (1879) 1 Ch.D. 363

427 *Behn v. Burness* (1863) 1 B & S 751, 754 which concerned a statement in charterparty as to position of a ship.

428 [1974] 80 Ll. L.R. 286

A Statement would be regarded as a term of the contract if it is intended to prevent the other party from finding out the truth. In *Schawel v. Reade*,[429] a buyer of a horse was about to examine it when the seller said, "You need not look for anything: the horse is perfectly sound. If there was anything the matter with the horse I should tell you." The buyer, in reliance on this statement bought the horse without examination. It was held by the British House of Lords that this was a warranty.

Importance

A Statement is likely to be a term of the contract if its importance is such that if it had not been made the representee would not have entered into the contract at all. Thus in *Bannerman v. White*[430] an intending buyer of hops asked whether sulphur had been used in their cultivation. He added that if sulphur had been used, he would not bother to ask the price. It was held that the assurance by the seller that sulphur had not been used was a term of the contract. This type of statement can be a term of the contract even though it conflicts with a previous statement. Thus in *Couchman v. Hill*,[431] a heifer was presented for auction. Printed conditions of sale provided that no warranty was given. The plaintiff asked whether the heifer was in calf and that if she was he would not bid. He bought the heifer after being assured that she was not in calf. It was held that the assurance was a term of the contract.

Special knowledge

The capacity of a representor and representee to ascertain the truth of what was stated is relevant in distinguishing between contractual terms and mere representations. Thus in *Oscar Chess Ltd. v. Williams*,[432] the seller was a private person to whom the car had been previously sold as a 1948 model with a forged logbook. The main reason why the seller's statement as to age of the car was not regarded as a term of the contract was that he had no special knowledge as to the age of the car while the buyers who were car dealers were in at least as good a position as the seller to know whether the statement was true. This case may be contrasted with *Dick Bentley productions Ltd. v. Harold Smith (Motors) Ltd.*,[433] where a dealer sold a Bentley car, representing that it had only done 20,000 miles since a replacement engine was fitted. In fact it had done nearly 100,000 miles since then. It was held that the representation was a warranty.

The two cases are usually reconciled by saying that the sale in the first was by a private seller and in the second by a dealer, although this had been ignored in some cases where the *Oscar Chess* case was not cited to the Court.[434]

Opinion

Statements of opinion which are so vague that they cannot be verified are mere puffs and of no effect. However, a statement of opinion which is difficult but not impossible to verify may be a term of the contract. Thus in *Power v. Barham*[435], it was held that a statement that certain pictures were by Canaletto could be a warranty. Similarly, in *Leaf v. International Galleries*[436] a representation made that a picture was a Constable could be a warranty.

(ii) Collateral contract

A statement made during negotiations leading up to the contract may not take effect as one of its terms. For instance, the contract may be in writing so that extrinsic evidence cannot be used to

---

429 [1913] 2 I.R. 64
430 (1854) 15 C. B. (N.S.) 844
431 [1947] K.B. 554; [1947] 1 All E.R. 103
432 [1957] 1 W.L.R. 370;
433 [1965] 1 WLR 615; [1965] 2 All E.R. 65
434 *Beale v. Taylor* [1967] 1 WLR 1193; [1967] 3 All E.R. 253
435 (1836) 4 A & E 473
436 [1950] 2 K.B. 86; [1950] 1 All E.R. 693

add to it or to vary it[437] or the statement may be oral and the contract is one which the law requires to be in writing.[438]. In such cases the oral statement may be enforceable as a collateral contract. The effect of this is that there are two contracts between the parties in the main (written) contract and the collateral (oral) contract both relating to the same subject matter. Thus in *Lassalle v. Guildford,*[439] the intending lessee of a house refused to execute a lease unless the landlord first assured him that the drains were in a good order. The landlord gave the assurance but it was not incorporated in the lease. It was held that the landlord was liable for breach of contract when the drains were found to be defective.[440]

It would appear that a statement takes effect as a collateral contract if two conditions are satisfied. First, it must have been intended to have contractual effect. Second, there must be some indication that the parties intended the statement to take effect as a collateral contract and not simply as a term in the main contract.

5. Rescission for misrepresentation

(a) Variety of meanings of "rescission"

The term "rescission" can mean a variety of things.

(i) Rescission for misrepresentation and breach

Where misrepresentation is not a term of the contract, the process referred to as "rescission for misrepresentation" means setting the contract aside for all purposes so as to restore, as far as possible, the state of things which existed before the contract. However if misrepresentation is a term of the contract, the victim may seek rescission for breach and this may also result in the restoration of the state of things which existed before the contract. The vital difference between the two processes is that a person who rescinds for breach can also claim damages for breach of contract,[441] whereas the one who rescinds for misrepresentation has, by treating the contract as if it never existed *prima facie* loses the right to claim damages for its breach.

(ii) Rescinding and pleading misrepresentation as a defence

Rescinding a contract, (whether for misrepresentation or breach) may take active steps to this end. For instance the victim may seek the return of money or property which he had given away under the contract or restoring what he obtained under it. Alternatively, he may seek cancellation of the contract or declaration of its invalidity. Furthermore, he may rely on the misrepresentation as a defence to an action on the contract.

(b) Rescission for misrepresentation

(i) Contract voidable

The general rule is that misrepresentation makes the contract voidable at the option of the representee.[442] Thus in *Redgrave v. Hurd*[443], the defendant was induced to buy a solicitor's house and practice by an innocent misrepresentation as to the value of the practice. It was held that he

---

437 Ss.90, 91 Evidence Act. See also *supra* Chap.6 and discussion on Parol evidence.

438 *supra* Chap.6

439 [1901] 2 K.B. 215

440 See also *Esso Petroleum co. Ltd. v. Mardon* [1976] Q.B. 312 discussed *supra*, where a statement made on behalf of the landlord was also held to constitute a collateral contract.

441 *Buckland v. Farmar & Moody* [1979] 1 W.L.R. 221, 232; [1978] 3 All E.R. 929, 938 *Johnson v. Agnew* [1980] A.C. 367, 392-3 [1979] 1 All E.R. 883, 889

442 *Clough v. L & N.W. Ry* (1871) L. R. 7 Ex.26, 34

443 (1881) 20 Ch.D. 1

could rescind the contract and thereby get back the deposit he had paid. In this instance it is clear that misrepresentation makes the contract voidable and not void. This has important effects on third parties. Consequently, if a person obtains goods under a contract which is void for mistake, property in the goods may not pass to him and the goods may be recovered by the owner from the third party in possession.[444] However, if a person obtains goods under a contract which is voidable for misrepresentation a voidable title passes to him and the former owner's right to avoid it is lost when an innocent third party for value acquires interest in the goods.

(i) Mode of rescission

Sometimes a contract is rescinded by bringing legal proceedings. However, rescission can also be effected informally by simply giving notice to the other party. Legal proceedings may nonetheless be necessary in order to work out the consequences of rescission. For instance it may be desirable to have a court order stating that a formal transaction (such as a lease or transfer of shares) has been or ought to be set aside. Even then rescission is the act of the representee and not that of the court and takes effect when the representee gives notice or commences legal proceedings - not the time of the Court's order.[445] In other cases, legal proceedings are unnecessary for example where goods have been obtained by fraud rescission can be effected by simply taking them back.[446]

All the modes of rescission considered hitherto, involve some degree of notice to the representor. However, it was held that this is not necessary. thus in *Car & Universal Co. Ltd v. Caldwell,*[447] the owner of a car was induced by fraud to sell to a rogue who absconded and could not be traced. Upon discovery of the fraud, the owner notified the Police and Automobile Association (AA) and asked them to help in recovering the car. It was held that the owner had, in these circumstances done enough to rescind the contract. The effect of this was that an innocent third party who later bought it got no title to it.

The decision has been described[448] as capable of causing hardship on the third party and was recommended for reversal in Britain.[449] However the Courts have held that such a case will only apply where the representor has disappeared or for some reason cannot be reached.[450]

(iii) Misrepresentation as a defence

Misrepresentation is a defence to an action to enforce a contract. In *Redgrave v. Hurd*[451] , the defendant successfully relied on the misrepresentations as to the value of the practice as a defence to the vendor's claim to specific performance.

When misrepresentation is pleaded as a defence, this is regarded as a form of "rescission" and, therefore, subject to the requirement that the representee must return what he got under the contract.[452] This however, will not apply where the representor is guilty of actual fraud. For instance an insurer can repudiate liability under a policy of insurance obtained by the fraud of the assured and also keep the premiums. The rule is based on the need to deter fraud.[453]

---

444 *Cundy v. Lindsay* (1878) 3 App Cas 459 discussed *supra* Chap.7

445 *Reese Silver Mining Co. V. Smith* (1869) L. R. 4 H.L. 64

446 *Re Eastgate* [1905] 1 K.B. 465. See also *Shirima V. Lalaito Kirikengori* Civ App. 3 A67 (Tanzania); Hodgin, *supra* p.121

447 [1965] 1 Q.B. 525

448 Treitel, *supra* n.2, pp.332 - 333

449 Law Reform Committee 12th Report (1966) Cmnd 2958 para 16. See also the Scottish Case *Macleod v. Kerr*1965 S.C. 253 where a similar case to *Caldwell* was decided in favour of the third party.

450 *Empresa Cubana de Fletes v. Lagonisi Shipping Co. Ltd.* [1971] 1 Q.B. 485, 505 though overruled in the *Laconia* [1977] A.C. 850

451 (1881) 20 Ch.D. 1

452 See discussion *supra* n.443 and text thereof.

453 Treitel *supra*, p.333

6. Limits of right to rescind

(a) Restitution impossible

The aim of rescission for misrepresentation is to restore to the other party any benefits that he has obtained under the contract. For instance, a buyer who wants to rescind in order to recover the price must give back the goods. If the benefit obtained is a sum of money there is no difficulty in complying with this requirement. All that the representee does is to restore the sum or its equivalent. However, where the benefit is other than money, he may be for some reason unable to restore it. The impossibility of restitution may, therefore, bar the right to rescind as enumerated below.

(i) Changes made by misrepresentee

Where a contract of sale has been induced by a misrepresentation of the seller, the buyer may lose the right to rescind if he has so changed the subject matter that he cannot restore what he obtained under the contract. For instance, a buyer of an animal who has slaughtered it cannot rescind by returning the carcass.[454] Furthermore, a purchaser of a business cannot get back his purchase money after carrying on business for four months and disposing of some assets,[455] or after changing the partnership into a limited company.[456] Similarly a buyer of a mine cannot rescind after he has marked it out.[457]

(ii) Deterioration or decline in value

A person who receives property under a contract does not lose the right to rescind just because property has deteriorated or declined in value without any fault on his part. Thus in *Adam v. Newbigging*,[458] a person was induced to enter a partnership by a misrepresentation as to its solvency. It was held that he could rescind the contract following the bankruptcy of the firm. In *Armstrong v. Jackson*[459], a broker purported to buy shares for a client, but in fact sold his own shares to the client. Five years later, when the shares had fallen in value from nearly Three British Pounds to 5s. It was held that the client could rescind. He still had the identical shares and was able to return them together with the dividends he had received.

Furthermore, the right to rescind is also not lost just because the subject matter deteriorates without the fault of the party claiming the right to rescind. Thus in *Head v. Tattersall*,[460] a buyer of a horse was allowed to return it for breach of "warranty" although it had been previously injured through no fault of his. Bramwell B. explained that the right to reject would not be lost if "the injury were caused by reason of a trial necessary to test the warranty."[461]

(iii) Changes made by misrepresentor

Where the sale is induced by the misrepresentation of the buyer e.g. as to his solvency or as to the value of the subject matter the issue arises as to whether rescission is possible. This will depend on whether the buyer, a fraudulent misrepresentor cannot rely on his dealings with the subject matter to bar the right to rescind. Thus in the *Spence v. Crawford Case*[462], A was induced by the fraud of B to enter into a contract by which (i) A sold to B shares in a company and (ii) B undertook to relieve A of his liability under a guarantee of the company's bank overdraft and to procure the

---

454 *Clarke v. Dickson* (1858) E.B. & E. 148, 155

455 *Sheffield Nickel Co. Ltd. v. Unwin* (1877) 2 Q.B.D.215

456 *supra* n.454

457 *Ibid.*, *Lagunas Nitrate Co. v. Lagunas Syndicate* [1899] 2 Ch. 392

458 (1886) 34 Ch.D. 582; (1888) 13 App. Cas 308

459 [1917] 2 K.B 822.

460 (1871) L.R. 7 Ex.7

461 *Ibid.* at p.12

462 *Spence v. Crawford* [1939] 3 All E.R. 271

release of securities deposited by A with the bank. A duly transferred the shares and B relieved A of his liability to the bank and freed the securities by giving his own personal guarantee to the bank. The Constitution of the Company was later altered and some of the shares in it were sold. It was held that the dealing with the shares did not bar A's right to rescind.

(iv) Benefit to misrepresentee

The fact that the misrepresentee has received a benefit under the contract does not bar the right to rescind if the misrepresentor has not been put to any expense in conferring the benefit. Thus in *Spence v. Crawford,*[463] the fact that B relieved A of his liability to the bank and freed his securities did not bar A's right to rescind. This is because B was not put to any expense by merely giving the guarantee, nor was he asked to pay anything under it as the company prospered.

Conversely the right to rescind is not lost *merely* because the representor has acted on the contract to his prejudice. Thus in *Mackenzie v. Royal Bank of Canada,*[464] a wife was induced by misrepresentation to deposit share certificates with a bank as security for the overdraft of a company controlled by her husband. It was held that she could rescind although the bank had advanced the company more money. It was indicated that she did not have to restore the money since it was not received by her. The decision casts doubt on the principle that the aim of rescission is to restore parties to the situation in which they have been had the contract never been made. It is significant in this respect that the essence of restitution is that the representee should not be unjustly enriched at the representor's expense.

(v) Precise restitution impossible

At common law the general rule that the representee had to restore what he had got under the contract was applied strictly with the result that a person who had agreed to buy land could not recover his money if he had merely gone into possession under the contract. It was felt that the benefit even of the temporary possession made restitution impossible.[465]

Equity developed a more flexible rule which now prevails. This is to the effect that a representee who can make substantial though not precise restitution can rescind if he returns the subject-matter of the contract in its altered state, accounts for any profits derived from it and makes allowance for deterioration by his dealing with it. It follows that a person who has gone into possession under a contract to buy or take a lease of land can rescind[466] on terms of paying rent for the period of his occupation.[467] In *Erlanger v. New Sombrero Phosphate Co.,*[468] a company bought and worked a phosphate mine, but did not so work it out as to make restitution utterly impossible. It was held that the company could rescind the sale for breach of fiduciary duty by one of its promoters on terms of returning the mine and accounting for the profits of working it.

These powers of adjustment are exercised where the misrepresentee is a buyer who claims back his money. The remedy is also available conversely where the misrepresentee is a seller who claims back his property as was the case in *Spence v. Crawford.*[469] The fraudulent buyer in that case had performed his contractual undertaking to relieve the seller of certain obligations to a bank. He was asked by the bank to sell some stock to maintain his liquidity, and the sale resulted in a loss to him of One Thousand British Pounds. The final order made in that case was that the seller should recover back his shares plus the dividends received by the buyer, but that he should repay the purchase price plus interest, and make allowance in respect of part of the One Thousand Pounds lost by the buyer on the sale of his stock.

---

463 *Ibid.*
464 [1934] A.C.468
465 *Hunt v. Silk* (1804) 5 East 449; *Blackburn v. Smith* (1848) 2 Ex. 783
466 *Redgrave v. Hurd* (1881) 20 Ch.D. 1
467 *Hulton v. Hulton* [1917] 1 K.B. 813, 826
468 (1878) 3 App. Cas 1218
469 *Supra* n.462

In ordering rescission the court can set off benefits received by one party against those received by the other. Thus in *Hulton v. Hulton,*[470] a wife set aside a separation deed on the ground of her husband's fraud. It was held that she need not repay Five Hundred British Pounds per annum which she had received under the deed since the husband had received corresponding advantages viz. freedom from his obligation to maintain the wife and destruction of certain letters at his request. However, she had to account for a debt owed by her to the husband which had been released by the deed since no benefit corresponding to the release had been received by the husband.

(vi) Improvements in subject-matter

In the cases so far considered, it has been assumed that dealings with the subject-matter have decreased its value. Those may also improve it and this may give rise to two problems. First, is whether such dealings bar the right to rescind. Second what allowance, if any, is to be awarded in respect of the improvements. These may be made either by the misrepresentee or by the misrepresentor.

(vii) Improvements by misrepresentee

This is illustrated by *Boyd & Forrest v. Glasgow & S. W. Ry*[471]. Contractors alleged that they had been induced to enter into a contract to build a railway by misrepresentations as to the strata. Following the construction of the railway, they claimed to rescind with a view to recovering a *quantum merit* (exceeding the contract price) for the cost of the work. The claim failed on a number of grounds. One was that the right to rescind was barred since it was no longer possible to restore the railway company to its original position. It has been observed[472] that this was an unusual requirement of restoration which prevents the representee from rescinding unless he can *give back* benefits that he has received. In this case, the principle operated to prevent rescission because the representee could not *take back* benefits that he had *conferred.* In this regard, rescission is senseless and the only convenient remedy is damages.

A second illustration is where a person is induced by misrepresentation to buy something which he improves before discovering the truth. In such a case the improvements would probably not bar the right to rescind and their cost can be claimed as damages. Where the misrepresentation is wholly innocent and the contract has been rescinded, there will be no such claim but the representee might be able to set off the cost of the improvements against his liability to make allowance for benefits received by him under the contract.[473]

(ii) Improvements by the Misrepresentor

This is illustrated by the *Spence v. Crawford* Case.[474] It can be concluded[475] that if the seller claims rescission he should make some allowance (based on the increase in value rather than the cost of work of the buyer). Where the seller is unwilling or unable to pay the allowance he can fall back on the alternative remedy of damages.

(b) Third party rights

The right to rescind a contract may be barred by the intervention of third party rights. For instance a person who has been induced by fraud to sell goods cannot rescind after the goods have been bought by an innocent third party.[476] Similarly, a person cannot rescind an allotment of

---

470 [1917] 1 K.B. 813.
471 1915 S. C. (H.L.) 20.
472 Treitel, *supra* n.368 p.342
473 *Ibid.*
474 [1939] 3 All E.R. 271 discussed *supra*
475 Treitel, *supra* n.368 , p.343
476 See discussion under Chap.7. See also Hodgin, *Law of Contract in East Africa* (1975) pp.122-123.

shares in a company after the company has gone into liquidation. At that point the rights of third parties intervene in that the assets of the company have to be collected for distribution among the creditors.[477] This should be contrasted with the rule in bankruptcy of an individual that the trustee in bankruptcy takes the property "subject to equities" including the right to rescind. Thus in *Load v. Green*[478], the plaintiff was induced by fraud to sell goods to one Bannister who went bankrupt. It was held that the plaintiff could disaffirm the contract and recover the value of the goods from Bannister's trustee in bankruptcy. Professor Treitel has observed in this respect[479] that it is difficult to rationalise the distinction between winding up insolvent companies and individual bankruptcy. He argues that this may be based on the assumption that third parties place greater reliance on the company's nominal capital (especially if the company is a new one, or has just raised new capital) than on an individual's appearance of wealth.

(c) Affirmation

A contract cannot be rescinded for misrepresentation if the representee expressly or by conduct affirms it after discovering the truth. Consequently, a person who is induced by misrepresentation to buy the goods cannot rescind if after discovering the truth, he uses them.[480] In this context, a person who is induced by misrepresentation to subscribe for shares in a company cannot rescind, if after discovering the truth, he accepts dividends, votes at a meeting or tries to sell the shares.[481] Furthermore, a person who is induced by misrepresentation to take a lease cannot rescind, if after discovering the truth, he stays on and pays rent.[482] Additionally, a mining lease cannot be rescinded if after discovering the truth, the lessee continues to work the mine.[483] However, use of the subject-matter for the sole purpose of testing the accuracy of the representation does not amount to affirmation.[484] In *Lindsay Petroleum Co. v. Hurd*[485] the sinking of an exploratory well was held not to bar rescission.

It is significant that a person cannot set aside one part of the contract while affirming the rest. Thus in *Urquart v. Macpherson* [486], a deed dissolving a partnership contained a clause by which each partner released his claims against the others. One partner sought to set aside the release on the ground of fraud. It was held that he could not do so while affirming the rest of the deed. Furthermore, in *West v. National Motors & Accident Insurance Union Ltd.*[487] it was held that an insurance company can rescind a policy of non-disclosure, but it cannot repudiate a particular claim while purporting to recognise the policy still in force.

For effective affirmation, a person must know all the facts from which a reasonable man would deduce the truth . Affirmation will not be deemed possible if a person has relied on rumours in doing so.[488]

Affirmation may be inferred from failure to rescind. Courts usually draw this inference where a person wishes to rescind an allotment of shares in a company. It is not enough for him to tell the

---

477 *Re Scottish Petroleum co.* (1883) 23 Ch.D. 413

478 (1846) 15 M & W 216

479 Treitel *op.cit.* p.343

480 *United Shoe Machinery Co. of Canada v. Brunet* [1909] A.C.330.

481 *Western Bank of Scotland v. Addie* (1867) L.R.1 Sc. & Div. 145, *Scholey v. Central Ry of Venezuela* (1870) L.R.9 Eq.266

482 *Kennard v. Ashman* (1844) 10 T.L.R. 213

483 *Vigers v. Pike* (1842) 8 Cl. & F. 562. See also the Nigerian Case, *Ajayi v. Ebern* 1964 (1) A.L.R. Comm 155

484 c.f. *Long v. Lloyd* [1958] 1 W.L.R. 753 where the buyer made a first trip.

485 (1874) L.R. 5 PC 221

486 (1878) 3 App.Cas 831

487 [1955] 1 W.L.R. 343

488 *Scholey v. Central Bank of Venezuela* (1870) L.R 9 Eq. 266 n; *Long v. Lloyd* [1958] 1 W.L.R. 753, 760; *Central Ry of Venezuela v. Kisch* (1867) L.R. 2 H.L.99.

company that he is rescinding. He must take active steps to remove his name from the company's register. He is not allowed to wait and see whether the company would prosper.[489]

(d) Lapse of time

Where the misrepresentation is fraudulent or made in breach of a fiduciary duty, lapse of time will not bar rescission. It is simply evidence of affirmation. This is supported by the rule that time only begins to run from the discovery of the truth.[490] It is further supported by the rule that the time spent in negotiations to settle a dispute does not bar rescission.[491] In contrast, in *Leaf v. International Galleries*[492], the plaintiff was induced to buy a picture by the innocent misrepresentation that it was by "J. Constable". Five years later he sought to rescind, but it was held that his right to do so was barred by lapse of time. Since he claimed rescission immediately upon discovering the truth, the lapse of time cannot be regarded as evidence of affirmation. The rationalisation of this approach is that to rescind for innocent misrepresentation is barred by lapse of time even though there is no evidence of affirmation.

7. Non-disclosure

(a) General Rule

(i) No Duty of disclosure

The general rule is that a contracting party is under no duty to disclose material facts known to him but not the other party. In this vein it has been held that a landlord is not liable in deceit if before letting his house he fails to tell the tenant that it is in bad condition.[493] Furthermore, it has been held that a person who applies for the post of governess is not bound to disclose the fact that she is a divorcee.[494] However, if a party lies this amounts to a misrepresentation or a breach of contract.[495] Although this rule would appear to operate harshly, if there was a general duty of disclosure, it would be difficult to say exactly what must be disclosed in any particular case.

(ii) Representation by Conduct

A person may make a representation by conduct[496] and if he fails to correct the impression given by his conduct he cannot rely on the general rule that there is no duty of disclosure.[497] Active concealment of a defect amounts to misrepresentation.[498] Furthermore, even conduct falling short of this may suffice. As is put by Blackburn J.:[499]

> The defendant, by taking the cow to a public market to be sold ... thereby furnishes evidence of a representation that so far as his knowledge goes, the animal is not suffering from any infectious disease ... The case might be different where the sale takes place privately.

---

489 *First National Reinsurance Co. Ltd. v. Greenfield* [1921] 2 K.B. 260

490 *Armstrong v. Jackson* [1917] 2 K.B. 822; *Lindsay Petroleum Co. v. Hurd* [1874] L.R. 5 P.C. 221, 241; *Aaron Reefs Ltd. v. Twiss* [1896] A.C. 273, 287

491 *Earlanger v. New Sombrero Phosphate Co.* (1878) 3 App. Cas. 1218, 1248

492 [1950] 2 K.B. 86. See also the Kenyan Case *Isherwood's Ltd. v. Blue Reefs Ltd.* 16 K.L.R. 17 Hodgin *op.cit.* pp.123-124

493 *Heates v. Cadogon* 1851 10 C.B.591

494 *Fletcher v. Krell* (1872) 42 L.J. Q.B. 55

495 *Omer Ali Mohammed v. Abdel Gardir Abu Regcilla* 1964(1) A.L.R. Comm. 103.

496 *Curtis v. Chemical Cleaning & Dyeing Co. Ltd.* [1951] 1 K.B. 805, 808; [1951] 1 All E.R. 631

497 *Walter v. Morgan* (1861) 3 D & F & J. 718, 723

498 *Schneider v. Heath* (1813) 3 Camp.506.

499 *Bodger v. Nicholls* (1878) 28 L. T. 441, 445

(iii) Latent defects

It has ben suggested that a person should disclose latent defects in the subject-matter of a contract which are known to him.[500] However, it appears that there is no general duty to disclose latent defects in English Law. Thus in *Ward v. Hobbs*,[501] the defendant took some pigs to a market and sold them there "with all faults". He knew that the pigs were diseased but did not disclose this fact to the buyer. It was held that the buyer had no remedy as there was no general duty to disclose known latent defects and any representation that might be inferred from the defendant's conduct in taking the pigs to market was negatived by the words "with all faults".

The general rule of non-disclosure of latent defects applies where land is sold subject to a latent defect such as an under ground water-course,[502] where there are latent defects in title on a sale of land[503] and where the buyer knows (but the seller does not) of some latent quality which makes the subject-matter of the contract *more* valuable.[504]

(b) Exceptions

There are some exceptions to the rule that there is no liability for non-disclosure. In these exceptional cases, a person is generally only bound to disclose facts known to him.[505] A person may also be under a duty to disclose facts known to his agent if the knowledge has been acquired within the scope of the agent's authority and if it was the agent's duty to communicate to the principal.[506] He may also be under a duty to disclose facts which he ought to have known if there is a "special relationship" between the parties as was the case in *Hedley Byrne & Co. Ltd. v. Heller & Partners Ltd.*[507]

If there is a duty of disclosure, it continues until the contract becomes binding.[508] Thus in a contract of insurance, the duty ceases where the insurer signs that he will accept the risk, although there is no legally binding contract until the policy is executed.[509] Alternatively it is possible for the duty of disclosure to continue even after the conclusion of the contract[510] or throughout the currency of the contract.[511]

The duty of disclosure exists in the following cases.

(i) Representation falsified by later events

A person has to disclose material facts which come to his notice before the conclusion of the contract if they falsify a representation previously made by him. Thus in *With v. O'Flanagan*[512] negotiations for the sale of a medical practice begun in January when the practice was worth Two Thousand British Pounds. By May 1, when the contract of sale was concluded, the practice had become worthless because of the intervening illness of the vendor. It was held that the contract should be set aside on the ground that the vendor ought to have communicated his change of circumstances to the buyer.

---

500 *Horsfall v. Thomas* (1862) 1 H & C 90, 100
501 (1878) 4 App. Cas 13.
502 *Shepherd v.Croft* [1911] 1 Ch. 521
503 Megarry & Wade, *The Law of Real Property* (5th Edn.) p.622 n.75
504 *Smith v. Hughes* (1871) L.R. 6 Q.B. 587, 604
505 *Blackburn Low & Co. v. Vigors* (1887) 12 App. Cas 531
506 *Joel v. Law, Union & Crown Insurance Co.* [1908] 2 K.B. 863
507 [1964] A.C. 465 discussed *supra*
508 *Container Transport International Inc. v. Ocean US Mutual etc., Association* [1984] 1 Lloyd's Rep. 476, 486
509 *Cory v. Patton* (1872) L.R. 7 Q.B. 304; *Citadel Insurance Co. v. Atlantic Union Insurance Co.* [1984] 2 Lloyd's Rep 543, 548
510 *Phillips v. Foxall* (1872) L.R. 7 Q.B. 666
511 *The Listian Pride* [1985] 1 Lloyd's Rep. 437, 512
512 [1936] Ch. 575

There are conflicting cases on the issue of whether a duty of disclosure arises where during negotiations a party makes a representation as to his present intention but changes his mind before the conclusion of the contract. Thus in *Traill v. Baring,*[513] an insurance company made a proposal for reinsurance to a second company stating that it would retain part of the risk. This was its intention at the time of the proposal but before acceptance of the proposal it disposed of part of that risk. It was held that the "change of intention" of the first company should have been disclosed to the company. However, in *Wales v. Waldham*[514], a husband who had left his wife made her an offer of financial provision after she had declared her intention of remarrying. She accepted the offer after having decided to remarry again. If the husband had known of this, he would have made a lower offer. It was held that the wife was not bound to disclose her change of mind because the duty to disclose changed circumstances only applied where the original representation was one of *fact*, not where it was one of *intention*. This approach has been subsequently disapproved in the House of Lords,[515] but only on the ground that the agreement for financial provision had been embodied in a consent order made in matrimonial proceedings and that the parties seeking such an order were, by statute[516] under a duty to make full and frank disclosure to the Court which made the order. Professor Treitel has nonetheless argued[517] that the principle in *Traill v. Baring* is preferable because what was originally a misrepresentation of intention becomes by the time of contracting one of fact *viz.* as to the representor's state of mind at that time.

(ii) Statements literally true but misleading

A person is guilty of misrepresentation, though all the facts stated by him are true, if the statement is misleading as a whole because of his failure to refer to the other facts affecting the weight of those stated. Thus in *Notts Patent Brick & Tile Co. v. Butler,*[518] a buyer of land asked the vendor's solicitor whether the land was subject to restrictive covenants. The solicitor replied that he was not aware of any. However, he failed to add that this was because he had not troubled to read the relevant documents. The solicitor's reply though literally true amounted to a misrepresentation entitling the purchaser to rescind. A similar approach is evident in some East African cases. Thus in *Gurdit Singh v. United Motor Works,*[519] the appellant bought a new car from the respondents and signed a proposal for insurance with a company of which the respondents were agents. The respondents issued a temporary cover note and accepted payment of the first annual premium. the respondents having mislaid the signed proposal form lodged with the insurance company another form which was incomplete in certain details and before the company had decided whether to accept the proposal, the appellant's car was badly damaged. It was held that the respondents by preparing and submitting a substitute proposal which lacked all the information required by the company and which was signed in the appellant's name were guilty of misfeasance. In *Pandya v. Oriental Fire and General Insurance Co.*,[520] the respondents insured a car in the names of a non-existent company, Dhanji Jasmat Ltd. and also misrepresented that the prospective driver did not suffer from any defect. In fact Dhanji Jasmat was an undischarged bankrupt and had lost an eye. When he met the appellant he was wearing dark glasses and the

---

513 (1864) 4 D.J. & S. 318

513 (1864) 4 D.J. & S. 318

514 [1977] 1 W.L.R. 199; [1977] 2 All E.R. 125. See critique thereof Phillips 40 M.L.R. 599

515 *Jenkins v. Liversey* [1985] A.C. 424

516 Matrimonial Causes Act, 1973, Ss.23 - 25 (U.K.)

517 Treitel *op.cit.* p.353

518 (1886) 16 Q.B.D.778. See also *Kirima Estates (U) Ltd. v. Korde* [1963] E.A. 636 discussed *supra* where the advocate mentioned a value to the plaintiff without recourse to professional valuation. See also *Motor Union Insurance Co. v. A. K. Ddamba* [1963] E.A. 271.

519 [1969] E.A. 200

520 [1957] E.A. 21

appellant was unaware of these material facts. The proposal form was warranted complete and accurate and to be the basis of the policy. It was held that these facts rendered the policy voidable for misrepresentation and non-disclosure.

(iii) Custom

In *Jones v. Bowden*,[521] the plaintiff bought a pimento which had been damaged by sea water. It was usual in the trade when pimento had been damaged to declare this, but the seller failed to make such a declaration. It was held that he was liable in deceit since, in view of the custom, his silence amounted to misrepresentation.

(iv) Contracts uberimmae fidei

A duty exists to disclose material facts in some types of contracts, particularly where one party is in a particularly strong position, and the other in a weak one, to know the material facts.

Insurance

In *Rozanes v. Bowen*[522] it was thus stated:

> It has been for centuries in England the law in connection with insurance of all sorts, marine, fire, life, guarantee and every kind of policy, that, as the underwriter knows nothing and the man who comes to him to ask him to insure knows everything, it is the duty of the assured .... to make a full disclosure to the underwriters, without being asked, of all the material circumstances.

Material facts to be disclosed

The assured must disclose all such facts as a reasonable or prudent insurer might regard as material.[523] A policy of insurance can, therefore, be avoided for non-disclosure in the following situations: where in the policy of marine insurance the assured conceals the real value of the cargo;[524] where the assured does not declare that the cargo may be carried on deck thereby increasing the risk;[525] where the assured does not declare that the ship carrying the cargo is already stranded.[526] A policy of life insurance can also be avoided if the assured fails to disclose that a number of other insurance offices had declined proposals to insure his life[527] or that there was doubt as to his mental health.[528] A policy of insurance of jewellery can be avoided if the insurer is not told that the jewellery had on several occasions been stolen from the assured.[529] A policy can also be avoided on ground of non-disclosure of facts material to the risk[530] by the insurer e.g. if he accepts a premium for insuring a voyage which he knows to have been safely accomplished.[531]

Facts which need not be disclosed

The assured need not declare facts which the insurer himself knows or ought to know or facts which both parties have equal means of knowing as well as facts the disclosure of which is waived by the insurer.[532]

---

521 (1813) 4 Taunt 847

522 (1928) 32 Ll.L.R. 98, 102

523 *Woolcott v. Sun Alliance etc. Insurance Ltd.* [1978] 1 W.L.R. 493, 498; [1978] 1 All E.R. 1253 *Singh v. United Motor Works* [1969] E.A. 200.

524 *Ionides v. Pender* (1874) L.R. 9 Q.B. 531

525 *Hood v. West End Motor Car Parking Co.* [1917] 2 K.B. 38

526 *Proudfoot v. Montefiore* (1867) L.R. 2 Q.B. 511

527 *London Assurance v. Mansel* (1879) 11 Ch.D. 363

528 *Lindenau v. Desborough* (1828) 8 B & C 586

529 *Rozanes v. Bowen* (1928) 32 Ll.R. 2Q.B. 511

530 *Banque Keyser Ullmann S.A. v. S. Kandia (U.K.) Insurance Co. Ltd.* [1990] 2 All E.R. 947; *Oriental Fire & General Assurance Ltd. v. Govinder & Ors* [1969] E.A. 116.

531 Treitel, *op.cit*, p.355

532 *Carter v. Boehm* (1766) 3 Burr 1905, 1910

Basis of contract clauses

The duty of disclosure protects insurers. However, insurers usually add to the contract the provision that the accuracy and completeness of the answers given by the assured to questions in the proposal form shall be the basis of the contract. The effect of this is that failure to disclose a trivial matter can vitiate the policy.[533] This is regarded as going too far by the insurance companies and courts have, therefore, construed basis of the contract clauses strictly against insurance companies.[534] The Law Commission in Britain recommended abrogation of these type of clauses.[535]

Insurance distinguished from suretyship or guarantee

A promise to pay another person's debt if he fails to pay it is a contract of guarantee. However, it is possible to insure against non-payment of a debt or against some other breach of contract. In *Seaton v. Heath*[536], A guaranteed a loan of Fifteen Thousand Pounds by B to X. U then promised B "in consideration of a premium of 50s per cent" to "guarantee" A's solvency. The contract between B & C was held to be one of insurance. However, in *Trade Indemnity Co. Ltd. v. Workington Harbour Board,*[537] A agreed to build a dock for B. C gave B a "guarantee" of Fifty Thousand Pounds that A would complete the work. It was held that this was not a contract of insurance.

The main distinction between the two types of contract is that a guarantor is usually selected by the debtor, while an insurer is usually selected by the creditor. Therefore, a guarantor is likely to know as much as (if not more than) the creditor about the credit worthiness of the debtor, but an insurer is likely to know less about this than the creditor as he has probably had no previous dealings with the debtor. Hence a higher duty of disclosure is owed to the insurer.[538]

Family arrangements

There exists a duty to make full disclosure in certain family arrangements, e.g. agreements between members of a family for settling disputes as to the family property. Consequently, the parties to an agreement for the division of the property of a deceased member must disclose to each other all the facts known to them which bear on their rights to the estate or its value.[539]

(v) Contractual duty to disclose

It was stated in *William Pickersgill & Sons v. London etc. Ins Co.*[540] that:

> the rule imposing an obligation to disclose upon the intending assured does not rest upon a general principle of common law, but arises out of an implied condition contained in the contract itself, precedent to the liability of the underwriter to pay.

Although this view has been questioned, it has been said[541] that it enables the Courts if they wished to do so, to extend the duty of disclosure.[542] The effect is that the categories of contracts *uberrimae fidei* may then be flexible but not be closed.

533 *Dawsons Ltd. v. Bonnin* [1922] A.C. 413

534 *Joel v. Law, Union & Crown Insurance Co.* [1908] 2 K.B. 863, 885 per Fletcher - Moulton L. J. *Pandya v. Oriental Insurance Co.* [1957] E.A. 21

535 Law Comm 104 par. 7.4

536 [1899] 1 Q.B. 782; [1900] A.C. 135

537 [1937] A.C. 1

538 c.f. *Re Denton's Estate* [1904] 2 Ch.178, 188.

539 *Gordon v. Gordon* (1817) 3 Swan 400; *Greenwood v. Greenwood* (1863) 1 D. J. & S.28

540 [1912] 3 K.B. 614

541 Treitel, *op.cit.* p.356

542 *Cie Algerienne de Mennerio v. Katana* [1960] 2 Q.B. 115

(vi) Contracts where there is limited duty of disclosure
There are situations where there is a duty to disclose certain specified or unusual facts.

Suretyship or guarantee
It is thought that contracts of suretyship or guarantee are *uberrimae fidei*,[543] although the better view is that they do not fall into this category.[544] The creditor is only bound to disclose unusual circumstances which the surety would not commonly expect.[545] However, an employer who takes a fidelity bond by which the honesty of an employee is guaranteed is under a somewhat higher duty: he must disclose to the surety any acts of dishonesty by the servant of which he has notice,[546] even if they occur after the execution of the bond.

Sale of land
Generally, there is no duty on the seller of land to disclose latent physical defects. However, there may be a duty to disclose unusual defects of title which a reasonably provident tax-payer would not be expected to discover.[547]

Compromises
A claim which is bad in law can be compromised if the compromise is made in good faith. However, the compromise is only valid if the person making the claim discloses to the other party all facts known to him which affect the validity of the claim.[548]

Exemption clauses
The failure to disclose or draw attention to terms of a contractual document may deprive one party of the exclusion clause.[549]

Fiduciary relationship
A duty of disclosure may arise from the relationship of the parties. The duty does not arise where the relationship is one to which the equitable doctrine of undue influence applies.[550] Examples of situations where such disclosure is required are the relationships between agent and principal,[551] partners[552] and between a company and its promoters.[553] A company promoter owes no common law duty to persons who subscribe for shares in the company on the faith of a prospectus issued by him,[554] but he owes them an extensive statutory duty of disclosure.[555]

(vi) Statute
Payments to promoters must be disclosed in the company's prospectus in the case of a public company[556] in addition to other information and reports relating to shareholding, directorship and details affecting shares indicated in the third Schedule to the Companies Act.[557]

---

543 *Gordon v. Gordon* (1817) 3 Swan 400; *Greenwood v. Greenwood* (1863) 1 D. J. & S. 28 c.f. *Wales v. Wadham* [1977] 1 W.L.R. 1 where the rule did not apply as the parties bargained at arms length.

544 *Davies v. London & Provincial Marine Insurance Co.* (1878) 8 Ch.D. 469, 475; *L.G.O.C. v. Holloway* [1912] 2 K.B. 72, 81, 83.

545 *National Provincial Bank of England Ltd. v. Glanusk* [1913] 3 K.B. 335; *Cooper v. National provincial Bank* [1946] K.B. 1, 7

546 *L.G.O.C. Ltd v. Holloway supra* n.79

547 See discussion *supra*

548 Treitel, *op.cit.* p.358

549 See Chap. 6 and discussion on exemption clauses

550 *infra* Chap.9

551 *Armstrong v. Jackson* [1917] 2 K.B. 822 discussed *supra*. See also *infra* Chap.12.

552 Bakibinga, *Partnership Law In Uganda* (1992) Chap.4.

553 Bakibinga, *Company Law In Uganda* (1993) Chap.3

554 *Heyman v. European Central Ry* (1868) L.R. 7 Eq. 154. See also Bakibinga *Company Law In Uganda* Chap.6.

555 Bakibinga, *Ibid.* Chap 6 and 7.

556 Companies Act Cap.85, Section 40; Schedule 3 para 13.

557 See generally, Bakibinga *Company Law In Uganda* (1993) pp.33, 92 - 93, 95, 106 - 107, 137.

(vii) Duty to clarify legal relationship
A duty of disclosure arises where A sees B acting in reliance on a view of a legal relationship between them which is to A's knowledge false.[558] The effect of breach of the duty gives rise to an estoppel although it may also invalidate the contract. The duty essentially is to disclose the true legal relationship or lack of it between A & B.

(c) Effect of non disclosure

Two kinds of non-disclosure may be considered from the point of view of effect. First the situation where no misrepresentation has been made as such but may be inferred from conduct or surrounding circumstances e.g. where a representation is falsified by later events or where a statement is literally true but misleading or where disclosure is required by custom. In this case non-disclosure can give rise to the same remedies as active misrepresentation that is, to a right to rescind and to a common law right to damages for deceit or for negligence.

The second situation consists of "pure" non-disclosure in which no inference is drawn e.g. in contracts of insurance or by statute. In contracts *Uberrimae fidei,* non-disclosure gives rise to a right to rescind, but not to one to damages either for breach of contract or for negligence at common law. Conversely, breach of the statutory duty of disclosure imposed on persons issuing a company prospectus has been held to give rise to a right to damages, but not one to rescind.[559] Essentially, though the effects of "pure" non-disclosure depend on the purpose of the rule of law by which the duty of disclosure is imposed.[560]

8. Misrepresentation and estoppel

By the doctrine of estoppel by representation,[561] a person who makes precise and unambiguous [562] representation[563] of fact[564] may be prevented from denying the truth of the statement if the person to whom it was made was intended to act on it to his detriment.[565] It is accepted that the doctrine does not give rise to a cause of action[566] but only to a defence.

Apart from providing a defence to the representee, estoppel may remove one that would otherwise be available to the representor. Consequently, it may help a plaintiff no less than a defendant. Thus in *Burrowes v. Lock*[567], beneficiary under a trust fund proposed to assign his share for value to the plaintiff, who, before advancing any money, asked the trustee whether the beneficiary had previously encumbered his share. The trustee replied that there was no encumbrance, having forgotten that 10 years earlier the beneficiary had in fact encumbered his share. It was held that the trustee was estopped from denying the truth of his statement. Consequently, he was liable to pay the assigned share to the plaintiff, free from the earlier encumbrance. The assignee, therefore had an independent cause of action against the trustee based on the assignment. Conversely, the trustee was, by his representation, deprived of the defence that he was already bound to pay part of the fund to the previous encumbrancer.

---

558 *Bell v. Marsh* [1903] 1 Ch. 528, 541; *Spiro v. Lintern* [1973] 1 W.L.R. 1002, 1010 - 1011. *The Henryksif* [1982] 1 Lloyd's Rep. 456; *The Lutetian* [1982] 2 Lloyd's Rep. 140, 158.

559 *Re South of England Natural Gas Co.*[1911]1 Ch.573. See also *Palmer's Company Law* (24th Ed.) paras 27-170.

560 Treitel, *op.cit.* p.360

561 as distinguished from estoppel by negligence: *Cross on Evidence* (7th Edn.) pp. 96 - 98; *Moorgate Mercantile Co. v. Twitchings* [1977] A.C. 890.

562 *Low v. Bouverie* [1891] 3 Ch.82

563 Non-disclosure or inaction is insufficient for this purpose: *Laurie & Morewood v. Dudin & Son* [1926] 1 K.B. 223.

564 As distinguished from Law : *Territorial & Auxilliary Forces Association v. Nichols* [1949] 1 K.B. 35; *The Argo Hellas* [1984] 1 Lloyd's Rep 296, 304.

565 e.g. *Lombard North Central Plc v. Stobart* [1990] Tr. L.R. 105

566 *Low v. Bouverie* [1891] 3 Ch.82 and discussion *supra* Chap.3; *The Anemone* [1987] 1 Lloyd's Rep. 546, 557.

567 (1805) 10 Ves 70 Which was explained in *Low v. Bouverie Ibid.* See also Sheridan, *Fraud In Equity,* pp. 31-36. c.f. *United Overseas Bank v. Jiwani* [1977] 1 All E.R. 733.

9

DURESS AND UNDUE INFLUENCE

The consent of a contracting party may be obtained by some form of pressure which the law frowns upon. The victim of such pressure may be entitled to relief under the common law of duress and under the equitable rules of undue influence. He may also be protected by certain special statutory provisions.

1. Duress at common law

A contract is voidable at common law if it was procured under duress.[1] At one stage the common law concept of fraud was a very narrow one. It was restricted to actual or threatened physical violence to, or unlawful constraint of the person of the contracting party. Thus in *Latter v. Bradell,*[2] a housemaid was ordered by her mistress to submit to a medical examination, on a suspicion of pregnancy which turned out to be unfounded. She cried and protested but submitted. Her claim for damages for assault failed and it was held that her consent to the examination had not been vitiated by duress as no physical violence was threatened or inflicted. However, this approach has been rejected in relatively recent cases. In *The Siboen and the Sibotre*[3], it was stated that a plea of "compulsion or coercion" would also be available e.g. where a person has been forced to enter into a contract under an imminent threat of having his house burnt down or a valuable picture slashed.[4] This approach has been endorsed in later cases with the result that the issue is whether there has been "coercion of the will, which vitiates consent".[5] Thus in *The Universe Sentinel*[6] trade union officials threatened to induce the crew of a ship to break their contracts of employment and so to prevent the ship from leaving port. In view of the "catastrophic"[7] financial consequences which the shipowners would suffer if these threats were carried out, it was conceded that they constituted "economic duress"[8] vitiating the shipowners' consent to an agreement to make certain payments to the Union. It should be stressed that for duress to occur the threat must be illegitimate either because what is threatened is a legal wrong or because the threat is wrongful e.g. where a black mailer threatens to disclose his victim's conduct to third parties[9] or because it is contrary to public policy[10].

In the East African case of *Hassanali Issa & Co. v. Jeraj Produce Store*[11], a garage owner carried out repairs to Y's motorcycle and stored it until collection. Y objected to the bill but

---

1 *Somali Democratic Republic v. Anoop Sunderial Treon* [1992] VIKALR 59 *Pao On v. Lau Yiu Long* [1980] A.C.614, 634 [1979] 3 All E.R. 65, 79; *The Universe Sentinel* [1983] 1 A.C. 366, 383, 400.

2 (1880) 50 L.J.C.P. 166; (1881) 50 L.J.Q.B. 448

3 [1976] 1 Lloyd's Rep 293; Beatson, 92 L.Q.R. 496

4 *Ibid.* p.335.

5 *Pao On v. Lau Yiu Long* [1980] A.C. 614, 636

6 [1983] 1 A.C. at p. 383

7 [1983] 1 A.C. at p.383

8 *Ibid.*

9 *Ibid.* at p.401

10 *The Evia Luck* (No.2) [1990] 1 Lloyd's Rep 319, 329

11 [1967] E.A. 555

realised that the garage would not release the motor-cycle until he paid. He gave a cheque and obtained the bike. He immediately cancelled the cheque. When he was sued, he alleged that the cheque had been obtained by duress. The Court of Appeal held that there was no duress since the garage owner was merely exercising his possessory lien over the motor-cycle until the bill was paid.

Situations where a party is induced to enter into a contract by a threat to break an earlier contract may amount to duress.[12] In *B & S Contracts & Designs Ltd. v. Victor Green Publications Ltd.*[13], a contractor who had undertaken to erect stands for an exhibition at Olympia told his client, less than a week before the exhibition was due to open, that the contract would be cancelled unless the client paid an additional sum to meet claims which were being made against the contractor by his workforce. The consequence of not having the stands erected in time would have been disastrous for the client in that it would have gravely damaged his reputation and might have exposed him to heavy claims for damages from exhibitors to whom space on the stands had been let. In these circumstances it was held that the payment had been made under duress and that the client was entitled to recover it back.

However, not all threats to break a contract would amount to duress.[14] Thus in *Pao On v. Lau Yiu Long*[15], the plaintiffs threatened to break a contract with a company unless the defendants, who were shareholders in the company, gave them a guarantee against loss resulting from the performance of that contract. The defendants, thinking that the risk of such loss was small, gave the guarantee to avoid adverse publicity which the company might suffer if the contract was not performed. It was held that in these circumstances there was no "coercion of the will", so that the guarantee was not vitiated by duress. In deciding whether the threat actually coerced the person to whom it was addressed, the Court will also consider what alternative courses of action were reasonably available to the person, for example there will be no economic duress if it would have been reasonable for him to have resisted the threatened wrong by taking legal proceedings.[16]

The nineteenth century view that unlawful violence to the person was necessary to constitute duress also led to the conclusion that a contract could not be vitiated by "duress of goods." The effect of this was that a contract to pay money for the release of goods unlawfully detained or to prevent their unlawful seizure was valid,[17] although it had also been held that money which had actually been paid for such a purpose could be recovered back.[18] However recent cases support the view that the "duress of goods" cases now depend on the "modern, flexible test of duress"[19] *viz* whether there had in fact been "coercion of the will".[20] This test governs both the validity of the contract and the right to recover back money under it.[21]

Similar to misrepresentation, it is unnecessary to show that duress was the sole cause inducing the contract.[22] It is sufficient if it was an inducement and once duress is established the burden is on the party exerting duress to show that it did not in fact induce the contract.[23]

---

12 *D & C Builders v. Rees* [1966] 2 Q.B. 617; [1965] 3 All E.R. 837

13 [1984] 1 C.R. 419

14 *The Siboen & The Sibotre, supra* n.3 at p.335

15 *supra* n.5

16 *Hennesy v. Craigmyle & Co.* [1986] 1 C.R. 461. See also Treitel, *Law of Contract* (8th Edn. 1991) p.365.

17 *Skeate v. Beale* (1841) 11 A & E 983

18 *Green v. Duckett* (1883) 11 Q.B.D. 275; *Maskell v. Horner* [1915] 3 K.B. 106; *T.D. Keegan Ltd. v. Palmer* [1961] 2 Lloyds Rep 449, 457.

19 Treitel, *supra*, n.16, p.365

20 *Pao On v. Lau Yiu Long supra* n.5 at p.636

21 *The Universe Sentinel* [1983] 1 A.C. 366; *Lloyds Bank Ltd. v. Bundy* [1975] Q.B. 326, 337

22 See discussion *supra* Chap. 8

23 *Barton v. Armstrong* [1976] A.C. 104

2. Undue influence in equity

(a) Actual pressure

Equity provides relief on the basis of undue influence where an agreement has been obtained by certain kind of improper pressure which were insufficient to constitute duress at common law because of the absence of an element of violence.[24] A party who claims relief on the ground of actual undue influence must show that such influence existed and had been exercised.[25] He should also show that the transaction resulted from that influence and that the transaction was manifestly to his disadvantage.[26]

(b) Special relationships

There are a number of situations in which the relationship between the parties is such as would give rise to a presumption of undue influence.[27] Equity would in those cases give relief based on the victimisation of one party by another.[28]

Relief can also be given on ground of undue influence even though the person to whom the gift or promise was made obtained no personal benefit from it. It would, therefore, apply where the head of a religious order uses a gift wholly for the purposes of the order and where a trustee extracts a promise from one beneficiary solely for the benefit of the other.[29]

(i) Relationships in which the presumption applies

The presumption of undue influence applies between parent and child[30], guardian and ward,[31] religious adviser and disciple[32], doctor and patient,[33] solicitor and client[34] and trustee and *cestui que trust*[35]. It also applies to some, but not all transactions between fiance and fiancee.[36] The rule does not apply between husband and wife[37] or between employer and employee[38]. Neither does it apply to all relationships which are fiduciary in the sense they give rise to a duty of disclosure. Consequently it does not apply between agent and principal.[39] the rule may apply even after the relationship has ceased if the influence continues for example between solicitor and ex-client,[40] and between parent and child for a "short" time[41] after the child has come of age, but not once the child is "emancipated" from parental control.[42] Even the marriage of a child does not necessarily have this effect.[43]

---

26 *Bank of Credit & Commerce International S. A. v. Aboody* [1990] 1 Q.B. 923. See also Cretney, 105 L.Q.R. 169 (1989); Dixon [1989] C.L.J. 359.

27 *Allcard v. Skinner* (1887) 36 Ch.D. 145. See also Tanganyika *Contract Act*, Ss.15, 16.

28 *National Westminster Bank PLC v. Morgan* [1985] A.C. 686, 706.

29 *Allcard v. Skinner, supra*, n.27; *Ellis v. Barker* (1871) L.R. 7 Ch. App. 104

30 *Bullock v. Lloyds Bank* [1955] Ch. 317; *Ottoman Bank v. Mawani* [1965] E.A. 464

31 *Hylton v. Hylton* (1754) 2 Ves. Sen 547; *Archer v. Hudson* (1846) 15 L.J. Ch.211

32 *Allcard v. Skinner, supra* n.27

33 *Dent v. Bennett* (1839) 4 My & Cr. 269.

34 *Wright v. Carter* [1903] 1 Ch. 27.

35 *Ellis v. Barker supra* n.29

36 *Zamet v. Hyman* [1961] 1 W.L.R. 1442

37 *Howes v. Bishop* [1909] 2 K.B. 390; *National Westminster Bank Plc v. Morgan supra* n.28 at p.703; *Midland Bank Plc v. Shephard* [1988] 3 All E.R. 17

38 *Matthew v. Bobbins* (1980) 256 E.G. 603

39 *Re Coomber* [1911] 1 Ch.723

40 *McMaster v. Byrne* [1952] 1 All E.R. 1362

41 *Re Paulings Settlement Trusts* [1964] Ch.303, 337

42 *Bainbridge v. Browne* (1881) 18 Ch.D.188

43 *Lancashire Loans Ltd. v. Black* [1934] 1 K.B. 380

The presumption also applies whenever the relationship between the parties is such that one of them is by reason of the confidence reposed in him by the other able to take unfair advantage of the other. In *Tate v. Williamson*,[44] the defendant became financial adviser to an extravagant Oxford undergraduate who sold him his estate for half its value and then drank himself to death at the age of 24. His executors successfully claimed that the sale of the estate should be set aside. In *O'Sullivan v. Management Agency & Music Ltd.*[45], a relationship between the plaintiff (then a young and unknown composer and performer of music) and his manager was held to be one giving rise to a presumption of undue influence; and transactions which turned out to be unfair to the plaintiff when he later became a celebrity were accordingly set aside.

The issue arises as to whether the presumption applies between banker and customer where the bank is asked to lend money on the security of the customer's home. In *Lloyds Bank Ltd. v. Bundy*,[46] a father gave his bank a guarantee of his son's business debts and mortgaged his house to the bank as security for the guarantee. It was held that the presumption applied since, for the purpose of the transaction the father had placed himself entirely in the hands of the bank manager and had been given no opportunity of seeking independent advice. However, this is regarded as an exceptional case which turned on its "very special facts."[47] since normally the presumption does not apply between banker and customer. Thus in *National Westminster Bank Plc v. Morgan*[48], a wife joined her husband in mortgaging the family home to their bank, after being assured by the bank manager that the mortgage covered no more than the amount of the original advance. This assurance was honestly given but it was mistaken because the mortgage extended to all further liabilities of the husband to the bank. No such further liabilities were in fact incurred; and after the husband's death it was held that the mortgage could not be set aside on the ground of undue influence since the bank manager had not acquired a sufficient degree of influence[49] over the wife, nor was the transaction unfair to her. If she had suffered loss as a result of the bank manager's misstatement, her remedy would have been to claim damages for negligence or for misrepresentation[50] not to have the mortgage set aside.

Where the necessary relationship is alleged to exist, the burden of proving that it does exist is on the party seeking to set the transaction aside.[51] Once the burden is discharged, it is up to the party benefitting from the transaction to rebut the presumption of undue influence[52] in one of the ways we are about to examine.

(ii) Rebutting the presumption

The presumption of undue influence is rebutted if the party benefitting from the transaction shows that it was "the free exercise of independent will".[53] The most common way of doing this is to show that the other party had independent advice before entering the transaction.[54] The advice must be competent and based on knowledge of all the relevant facts.[55] It is further

---

44 (1866) L.R. 2 Ch. App.55. See also *Inche Noriah v. Shaik Allie bin Omar* [1929] A.C. 127; *Re Craig* [1971] Ch.95

45 [1985] Q.B. 428

46 [1975] Q.B. 326, 342; Carr 38 M.L.R.463; Sealy [1975] C.L.J. 17.

47 *National Westminster Bank Plc v. Morgan* [1985] A.C. 686, 698, 709.

48 *Ibid.*

49 *Ibid.* at p.708

50 See *Cornish v. Midland Bank Plc* [1985] 3 All E.R. 513

51 *Lloyds Bank Ltd. v. Bundy* [1975] Q.B. at p.342

52 *Allcard v. Skinner* (1887) 36 Ch.D. 145; *Re Craig* [1971] Ch.95

53 *Inche Noriah Case supra* n.53

54 *Allcard v. Skinner, supra* n.52; *Bullock v. Lloyds Bank* [1955] Ch.317; *Horry v. Tate & Lyle Refineries Ltd.* [1982] 2 Lloyd's Rep. 417, 421

55 *Inche Noriah Case supra* n.53

contended that the independent adviser must also approve the transaction, and that his advice must be followed,[56] although this is not necessary in every case.[57]

Stringent rules apply where a solicitor buys from his client. The solicitor must show that the client was informed of all relevant facts; (generally) that the client was separately advised; and that the transaction was a fair one. It can for instance be set aside on the ground of undervalue.[58] A solicitor must make full disclosure even where the presumption of undue influence has been rebutted.[59]

(c) Unconscionable bargains

Equity provides relief against unconscionable bargains in certain cases in which one party is in a position to exploit a particular weakness of the other. The burden of justifying such a transaction is on the former party.[60]

It has been argued that in the East African context, courts are unwilling to extend the concept of undue influence in such situations.[61] In this respect, in *S. K. Ndugwa v. The Baganda Butchers Ltd.*[62] the interest rate on a loan was agreed to at 60%. The Court held this was not an example of undue influence. While this was indeed a hard bargain as far as the borrower was concerned, Section 16 of the Indian Contract Act[63] (then applicable) was clear in its scope. Thus the Court stated:

> (It) appears to me to take the place of the English rules of equity as to unconscionable bargains (and) would seem to leave untouched hard bargains, even ruinous bargains where there has been nothing in the nature of unconscientious use of power by one of the parties.

It is notable, though that the Indian Contract Act is no longer applicable in Uganda.[64] Consequently, it could be argued that, presently, equitable rules could be used to upset an unconscionable contract, although it has been doubted whether equitable intervention could be more bold or effective than Section 16 of the Indian Contract Act.[65] In the *Ndugwa* case itself, though, the Court resorted to the Courts Ordinance 1911[66] to mitigate the resultant hardship. Section 63, thereof provided:

> Where an agreement for the payment of interest is sought to be enforced, and the Court is of the opinion ;that the rate agreed to be paid is harsh and unconscionable and ought not to be enforced by legal process, the court may give judgment for the payment of interest at such a rate as it may think just.

(i) Catching bargains[67]

Equity can set aside or modify an agreement with "an expectant heir" made in anticipation of his expectations. The transaction need not amount to a sale of or charge on the expectation.[68]

---

56 *Powell v. Powell* [1900] 1 Ch.243, 246; *Wright v. Carter* [1903] 1 Ch.27

57 *Re Coomber* [1911] 1 Ch.723, 730

58 *Wright v. Carter* [1903] 1 Ch.27

59 *Moody v. Cox & Hatt* [1917] 2 Ch.71

60 *Aylesford v. Morris* (1873) L.R. 8 Ch. App.484

61 Hodgin, *Law of Contract In East Africa* (1975), p.132

62 6 U.L.R. 150; Hodgin *Ibid.* pp.132 - 133. See also *Gandhi v. Mehta* 2 U.L.R. 193.

63 See also Section 16 Tanganyika Contract Act

64 See Contract Act Cap.75

65 Hodgin, *supra* n.61, p.133. See also the Privy Council decision in the Indian Case of *Dhanipal Das v. Maneshar Bakhsh Singh* (1906) 3 I.A. 118.

66 See now Civil Procedure Act Cap.65, S.26

67 See also Dawson, 45 Mich. L. Rev 267 - 279

68 *Aylesford v. Morris* (1873) L.R. 8 Ch. App. 484

Therefore, equity can relieve against a *post-obit* bond, by which a debtor promises his creditor a certain sum if the debtor survives a named person and becomes entitled to a share in his estate.[69] Relief can also be given to a young man whose sole expectation of wealth is from his father who is still alive.[70]

Undervalue in a transaction has also been said to be "a material element in cases in which it is not the sole equitable ground for relief"[71] and may form the sole ground for relief if it is "so gross as to amount of itself to evidence of fraud.[72] Fraud here is not used in its common law sense but refers to "an unconscientious use of the power arising out of "the relative positions of parties.[73]

(ii) Dealing with poor and ignorant persons

In *Evans v. Llewellin*[74], a poor man became entitled to a share of an estate worth One Thousand, Seven Hundred British Pounds. He sold it for Two Hundred guineas cash. He was later able to set the transaction aside as it was "improvidently obtained". it appears that equity provides relief when unfair advantage it taken of a person who is poor, ignorant or weak-minded, or is for some other reason in need of special protection.[75] Specific performance may be refused on similar grounds.[76] It should be stressed that the equitable rule is based on unconscientious conduct by the stronger party. Consequently, relief will not be granted merely because the transaction is unfair.[77] In a similar vein, mere inadequacy of consideration is not a ground for relief where the parties have bargained on equal terms.[78]

(iii) Inequality of bargaining power[79]

There is judicial support for the view that a party to a contract may be entitled to relief if the other has taken unfair advantage of the fact that there is inequality of bargaining power between them.

The first approach relates to the validity of covenants in restraint of trade,[80] which depends on whether the covenant is reasonable and the adequacy of consideration is considered in determining the issue of reasonableness.[81] The fairness of the bargain will, in this context, be relevant to the validity of restraint. This does not, however, support a general principle of relief against harsh bargains on the ground of inequality of bargaining power.

There has, however been an attempt to formulate such a principle. Thus in *Lloyds Bank v. Bundy*[82] Lord Denning M.R. (as he then was) formulated the principle as follows:[83]

> The English law gives relief to one who, without independent advice, enters into a contract upon terms which are very unfair or transfers property for a consideration which is grossly inadequate, when his bargaining power is grievously impaired by reason of his own needs or desires, or by his own ignorance or infirmity coupled with undue influence or pressures brought to bear on him by or for the benefit or for the benefit of the other.

---

69 *Chesterfield v. Janssen* (1750) 2 Ves Sen 125

70 *Nevill v. Snelling* (1880) 15 Ch.D. 679

71 *O'Rorke v. Bolingbroke* (1877) 2 App. Cas 814, 833

72 *Fry v. Lane* (1888) 40 Ch.D. 312, 321

73 *Aylesford v. Morris, supra* n.68 at p.491

74 (1787) 1 Cox C.C. 333. See also *Lloyds Bank Ltd. v. Bundy* [1975] Q.B. 326, 337.

75 *Cresswell v. Potter* [1978] 1 W.L.R. 255n. See also the Illiterates Protection Act Cap 73.

76 *Falcke v. Gray* (1859) 4 Drew 651

77 *Alec Lobb (Garages) Ltd. v. Total Oil (Great Britain) Ltd.* [1985] 1 W.L.R.173 *Hart v. O'Connor* [1985] A.C.1000

78 *Collier v. Brown* (1788) 1 Cox C.C. 428; *Coles v. Trecothick* (1804) 9 Ves.

79 Se also Clark, *Inequality of Bargaining Power* Thal 80 J.L.S. 17

80 *A. Schroeder Music Publishing Co. v. Macaulay* [1974] 1 W.L.R. 1308, 1315

81 *Infra.* Chap.10

82 [1975] Q.B. 326; [1974] 3 All E.R. 757 discussed *supra* n.46 & text thereof.

83 *Ibid.* Q.B. p.339; All E.R. at p.765

Although the statement was made *obiter* and was neither approved nor disproved by the other members of the English Court of Appeal it is regarded as "a fruitful source for future development of the law"[84] in this area. The formulation has in later cases been rejected as likely to render the law uncertain[85] and unnecessary in view of legislation dealing with specific instances in which superior bargaining power may be abused[86] and the widening of the scope of duress.[87]

(d) Bars to relief

Relief for due influence is restricted on grounds similar to those which limit the right to rescind for misrepresentation.

(i) Impossibility of restitution

The party seeking rescission must restore benefits which he has obtained under the contract, although he is not required to make *precise* restitution. Rescission will also be permitted in circumstances where equity can achieve a "practically just"[88] result. Thus in *O'Sullivan v. Management Agency & Music Ltd.*[89], the plaintiff sought to set aside for undue influence a number of management, sole agency, recording and publishing agreements and transfers of copy rights. The defendants argued that rescission should not be permitted as they could not be restored to their pre-contract position in view of the work which they had done to promote the plaintiff's success. However, the plaintiffs argued that rescission for undue influence (as distinguished from that for misrepresentation) was not subject to the requirement of restitution at all. The Court rejected both arguments and held that, even though precise restitution was impossible, rescission could be ordered so long as the Court could do substantial justice. This could be achieved by upholding the plaintiff's claim for rescission while allowing the defendants reasonable remuneration for their work on behalf of the plaintiff. It is argued that in this respect, the case resembles those in which contracts have been rescinded for misrepresentation subject to similar allowances in respect of improvements made to the subject-matter by the misrepresentor.[90]

(ii) Affirmation

A claim for relief on the ground of undue influence is barred by affirmation of the transaction after the influence (or the relationship giving rise to a presumption of influence) has ceased. In this respect, affirmation is effective though made without independent advice and ignorance of the right to have the transaction set aside.[91]

(iii) Delay

The victim of undue influence must "seek relief within a reasonable time after the removal of the influence under which the gift was made."[92] Consequently, if with knowledge or means of knowledge of his rights he fails to seek relief, he is assumed to have ratified the transaction.

(iv) Third party rights

The right to set the transaction aside cannot be exercised against a third party who in good faith acquires an interest for value in the subject matter. Thus in *Bainbridge v. Browne,*[93] children

---

84 Cheshire & Fifoot, *Law of Contract* (12 Edn., 1991) p.314. See also Sealy [1975] C.L.J. 21; Carr, 38 M.L.R. 463; Tiplady;, 46 M.L.R. 601.

85 *Pao On v. Lau Yiu Long* [1980] A.C. 614 (P.C.)

86 Unfair Contract Terms Act 1977 discussed by Treitel, *supra* n.16, pp.226 - 244.

87 *The Siboen & the Sibotre supra* n.3

88 *Erlanger v. New Sombrero Phosphate Co.* (1878) 3 App. Cas. 1218, 1279 discussed *supra* Chap.8

89 [1985] Q.B. 428

90 Treitel, *supra* pp.374, 342 - 343. See also *supra* Chap.8

91 *Mitchell v. Homfray* (1882) 8 Q.B.D. 587.

92 *Allcard v. Skinner* (1887) 36 Ch.D. 145, 187.

93 (1881) 18 Ch.D. 188, considered *supra* n.42 and text thereof.

who were not yet emancipated charged their property as security for their father's debts. It was held that they could not set this transaction aside against the father's creditors who did not know that they were not emancipated and gave value (presumably) by forebearing to sue the father. Furthermore, in *Coldunell Ltd. v. Gallon*[94], a son had by influence induced his parents (aged 86 and 91) to mortgage their house to enable his father to borrow Twenty Thousand Pounds for the purpose of providing financial help to the son in his business. The lender was unaware of the son's influence over the parents and had done his best to warn them to seek independent advice. It was held that the parents were not entitled to have the transaction set aside against the lender. Similarly in *O'Sullivan v. Management Agency & Music Ltd.*[95] relief was refused against a company which had acquired some of the plaintiff's copyrights and tapes in good faith and for value.

A transaction can, however, be set aside against a third party who does not give value, and against one "with notice of the equity ... or with notice of the circumstances from which the Court infers the equity".[96] In this vein, if an emancipated child guarantees his parent's debt he can set the guarantee aside against a creditor who knows of the nature of the relationship or deliberately shuts his eyes to it.[97]

3. Money lending

Statutory powers to control money lending contracts are given to the Courts by the Moneylenders Act.[98] The Courts may, therefore review transactions governed by the Act and alter the interest rate. Section 12(1), provides *inter alia:*

> Where ... there is evidence which satisfies the Court that the interest charged in respect of the sum actually lent is excessive, or that the amounts charged for expenses, inquiries, fines, bonus, premium, renewals or any other charges, are excessive, and that, in either case, the transaction is harsh and unconscionable or is otherwise such that a court of equity would give relief, the court may re-open the transaction... and relieve the person sued from payment of any sum in excess of the sum adjudged by the Court to be fairly due ... having regard to the risk and all the circumstances ...

The Section further requires that it the money paid is excessive the Court may order the creditor to repay it to the borrower or to indemnify him or other person sued. Section 13 provides that a rate of interest in excess of 24% is presumed to be excessive and that the transaction is harsh and unconscionable. Presumably the Court can also decide that a rate less than 24% is also unreasonable.[99] However, the rate of 24% may be out of keeping with present circumstances. Consequently it has been provided in Britain that factors to be taken into account in determining whether a credit bargain is extortionate include the prevailing level of interest rates, matters affecting the debtor (such as his age and business capacity, and the degree to which he was under financial pressure when he made the bargain); and the degree of risk accepted by the creditor.[100]

94 [1986] 1 All E. R. 1184

95 *supra* n.89

96 *Bainbridge v. Browne* (1881) 18 Ch.D. at p.197.

97 *Maitland v. Irving* (1846) 15 Sim 437; *Lancashire Loans Ltd. v. Black* [1934] 1 K.B. 380; *Turnbull & Co. v. Duvall* [1902] A.C. 429; *Chaplin & Co. Ltd. v. Brammall* [1908] 1 K.B. 233; *Coldunnel Ltd. Case supra* n.94 at p.1197; *Avon Finance Co. v. Bridger* [1985] 2 All E.R. 281. See also Oldham [1989] C.L.J. 184.

98 Cap 264

99 *C.B. Lalobo v. Baganda Butchers Ltd.* 14 E.A.C.A. 12, where the Court indicated that no hard and fast rule could be laid down to determine what was or was not unconscionable. The rate of 48% was reduced to 24% under Section 26 of the Civil Procedure Act Cap 65.

100 Consumer Credit Act 1974, S.138(2)-(4); *Davies v. Direct Loans Ltd.* [1986] 1 W.L.R. 823 *Ketley v. Scott* [1981] 1 C.R. 241.

10
ILLEGALITY

1. Introduction

A contract which is illegal is void. Illegality may manifest itself in four main ways. First, in the formation of the contract e.g. where an unlicensed money lender makes a loan. Second, in the performance of the contract e.g. a contract to commit a crime. Third, in the consideration for the contract. Finally, illegality may be evident in the purpose for which the contract is made; for instance where a vessel is hired for the purposes of smuggling items into the country.

A contract is illegal if it is (i) contrary to public policy and (ii) forbidden by statute. A contract is contrary to public policy when it is in the interest of the public that it should not be enforced. Illegality is a question of degree. For this purpose two types of illegal contracts should be distinguished. First, those which contain elements of moral turpitude such as an agreement to commit a crime. Second, those in which the turpitude is absent such a contract in restraint of trade. The second category of contracts are treated more leniently than those in the first category.

2. Types of illegality

(a) Contracts tending to injure the public service

These include agreements for (i) the sale of public offices;[101] (ii) the assignment of salaries of public officials; (iii) sale of pensions for public services; (iv) to procure titles of honour.[102] Contracts of this nature are contrary to public policy because of their tendency to lead to corruption and inefficiency.

In *Parkinson v. College of Ambulance Ltd,*[103] the Secretary of the College of Ambulance promised Colonel Parkinson that, if he made a large donation to the college, which was a charitable institution, he would receive a knighthood. The Colonel made a large donation. When he did not get the knighthood, he sued for the return of his money. It was held that the action could not succeed because the contract was against public policy and illegal. The Court further observed that such a contract was "derogatory to the dignity of the Sovereign."[104]

Similarly, a contract by a person to use his position/influence with Government to procure a benefit for another is void for being contrary to public policy.[105] furthermore, a contract to restrain a person to serve in the military forces is also void.[106]

---

101 Sale of Offices Act, 1551, Sale of Offices Act, 1809 (U.K.)

102 *Parkinson v. College Ambulance Ltd.* [1925] 2 K.B.1

103 *Ibid.*

104 *Ibid.* at p.14

105 *Montefiore v. Monday Motor Components Ltd.* [1918] 2 K.B.241; *Lamenda Trading Co. Ltd. v. African Middle East Petroleum Co.* [1988] Q.B. 448, 458. See also Prevention of Corruption Act No.8 of 1970, S.4

106 *Re Beard* [1908] 1 Ch.383

In the Ethiopian Case of *Tekele Gebre Sellassie v. Sebhatu Woldemariam*[107], the contracting parties were potential candidates in an election. They agreed to draw lots to determine who would stand with the proviso that should the loser not keep the agreement then he should pay $ E 5,000 to the winner. The loser did in fact contest the election and was sued. The Court held that the contract was immoral and unlawful. It explained thus:

> Every citizen has both the right and full freedom conferred upon him by law to stand for election ... This right or freedom cannot be sold; nor can it be made an item of transaction. Further, one cannot acquire the right to become a representative of the people through money or deceit.

(b) Contracts tending to impede the administration of Justice

(i) Contracts relating to criminal prosecution and bankruptcy

An agreement to stifle a prosecution for a criminal offence is void since the public has interest in the proper administration of justice.[108] However, if the offence is one for which the aggrieved party could sue, then the agreement for compromise of the action for instance as to damages is valid.[109]

A contract whose aim is to defeat bankruptcy law is void. Thus in *John v. Mendoza*[110], Mendoza owed John Eight Hundred and Fifty two Pounds and promised that if John would tell Mendoza's trustee in bankruptcy that the money was present, Mendoza would, not withstanding still be John's debtor. It was held that the agreement was void.

(ii) Contracts of maintenance/champerty

Contracts aimed at improperly stirring up litigation and strife by giving aid to one party to bring or defend a claim is illegal.[111]

Champerty is an arrangement whereby a person obtains a promise of a share in the proceeds of an action in return for providing evidence or financial assistance to the person who conducts litigation. A contract with such an object is illegal. However, an act will not amount to maintenance when a person giving the assistance is a relative or friend acting from motives of charity or has a common interest with the person assisted.[112]

Torts of maintenance and champerty largely feature in solicitor/client relationships. A contract to commit such torts is contrary to public policy and therefore void.[113]

(c) Contracts to oust the Jurisdiction of the Court

A contract to oust the jurisdiction of the Court on a question of law is illegal since it is contrary to public policy and therefore, void.[114] In *Bennett v. Bennett*[115], a wife agreed not to apply for maintenance to Court in return for a promise by the husband to give her a certain allowance. It was held that the agreement was contrary to public policy since it usurped the statutory power of the Courts over the matter.

---

107 1965 A.L.R. Comm.593. Hodgin, *Law of Contract In East Africa (1975)* p.152

108 *Collins v. Blantern* (1767) 2 Wils K.B. 341; *Howard v. Odham's Press Ltd* [1938] 1 KB 42; *R. v. Andrews* [1973] Q.B. 422; *R. v. Panayiotou* [1973] 3 All E.R. 112.

109 *McGregor v. McGregor* (1888) 21 Q.B.D. 424; *Fisher & Co. v. Apollinaris Co.* (1875) L.R. 10 Ch.App. 297.

110 [1939] 1 K.B. 41. See also *Elliot v. Richardson* (1870) L.R. 5 C.P. 744

111 *Re Trepca Mines Ltd.* (No.2) [1963] Ch.199, 219; [1962] 3 All E.R. 351, 355 E

112 *Martell v. Consett Iron Co. Ltd.* [1955] Ch.363;

113 *Abdallah v. S. J. S. Barlatt* [1931] 1 W.A.C.A. 137; *Rees v. De Bernady* [1896] 2 Ch.437. For exceptions see *Wallersteiner v. Moir* (No.2) [1975] Q.B. 373; [1975] 1 All E.R. 849

114 *Thompson v. Charnock* (1799) 8 Term Rep 139. *Lee v. Showmen's Guild of Great Britain* [1952] 2 Q.B. 329, 342 [1952] 1 All F.R. 1175, 1181 per Lord Denning.

115 [1952] 1 All E.R. 413 [1952] 1 K.B. 249

However, an agreement requiring arbitration before recourse to the Courts is valid. Thus in *Scott v. Avery*,[116] a clause requiring arbitration in the first instance was upheld since it did not purport to overt the jurisdiction of the Court but simply to lay down at what stage the cause of action upon which that jurisdiction might be exercised arose.

(c) Contracts for trading with the enemy

A contract made with enemies as contracting parties is against public policy and, therefore, illegal. Two reasons are given for this. First, further performance of the contract would involve intercourse with the enemy. Second, continued existence of the contract would confer upon the enemy an immediate future benefit.[117] An enemy, for this purpose, is a person voluntarily resident or carrying on business in enemy-occupied territory.[118]

It is notable that war does not expropriate accrued rights of an enemy. These are normally preserved until the end of the war. The administration of such interest is normally given to an administrator or custodian of enemy property.[119]

(d) Contracts to commit a criminal offence or a civil wrong

The following contracts are illegal and void.

(i) Contract to defraud revenue by tax evasion

In *Miller v. Karlinski*[120], the plaintiff received a salary and expenses. He was allowed to include in his expenses the sum of money that he had paid as tax. He sued for arrears and it was held that the expenses/income tax arrangements was a fraud on the revenue and, therefore, he could not enforce the sum owed. However in *Jhevanjee v. Jamal*[121], the Courts found the tax arrangement legal. In that case, X bought a house from Y and sold it to Z. He merged the two contracts into one, thus saving on the stamp duty which would go to the Treasury. Z refused to pay X's commission and alleged that the contract was illegal. It was held by the Court of Appeal for East Africa that the agreement was not itself illegal.

(ii) Contract to defraud local rating authority

A contract to defraud a local rating authority is illegal. Thus in *Alexander v. Rayson*,[122] A let a flat to R at a rent of One Thousand, Two Hundred British Pounds per annum. With the object of getting a low rateable value for the flat, 2 written agreements were entered into: one purporting to let the flat at Four Hundred and Fifty Pounds per annum; the other being an agreement to pay Seven Hundred and Fifty Pounds per annum for services in connection with the flat. A sued R for an instalment of Seven Hundred and Fifty Pounds. It was held that since the agreement was made to defraud the rating authority, it was void and the defendant could not succeed.

(iii) Deceptive offer to take shares in a company

An agreement to take shares in a company for the purpose of fraudulently inducing the public to believe that there is a market for shares is a criminally indictable conspiracy which is illegal.[123]

---

116 (1856) 5 H.L.C. 811. See also *Czarnikow v. Roth Schmidt & Co.* [1922] 2 K.B. 478 *Re Davstone Estates Ltd.'s Leases* [1969] 2 Ch.378; [1969] 2 All E.R. 849 c.f. *Tanzanian Case Wendt v. Jiwan & Mulji* 1 T.L.R. (R) 460.

117 *Re Badische Co. Ltd.* [1921] 2 Ch. 331 per Russel J.

118 *Porter v. Freudenberg* [1915] 1 K.B. 857

119 *Arab Bank v. Barclays Bank* [1954] A.C. 495

120 [1945] 62 T.L.R. 85. See also *Napier v. National Business Agency Ltd.* [1951] 2 All E.R. 263

121 1967(1) A.L.R. Comm.395

122 [1936] 1 K.B. 169

123 *Scott v. Brown* [1892] 2 Q.B. 724

(iv) Agreement to indemnify against libel claims

An agreement by proprietors of a newspaper to indemnify the printers against claims arising out of libels published in the newspaper is void.[124]

(v) Agreement for indemnity of assured against accidents caused by Him

An insurance policy indemnifying the assured against legal liability for accidents caused by him cannot be enforced. Thus in *Gray v. Barr* [125], Gray had an affair with Barr's wife. Armed with a loaded shotgun, Barr went to Gray's farm to search for his wife. In a struggle with Gray, Barr fell down the stairs, the gun was involuntarily discharged and the shot killed Gray. Barr was acquitted of murder and manslaughter. The administrator of Gray's estate sued Barr for damages under the Fatal Accidents Acts. By way of third party proceedings, Barr claimed to be indemnified by the Pentecostal Assurance under the accident liability policy. It was held that Bar was liable for having caused Gray's death by, gross negligence. Furthermore, that the killing was not an "accident" within the meaning of the insurance policy and that even if the killing was an "accident" it was caused by the deliberate and unlawful act of the assured. Consequently, it was against public policy to admit a claim for indemnity against the insurance company.

(vi) Effect of suicide on insurance policy

The suicide of the assured, while sane, can render it impossible to recover under a policy if the suicide is a crime. Thus in *Baresford v. Royal Insurance Co. Ltd.*[126], X who had insured his life with the defendant company for Fifty Thousand Pounds, shot himself two or three minutes before the policy would have been invalidated by non-payment of the premium. He was sane at the time of his death. As the law then stood, suicide was a crime.[127] On the true construction of the contract, the company had agreed to pay the money to X's representatives even though he should die by his own hand and whether he should then be sane or insane. An action in which X's executor claimed payment of Fifty Thousand pounds failed on the ground that to allow a person or his estate to benefit from his own crime was against public policy.[128]

(vii) Contract to perform illegal act in friendly foreign country

An agreement to perform in a foreign friendly country an act which is illegal in that country is void for being contrary to public policy and international comity.[129] In *Regazzoni v. K.C. Sethia (1944) Ltd.*,[130] a contract was made for the export of Indian jute to Italy, with a view to re-export to South Africa. The Court refused to enforce the contract as it contravened an Indian law prohibiting the export of goods produced in India to South Africa, and as it could only be performed by making false declarations in India.

---

124 *W.H.Smith & Son v. Clinton* (1908) 25 T.L.R. 34

125 [19‾1] 2 Q.B. 544, 568, 581 C.A. c.f *Tinline v. White Cross Insurance* [1921] 3 K.B. 327; *James v. British General Insurance Co. Ltd.* [1927] 2 K.B. 311. The Gray case is reconcilable with *Gardner v. Moore* [1984] A.C. 548, 560; [1984] 1 All E.R. 1100.

126 [1937] 2 K.B. 197; [1937] 2 All E.R. 243 affd. [1938] A.C. 586; [1938] 2 All E.R. 602

127 In Britain this is no longer the case: Suicide Act 1961, S.1.

128 See also *Hardy v. Motors Insurers Bureau* [1964] 2 Q.B. 745, 760 per Lord Denning; *Dewitt v. Titcumb* [1990] Ch.110; [1989] 3 All E.R. 417; Furmston, 16 *U. Toronto L. J.* 267, 269 - 272.

129 *Foster v. Driscoll* [1929] 1 K.B. 470, 510, 520 - 522

130 [1958] A.C. 301; [1957] 3 All E.R. 286 H.L. See also Mann 21 *M.L.R.* 130; 73 L.Q.R. 32; *Fielding & Platt v. Selim Najjar* [1969] 2 All E.R. 150; [1969] 1 W.L.R. 357; *National Westminster Ltd. v. Barclays Bank International Ltd.* [1975] Q.B. 654; [1974] 3 All E.R. 834 *Lamenda Trading Co. Ltd. v. African Middle-East Petroleum Co. Ltd.* [1988] Q.B. 448; [1988] 1 All E.R. 513

(e) Immoral contracts

Contracts relating to sexual immorality such as agreements for future illicit cohabitation are void. Similarly collateral contracts which are valid in themselves will be void if they are knowingly made to further an immoral purpose. Thus in *Pearce v. Brooks*,[131] A let a cab on hire to B, a prostitute knowing that it was to be used for immoral purposes. It was held that he could not recover the fee for hire as the contract was illegal.

Other immoral contracts include an agreement between husband and wife for future separation; an agreement between a man and woman who knows him to be married, for marriage after the wife's death.[132] However, a contract made between a *decree nisi* and *decree absolute* for marriage after dissolution of the existing marriage is valid.[133]

(f) Contracts affecting the freedom of marriage

Contracts in general restraint of marriage are void. This also applies to contracts unreasonably affecting freedom of choice in marriage.[134] In *Lowe v. Peers*[135] , a contract made by a man under seal to the following effect was held to be contrary to public policy:

> I do hereby promise Mrs Catherine Lowe, that I will not marry with any person besides herself: if I do I agree to pay to the said Catherine Lowe One Thousand Pounds within three months next after I shall marry anybody else.

However, contracts restraining marriage with a particular person or only partially restraining marriage is valid.[136]

(g) Contracts restricting personal liberty

A contract by a newspaper owner not to comment on the conduct of a particular person is void.[137] Similarly a contract which unfairly limits the freedom of an individual is void. Thus in *Horwood v. Millar's Timber Co.*,[138] a man agreed with a money-lender not to change his residence or employment or to consent to a reduction of his salary or to part with any of his property or to incur any obligations on credit or any obligations, legal or moral without the consent of the moneylender. It was held that the contract was void as it unduly restricted the liberty of the borrower.

(h) Contracts in restraint of trade

A contract in restraint of trade is one which restricts a person wholly or partially from carrying on his trade or business.[139] All such contracts are *prima facie* void. They are only enforceable if they are deemed to be reasonable.

Two types of contract in restraint of trade can be identified. First, those which are aimed at protecting a proprietary interest and second, those aimed at restraining competition.

(i) Contracts for protection of proprietary interest

These comprise contracts for the protection on sale of goodwill of business and prevention of a servant from revealing trade secrets. Contracts of this nature will be enforced if they satisfy

---

131 (1866) L.R. 1 Ex 213

132 *Wilson v. Carnley* [1908] 1 K.B. 729; *Spiers v. Hunt* [1908] 1 K.B. 720 c.f. *Shaw v. Shaw* [1954] 2 Q.B.429

133 *Fender v. Mildmay* [1938] A.C. 1; [1937] 3 All E.R. 402, 429, per Lord Wright.

134 Story, *Equity Jurisprudence*, S.274

135 (1768) 4 Bur. 2225. See also *Re Mitchellham's Will Trusts* [1964] Ch.550; [1963] 2 All E.R. 188. *Baker v. White* (1690) 2 Vern 215.

136 Treitel, *supra* p.390

137 *Neville v. Dominion of Canada News Co. Ltd.* [1915] 3 K.B. 556

138 [1917] 1 K.B. 305 c.f. *Denny's Trustee v. Denny* [1919] 1 K.B. 583

139 Heydon, *The Restraint of Trade Doctrine* 50 A.L.J. 290; Trebilcock, *The Common Law of Restraint of Trade*

two conditions. First if the contract is reasonable with reference to the person against whom it is made. Second, the contract must be reasonable with reference to the public. In *Nordenfelt v. Maxim Nordenfelt Gun Co.*[140] N was an inventor and manufacturer of guns and ammunition. He sold his business to a company and agreed that for 25 years he would not manufacture guns or ammunition in any part of the world. It was held that the agreement was binding.

However, if the restraint is wider than required to protect the person in whose interest it is imposed, the court will in most cases refuse to alter it to its proper limit in order to maintain a degree of certainty.[141] Nevertheless, if the agreement has several clauses, some of which are valid and others void, the court can sever the valid ones from the void ones and enforce them, provided that severance does not affect the meaning of the remaining part of the contract. Thus in *Scorer v. Seymour Jones*[142], S carried on business as an estate agent in Dartmouth and Kingsbridge. He employed S. J. as clerk and negotiator at the Kingsbridge office. S.J. signed a covenant whereby he undertook for 3 years not to set up in business within a radius of the Dartmouth or Kingsbridge offices of S. After the termination of the contract of employment S. J. immediately opened an office of his own within five miles radius of Kingsbridge. It was held that the restraint as agreed was too wide as S. J. had never worked at the Dartmouth office. However, the Dartmouth restraint was severable from the Kingsbridge restraint which was not too wide. While the former was invalid, the latter was valid and enforceable.

If a contract in restraint of trade is reasonable as between the parties, the burden of proving that it is unreasonable in the public interest is a heavy one.[143]

(i) Nature of public interest

Public interest refers[144] to a legal principle or proposition and not to economic theories. Therefore, reasonableness in the public interest refers to the interests as recognised in a principle or proposition of law and not to the interests of the public at large in terms of economic advantages or disadvantages. In this regard the categories of restraint of trade are not closed. The doctrine of restraint of trade is not restricted to contracts between employer and employee or vendor and purchaser of business. The doctrine also applies[145] to (i) restrictions intended to promote trade; (ii) restrictions on part only of a multiple business; (iii) restrictions in a trade or service contract during the existence of the trade or service; (iv) restrictions on trade on a particular piece of land.

In *MceEkistrim v. Bally Macelligot Co-op Soc.* [146], the respondent society manufactured cheese and butter from milk supplied by its members. The rules of the society provided that no member should sell milk to any other person without the consent of a committee; that no member should be entitled to withdraw from the society unless his shares were transferred or cancelled; and that the consent of the committee, which might be refused without giving reasons, should be essential to the effectiveness of such a transfer or cancellation. It was held that this arrangement was unreasonable between the parties as it restricted the right of members to supply milk in the free market.[147] The arrangement was an attempt to eliminate competition altogether and was void.

---

140 [1894] A.C. 535

141 Treitel, *supra* p.401

142 [1966]1 W.L.R. 1419; [1966] 1 All E.R.347. See also the *Nordenfelt Case supra* n.140; *T Lucas & Co. Ltd. v. Mitchell* [1974] Ch.129; *Amoco Australia Pty Ltd.v.Rocca Bros.*[1975] A.C. 561; [1975] 1 All E.R. 968.

143 *A-G of Australia v. Adelaide S.S. Co.* [1913] A.C. 781 *N.W. Salt Co. v. Electrolytic Alkalico* [1914] A.C. 461, 471 per Lord Haldane

144 *Texaco Ltd. v. Mulberry Filling Station Ltd.*[1972] 1 WLR 814, 828; [1972] 1 All E.R. 513 per Ungoed Thomas J.

145 *Evans (Joseph) & Co. v.Heathcote* [1918] 1 K.B. 518

146 [1919] A.C. 548

(ii) Solus agreement

An agreement whereby a garage owner binds himself to buy all his petrol from one particular oil company is not necessarily in restraint of trade and, therefore, is not bad. However, whether the agreement is reasonable depends on the nature and duration of the restrictions. Thus in *Petrofina (G.B.) Ltd v. Martin*,[148] M who was negotiating to buy a garage signed as a condition of the sale a solus agreement with P, an oil company. The agreement provided, *inter alia* that (i) M would obtain all petrol from P and sell no other brand of petrol; (ii) M would advertise only P's lubricating oil and use only that oil; (iii) M would not sell or otherwise dispose of the garage without first giving P first refusal and then only to a person willing to enter into a solus agreement on similar terms with P; (iv) the agreement would continue for twelve years and could be ended on the giving of three months notice after 600 gallons of petrol had been sold. It was held that (i) the agreement operated as a restriction on the way in which M could carry on his trade on his own land (since P had no interest therein by way of mortgage lease or sale) the doctrine of restraint of trade applied; (ii) the restriction of M's power to dispose of his property, the period of restriction and the restriction of the lubricating oils were all unreasonable restrictions; (iii) as these provisions were not severable, the agreement as a whole was in unreasonable restraint of trade and was unenforceable.

The doctrine of restraint of trade applies to mortgages but not to leases.[149]

(b) Contract in restraint of competition

A contract which is simply aimed at restraining business competition is unenforceable.[150] However, if the restraint of competition is necessary to prevent an employee from making use of the employer's confidential information such as trade secrets or connections, it may be enforced. This is provided the restraint is not wider than necessary to effect that purpose. Thus in *Attwood v. Lamont* [151], A, a tailor employed B as his assistant under a contract by which B agreed on the termination of his employment not to carry on his business as a tailor within ten miles of A. It was held that the agreement was simply to prevent B from using such skill as he possessed in competition with A and was, therefore, void. In contrast in *Fitch v. Dewes*,[152] X was a solicitor in Tamworth and Y was in turn his junior clerk, articled clerk and managing clerk. In his contract of service, Y agreed on leaving X's employment not to practice as a solicitor within 7 miles of Tamworth. It was held that the agreement was good because Y, during his service with Y had become acquainted with the details of the business of X's clients and therefore, could be restrained from using that knowledge to the detriment of X.

It appears that the extent of protection appears to depend on two factors. First, the nature of the employer's business and secondly the business position of the employee[153]

Contracts illegal by statute

Contracts which violate the provisions of a statute are regarded as void and not illegal.[154] The distinction between a void and illegal contract is that[155] a void contract is one where for instance

---

148 [1966] Ch.146; [1966] 1 All E.R. 126 distinguished in *Esso Petroleum Co. Ltd. v. Harper's Garage (Stourport) Ltd.* [1968] AC 269; [1967] 1 All E.R. 699.

149 *Esso Petroleum Co. v. Harpers Garage (Stourport) Ltd. ibid.* ; *Total Oil (Great Britain) Ltd. v. Thompson Garages (Biggin Hill)* [1972] 1 Q.B. 318; [1971] 3 All E.R. 1226

150 *Morris v. Saxelby* [1916] A.C. 668, 710

151 [1920] 3 K.B. 571

152 [1921] A.C. 158

153 See also *Strange v. Mann* [1965] 1 W.L.R. 629, *Gilford Motor Co. v. Horne* [1933] Ch.935; *Howe Counties Diaries Ltd. v. Skilton* [1970] 1 W.L.R. 528; *Marion White Ltd. v. Francis* [1972] 1 W.L.R. 1423; *Robb v. Green* [1895] 2 Q.B. 315; *Hivac Ltd. v. Park Royal Scientific Instruments Ltd.* [1946] Ch. 169

154 Infants Relief Act, 1874 (U.K.) S.1, *Ayo Solanke v. Abraham Abed & Ogunlowo* [1962] N.R.N.L.R. 92

155 Achike, *Nigerian Law of Contract*, pp.190-191. See also Cheshire, Fifoot & Furmston's *Law of Contract (12 Ed, 1991)* p.349, 353; *Bostel Bros Ltd. v. Hurlock* [1949] 1 K.B. 74; [1948] 2 All E.R. 312

a statute requires certain formalities to be carried out as a condition precedent for its validity, but without imposing penalty for non-performance. Failure to comply with the formalities renders the contract void. On the other hand, an illegal contract is one where a penalty is imposed thereby rendering the contract both void and illegal. Three situations may illustrate this.

(i) Void contracts which are declared to be illegal

Section 1 of the Life Assurance Act, 1774 (U.K.) provides that "no insurance shall be made by any person on the life of another or on certain other risks unless the assured has an interest in the subject-matter. Contracts in breach of this provision were declared both void and illegal. A similar approach was adopted to the Marine Insurance Act, 1745. However, when that Act was replaced by the Marine Insurance Act, 1906 where in particular Section 4(1) made such policies void, the contracts in question were held to be no longer illegal.[156]

(ii) Where formalities of breach of statute are not specified

The Companies Act (Cap.85) provides[157] that "no association or partnership shall be formed consisting of more than 20 persons unless it is registered under the Act." There is no penalty for breach of the section. However, sometimes an unregistered association of more than 20 persons has been regarded as illegal.[158]

(iii) Where formalities are required by statute

A Statute may require the observance of certain formalities in making a contract but fail to specify the consequences of the breach. In such situation the issue is whether the statutory requirement is regarded as *directory* only or *obligatory*. If it is *obligatory*, failure to comply therewith makes the contract void. If it is *directory*, the contract is not invalidated. Thus in the Nigerian case, *Kasumu & Ors v. Baba Egbe*[159], a moneylender lent money in contravention of Section 19 of the Moneylender Ordinance. The Ordinance required a lender to keep a book for recording the transaction and in default to be liable to a fine. It was held that a transaction which failed to comply with Section 19 was un enforceable and the lender could not in such circumstances recover the money lent.

In *Cope v. Rowlands* [160] a statute provided that a person who acted as a broker in the City of London without first obtaining a licence should forfeit and pay to the City Twenty five pounds for every such offence. The plaintiff, who was unlicensed, sued the defendant for work that he had done in buying and selling stock. In delivering judgment for the defendant, Parke B stated:[161]

> The legislature had in view, as one object, the benefit and security of the public in those important transactions which are negotiated by brokers. The clause, therefore, which imposes a penalty, must be taken ... to imply a prohibition of all unadmitted persons to act as brokers, and consequently to prohibit, by necessary inference, all contracts which such persons make for compensation to themselves for so acting.

The case may be compared with *Archbold (Freightage) Ltd. v. S. Spanglett Ltd.*[162], where the Road and Rail Traffic Act, 1933 provided that no person should **use** a vehicle for the carriage of goods unless he held an "A" or "C" licence. The former entitled him to carry the goods of

---

156 *Re London County Commercial Reinsurance Office* [1922] 2 Ch.67

157 Section 392

158 *Sykes v. Beadon* [1897] 11 Ch.D. 170

159 14 W.A.C.A. 444

160 (1836) 2 M & W 149

161 *Ibid.* p.159

162 [1961] 1 Q.B. 374; [1961] 1 All E.R. 417; Furmston 24 MLR 394

others for reward; the latter to carry his own goods but not the goods of others. The defendants who held a "C" licence, agreed with the plaintiffs to carry 200 crates of whisky belonging to third parties from Leeds to London. The plaintiffs were unaware that the defendants held no "A" licence. The whisky was stolen *en route* and the plaintiffs claimed damages for its loss. One issue *inter alia* which arose was whether the contract for carriage was prohibited by the Act, either expressly or impliedly. The Court of Appeal examined the purpose of the statute and concluded that the contract of carriage was not expressly prohibited since the Act did not strike at a contract to carry goods, but at the use of an unlicensed vehicle on the road. Furthermore, that there was no implied prohibition. In the words of Pearce L. J.[163]

> The object of the Road and Rail Traffic Act, 1933, was not (in this connection) to interfere with the owner of the goods or his facilities for transport, but to control those who provided the transport with a view to promoting its efficiency. Transport of goods was not made illegal but the various licence holders were prohibited from encroaching on one another's territory, the intention of the Act being to provide an orderly and comprehensive service.

(iv) Gaming contracts

Section 18 of the Gaming Act, 1845[164] provided that (i) contracts by way of gaming or wagering are null and void and (ii) no action can be brought to recover money upon any wager. Furthermore under the Gaming Act 1892, any promise, express or implied to (i) pay any person any sum of money paid by him in respect of any contract rendered null and void by the Gaming Act 1845 or (ii) pay any sum of money by way of commission, fee reward or otherwise in respect of any such contract or of any services connected therewith is null and void and no action can be brought to recover any such sum of money.

In Uganda, while gaming and wagering can give rise to criminal liability,[165] there are certain forms of gaming which are authorised.[166] Indeed a wagering contract *perse* is not illegal but the law does not enforce it except in the circumstances authorised by Parliament[167]. To that extent it is void.

Essentially, a wager is an agreement between two parties that on the happening or ascertainment of some uncertain event, one party shall pay a sum of money to the other. Which party is to pay depends on the happening of the event. For instance contracts for differences in stock exchange dealings i.e. where parties agree simply to pay or receive the difference between the price of shares on a particular day and their price on another day are void since they amount to wagers.

With respect to loans for gaming, money lent for purposes of gaming cannot be recovered.[168] However, if the money is lent to make bets in a country where betting is lawful it can be recovered.[169] Finally, money lent to pay bets which are already lost cannot be covered.[170]

---

163 *Ibid.* [1961] 1 Q.B. at 386; [1961 1 All E.R. at 423

164 Previously applicable to Uganda by virtue of the Judicature Act, 1962, but now not applicable: *Uganda Motors Ltd. v. Wavah Holdings Ltd.* Civil Appeal No.19 91 (Supreme Court of Uganda) decided 1st July 1992, interpreting Section 3(2) Judicature Act, 1967.

165 Penal Code Act, Ss. 157 - 160

166 National Lotteries Act, 1967; Pools Betting Act, 1968

167 *Ibid.*

168 *Carlton Hall Club v. Lawrence* [1929] 2 K.B. 153

169 *Saxby v. Fulton* [1909] 2 K.B. 208

170 *Macdonald v. Green* [1951] 1 K.B. 594; *C.H.T. Ltd. v. Ward* [1965] 2 Q.B. 63 *Hill v. William Hill (Park Lane) Ltd.* [1949] A.C. 530

3. Effects of illegality

Illegality generally renders a contract void, although a distinction is made between a contract which is unenforceable by one party and one which is unenforceable by both parties thereto. It has been said that where the contract is "wholly unenforceable because it is contrary to ... law, it may ... accurately be said to be void as a contract, that is, not to be a contract at all;"[171] or to be "illegal and void"[172]. In the restraint of trade cases, the illegality often affects only a single term of the contract and generally its effect is not to make the contract wholly void: it only makes the stipulation in restraint of trade unenforceable in so far as it has not been performed.[173] Furthermore, a contract in restraint of trade would only be "wholly unenforceable" and void (in the sense described above) where the restraint formed the sole or principal subject-matter of the contract.[174]

(a) Position of the guilty party

The law does not assist a guilty party in the case of an illegal contract.[175] The effect of this is that a guilty party cannot recover any money or goods supplied under such a contract.[176] Additionally he cannot also sue for damages or the price of the goods.[177] In *Berg v. Sadler & Moore,*[178] B a tobacconist, was placed on the stop list by a tobacco association for breach of its rules. Later on he concealed his identity and through an agent induced S to sell him cigarettes and paid Seventy two pounds 19s for them. Later S suspected the fraud and refused to deliver the cigarettes. It was held that B could not recover the money paid because it was paid for an illegal purpose i.e. to obtain goods from S by false pretences.

This approach is obviously severe and has consequently been mitigated.

(b) Where the parties are not in pari delicto

Where the parties are not in *pari delicto,* the innocent party can recover anything he has paid under the contract. Thus in *Hughes v. Liverpool Victoria Friendly Society,*[179] a person was induced by fraud to take over some insurance policies on a life in which he had no insurable interest. Such a contract was illegal. It was held that he was entitled to recover the premiums he paid under the illegal contract.

(c) Where illegal purpose not executed

The rule on unenforceability and non-recovery by the parties under an illegal contract will not apply where the illegal purpose has not been carried out. In these circumstances a party to the contract may repent the illegal purpose. If he does so before performance then the law can come to his aid.[180] However, if the non-performance is due not to his repentance but to other factors, then the law will not assist him. Thus in *Bigos v. Bousted,*[181] X wanted to send his wife to Italy on grounds of her health. He agreed with Y that Y should provide her in Italy with Italian currency to the value of One hundred and fifty pounds contrary to the Exchange Control

---

171 *Mackender v. Feldia* [1967] 2 Q.B. 590, 601

172 *Phoenix General Insurance Co. of Greece S.A. v. Halvanon General Insurance Co.* [1988] Q.B. 216, 249, 267, 268

173 *O'Sullivan v. Management Agency & Music Ltd.*[1985] Q.B. 428, 469

174 *Amoco Australia Pty v. Rocca Bros Motor Engineering Pty Ltd.* [1975] A.C. 561

175 *Holman v. Johnson* (1775) 1 Cowp 341, 343

176 *Cowan v. Milbourn* (1867) L.R. 2 EX.230;

177 *Yin v. Sam* [1962] A.C. 304

178 [1937] 2 K.B. 158; Allen, 54 L.Q.R. 201 See also *Saunders v. Edwards* [1987] 1 W.L.R. 1116

179 [1916] 2 KB. See also *Kiriri Cotton Co. Ltd. v. Dewani* [1960] 1 All E.R. 177 P.C. (Uganda)

180 *Taylor v. Bowers* (1876) 1 Q.B.D. 291.

181 [1951] 1 All E.R. 92

Act, 1947. He deposited shares with Y as security for repayment. X's wife went to Italy but Y failed to supply the currency. X tried to recover his shares from Y. It was held that as the contract was illegal and the failure of the contract was Y's conduct and not X's repentance, the action failed.

(d) Manner of performance of legal contract

The issue arises as to the effect of an illegal act committed in the course of performance of a legal contract. Its resolution depends on the construction of the statute which prohibits the illegal act. If the intention of the legislature is that illegality in performance amounts to nullification of the whole contract, then no action can be brought on the contract. This will be so especially if the parties know that the of performance is contrary to statute. Thus in *Ashmore, Benson, Pease & Co. Ltd. v. Dawson Ltd.*[182], a contract to carry two 25 -ton loads was performed by using lorries which could not lawfully carry loads of more than 20 tons. This was known both to the carrier and to the owner of the goods, whose claim for damage done to them in the course of transit was rejected as he not only knew the illegality but "participated" in it. "Participation" in this context meant that he assented to a method of performance which he knew to be illegal, and that he hoped to benefit from it by saving the extra expense of having the goods carried on different vehicles.

However, if the legislature intended that illegality should have other consequences, then the contract will not be affected by the illegality and is enforceable in law. Thus in *St John Shipping Corporation v. Joseph Rank Ltd.*[183] , the *St John*, a ship which was registered in Panama carried a consignment of grain from the United States to England. When the ship arrived in England, it was discovered that she was overloaded and her loadline was submerged. This contravened the Merchant Shipping (Safety & Loadlines Conventions) Act, 1932. The defendants, who were holders of a bill of lading refused to pay freight on the overloaded portion of the cargo. It was held that on a true construction of the Act of 1932, the contracts of carriage of goods were not within its ambit and the defendants were liable to pay the retained part of the freight.

(e) Severance

Where only part of the contract is illegal, the whole contract will not be void if the illegal portion can be severed from the rest of the contract. Thus in *Ailion v. Spiekermann*[184] Ailion was the lessee of a flat which he occupied as a protected tenant. He agreed to assign the remainder of his lease to S and his wife. The rent was Eight Hundred and Fifty pounds per annum and the purchasers agreed to pay Three Thousand, Seven Hundred and Fifty pounds for certain furniture which was worth much less. The purchase price thus contained a premium which was prohibited by the Rent Act, 1968. It was held that the illegal element (i.e. the premium) was severable and consequently the lease was valid and S and his wife were entitled to specific performance without payment of the illegal premium.

However, the severance should not alter the nature of the original contract. Thus in *Goldsoll v. Goldman,*[185] the seller of an imitation jewellery business in New Bond Street, London promised that he would not for two (2) years deal in real or imitation jewellery in the United Kingdom and certain places abroad. The covenant was too wide as the seller had not traded abroad and

---

[182] [1973] 2 All E.R. 856; [1973] 1 All E.R. 909 Critique: Hamson [1973] C.L.J. 199

[183] [1957] 1 Q.B. 267; [1956] 3 All E.R. 683. See also *Archbolds (Freightage) Ltd. v. Spanglett* [1961] 1 Q.B. 374 [1961] 1 All E.R. 417, *Shaw v. Groom* [1970] 2 Q.B. 504; [1970] 1 All E.R. 702; *Curragh Investments Ltd. v. Cook* [1974] 1 W.L.R. 1559.

[184] [1976] Ch.158; [1976] 1 All E.R. 497

[185] [1915] 1 Ch.292

in respect of the subject matter had not dealt in real jewellery. It was held that references to foreign places and real jewellery could be severed from the restraint in respect of imitation jewellery in the United Kingdom, which could be enforced.

Where the whole purpose of the contract is illegal, then severance cannot save it. Thus in *Napier v. National Business Agency Ltd.*[186], N was employed as a Secretary and accountant at a salary of Thirteen pounds per week with Six pounds per week as expenses. Both parties knew his expenses were less than One pound a week. It was held that the contract was to evade tax and, therefore, illegal. It was impossible to sever the part dealing with salary from the part dealing with expenses so that the whole contract was unenforceable.

(f) Passage of title under fully executed illegal contract

Title can pass under an illegal contract. When it passes, the buyer has normal remedies available to the owner such as suing for trespass and detinue.[187] Conversely, a plaintiff may recover money, chattels or land transferred under an illegal contract to the defendant, if he can frame a cause of action, entirely independent of the contract, since in these circumstances he is not compelled to disclose the illegality. It has been stated that "any rights which he may have irrespective of his illegal interest will, of course, be recognised and enforced". In *Amar Singh v. Kulubya,*[188] a statutory ordinance in Uganda prohibited the sale or lease of "Mailo" land by an African to a non-African except with the written consent of the Governor. Without obtaining this consent, the plaintiff, an African, agreed to lease such land of which he was the registered owner to the defendant, an Indian, for one year and thereafter on a yearly basis. The agreement, therefore, was void for illegality, and no leasehold interest vested in the defendant. After the defendant had been in possession for several years, the plaintiff gave him seven weeks' notice to quit and ultimately sued him for recovery of the land. He succeeded. His claim to possession was based not upon the agreement, to the illegality of which on his own admission he had been a party, but on the independent and untainted ground of his registered ownership. He was not forced to have recourse to the agreement.

---

186 [1951] 2 All E.R. 264

187 *Singh v. Ali* [1960] A.C. 167 (P.C. (Malaysia) c.f. *Singh v. Kulubya* [1963] 3 W.L.R.513; [1964] A.C. 142; [1963] 3 All E.R. 499. Criticised. Cornish 27 MLR 225

188 *Scott v. Brown, Doerring, Mc Nab & Co.* [1892] 2 Q.B. 724 at 729 per Lindley L.J.; Gooderson [1958] CLJ 199; *Iraqi Ministry of Defence v. Arcepey Shipping Co. SA* [1980] 1 All E.R 480; [1980] 2 W.L.R. 488.

11
PRIVITY OF CONTRACT

1. Background and rationale of the doctrine

In the middle of the nineteenth century English Common law judges formulated the rule that no one may be entitled to or bound by the terms of a contract to which he is not an original party.[189] Although a concrete proposition under the common law, the doctrine is subject to some reservations.

First, the principle was not accepted as universally true in the earlier common law. In the Middle Ages the actions of debt and account had been available to third parties who wanted to benefit from an arrangement made by others on their behalf, and after the development of assumpsit,[190] it was for a long time unclear whether a similar view would be adopted.[191] Second, there was a recognised exception to the rule in the first half of the eighteenth century. Thus of A has made a contract with B, C may intervene and take A's place, if A was acting throughout as his agent, and it is immaterial that B entered into the contract in ignorance of this fact. This right of intervention, known normally as the doctrine of undisclosed principal, has, indeed been attacked on the ground that it offends the common law doctrine of privity. However, this criticism has been fruitless and the *undisclosed principal* is a well-established character in the modern law of agency.[192] Third, the rule is strictly a creation of the common law. Equity in its essence tends to take a less rigid view of the boundaries of contract and has sometimes sought to overreach them although its approach tends to be tentative. Fourth, while the doctrine of privity is a natural inference from a strict theory of contract, it has conflicted with the needs and concepts of the law of property. For instance, a lease, is a contract, but it creates rights of property that cannot be restricted to contractual notions. Thus if A lets land to B, the lease will contain mutual rights and duties - to pay rent, to keep the premises in repair and many other obligations. As between the parties themselves, there is privity of contract, but if either transfers his interest to a stranger, convenience demands that he, in his turn, shall take the benefit and burden of the original covenants. Similarly, a freeholder who sells his land intends to restrict its use not only by the purchaser but by anyone to whom it may be transferred.[193] In *Smith and Snipes Hall Farm Ltd. v. River Douglas Catchment Board,*[194] by deed made in 1938, the defendants agreed with eleven owners of land adjoining a certain stream to improve its banks and to "maintain for all time the work when completed". The landowners agreed to pay a proportion of the cost. In 1940 one of the landowners conveyed her land to Smith, the first plaintiff, and in 1944 Smith leased it to Snipes Hall Farm Ltd, the second plaintiff. In 1946, owing to the defendant's negligence, the banks burst and the land was flooded. Both plaintiffs

---

189 *Price v. Easton* (1833) 4 B & Ad 433, *Tweddle v. Atkinson* (1861) 1 B & S 393.

190 See *supra*, Chap 1

191 Simpson, *History* pp 475 - 485, *Coulls v. Bagot's Executor & Trustee Co. Ltd.* [1967] ALR 385, 407 - 9

192 See Chap 12 *infra* for discussion thereof

193 Cheshire & Burn *Modern Law of Real Property* (14th Edn.), pp.582 ff.

194 [1949] 2 K.B. 500; [1949] 2 All E.R. 179

were strangers to the contract. However, the Court of Appeal held that the covenants undertaken by the defendants affected the use and value of the land, that they were intended from the outset to benefit anyone to whom the land might be transferred and that the defendants were liable. The effect of such a decision is to diminish the importance of the doctrine of privity. Fifth, the doctrine only means that a non-party cannot bring *an action on the contract.* This does not exclude any other cause of action which he may have. Thus if A buys a car from B and gives it to his wife, she will have no rights under the contract against B but she could have an action in tort if she suffered personal injuries because of B's negligent pre-delivery inspection.[195] Similarly, if A threatens to break his contract with B unless B dismisses his servant C, C may be able to sue in the tort of intimidation.[196]

2. Measures to avoid the doctrine

(a) Attempts to confer benefits on strangers

(i) Discharge of debt to third party

The aim under a contract maybe that a debt due to a third person from one of the contracting parties shall be discharged by the other party. Thus if B owes money to X he may contract with A, whereby A agrees for good consideration, to discharge this debt. Can X sue A for failure to keep his promise? In *Crow v. Rogers,*[197] Hardy owed Crow Seventy Pounds. By an agreement between Hardy and Rogers, Rogers promised to discharge this debt in return for Hardy's undertaking to convey a house to him. Crow sued Rogers on the promise and failed.

(ii) Conferring benefit on third party

It may be desired to confer a benefit upon a third party towards whom no antecedent liability exists. A may promise B, for god consideration to pay X Shs.100,000/=. This type of situation was considered in *Tweddle v. Atkinson,*[198] where in consideration of an intended marriage between the plaintiff and the daughter of William Guy a contract was made between Guy and the plaintiff's father, whereby each promised to pay the plaintiff a sum of money. Guy failed to do so and the plaintiffs sued his executors. The action was dismissed on the ground that "no stranger to the consideration can take advantage of a contract, although made for his benefit".[199]

Furthermore, in *Dunlop v. Selfridge,*[200] the plaintiffs sold a number of their tyres to Dew & Co., described as "motor accessory factors," on the terms that Dew & Co. would not resell them below scheduled prices and that, in the event of a sale to trade customers, they would extract from the latter a similar undertaking. Dew & Co. sold the tyres to Selfridge, who agreed to observe the restrictions and to pay Messrs Dunlop the sum of Five Pounds for each tyre sold in breach of this agreement. Selfridge in fact supplied tyres to two of their own customers below the listed price. Dunlop sued to recover two sums of Five pounds each as liquidated damages and asked for an injunction to restrain further breaches of the agreement. The action was resisted on the ground that Dunlop were not a party to the contract and had furnished no consideration for the defendants promise. In reply, plaintiffs' Counsel evasively

---

195 *Donoghue v. Stevenson* [1932] A.C. 562. Jolowicz 32 Mod L.R. 1; Pasley 32 Mod. L.R. 241; Leigh-Jones [1969] Camb. L. J. 54

196 *Rookes v. Barnard* [1964] A.C. 1129; [1964] 1 All E.R. 367; Hoffman, 81 L.Q.R. 116

197 (1724) 1 Str. 592

198 (1861) 1 B & S. 393

199 *Ibid.* pp. 397-98. See also the Uganda Case of *Barugahare v. Ntarantambi* [1987] H.C.B. 95 where it was held that the respondent plaintiff had no right to sue on a contract to which she had given no consideration at all.

200 [1915] A.C. 847

pleaded that their clients were in the position of undisclosed principals. The House of Lords decided for the defendants.

While the *Dunlop case* strictly followed the common law, its effect is inconvenient and unjust. Thus it is common for insurance policies to be taken out by one person on behalf of another - a husband for his wife, or a parent for his child. Yet even if the policy expressly confers benefits on the third party, the latter has no claim at common law.[201] This is inconsistent with the needs of modern times and invites the intervention of parliament. Consequently, from time to time statutes have been passed to redress a particular grievance arising from the strict application of the doctrine of privity. In this vein, husband and wife have been enabled to take out life insurance policies in favour of each other or of their children;[202] third parties have been allowed in certain circumstances to sue on marine or fire insurance policies,[203] or on policies. It has been observed that:[204]

> these statutes are only so many isolated exceptions to the general rule of the common law, rendering its operation uncertain, but not impairing its ultimate validity...

The resultant persistent injustice of the rule have led to attempts to induce courts to evade it with considerable success. The application of the doctrine of undisclosed principal is one example,[205] while allowing a beneficiary to sue on a policy of insurance is another.[206] Furthermore, under the rules governing negotiable instruments it has been established first by custom of the law merchant, then by judicial decision and finally by statute[207] that a third party can sue on a bill of exchange or cheque. The usages of trade and commerce have, therefore, contributed to modification of the rigour of the strict application of the common law doctrine. Additionally, where it is clear in a particular case that a commercial practice exists in favour of third party rights and that all litigants have based their relations on it, the court endeavours to support and sanction it.[208]

(iii) Effect of Constructive Trust

With the exception of the areas of law of property and the commercial world (*supra)* few if any exceptions have been permitted at common law to the doctrine of privity. Litigants have, therefore, sought the assistance of equity. Thus in 1753 Lord Hardwicke indicated the possibilities of the trust as a way out. He was prepared, in a case where A promised B to pay money to C to regard B as a trustee for C of the benefit of the contract.[209] In *Gregory and Parker v. Williams*,[210] Parker owed money both to Gregory and to Williams. He agreed with Williams to assign to him the whole of his property, if Williams would pay the debt due to Gregory. The property was duly assigned, but Williams failed to implement his promise. Gregory and Parker filed a

---

201 *Cleaver v. Mutual Reserve Fund Life Association* 1892] 1 Q.B. 147, 152; *M/S Peter S.S. Kirumira Oil Millers Industry v. Uganda American Insurance Co. Ltd.* [1976] H.C.B. 54

202 Married Women's Properties Act, 1882, S.11 (U.K.)

203 Marine Insurance Act 1906 S.14(2) (U.K.); Motor Vehicle Insurance (Third Party Risks) Statute, 1988 as amended by Statute No.5 of 1991 (Uganda), Traffic & Road Safety Act, 1970

204 Cheshire, Fifoot & Furmston's *Law of Contract* (12th Ed 1991) P.454

205 See *infra* Chap.12

206 *supra* notes 16, 17; *P. Samuel & Co. v. Dumas* [1923] 1 K.B.592; [1924] A.C. 431; *Hepburn V. A. Tomlinson (Hauliers) Ltd.* [1966] A.C. 451; [1966] 1 All E.R. 418

207 Bills of Exchange Act, Cap.76, S.29. See also discussion *infra* Chap.13.

208 *United Dominions Trust Ltd. v. Kirkwood* [1966] 2 Q.B. 431, 454 - 455; [1966] 1 All E.R. 968, 980 per Lord Denning M.R.

209 *Tomlinson v. Gill* (1756) Amb. 330; Corbin, 46 L.Q.R. 12; Williams 7 M.L.R.123

210 (1817) 3 Mer. 582

bill in equity to compel performance of the promise and succeeded. Sir William Grant held that Parker must be regarded as trustee for Gregory, and that the latter "derived an equitable right through the mediation of Parker's agreement." In Britain, after the Judicature Act 1873, the propriety of the device was affirmed and its use sanctioned in any division of the High Court. Thus in *Lloyd's v. Harper*, Lush L. J. stated:[211]

> I consider it to be an established rule of law that where a contract is made with A for the benefit of B, A can sue on the contract for the benefit of B and recover all that B could have recovered if the contract had been made with B himself

Implicit in this statement is the view that if A fails in his duty, B, the beneficiary under the implied trust, may successfully maintain an action to which A and the other contracting party are joint defendants.

In the Ugandan context, it is notable that the rules of common law and equity are administered concurrently,[212] thereby importing for purposes of modifying the privity doctrine, the constructive trust concept.

Equitable intervention has also been applied to a charterparty. Thus in *Walford's Case*,[213] Walford, as broker had negotiated a charterparty between the owners of the SS Flore and the Lubricating and Fuel Oils C. Ltd. By a clause in the charterparty the owners promised the charterers to pay Walford a commission of 3 per cent on the estimated gross amount of hire. Walford brought an action against the owners to obtain this commission. The charterers were not joined to the action, but, when Walford applied to join them as such, the owners agreed to raise no objection and the action proceeded as if they had in fact been joined. The House of Lords affirmed the judgment in Walford's favour. Lord Birkenhead considered previous decisions and declared that "in such cases charterers can sue as trustees on behalf of the broker."[214]

However, the device of the trust has in practice proved a disappointing and unreliable instrument. Thus in *Re Schebsman*,[215] S was employed by two companies. By a contract made between him and them, one of the companies agreed in certain eventualities to pay Five Thousand and Five Hundred Pounds to his widow and daughter. It was held that the contract did not create a trust in favour of the widow and daughter on the ground that there was no intention to create a trust. No such intention could be gathered from the language used and the circumstances of the case. To hold that there was a trust would be to undermine the parties common law right to vary consensually the terms of the obligation undertaken by the company.

It may be concluded that while the application of the trust concept to mitigate the rigours of the common law rule looked at one time to be promising the last fifty years in Britain have shown that, "without locking the door, the Courts have consistently failed to open it."[216] The result is that a trust will not now be inferred simply because A and B make a contract with the intention of benefiting C. Strong indicators for holding that a trust exists have been required.[217] This has resulted from the view that the trust was a "cumbrous fiction";[218] an insistence that intention to create a trust be affirmatively proved and a concern lest the irrevocable nature of the trust should prevent the contracting parties from changing their minds.[219]

---

211 (1880) 16 Ch.D. 290 at 321; *Flavell Murray v. Flavell* (1883) 25 Ch.D.89

212 Judicature Act, 1967, S.3(2) (b)

213 *Les Affre'iturs Reu'nis SA v. Walford* [1919] A.C. 801

214 See also Maitland, *Equity*, p.44

215 [1944] Ch.83; [1943] 2 All E.R. 768. See also *Green v. Russel* [1959] 2 All E.R. 525; [1959] 2 Q.B. 226. Furmston 23 Mod. L.R. 373, 377 - 385.

216 Cheshire, Fifoot & Furmston, *op.cit.. supra.* n.18, p.457

217 *Re Webb* [1941] Ch.225; [1941] 1 All E.R. 321. *Re Forster Clark's Indenture Trusts* [1966] 1 All E.R. 321; [1966] 1 W.L.R. 125

218 Lord Wright, 55 LQR 189, 208

219 *Re Schebsman, supra,* n.215. c.f. *Wilson v. Darling Island Stevedoring & Lighterage Co.* (1956) C.L:R. 43, 67 per Fullager J.

(b) Imposition of contractual obligations on strangers

While the doctrine of privity prevents a third party beneficiary from suing on a contract, it, by the same logic, forbids the contracting parties to enforce obligations against a stranger. Put simply, a contract between A and B cannot impose a liability upon C.

The rule was found to be inconvenient in cases of contracts concerning land and this was rectified by allowing covenants on the original contract to run with the land.[220] Secondly, the rule was modified by equity which dealt with the issue of whether a restrictive covenant, voluntarily accepted by the purchaser of land as part of the contract of sale, bound persons who later acquire the land. Thus in *Tulk v. Moxhay*,[221] the plaintiff, the owner of several plots of land in Leicester Square, sold the garden in the centre to one Elus, who agreed not to build upon it but to preserve it in existing condition. After a number of conveyances the garden was sold to the defendant Moxhay, who, though he knew of the restriction, proposed to build. The plaintiff, accepting his inability at common law to recover damages from one who was not a party to the contract, sought an injunction against the erection of the proposed buildings. The injunction was granted. The decisive factor in the view of the Court was the knowledge by the defendant of the existence of the covenant. Consequently, a court of equity, being a court of conscience could not permit him to disregard a contractual obligation affecting the land of which he had notice at the time of his purchase. This established the doctrine that a restrictive covenant, binding a purchaser not to perform certain acts of ownership upon the land bought, may be enforced, not only against him as the contracting party but also against third parties who later acquire the land. It is notable that the liability of the third party ceased to be based exclusively on notice. Something more than mere notice by the third party of the existence of the covenant is necessary to render him liable. Particularly, it is essential that the covenantee or original vendor, should have retained other land in the neighbourhood for the benefit and protection of which the restrictive covenant was taken. Thus if an owner sells only a portion of his property, the selling value of what he retains will often depreciate unless restrictions are placed upon the enjoyment of the part sold, and it is only where the covenantee has retained land capable of being benefited in this way that equity enforces a restrictive covenant against a third party.[222]

The issue arises as to whether the equitable doctrine can be applied where the subject-matter of the contract is property other than land.[223] Two situations present themselves in trying to tackle this issue.[224] First, attempts to enforce against third parties restrictions upon the use of goods. Second, attempts to enforce against third parties restrictions upon the price at which goods may be resold.

(i) Restrictions upon use

Tulk v. Moxhay[225] enforced a restriction upon use. The propriety of a similar restriction was considered relative to a ship in *De Mattos v. Gibson*.[226] In that Case, A chartered a ship from X. During the currency of the charterparty, X mortgaged the ship to B, who knew at the time that this charterparty existed. A alleged that B now threatened, as mortgagee, to sell the ship in disregard of his contract rights and he applied for an interlocutory injunction to restrain B from doing so. The application was refused by Vice-Chancellor Wood, but allowed on appeal by Knight-Bruce & Turner LJJ. Knight Bruce L. J. thus observed:[227]

---

220 *supra* notes 5 and 6 and text thereof

221 (1848) 2 Ph.774

222 *Formiby v. Baker* [1903] 2 Ch.539; *LCC v. Allen* [1914] 3 K.B. 642

223 Gardener 98 LQR 279

224 Formulated by Wade 44 L.Q.R. 51

225 *supra* n.35

226 (1858) 4 De G & J 276

227 *Ibid.* p.282

> Reason and justice seem to prescribe that, at least as a general rule, where a man by gift or purchase, acquires property from another, with knowledge of a previous contract, lawfully and for valuable consideration made y him with a third person, to use and employ the property for a particular purpose in a specified manner, the acquirer shall not, to the material damage of the third person, in opposition to the contract and inconsistently with it, use and employ the property in a manner not allowable to the giver or seller.

The case was remitted back to Wood V.C. for the cause to be heard. Wood V. C. disallowed the application and was upheld by the Lord Chancellor, Lord Chelmsford. The Plaintiff's application, thereby failed. Lord chelmsford stressed that his decision was based on the finding that the defendant had not in fact interfered with the performance of the charterparty. Had he done so an injunction might well have been granted.

Subsequently, in *Messageries Imperiales Co. v. Baines*,[228] the plaintiff had chartered a ship to the defendant who knew at the time of the existence of the charter but declined to allow the ship to fulfil the charter obligations. Wood V. C. was constrained by the observations of his brothers in the superior Courts and granted the injunction requested by the plaintiff.

It is notable that for the next fifty years the assertion by Lord Justice Knight Bruce[229] was cited from time to time. However, in 1914, the Court of Appeal refused to accept it as offering a catholic principle upon which it was safe to depend. In *LCC v. Allen* it was thus observed:[230]

> Notwithstanding what was said by Knight Bruce L J in De Mattos v. Gibson, it is not true as a general proposition that a purchaser of property with notice of a restrictive covenant affecting the property is bound by the covenant.

However, the Judicial Committee of the Privy Council took a different view in the Canadian case, *Lord Strathcona SS Co. v. Dominion Coal Co.*[231] In that case, B, the owner of the steamer, *Lord Strathcona,* chartered her to A on the terms that, for a period of years, A should be free to use her on the St. Lawrence river for the summer season and should surrender her to B in November of each year. During the currency of the charterparty, but while the ship was in B's possession, B sold and delivered her to C, who in turn resold her to D. D, though he knew of the charterparty, refused to deliver the ship to A for the summer season. A obtained an injunction against D in the courts of Nova Scotia restraining him from using the ship in any way inconsistent with the charterparty and D's appeal to the Privy Council was dismissed. The Privy Council quoted with approval the words of Knight Bruce L.J.[232] The advice of the Judicial Committee has often been interpreted as deciding in effect that the defendant in the case before them was caught by the rule in *Tulk v. Moxhay* because he had bought a ship with notice that she was affected by a restrictive covenant in favour of the plaintiff and was, therefore, in their view in the same position as if he had bought an estate in land with notice of a similar restriction. However, since the case of *De Mattos v. Gibson*[233] the rule in *Tulk v. Moxhay* had been radically developed by the Courts and had ceased to depend solely upon notice. Consequently, a restrictive covenant imposed on land could no longer be enforced against later purchasers unless the original covenantee had retained a proprietary interest in other land for the benefit of which the covenant was taken. In the light of this requirement, the decision in the *Strathcona case* has been described as "indefensible and ... startling".[234] It has also been observed that[235] the interest sought to be enforced in the

---

228 (1863) 7 L.T. 763
229 *Supra* n.227
230 [1914] 3 K.B. 642, 658 - 59. See also *Barker v. Stickney* [1919] 1 K.B 121
231 [1926] A.C. 108
232 *Supra* n.227
233 *Supra* n.226
234 Achike, *Nigerian Law of Contract* (1981) p. 222
235 Cheshire, Fifoot & Furmston, *supra* n.204 p.464

Strathcona case was "not the independent proprietary interest which equity requires in the case of restrictive covenants over land". Furthermore, that in the context of the Case, it was trite law that a charterparty creates no right of property in a ship.[236]

The *Strathcona* decision was challenged in *Port Line Ltd. v. Ben Line Steamers Ltd.*[237] In that Case, the plaintiffs chartered a ship from the owner, for a period of 30 months. The ship was to remain in the owner's possession but to be at the complete disposal of the plaintiffs. In February 1956, the owner sold the ship to the defendants. The defendants immediately chartered it back to the previous owner so that it never ceased to be in his possession. The plaintiffs knew of the sale and acquiesced in it since the ship was to remain available under their own charter. The charter between the previous owner and the defendants contained a clause that "if the ship is requisitioned, the charter shall thereupon cease." There was no such clause in the plaintiff's charter. The defendants, when they bought the ship, knew of the existence of the plaintiff's charter but not of its terms. In August 1956 the Ministry of Transport requisitioned the ship and paid compensation to the defendants as owners. In November 1956, the requisition ended. The plaintiffs sued the defendants to obtain the compensation received by the defendants from the requisition. They relied on the *Strathcona Case* and the dictum in *De Mattos v. Gibson.*[238] Diplock J found for the defendants and felt that the *Strathcona* Case was not good law because it was essential to have some proprietary interest to support a claim based on *Tulk v. Moxhay* which was missing in the *Strathcona Case*. Second, even if *Strathcona* could be supported in principle, the facts before him did not fall within its scope because the defendants, when they bought the ship, had no actual knowledge of the plaintiff's rights and although they knew that a charter existed, they did not know its terms. Furthermore, they were not in breach of duty and it was not their act but by the act of the Crown that the ship had been used inconsistently with the plaintiff's charter. Third, that the only remedy possible under the doctrine of *Tulk v. Moxhay* and consequently the *Strathcona Case* was the grant of an injunction. No damages or money compensation could be obtained.

However, in the subsequent case of *Swiss Bank Corpn. v. Lloyds Bank Ltd.*,[239] Browne-Wilkinson J thought both *De Mattos v. Gibson* and the *Strathcona Case* correctly decided, although he found some of the reasoning in *Strathcona* difficult to follow. He proffered two additional lines of reasoning in addition to the restrictive covenant one. First, that a purchaser who takes expressly subject to the terms of an earlier contract as to the use of the property may be held to be a constructive trustee.[240] Secondly he felt that the granting of the injunction in *De Mattos v. Gibson*[241] was the "counterpart in equity of the tort of knowing interference with contractual rights."[242]

It has been observed[243] that "the discussion of the application of real property analogies to personal property has concentrated on restrictive covenants to the exclusion of other interests, perhaps more readily applicable to chattels" In this vein it has been remarked that:

> ... an option to purchase land creates an equitable interest in the land capable of being enforced against the purchaser of the land[244] ... there is authority for the

---

236 *Federated Coal & Shipping Co. v. R.* [1922] 2 K.B.42, 46 per Bailhache J.

237 [1958] 2 Q.B. 146; [1958] 1 All E.R. 787

238 *Supra* n.227

239 [1979] Ch.548; [1979] 2 All E.R. 853

240 Se also *Binnions v. Evans* [1972] Ch.359; [1972] All E.R.70

241 *Supra* n.226

242 [1979] Ch.548, 575; [1979] 2 All E.R. 853 at 874. See also *Sefton v. Tophams* [1965] Ch.1140; [1965] 3 All E.R.1

243 Cheshire, Fifoot & Furmston, *supra* n.204, p.465

244 *London & South Western Rlwy Co. v. Gomm* (1882) 20 Ch.D.562.

> application of the same principle to options to purchase chattels and choses in action, such as copyrights.[245]

An issue of practical concern, is whether a contract under which possession of a chattel is transferred for a fixed term creates property rights similar to a lease. This was resolved by Holdsworth's postulation thus:[246]

> it is obvious that if A let or pledged his chattel to B and has transferred its possession to B and if he then sells it to C, C can only take it subject to B's legal rights, and since they are legal rights whether C has notice of those rights or not.

(ii) Restrictions price

The issue arises as to whether a price restriction can be enforced against a third party. In *Taddy v. Sterious,*[247] the plaintiffs were manufacturers of "Myrtle Grove" tobacco. They sought to prevent retailers from selling it below a minimum price. They attached to each packet a printed sheet, stating that the tobacco was sold "on the express condition that retail dealers do not sell it below the prices above set forth" and adding that "acceptance of the goods will be deemed a contract between the purchaser and Messrs Taddy & Co. that he will observe these stipulations. In the case of a purchase by a retail dealer through a wholesale dealer, the latter shall be deemed to be the agent of Taddy & Co." The plaintiffs sold tobacco under these conditions to Messrs Nutter, wholesale dealers, who resold it to the defendants retail tobacconists. The defendants, despite having notice of the conditions, resold below the minimum price. The plaintiffs sued for a declaration that the defendants were bound by the conditions. They based their claim on two premises. First, that the printed sheet constituted a contract between themselves and the defendants and that Messrs Nutter were their agents. The Court dismissed this attempt to create a contract by ultimatum. There was no contract between Taddy and Sterious, Messrs Nutter were not Taddy's agents and no unilateral declaration, however peremptory, could alter the legal position. Second, the plaintiffs requested the Court to extend to them the protection of the rule in *Tulk v. Moxhay*. This was summarily rejected. As put by Swinfen Eady J.:

> Conditions of this kind do not run with goods and cannot be imposed upon them. Subsequent purchasers, therefore, do not take subject to any conditions which the Court can enforce.

Another attempt to enforce a price restriction against a third party were similarly and uncompromisingly rejected by the Court in the same year.[248]

3. Proposals for reform

The doctrine of privity of contract to the effect that no one apart from a party to the contract can enforce it may cause inconvenience by preventing a person most interested in the contract from enforcing it.[249] While the many exceptions to it make it tolerable in practice, these have in turn ›voked the question of whether it is not preferable to modify the doctrine or abolish it altoge.. ›r.

---

245 *Falcke v. Gray* (1859) 4 Drew 651; *MacDonald v. Eyles* [1921] 1 Ch. 631

246 49 L.Q.R. 576, 579

247 [1904] 1 Ch. 354

248 *McGruther v. Pitcher* [1904] 2 Ch. 306

249 as was the case in the *Dunlop Pneumatic Tyre Co. Case, supra* n.200

In Britain in 1937, the Law Revision Committee recommended[250] that:

> Where a contract by its express terms purports to confer a benefit directly on a third party it shall be enforceable by the third party in his own name subject to any defences that would have been valid between the contracting parties.

Furthermore, to deal with the difficulty that this might unreasonably restrict the freedom of the contracting party to vary the contract[251] the Committee added that:

> Unless the contract otherwise provides, it may be cancelled by the mutual consent of the contracting parties before the third party has adopted it either expressly or by conduct.

The law Revision Committee's proposal has been criticised on the ground that it does not go far enough. There are cases in which it is arguable that the third party's rights should not be subject to the contracting parties right of cancellation, such as where an insurance policy is taken out for the benefit of a third party. The third party should at least receive notice of cancellation. Furthermore, the recommendation appears not to affect the law as to exemption clauses and third parties which is in need of clarification.[252]

---

250 6th Interim Report (Cmnd.5449), Section D, partly adopted in the Republic of Ireland; see Dowrick 21 Mod. L.Rev. 98. See also New Zealand Contract (Privity) Act, 1982.

251 as was the case in *Re Schebsman, supra* n.215

252 Treitel, *Law of Contract* (8th Edn. 1991), pp.552 - 561, 575

12
AGENCY

1. Purpose of agency

In most cases, especially in business transactions, it is impossible for a businessman to make contracts alone and individually. He therefore, employs agents to make contracts on his behalf. Alternatively, a businessman may engage other persons as partners in the business. The result is that each partner becomes an agent of the others in running the business of the firm.[253] A third instance in which agency may occur is where business people form a limited liability company by filing documents with the Registrar of Companies. A company registered under the Companies Act[254] is a distinct legal person separate and set apart from its members.[255] Since it is legally a fictitious person, it can only transact business through agents such as its directors and managerial staff.

2. Nature and definition of agency

(a) Definition

Agency may be defined as the relationship which exists whenever one person (the agent) acts on behalf of another person (the principal) and has power to affect the principal's legal position with regard to a third party.

Practically an agent has two principal functions. First to make contracts on behalf of the Principal. Second to dispose of the principal's property. Considering that the agent practically brings his principal into a relationship with third parties, three different relationships may be considered; namely the relationships between a principal and agent; principal and third party and agent and third party. However, before such analysis is undertaken a few preliminary points should be disposed of.

(i) Legal and commercial conception

It is critical to distinguish the legal conception of agency from its commercial understanding. Legally, an agent is a person who acts on behalf of another in his dealings with third parties. Commercially, a "sole agent" may simply be a person who is given the sole selling rights by a particular manufacturer. When such a person contracts with third parties, he does so as a principal. Thus in the English Case of *Lamb (W.T.) & Sons v. Goring Brick Co. Ltd.*[256], the defendants appointed the plaintiffs sole selling agents of their goods for a fixed period. Before the end of that period, they informed the plaintiffs that in future they would sell the goods

[253] Partnership Act, Cap 86, S.7

[254] Cap 85

[255] *Salomon v. Salomon & Co.* [1897] A.C. 22; *Sentamu v. U.C.B.* [1983] H.C.B.59; *Katate v. Nyakatura* (1956) 7 U.L.R. 47; Companies Act, S.16.

[256] [1932] 1 K.B. 710

themselves. If this had been a true agency contract, it would not have prevented the defendants from selling their own goods. It was held that this was a contract giving sole selling rights for a fixed period. The defendant's letter amounted to a breach of contract.

(ii) The authority to Act through an agent

The common law rule is that any person can act through an agent - *qui facit per alium facit perse*, the reason being the obvious one of practical convenience.[257]

An exception to the rule arises where a person occupies a position requiring personal performance or where parties make a contract which expressly or impliedly prohibits delegation to an agent as was the case in *Bevan v. Webb*.[258] Some statutes expressly adopt the common law rule.[259] Other statutes are silent. Where they are silent, there is a presumption in favour of the common law rule.

(iii) Agency distinguished from other relationships

Agents and Trustees

Agents are like trustees in that they both stand in a fiduciary position. This means firstly that they must not make secret profits. Secondly, they must not allow their interests to conflict with their duty. However an agent is different from a trustee in a number of ways. First, a trustee is the legal owner of property, whereas an agent has at most, a legal power to dispose of it. Second, an agent genuinely represents his beneficiaries. Third, the relationship of principal and agent is consensual in origin except in a few cases such as one of necessity. However, a trust, except in minor cases is created without the consent of the beneficiaries (*cestui que trust*). Fourth, an agent is appointed by the principal. The trustee is never appointed by the *cestui que trust*. Fifth, there are many cases where the principal - agent relationship is merely that of creditor and debtor. Hence, an agent who receives a bribe from a third party is under a personal duty to pay it over to his principal, but this does not give the principal any proprietary interest in the bribe nor in any property bought with it.[260]

Agents, servants and independent contractors

The distinction between an agent on the one hand and a servant and independent contractors on the other is one of function. Agents are employed to make contracts to dispose of property. Servants and independent contractors are employed for other tasks. Case law[261] suggests that an agent is a person with greater independence and freedom from control than a servant. In a servant-master relationship, the master at all times controls the execution by the servant of the terms of his employment. Thus while the servant works for his master, an agent acts for and in place of his principal to effect legal relations with a third party. Thus the distinguishing features of an agency relationship are its representatives and derivative authority which give the agent a degree of discretion in executing the terms of his agency which a servant would not have.

An independent contractor renders services to his employer in the course of an independent occupation or calling. He contracts with his employer only as to the results to be achieved not to the means whereby the work is done. Hence, he employs his own means and skill and is entirely independent of control and supervision of his employer. In *Haji Khamisha Juma Essak v. High Commissioner for Transport,*[262] the plaintiff sued to recover certain charges he had paid for storage facilities at Mombasa. He argued that he was not liable for the charges as these had

---

257 *Bevan v. Webb* [1901] 2 Ch.59, 77.

258 *Ibid.*

259 Bills of Exchange Act, Cap.76, S.91; Sale of Goods Act Cap.79, S.59

260 *Lister v. Stubbs* (1890) 45 Ch.D.1

261 *R v. Negus* (1873) L. R. 2 CCR 34 *Hayman v. Flewker* (1863) 13 C.B.; *Baillie v. Goodwin* (1886) 33 Ch.D. 604

262 20 K.L.R.1 (Kenya).

been incurred by two clearing clerks who were not in law his agents but were acting as independent contractors. The Court dismissed the plaintiff's claim. The Court took into account the fact "that they were put into funds by the plaintiff to pay the wharfage charges, they were not the owner of the goods; they were under a duty for which remuneration was payable to clear the plaintiff's goods and to hand them over to the plaintiff. The fact that they did similar work for others at the same time did not make them independent contractors".

Agent and Bailee

A bailee is person who receives possession of goods from (or for) the owner for a specific purpose. The concept of bailment overlaps with agency where the agent receives possession, as in the case of factors and other mercantile agents (for sale only). Many agents (such as brokers and estate agents) are not bailees since they do not receive possession. Conversely, many bailees are not agents since they do not represent their bailors (as in cases of bailees for storage, hire, work and labour.)

The main distinctions between an agent and a bailee are first that whereas an agent represents his principal, a bailee does not become a representative of the bailor. Second, an agent has authority to contract on behalf of the principal and can make him liable in tort. However, a bailee essentially has no authority to bind the bailor in contract except to preserve the bailed property and cannot make the bailor liable in tort.

(b) Nature of agency

(i) Formalities for creation of agency

The principal feature of the agency relation is the agent's power to alter his principal's legal position by making contracts on his behalf or disposing of his property. Such power can arise in three ways. First, by consent; secondly by operation of law and thirdly by the doctrine of apparent authority. Normally an agent's power to bind his principal is consensual; the principal authorises the Agent to do an act on his behalf and he does it. The authority can be express or implied; precedent or subsequent as in the case of ratification.

There are generally two situations where the Principal can be bound by the agent's act even if he did not consent to it. These are through agency of necessity and agency arising through apparent authority (i.e. authority which appears to the public to exist)

(ii) Appointment of Agent

The general rule is that no formalities are required for the appointment of an agent. The relationship between the principal and agent may be by word of mouth, conduct or in writing.[263] An agent appointed to execute a deed on the sale of land must be appointed by deed or what is commonly called a power of attorney.[264] In *Alexander Logios v. A-G Nigeria*[265] it was observed by Webb C.J. that:

> it was settled that an agent may be appointed or his authority conferred by word of mouth save only where he is appointed to execute an instrument under seal on behalf of his principal.

In *Stevens v. Biller*[266], there was no clearly defined contract either with a factor or the defendant. At first, the plaintiffs made cash advances to the factor and the factor instructed the defendant to buy cotton for the plaintiffs. In 1956, the plaintiffs started paying advances direct to the defendant. The plaintiffs claimed for amounts outstanding upon a stated account. The defendant

---

263 *Pole v. Leask* (1863) 33 L.J. Ch. 155, 161-162

264 per Agbaje J. in *Attorney General of Western State of Nigeria v. Ogundana* [1970] N.C.L.R. 131 at p.135.5

265 4 W.A.C.A. 162

266 (1884) 25 Ch.D. 31

alleged that he was a sub-agent of the factor and not agent of the plaintiffs. The defendant counter-claimed for his commission and expenses. It was held that the relationship between the plaintiffs and the factor, and factor and defendant was that of principal and agent and sub agent respectively. Secondly that there was no privity of contract between the principal and sub-agent. Consequently, the plaintiff's claim failed.

The case shows that the agreement constituting the agency relationship need not be in writing. A proven oral agreement is sufficient. Furthermore, where the terms of the oral agreement are not clear, evidence of subsequent dealing between the parties may be admitted as a term of such agreement.

(ii) Capacity to appoint agents

Infants

A minor or an infant cannot appoint an agent to dispose of property so as to bind him irrevocably.[267] It has also been held that a minor cannot give a valid power of attorney unless a minor is a married woman.[268] However, a minor can appoint an agent to make a contract which would have bound him if he had made it personally as in the case of necessaries.[269]

Persons of unsound mind

The general rule is that where a party to the contract is of unsound mind, the contract is still binding on him unless he can prove that he was so insane as not to know what he was doing and this was known to the other party.[270] In *Yong v. Toynbee*,[271] the insanity of the principal was held to terminate his agent's authority automatically although the agent was unaware of the insanity.

It should be observed that since the agent was a mere link between the contracting parties, he need not have full contractual capacity[272] and would be immune from any action that would normally be successful against an adult agent.

Companies

Companies can be appointed as agents of individuals or of other companies. No special formalities are required to achieve this end. Thus in *Lwajali Coffee Growers Ltd. v. Leslie & Anderson (E.A.) Ltd., Mackenzie & O'Neill*[273], the plaintiff company had appointed the first defendant company as their agents for selling coffee. Various financial difficulties arose and the plaintiffs claimed an agreement whereby the first defendants had been appointed as managing agents of their affairs by the second and third defendants was not binding as it had not been made in writing. The Court rejected this argument and explained that for practical reasons such contracts need not be in writing.

(iii) Consideration

Although the general law of contract requires the existence of consideration for a valid contract, agency may be gratuitous. In other words the principal need not pay any remuneration to the agent. An example is where a wife buys goods on the husband's behalf.

(iv) Ratification

An agency relationship can be created by ratification. This means that an agent does an act without the principal's authority but on his behalf. If the principal adopts the act, this is called ratification. Ratification is retrospective in effect.[274]

---

267 *G v G* [1970] Q.B. 643, 652

268 *Ibid.*

269 Webbs 18 M.L.R. 861; R.E.M. 69 L.Q.R. 446

270 *Imperial Loan Co. v. Stone* [1892] 1 Q.B. 599

271 [1910] 1 K.B. 215

272 *Stevenson v. Hardie* (1773) 2 Wm Bl.872; Treitel, *Law of Contract* (8th Edn. 1991) p.612.

273 1967 (1) A.L.R. Comm. 323

274 discussed in more detail *infra* under Agent's Authority.

(b) Duties of an agent

(i) Obedience

Where an agent is carrying out the terms of the agency, he is obliged to carry out instructions from the principal. If he fails to do so, he is liable in damages to the principal. Thus in *Fraser v. B.N. Furman (Productions) Ltd.*,[275] the plaintiff obtained damages for personal injuries from employers. The employers claimed indemnity from a broker who had agreed to effect an employer's liability policy but had failed to do so. It was held that the employers were entitled to indemnity.

An agent is also required to stay within the limits of his instructions. Thus in *Bertram Armstrong & Co. v. Godfrey*,[276] A was instructed to sell stock when valued at Eighty five pounds or above that price. The price came up to Eighty five pounds, but A failed to sell the stock. It was held that the agent had no general discretion to wait for a higher price and was liable for not having sold as instructed.

However, an agent will not be liable if the instructions are illegal or void,[277] ambiguous[278] or the agent is a professional agent whose instructions are subject to the customs or usage of a particular trade.

(ii) Care and Skill

A gratuitous agent is only bound to show the skill and care which he in fact possesses[279] and would be liable only where he commits an act of gross negligence.[280] On the other hand, a paid agent must show the degree of skill which an agent in his position usually shows. Such a distinction has been doubted[281] and it has been suggested that the basic principle is that a person professing a particular calling must show the degree of skill necessary for that calling.[282] In *Olatunji Omotayo v. A. Y. Ojikutu*, [283] the appellant and respondent were general traders and members of a syndicate in Lagos. The appellant visited London where he acted as agent for the respondent for purchase of some motor trucks. Following a contract negotiated by the appellant on behalf of the respondent, the latter suffered financial loss. He sued the appellant to recover the loss alleging that the appellant had been negligent in negotiating the contract. It was held by the Privy Council that a principal who appoints an agent knowing his skill and experience is not entitled to expect or require from the agent a higher measure of skill or knowledge than one of his position and experience could reasonably be expected to possess. Furthermore, an agent is not required to ensure successful outcome of the transaction undertaken on behalf of the principal. All that is required of him is honesty and measure of skill and diligence expected of his position and experience. The care and skill is judged on particular facts and circumstances. In this instance, the plaintiff knew the defendant as a general trader in Lagos, fellow member of a syndicate and a produce dealer with no special qualification as a motor-dealer. Consequently, he could only expect from the defendant only the skill and care and knowledge reasonably possessed by the defendant. Similarly in *Spiropolous Co. Ltd v. Nigeria Rubber & Co. Ltd. & Anors,*[284] it was held that the prudence which an agent is expected to show in the affairs of his

---

275 [1967] 3 All E.R. 57. See also *Otto Hamman v. Alade Senbanjo & Anors* [1962] 2 All N.L.R. 139

276 (1830) 1 Knapp 381, P.C.

277 *Cohen v. Kittel* (1889) 22 Q.B.D. 680 (betting)

278 *Ireland v. Livingstone* (1872) L.R.H.L.; *Pariente v. Lubbock* (1856) 8 DeGM & G 5

279 *Otto Haman* Case, *supra* n.215; *Davis v. Tooth Co. Ltd.* [1937] 4 All E.R. 118, 128

280 *Coggs v. Bernard* (1703) 2 L.d. Raym 999; (1558 - 1774) All E.R. Rep. 1; *Wilkinson v. Coverdale* (1793) 1 Esp. 74; [1775 - 1802] All E.R. Rep.339

281 *Houghland v. R. Low (Luxury Coaches) Ltd.* [1963] 1 Q.B. 694; [1962] 2 All E.R. 159

282 *Grill v. General Iron Screw Collier Co.* (1866) L.R.1

283 [1961] All N.L.R. 901 (Nigeria)

284 1970 N.C.L.R. 94 (Nigeria)

principal requires that the agent should not involve his principal in heavier financial burden where he could lessen the burden. The insurance policy should in this case have been effected at an economic rate.

The Kenyan case, *Marianne Winther v. Arbon Langrish & Southern Ltd.*[285] shows what skill a professional agent must exercise. An insurance broker wrote to a policy holder suggesting a discussion concerning the renewal of an aircraft policy and a personal accident policy. The wife of the policy holder called at the brokers' and asked for both policies to be renewed with Lloyds Underwriters. Through some misunderstanding on the part of the broker the personal accident policy was not renewed. The husband was later killed in a plane crash and the wife lost Two Thousand pounds that would have been paid had the policy been renewed. She sued the broker for breach of duty of care. The Court held[286] in her favour on the ground that the broker possessed special skill and experience in the matter of aircraft insurance and in his dealings in this matter must be assumed to have undertaken to apply that skill and experience for the benefit and assistance of the plaintiff. This case may be contrasted with *Uttamchand & Co Ltd. v. F. J. Hawkers & Co. Ltd.*,[287] where P employed A to buy 1,920 yards of material in England. This was done but owing to the scarcity of shipping space, the material could not be dispatched for five months. When that time arrived P purported to cancel the order arguing that A had exceeded the deadline for buying the material by two days; also he had purchased fifty three yards too much. The Court held that A had acted with reasonable skill and diligence in the circumstances.

(iii) Personal performance

An agent must perform personally and is not permitted to delegate his duties except with express permission or unless such can be implied from that trade or business in which the agent is engaged, or where in the course of employment the agent finds that he has to delegate.[288]

The agent may also delegate where the act required to be done is ministerial and does not require the Agent's skill and discretion as in the case of signature on his behalf.[289]

(iv) To Act in good faith

An agent stands in a fiduciary position to the principal, must act in good faith and should not allow his interest to conflict with his duty. If he takes a bribe he is liable to account for it to the principal.[290]

In the Nigerian case of *Igben & Oke v. Etawarie*,[291] the High Court of Benin held that it was a rule of general application that an agent should not be allowed to enter agreements in which he has, or can have a personal interest conflicting with that of his principal. This was positive law and not a principle of morality.

Where an agent makes a secret profit, he must disclose and account for it to the principal. Thus in *I. T. Palmer of Nigeria Ltd. v. Julie Fonseca*,[292] the plaintiff was an owner of rubber estates. It employed the defendant as a manager to sell rubber and was to be paid an agreed salary and commission. The defendant made an agreement with a firm by which she was to receive an additional commission from the firm to which she was selling the rubber. It was

---

285 [1966] E.A. 292

286 applying *Candler v. Crane Christmas Co.* [1951] 2 K.B. 164 per Denning L.J. (dissenting)which was approved in *Hedley Byrne & Co. Ltd. v. Heller & Partners Ltd.* [1963] 2 All E.R. 575

287 (1955) 22 E.A.C.A. 197

288 *De Bussche v. Alt* (1878) 8 Ch.D. 286; [1874-80] All E.R. Rep 1247

289 *Marsh v. Joseph* [1897] 1 Ch.213; *Allan v. Europa Poster Services* [1968] 1 All E.R. 826.

290 *Cook v. Deeks* [1916] A.C. 240 (Company Directors); *Gluckstein v. Barnes* [1900] A.C.554 (Promoters).

291 [1971] 1 N.C.L.R. 85. See also *Boardman v. Phipps* [1967] 2 A.C. 46

292 [1946] 4 N.L.R. 49

held that the plaintiff was entitled to recover from the defendant the secret commission. This case may be contrasted with *Ramzanali H. Ebrahim v. Astridger,*[293] where P wished to sell three plots of land at Bamburi. P asked X an advocate, to find a purchaser and X put the matter in the hands of A, A buyer was found and negotiations took place between the buyer and X and a price agreed upon and a deposit paid. Afterwards, the buyer returned and on A's prompting gave X Shs.2,000/=. X told P what had happened and advised her that in his opinion, the Shs.2,000/= was an illegal consideration and that she should rescind the contract if she wished. This was not done and the transaction was completed. P however refused to pay A the commission and expenses incurred by A. The Court indicated that the critical issue was whether the sum had been paid "in effecting such sale corruptly and secretly". Connell J. decided that the Shs.2,000/= had not been paid to effect "such sale" and A was entitled to his commission since there was no fraud.[294]

An agent is also required to disclose to the principal any opportunity or information which he comes across in his position as agent. It has been held by the British House of Lords that[295] an agent is liable if he makes use of information or knowledge acquired in his capacity as agent for the principal. Mere use of the information, will not, however make the agent liable.[296] The information must be useful to the principal.[297]

The duty to act in good faith further requires that an agent must act *bona fide* in the interest of the principal. He should also not allow his interest to conflict with his duty. Where this is likely to happen, then he must disclose the fact to the principal. If he does not disclose any profit made out of the transaction this must be accounted for. Thus in *Hippisley v. Knee Brothers,*[298] the principal appointed an auctioneer to sell goods and agreed to pay the auctioneer's advertising and printing expenses. The auctioneer charged the full price of these items to the principal without disclosing that he had received certain trade discounts. It was held that he must account for the difference.

It is notable that a secret profit may cover a bribe, although a distinction exists between the two. A secret profit is profit made by the agent without the connivance of the other party to the transaction. A bribe, on the other hand, is a profit made with the connivance of the other party to the transaction. The rationale for the distinction is that an agent who receives a bribe cannot claim a commission, whereas one who receives a secret profit, can claim a commission on the transaction. In *Hippisley case,*[299] the agent was allowed to claim his commission although he was in breach of duty in making a secret profit for which he had to account.

Furthermore, if an agent performs several acts, some of which are unlawful he may still be entitled, to a commission if the acts can be separated or severed. Thus in *Nitedals Taendstikfabrik v. Bruster,*[300] a principal appointed an agent to sell his goods. The agent did so. However, in breach of contract, he sold goods to the principal's competitors. In an action by the agent for the commission; it was held the agent's acts were severable. Consequently, the agent was entitled to the commission on sales for the principal but had to account for all the profit made on other sales.

---

293 25 K.L.R. 29 (Kenya)

294 relying on *Hippsley v. Knee* [1905] 1 K.B.1 per Lord Alverstone, C.J.

295 *Regal (Hastings) Ltd. v. Gulliver* [1942] 1 All E.R. 378

296 *Thomas Marshall (Exporters) Ltd. v. Guinle* [1979] 1 Ch.227

297 *Igben & Oke Case, supra* n.291

298 *supra* n.294. See also *Ramazanali case, supra n.293*

299 *supra* n.294, 298

300 [1906] 2 Ch.671

The liability to account may extend to the agent's acts even if they are unconnected with his duties. Thus in *Reading v. A-G,*[301] a Sergeant in the British Army in Egypt agreed to accompany lorries carrying illicit spirits. Since he was in uniform, the vehicles would not be searched. He was paid Twenty Thousand pounds for this service. It was held that since he had made this profit through use of his position, he was bound to account to his employer for the money paid to him.

Other instances where the agent will be required to account is where, he sells to himself without full disclosure;[302] he acts for the purchaser;[303] he buys for himself without full disclosure in his capacity as agent;[304] he makes use of confidential information or for his own benefit by compiling a list of his principal's customer.[305] An agent can, however, sell property to his principal on making full disclosure of material fact. The relationship then becomes that of vendor and purchaser.[306]

The duty of good faith does not automatically end with the termination of the agency. It may continue even after termination.[307]

(v) Duty to account

An agent is under a duty to keep and render appropriate account of his stewardship to his principal. This means that he must pay over to the principal all sums received by him for the use of the principal. The agent must do this even if the transaction giving rise to the payment is illegal or void,[308] although he need not do so if the contract of agency is illegal.[309]

In the Nigerian case, *Akibola v. Neburagho*[310], the plaintiff was a proprietress of a nursery school in Warri. When she went overseas for further studies, she left the management of the school to the defendant. In her absence the defendant failed or neglected to communicate with her and demands by her of an account of the state of her business were ignored. It was held that she was entitled to an account of the management of her business from the defendant on her return overseas.

The obligation by the agent to account to the principal entail the following. First, he must keep proper account of all his dealings and transactions in the course of execution of the agency. Second, he must make available to the principal or any other person appointed by the principal all books and documents in his custody relating to the agency. Third, he should keep any money or property of his principal separate from his own and from other persons. If he mixes the property then he is liable to the principal for everything in the mixture which he could not prove to be his own. Fourth, he must pay money and property held on behalf of the principal to the principal regardless of third party claims. In other words, the agent is estopped from denying the title of the principal to any property or money which is the subject of the agency.

In the Nigerian case, *Akande v. Akande*[311], the plaintiff (respondent) claimed from the defendant (appellant) an account for plots or parcels of land out of Ajanla family land sold by

---

301 [1951] 1. All E.R. 617. See also *Abbey Glen Property Corp v. Stamborg* (1978) 85 D.L.R. (3rd) 35; *Industrial Development Consultants v. Cooley* [1972] 2 All E.R. 162.

302 *De Bussche v. Alt supra* n.288

303 *Fullwood v. Hurley* [1928] 1 K.B. 498

304 *Armstrong v. Jackson* [1916 - 17] All E.R. 1117

305 *Lamb v. Evans* [1893] 1 Ch.318. See also *Thomas Marshall Case, supra,* n.296

306 *Regier v. Campbell - Stuart* [1939] 3 All E.R. 235

307 *Thomas Marshal case , supra* n.296; *Industrial Development Consultants Case, supra* n.301; *Canadian Aero Services v. O'malley* [1974] 40 D.L.R. (3d) 371

308 *De Mattos v. Benjamin* (1894) 63 L.J.Q.B. 248

309 *Harry Parker Ltd. v. Mason* [1940] 2 K.B. 590; [1940] 4 All E.R. 199

310 High Court of Warri Suit No. W 171/74 Decided 26 January 1977.

311 [1967] N.M.L.R. 96. See also *Misr (Nig) Ltd. v. Mallam Yusuf Ibrahim* [1974] S.C. 55

the defendants and an account of money had and received from the then Western Nigerian Government by the defendants for portions of Ajanla land acquired by Government. The first defendant was head of the Ajanla family. The trial court held that the third defendant (appellant) was at all times the agent of the first defendant and he acted in that capacity. However the third defendant was accountable to the first defendant. On appeal, the issue was whether the third defendant (appellant) was accountable to other members of Ajanla family. The Appeal Court held that he was not an agent of other members of the Ajanla family and was not liable to repay money which he had received for the use of the plaintiff. Accordingly the order against the third defendant to account to the plaintiff was unjustified both in English and Customary law.

(vi) Remedies of Principal for Agent's Breach of Duty

Where the agency is contractual, the principal can sue the agent for damages for breach of contract. If the agent commits a tort (as in the case where he refuses to return the principal's property or obtains a bribe from a third party), the principal can sue him for damages in tort. If the agent has received a bribe, secret profit or money for the principal the principal can sue the agent for money had and received or for an account.[312] In *T. Maheson S/O Thambriah v. Malaysian Govt. Officers' Housing Society,*[313] T was an employee and director of the respondent. A third party bought land for M $456,000 with the connivance of T, spent $45,000 on it and then sold it to the respondent for $944,000. He then paid T a bribe of $122,000. The common law and equitable principles apply in Malaysia in the same way they apply in England. R claimed from T the amount of the bribe and damages of Four Hundred and Eighty Eight Thousand pounds (third party's profit on the sale disregarding the bribe and expenses). The Malaysian Federal Court upheld both claims but reduced the damages by $45,000 being amount spent by the third party. T appealed to the Privy Council. The Judicial Committee of the Privy Council held that the principal could claim the amount of the bribe as money had and received or damages. The damages would be for fraud and would be equal to the principal's actual loss of Four Hundred and Forty-three Thousand pounds. Consequently, the Federal Court was wrong to award both remedies since this amounted to double recovery. The election between the two claims need not be made by the principal until the time when judgment is to be entered.

Finally, a principal can dismiss the agent who is guilty of breach of duty and is not bound to pay him compensation.[314]

(c) Principal's duties to an Agent

(i) Agent's right to remuneration

An agent is normally entitled to be paid for his services and this normally takes the form of a commission. Three aspects relating to the payment of a commission may be considered.

(ii) Whether commission is payable

Whether a commission is payable depends on the terms of the agreement between a principal and his agent. Thus in *Taylor v. Brewer*[315], A was to receive "such commission as should be deemed right by the principal." It was held tat the agent had no legal right to commission. Where the agency is commercial, courts would deem reasonable payment for the agent in the absence of express provision for payment.[316] If the agreement stipulates that the amount of the commission is to be left to the principal's discretion and he refuses to fix the amount, then the

312 *Christoforides v. Terry* [1924] All E.R. Rep.815

313 [1978] 2 W.L.R. 444; [1979] A.C. 374

314 *Harris v. Power Packing Services Ltd.* [1970] 2 Lloyd Rep 65; *Boston Deep Sea Fishing 7 Ice Co. v. Ansell* (1889) 39 Ch.D. 339 C.A.

315 (1813) 1 M & S 290

316 *Kofi Sunkersette Oba v. Strauss & Co. Ltd.* [1951] A.C.543

court may force him to pay a reasonable sum.[317] In case of a company, a director may agree to work for it for such remuneration as the other directors may determine and subject to the company getting on its feet. If the company does not find its feet, the director cannot claim reasonable remuneration for his work.[318]

The right to payment may be implied from the circumstance of the relationship of agency. For instance, employment of a professional agent raises the presumption that he should be paid his professional fees, unless circumstances show otherwise.[319]

(iii) Whether agent has earned the commission

A commission is payable in respect of a transaction which the agent was employed to bring about. Thus in *Toulmin v. Millar*[320], the owner of a house employed an agent to find a tenant, who later bought the house. His claim for a commission on the sale of the house failed since he was only employed to let the house.

An agent only earns commission on a transaction caused by his efforts. Thus in *Tribe v. Taylor,*[321] a principal employed an agent to raise a loan money. The lender later entered into a partnership with the principal on this occasion and made a further loan. The agent's claim for a commission on the second loan failed since this was not brought about by his efforts. Furthermore, in the Nigerian case of *Odufunade v. Rossek*[322], the agent was engaged to find a lessee of the principal's property and was to receive 10% commission on what the client paid. The agent negotiated with the Chief Federal Land Officer, but the outcome was that the Government acquired the property by means of a compulsory order. The agent's attempt to recover the commission failed. The Court explained that the agent did not complete his task on the introduction of prospective clients but only if he was the effective cause of the final contract. It is possible for the agent to earn a commission for an act falling short of the final contract but such a situation would have to be clearly expressed in the agency relationship. This issue has caused difficulties especially in cases involving estate agents. Thus in *Hodges v. Hackbridge Park Residential Motel Ltd.*[323], a firm of estate agents were asked by their client to find a purchaser for his hotel. They found Colonel Cannon who was looking for some land for erecting a hall with a sports ground. Negotiations took place for a sale at about Twelve Thousand, Five Hundred Pounds but came to nothing. Colonel Canon had been acting for the British War office which acquired it later under a compulsory purchase order for between Seven Thousand pounds and Eight Thousand Pounds. The agents claimed commission from their client. The Court of Appeal held that they were not entitled to it as they were not the effective cause of the sale. In *Luxor (Eastbourne) Ltd v. Cooper,*[324] the contract provided that the landowner should pay the estate agent a commission "on completion of the sale." There was no sale because the owner refused to deal with the prospective purchaser introduced by the agent. It was held that he was not entitled to the commission.

It has been observed[325] that it is unfair to the estate agent who may have gone to the trouble and expense in advertising a house and securing orders[326] not to be rewarded. On the other

---

[317] *Bryant v. Flight* (1839) 2 M & W 114; *British Bank for Foreign Trade v. Novinex* [1949] 1 K.B. 623

[318] *Re Richmond Gate Property Co. Ltd.* [1965] 1 W.L.R. 335; [1964] 3 All E.R. 939

[319] *Carbin v. Stewart* [1911] 28 T.L.R. 99

[320] (1887) 12 App. Cas.746

[321] (1876) 1 C.P.D. 505

[322] [1962] All N.L.R. 98; Hodgin, *Law of Contract in East Africa* (1975), p.262 see also *Luther v. Mandilas & Karaberis Ltd.* [1958] 3 F.S.C. 98; *Afolabi v. Polymera Industries (Nig.) Ltd.* [1964] T.L.R. 940; *Omoregie v. Attorney General* [1971] 1 N.C.L.R. 397; (1972) 2 U.I.L.R. 402; *Hodges case infra* n.323

[323] [1939] 4 All E.R. 347.

[324] [1941] A.C. 108; [1941] 1 All E.R. 33

[325] Treitel, *Law of Contract* (8th Edn. 1991), p.644

[326] as was the case in *Bernard Thorpe & Partners v. Flannery* (1977) 244 E.G.129 although there was in this instance a stipulation by the agent for reimbursement of advertising expenses.

hand, it is also unfair for a client to pay a commission when it is not his fault that a sale has taken place. The solution suggested by Denning L. J. in *Dennis Reed ltd. v. Goody*[327] would appear equitable in the circumstances. He suggested that as a general principle, a commission should be payable out of the purchase price. if the sale goes off through, the purchaser's or agent's fault, the vendor should not be liable to pay the commission. However, if as a result of the purchaser's default, a deposit is forfeited to the vendor, the agent should be entitled to a *quantum meruit* out of the forfeited sum.[328] If the sale does not take place owing to the vendor's fault, the agent should be entitled to his commission.[329]

(iv) Whether principal should give agent chance to earn commission

If a principal employs an agent for a fixed period, he is not bound to stay in business just to enable the agent to earn his commission. Indeed the general rule is that unless otherwise agreed, an agent is not entitled to a commission on transactions which take place after the termination of the agency.[330] In *Rhodes v. Forwood*,[331] a colliery owner employed an agent to sell his coal in Liverpool for seven years. It was held that the owner did not commit a breach of contract by selling his colliery and going out of business within seven years. However, in *Sellers v. London Counties Newspapers Ltd.*[332] an agent was employed to sell advertising space in a newspaper and was paid a commission on the sales. Some of the advertisements were placed on a recurring basis over a period of time. The agent was dismissed and the court held that he was entitled to claim the commission on those advertisements that appeared after he had left the newspaper. In contrast, in the Kenyan case of *Raghban Mohammed Siddique v. Eastern Federal Union Insurance Company*[333], the plaintiff was the chief agent of the defendant company and was paid a commission on the first premiums and also renewals of premiums. The agency was terminated and the plaintiff claimed that he was entitled to the commissions on the renewals of those policies effected by him. It was held against the agent and explained that the contract made no reference to this type of claim for continuing commission. Additionally, no evidence was led to show that this was the normal practice in the insurance business.

However, if a principal contracts to stay in business for the agent's benefit then he is liable in damages if he fails to do so. Thus in *Turner v. Goldsmith*,[334] a principal employed an agent for five years to obtain orders for shirts manufactured and sold by the principal. It was held that the principal was not justified in going out of business because the factory in which the shirts were manufactured was burnt down.

(v) Right to indemnity

The general rule is that an agent who incurs liability or uses his money in performing the agency is entitled to an indemnity from his principal, unless the agency contract excludes this right.[335] In *Adamson v. Jarvis*[336] a principal instructed his agent, an auctioneer, to sell goods by auction which the agent did. The principal did not in fact own the goods and the agent was compelled to pay damages for conversion to the owner. It was held that the agent was entitled to indemnity from the principal. Furthermore, in the Kenyan case, *Isaac Gundle v. Mohanlal Sunderji*,[337] the appellant claimed money expended by him as an agent of the respondent. The

[327] [1950] 2 K.B. 277;

[328] *Boots v. E. Christopher & Co.* [1952] 1 K.B. 89

[329] *Ibid.*

[330] *Levy v. Goldhill* [1917] 2 Ch.297; *Crocker - Harlock v. Lang & Co.* [1949] 1 All E.R. 526

[331] (1876) 1 App. Cas. 256

[332] [1951] 1 All E.R. 544

[333] Civil Case 141 of 1968 (Unreported) See also Hodgin, *Law of Contract In East Africa supra* p.262 - 263.

[334] [1991] 1 Q.B. 544

[335] *Thacker v. Hardy* (1878) 4 Q.B.D. 685; Tanganyika Contract Act, S.174

[336] (1827) 4 Bing 66.

[337] 18 K.L.R. 137

respondent (P) had used A as a confirming agent in London to obtain certain provisions to be dispatched to Mombasa. A purchased what he could, but some goods were unobtainable. P refused to accept delivery as the order was not complete and refused to indemnify A on the grounds that A had no authority to pay for less than was ordered. The appellant successfully appealed to the High Court which relied on Section 222 of the Indian Contract Act.[338] In *Dalgety & Co Ltd. v. Cluer,* [339] A's demand for indemnity was Shs.11,000/=, representing the arbitrator's award to the third party which A had paid him. P resisted the claim on the grounds that they had instructed A not to proceed to arbitration and therefore A had acted in disregard of their directive. In allowing A's claim, the Court of Appeal observed that an arbitration clause existed in the original contract, liability had been incurred and it was, therefore, too late to withdraw from A's powers the right to arbitration.[340]

The agent's right to indemnity is subject to three main qualifications. First there is no right to indemnity unless the agent's acts are authorised or ratified by the principal. Thus in *Barron v. Fitzgerald*[341] A was employed to effect some policies of life insurance and to do so in his own name or in that of his principal. A insured in his names and a certain X and then claimed indemnity from the principal. It was held that he was not entitled to the indemnity. Second, no right to indemnity accrues if the agent is in breach of his duties to the principal or if the loss in question is due to the agent's fault.

Thus in *Duncan v. Hill*[342], a stockbroker, bought goods for his principal. The principal asked him to defer payment until the next account. The Stockbroker became insolvent and the stock was sold at a loss. It was held that the principal was not bound to indemnify the stockbroker in respect of the loss since the cause of the loss was the agent's insolvency. Similarly, in *Lister v. Romford Ice & Cold Storage Co. Ltd.*[343], a lorry driver injured a third party through negligent driving in the course of his employment for P. The third party recovered damages from P who in turn obtained indemnity from the driver on the ground that he had broken an implied term in the agreement to drive with proper care. The holding would have been different if it was shown that P's fault led to the loss.[344]

Third, no indemnity can be claimed in respect of an illegal act. However, the agent can claim indemnity by showing that he was unaware of the illegality and that the act in question was not manifestly unlawful.[345] Relatively, the agent may be entitled to indemnity in respect of payments which he was not legally obliged to make. Thus in *Read v. Anderson*[346], A paid the amount of a bet which he made on behalf of P and lost. It was held that he was entitled to recover payment from P. The decision was reversed by the Gaming Act 1892 of Britain which prohibits indemnity in the case of a wagering contract. However, the principle of this case would probably still apply to a case not concerned with a wagering contract.[347] It, however, appears that the agent is only entitled to an indemnity in respect of a payment which though not legally due, was made in the usual course of business, or possibly if it was made under a moral obligation.[348] Furthermore, where the agent has incurred personal liability to a third party in the course of carrying out his principal's instructions, he is entitled to an indemnity from his

338 equivalent to Section 174 of the Tanganyika Contract Act

339 [1961] E.A. 178; Note 1969 E.A.L.R. 259 (Thomas)

340 applying S.204 Indian Contract Act (Section 156, Tanganyika Contract Act.)

341 (1840) 6 Bing (N.S.) 201. See also *Dalgety* case, *supra* n.339.

342 (1873) L.R. 8 Ex 242

343 [1957] A.C. 555; [1957] 1 All E.R. 125

344 *Lacey v. Hill* (1874) L.R. 18 Eq. 182

345 *Thacker v. Hardy* (1878) 4 Q.B.D. 685

346 (1884) 13 Q.B.D. 779

347 Treitel, *supra* n.325, p.646

348 *Ibid.*

principal to the extent of his liability. Thus in *Anglo Overseas Transport Ltd. v. Titan Industrial Corporation*[349], a firm of forwarding agents was employed by some shippers of goods to reserve shipping space for them on a vessel sailing from the port of London. The agents did so. However, the space was unfulfilled because the goods were late in arriving at the port. The agents had to pay to the shipowners damages for dead freight since, by custom of the port, they incurred personal liability in the circumstances. They claimed indemnity from the principals in respect of the sum they had to pay. It was held that the agents were entitled to the indemnity.

(vi) Right to Lien

An agent is (except where there is contrary agreement)[350] entitled to a lien on all the property of the principal which has come into his possession in the course of the agency. Every agent has a *particular* lien: that is, he can hold the property until the principal satisfies all claims of the agent arising out of the agency. An agent may, by custom or special contract also have a *general* lien, entitling him to hold the property until the principal satisfies all the claims of the agent, whether arising out of the agency or not.

In *Taylor v. Robinson*[351], A bought goods from T on behalf of P. It was agreed that the goods should remain on the premises of T. Later, without P's authority, A removed the goods to his own premises. P became bankrupt and A claimed lien. It was held that A was not entitled to lien because the goods had at all times remained in possession of P.

A lien cannot be claimed if it has been expressly excluded by the agency contract or if the goods have been delivered for a special purpose which is inconsistent with the lien.[352]

The right to lien may be lost in four main ways. First, by voluntary parting with possession by the agent. Second, a change in character of the possession may destroy the lien. Thus in *Barrat v. Gough-Thomas*,[353], a solicitor acted for A and had possession (and lien over) title deeds to A's land. A mortgaged the land to B and the deeds remained with the solicitor who acted for both parties. The Court of Appeal held that as soon as the mortgage was executed, the solicitor held the deeds as agent for B and this destroyed any lien which he (the solicitor) might have over the deeds as against A. Third, a lien is lost if the agent waives it, for instance where he takes security for his remuneration which is inconsistent with the lien. Thus in *Re Morris*[354], a client who owed money to solicitors deposited some share certificates as security for disbursements in certain matters. It was held that this was not inconsistent with the solicitor's lien over other papers in respect of outstanding profit costs. Finally, a lien is lost if the principal tenders to the agent the sum due.

A lien is said to survive if goods are obtained from the agent by fraud.[355] The lien will also survive if at the time of the transfer of possession the lien is expressly preserved.[356]

(vii) Remedies of Agent

Unless the parties otherwise agree, the agent may sue the principal to enforce the right to indemnity for losses, expenses or damages sustained in discharging the terms of the agency. Second, where the principal sues the agent, the latter has a right to set-off or counterclaim from the amounts due to him by way of payment, indemnity or reimbursement. Third the agent has right of lien over the goods in his possession belonging to the principal.[357] Fourth, if the agent

---

349 [1959] 2 Lloyds Rep, 152

350 *Rolls Razor Ltd v. Cox* [1967] 1 Q.B. 552

351 (1818) 8 Taunt 648.

352 *Brendao v. Barnett* (1846) 12 Cl. & Fin. 787

353 [1951] 2 All E.R. 48

354 [1908] 1 K.B. 473

355 *Northwestern Bank v. Poynter, Son & Macdonalds* [1895] A.C. 56.

356 *Caldwell v. Sumpters* [1972] 1 All E.R. 567

357 discussed *supra*

is in the position of an unpaid seller to the principal he may exercise the right to stoppage of the goods in transit against the goods of the principal.[358] He is said to stand in such a position if after buying goods from the principal, he pays the seller with his own money or otherwise incurs personal liability to the seller for the price.[359] Other remedies include requiring an account by the principal where there is reciprocal indebtedness by the parties; withholding further performance under the agency where the principal's breach of contract continues; where he is in possession of goods subject to conflicting claims of the principal and a third party, he may claim relief by way of interpleader summons i.e. by being joined to the action as a party.

3. The agent's authority

The agent's authority may arise in six instances: by express authority; through implied authority; through usual authority; by apparent or ostensible authority, ratification and through necessity. Each will be considered in turn.

(a) Express authority

An agent's authority may be conferred or given by express appointment between the principal and agent either orally or in writing.[360] There exists an exception where the agent is appointed to execute an instrument under seal for instance sale or conveyance of land. Such authority must be given in writing or under seal by an instrument called a power of attorney. Where the instructions are ambiguous the agent is not liable. Thus in *Weigall & Co. v. Runciman & Co.*,[361] the principal instructed A to "fix" a steamer. He intended A to let a steamer. Instead A hired a steamer. It was held that P was liable for the charges of hiring as his instructions were ambiguous.

(b) Implied authority

An agent has authority to do everything necessary for, or incidental to the execution of his express authority. This is otherwise known as implied authority. Implied authority is real in the sense that it arises from construction of express authority. Words of express authority must be looked at closely in each case. Thus in *Keen v. Mear,*[362] an agent was employed to sell but was held to have no authority to sign a contract containing special conditions. He had authority to sign an open contract. In contrast, in *Wragg v. Lovett,*[363] it was held that the agent had an implied authority to make a contract on any conditions he thought fit.

An agent who is employed to sell an item has generally no authority to receive payment for it. Thus in *Butwick v. Grant,*[364] the principal appointed an agent to sell coats for him. The purchaser of coats paid the agent but the agent did not pay money to the principal. The principal sued the purchaser for the price and succeeded on the ground that the agent had no authority to receive payment of the price.

Implied authority may be implied either from conduct on a particular occasion or from other relationship. It has been held that a husband who lives with his wife impliedly authorises her to pledge his credit for necessary household expenses.[365] This depends on the existence of a household which the husband permits the wife to manage. The authority will not arise if

---

358 Sales of Goods Act Cap 79, S.44

359 *Ireland v. Livingston* (1872) L.R.S.H.L. 395

360 See also Tanganyika Contract Act, S.139.

361 (1916) 85 L.J.K.B. 1187. Se also *John Holt (Liverpool) Ltd. v. Alhaji Jaafaru* (1958) NRNLR 29.

362 [1920] 2 Ch.574

363 [1948] 2 All E.R. 968 C.A.

364 [1924] All E.R. Rep. 483

365 *Jewsbury v. Newbold* (1857) 26 L.J. Ex. 247

there is no household for instance where the parties live in an hotel.[366] A mistress will also have implied authority to pledge goods on credit where there is a household.[367] In that case, death of the principal was held to terminate the implied authority of his mistress to pledge his credit.[368]

Since the authority is based on implied consent, it can be negatived if for instance the husband forbids his wife to pledge credit;[369] the husband gives her an adequate house keeping allowance;[370] the husband warns a trader not supply goods to his wife on credit or if the wife already has an adequate supply of the goods in question. Thus in *Miss Gray Ltd. v. Cathcart*,[371] a wife was supplied with clothes to the value of Two Hundred and Fifteen Pounds and the husband refused to pay for them. He was sued by a tradesman. The husband proved that he paid his wife Nine Hundred and Sixty Pounds a year as an allowance. It was held that the husband was not liable.

Implied authority can also arise from custom. A principal who employs an agent to act for him in a particular market impliedly authorises the agent to act in accordance with the custom of that market.[372] The principal will be bound by the custom even if he is unaware of it.[373] The inference of an implied authority according to custom may be negatived if the custom is inconsistent with instructions given by the principal to the agent or with the very relationship of principal and agent. In such a situation, the custom is "unreasonable" and the principal is not bound by it unless he knows of it. Thus in *Perry v. Barnett*,[374] A who was employed to buy bank shares failed to comply with an Act of Parliament which was in force. The act provided that such contracts were void unless the number of shares were stated in the contract note. P did not know of the custom of the stock exchange to disregard the Act (Banking Companies (Shares) Act 1867). It was held that P was not bound by the custom, which was inconsistent with A's instructions in so far as it resulted in his making a void contract when he was employed to make a valid one.

In some markets, there is a custom by which an agent is employed by several principals to buy in bulk to satisfy the needs of all. In *Robinson v. Mollett*[375], a custom to this effect in a tallow market was held to be unreasonable since its effect was to turn an agent into a seller. This was inconsistent with the relationship of principal and agent. Since the agent must buy for his principal as cheaply as he can, while a seller sells at the highest price he can get. In contrast, in *Scott v. Godfrey*[376] a custom of the stock exchange which permitted stock brokers to buy enough shares for several principals from a single seller was held to be reasonable because all the parties intended that contracts should be made between the seller and various buyers.

(c) Usual authority

The expression, "usual authority" has three possible meanings. First, it may mean implied or incidental authority (*supra*). Second, it may refer to cases where an agent has apparent authority because he has been placed by his principal in a situation in which he would have had incidental authority if this had not been expressly negatived by instructions given to him by the principal and not communicated to the third party. Third it may refer to a situation where the principal is bound by the agent's contracts even though there is no express, implied or apparent authority.

---

366 *Debenham v. Mellon* (1880) 6 App. Cas 24

367 *Blades v. Free* (1829) 9 B & C 167

368 *Ibid.*

369 *Jolly v. Rees* (1864) 15 CB (N.S.) 628; *Miss Gray Ltd v. Cathcart* (1922) 38 T.L.R. 562.

370 *Morel Bros v. Westmoreland* [1903] 1 K.B. affirmed [1904] A.C. 11.

371 *supra* n.369

372 *Graves v. Legg* (1857) 2 H & N 210

373 *Pollock v. Stables* (1848) 12 Q.B. 765

374 (1885) 15 Q.B.D. 388

375 (1875) L.R. 7 H.L. 802

376 [1901] 2 Q.B. 726

The third meaning is the one with which usual authority is associated here. In *Watteau v. Fenwick*[377]. Humble owned the Victoria Hotel. He sold it to Fenwick, who employed him as manager and allowed his name to remain over the door. Fenwick forbade Humble to buy cigars on credit. However, Humble bought some on credit from Watteau. Later, Watteau discovered the existence of Fenwick and claimed their price from him. The claim succeeded on the ground that it was within the usual authority of a manager of a hotel to buy cigars on credit. A principal whether disclosed or not, was liable for the acts of an agent acting within his authority . A secret limitation of such authority was useless where the principal was sued by a third party. Wills J. thus added:[378]

> The principal is liable for all the acts of the agent which are within the authority usually confided to an agent of that character, notwithstanding limitations as between the principal and his agent put upon such authority....

Other situations where the principal is bound include where a principal gives his agent documents and authorises him to borrow a fixed sum on security of them. In this case, he may be liable to a third party from whom the agent borrows more, even if the third party did not think that agent had any authority to borrow.[379] In addition, at common law, a person is bound by an unauthorised sale of his goods by a factor, although the factor sells in his own name.[380]

At common law, a principal is not bound by an unauthorised pledge of credit by his agent. However, under the Factors Act 1889[381] of Britain a principal is bound in certain instances by any disposition made by such agent. These rules are based on the principle in *Watteau v. Fenwick*, although the principal "seems to be more closely analogous to the doctrine of vicarious liability in tort (under which an employer may be liable even for forbidden acts if done by an employee in the course of employment)[382] than to the doctrine of apparent authority".[383]

The extent of the agent's usual authority depends on the class of agent to which he belongs and on the common understanding of the trade concerning such agents. In *Daun v. Simmins*[384], it was held that the manager of a tied public-house has no usual authority to order spirits from any person he likes. It is significant that where an agent does not belong to a well-known class of agents, but is simply appointed for an isolated transaction, the doctrine of usual authority does not apply. Thus in *Jerome v. Bentley & Co.*[385] a retired army officer to whom jewellery had been entrusted for sale was held not to have the usual authority which a mercantile agent would have in the same circumstances.

An attempt is now made to examine particular instances in which an agent is regarded as having usual authority of his principal to do an act.

(a) Auctioneers

An auctioneer is normally given instructions to sell certain items. As a result, by the application of the doctrine of usual authority he has authority to sign a memorandum of the contract of sale. Three aspects arise from this authority. First, it is irrevocable.[386] Second, an auctioneer

---

377 [1891-4] All E.R. 897

378 *Ibid.* p.898. See critique by Hornby [1961] Camb L.J. The case has been distinguished in a number of cases e.g. *The Rhodian River* [1984] 1 Lloyds's Rep 373, 379.

379 *Brocklesby v. Temperance* P.B.S. [1895] A.C. 173; *Fry v. Smellie* [1912] 2 K.B. 282.

380 (1875) L.R. 10 C.P. 354, 362

381 previously applicable to Uganda: Contract Act Cap 75 and Judicature Act, 1962. But see now Judicature Statute, 1996, S.16(2) and *Uganda Motors Ltd. v. Wavah Holdings Ltd.* Civil Appeal No.19/91 (Supreme Court of Uganda) per Platt J.S.C.

382 *Limpus v. L.G.O.C.* (1862) 1 H & C 526

383 Treitel, *Law of Contract supra* p.620

384 (1879) 41 L.T. 783 distinguishable from *Watteau v. Fenwick supra* n.377.

385 [1952] 2 T.L.R. 58

386 *Phillips v. Butler* [1945] 2 All E.R. 258

is deemed to be the agent of the purchaser and vendor and for the purpose of signing the memorandum of contract of sale. Consequently, he can sign the memorandum on behalf of the purchaser. The signature must be at the time of sale or soon thereafter[387] so as to be regarded as forming part of the transaction. Third, the power to sign extends to a licensed auctioneer employed by the auctioneers in question.[388] This power does not, however, extend to the auctioneer's clerk[389], unless the principal authorises him to sign. This is an exception to the general rule that a party to a contract cannot sign a memorandum as agent of the other, (that is a seller cannot sign a memorandum as agent for the buyer.)[390] However, in the case of an auctioneer it is suggested that the power to sue the buyer for the price is based on a lien and special property and not on contract. Consequently, if he signs the memorandum as agent for the buyer this does not prevent him from suing the buyer for the price.[391]

(b) Mercantile agents

A mercantile agent is one having in the ordinary course of his business authority to do three things. First, authority to sell goods. Second, authority to consign goods for the purpose of sale. Third, authority to buy goods or to raise money on security of the goods.[392]

There are three well known classes of mercantile agents.

(i) Factors

A factor is "an agent who is entrusted with possession of goods for purpose of sale" and has implied authority to sell in his own name.[393] A factor may also warrant or guarantee the goods if it is customary to warrant the type of goods in question.[394] Where a factor pledges goods which he receives on sale the position is that as between the principal and factor, the factor is in breach of duty; but as between factor and pledgee, the pledgee may have acquired good title under Section 2 of the Factors Act, 1889 of Britain.

(ii) Brokers

A broker is a mere agent, who in the ordinary course of his business is employed to make contracts with third parties for the purchase of goods or property for the sale of the principal's goods or property of which he is not entrusted with possession or documents of title thereto. A broker differs from a factor because he has no authority to sell in his own name. Furthermore, he is generally not entrusted with possession of the principal's goods.[395] A broker has authority to observe all reasonable and lawful customs prevailing at his place of work. It has been observed[396] that with the development of the doctrine of apparent authority and passing of the Factors Act, the distinction between factors and brokers has lost importance.

(iii) Del credere agent

A *del credere* agent is a broker who has implied authority to make contracts on his principal's behalf. A special feature of this agency is that the agent agrees, in return for a commission, to guarantee payment of the price. If the principal fails to recover the price, then the agent is liable for its payment.[397] Three aspects should be noted with regard to a *del credere* agent.

387 *Chaney v. Maclow* [1929] 1 Ch. 461

388 *Wilson v. Pike* [1948] 2 All E.R. 267

389 *Bell v. Balls* [1897] 1 Ch.663.

390 *Farebrother v. Simmons* (1822) 5 B & Ald. 333

391 *Benton v. Campbell, Parker & Co.* [1925] 2 K.B. 410

392 Factors Act, 1889 (U.K.), S.1(1).

393 *Stevens v. Biller* (1883) 25 Ch.D. 31, 34 per Cotton, L.J.

394 *Benmag Ltd v. Bard* [1955] 2 Lloyds Rep 354

395 *Borrie v. Corrie* (1818) 2 B & A.

396 Lowe, R. *Commercial Law* (1976), p.29.

397 *Gabriel (Thomas) & Sons v. Churchill Sim* [1914] 3 K.B.1272, 1278-79.

First a contract need not be evidenced in writing as a guarantee under Section 4 of the Contract Act[398] because the guarantee merely forms part of a larger transaction.[399] Second, a *del credere* agent merely guarantees payment and not performance of other obligations for instance failure under f.o.b. contract to name an effective ship.[400] Third a *del credere* agent is a guarantor of the buyer's solvency and not guarantor of the seller's duty to supply merchantable goods.[401]

(iv) Confirming Houses

A confirming house is important in sections of the export trade. It performs duties similar to those of a *del credere* agent. The rationale for using a confirming house is that a Ugandan exporter may be unwilling to deal directly with a foreign importer whose reputation and financial standing he does not know. The foreign importer may, therefore, instruct a Ugandan Confirming House (Bank) to assume personal responsibility for the price and to make necessary shipping arrangements. If the order is cancelled by a foreign importer then the confirming house is liable to pay for the goods if the sellers are ready and willing to deliver.[402] If the price is subsequently paid by the foreign importer, the confirming house can claim indemnity from the foreign importer and also claim the agreed commission.[403]

(v) Estate Agents

An estate agent who is instructed to negotiate the sale of a house privately has normally no authority to sign a contract on behalf of the vendor unless he is expressly employed to sell property in which case he can sign contracts of sale.[404] An estate agent has also an implied authority to receive a pre-contract deposit subject to the obligation to repay it on demand to a prospective purchaser without interest.[405] A vendor has no right to demand deposit from the agent without the prospective purchaser's consent.

(d) Apparent authority

In *Rama Corpn. v. Proved Tin & General Investments Ltd.*[406] Slade J. defined ostensible or apparent authority as a form of estoppel which depends on three conditions: (i) representation; (ii) reliance on the representation; (iii) alteration of the third party's position as a result of such reliance. A representation must be made by the principal since it is his act which produces the belief in the mind of the third party and gives rise to the principal's liability. Thus in *Attorney General v. Silva*,[407] a Crown Agent falsely represented that he had authority to sell steel plates which were crown property. The Privy Council held that the Crown was not bound by the sale since (i) the agent had no actual authority; (ii) apparent authority could only arise out of a representation made by the principal and not out of that made by the agent. The representation may be by word or conduct. For instance a letter written by a principal to his bank informing the bank that the agent has authority to draw cheques. Representation by conduct would arise where the principal places the agent in a position where he normally has authority to do a particular act or a husband creating the appearance of authority by paying for goods supplied to his wife.

398 Cap. 75

399 *Sutton v. Grey* [1894] 1 Q.B. 285

400 *Gabriel Thomas* case *supra* n.397.

401 *Churchill & Sim v. Goddard* [1936] 1 All E.R. 675

402 *Rusholme & Bolton & Roberts Hadfield Ltd. v. Road & Co. (London) Ltd.* [1955] 1 All E.R. 180.

403 *Anglo-Shipping Co. of New York v. J. Mortner Ltd.* [1962] 1 Lloyd's Rep 60 C.A.

404 *Spiro v. Lintern* [1973] 1 W.L.R. 1002, 1006; [1973] 3 All E. R. 319; *Sorrell v. Finch* [1977] A.C. 728; [1976] 2 All E.R. 371; Reynolds, 92 L.Q.R. 484

405 *Potters v. Loppert* [1973] 2 W.L.R. 469; [1973] Ch.399.

406 [1952] 1 All E.R. See also *President Clothing & Co. Ltd. v. J. Anyanwu* [1975] 1 C.C.H.C.J.1 (Lagos High Court, Nigeria).

407 [1953] A.C. 461

A representation may be intentional or negligent. For instance if the principal mistakenly signs a document giving authority to the agent, then he would be liable if a third party acts on the document.[408] In *Edmund Schulter & Co. (Uganda) Ltd. v. Patel*,[409] P sold land to Y through A who was P's agent. A deposit of Shs.50,000/= was paid to A and the balance paid direct to P. A, however disappeared with the deposit. P now claimed the deposit afresh arguing that A had no authority to receive such sums. The Court of Appeal dismissed the claim. It was explained that P had given A the duplicate documents of title and by such behaviour P was estopped from denying A's right to act.

A second consideration is that the representation must give a clear message that the agent has authority to do a particular action the plaintiff's behalf. Thus in *Colonial Bank v. Cody*[410], the deceased person owned shares which could be transferred by using a transfer form on the back of the certificates. On his death, the executors wanted to get themselves registered in the books of the company. Therefore, they signed the transfer in blank and sent it to a broker. The broker fraudulently pledged them with a bank which made no inquiry as to his authority. Later the executors discovered the fraud and sued the bank. It was held that they were entitled to recover the shares. The House of Lords observed that the transfer was ambiguous since it could mean that executors wanted themselves registered. Because of the ambiguity, the bank was under a duty to inquire. Consequently, the document did not raise an estoppel.

Thirdly, the representation must be made to the person seeking to hold the principal liable. Thus in *Farguharson Bros v. Kings Co.*,[411] a buyer's plea of apparent authority was rejected because the buyer had never heard of the principal or his clerk. A representation by the principal to the agent does not give rise to apparent authority.

Fourth, where an agent is acting under a power of attorney, a third party is required to examine the deed of attorney since the principal will not be liable for the agent's unauthorised act if the lack of authority was clear from the document.[412]

Fifth, a person or a third party raising the issue of estoppel or apparent authority should show not only that the representation was made to him but also that he actually acted upon it. If he had not acted at all or acted but not on the faith of the representation, there will be no agency by apparent authority or estoppel.[413]

Sixth, a third party who has relied or acted upon a representation must show that this altered his position. Consequently, if a third party has not altered his position at all or has done so but has not suffered any loss or has suffered loss but not one arising out of the representation then there is no agency by estoppel or apparent authority. Thus in *Swan v. North British Australasia Co. Ltd.*,[414] it was held that in order for a representation to operate as an estoppel, it must be the "proximate cause of the loss". In *Lloyds Bank v. Chartered Bank of India, Australia & China*[415] the plaintiff's employee drew cheques on the plaintiff's account and paid them into his personal account with the defendant bank. The plaintiff sued the defendant for conversion of the total amount paid into that bank by the employee. It was held upon the facts that the defendant could not plead that they had been misled by the acts of the employee which though irregular were not fraudulent because (i) the defendant had not in fact relied upon those acts and (ii) that the employee was authorised to commit subsequent irregular acts. Serutton L. J. observed that

---

408 *Saunders v. Anglia Building Society* [1970] 3 All E.R. 961

409 [1969] E.A. 259. See also Section 2(1) Factors Act, 1889 (U.K.)

410 (1890) 15 App. Cas. 267.

411 [1902] A.C. 325.

412 *Jacobs v. Morris* [1902] 1 Ch.816

413 *President Clothing Co. Ltd. v. Joseph Anyanwu* [1975] 1 C.C.H.C.J. 1 (Nigeria)

414 [1863] 2 H & C 175

415 [1929] 1 K.B. 40

the proximate cause of the defendant's bank's action was not the representation of the plaintiff bank that the employee had authority.

Finally, since the doctrine of estoppel is an equitable remedy, a person seeking to rely on the agency by estoppel or apparent authority must have acted honestly and without knowledge that the supposed agent had no authority or had exceeded his authority. Thus in *John v. Dodwell & Co.*[416], the respondent authorised their manager to draw cheques upon their banking account for the purpose of their business. The manager fraudulently drew some cheques in favour of the appellant upon the said account. The appellant had knowledge that the manager was without apparent authority and was drawing the cheques for his benefit. It was held that the respondent had a right of action in conversion and recovery of money because the notice would deprive the appellant of all titles to hold the cheques if the respondent company challenged the transaction. Such notice may be actual or constructive.[417]

(e) Ratification

Ratification occurs when a principal affirms or ratifies an act of the agent which at the beginning was not authorised. There are six main requirements for ratification.

(i) Principal to be in Existence

The principal must be in existence when the act in question was done. This condition normally gives rise to difficulties when promoters enter into contracts on behalf of a company which has not yet been formed. Thus in *Kelner v. Baxter*[418], Kelner agreed with Baxter, Calisher and Dales, who were promoters of an unformed company to sell them wine. The proposed company was to be called Gravesend Royal Alexandra Hotel Co. Ltd. Kelner delivered the wine to the hotel business which was then in existence. On 1st February, 1866, the proposed directors held a meeting at which they purported to ratify the purchase. The incorporation of the company was completed on 20th February, 1966. The company wound up before Kelner had been paid. He sued the promoters personally. It was held that they were liable on the contract personally. Furthermore it was observed that since the company had not yet come into existence it could not ratify a contract made before its incorporation.

(ii) The principal to be ascertainable

A principal on whose behalf an agent purports of act must have been named or ascertained by a third party when the act is done. An undisclosed principal cannot ratify. Thus in *Keighley Maxsted & Co. v. Durant*[419], the company instructed Roberts, a corn merchant to buy wheat from Durant on a joint account at 45s 3d per quarter. Roberts could not buy at this price, but he agreed to buy wheat from Durant at 45s 6d but did not disclose that he was buying on a joint account. The company purported to ratify the agreement. The price was not paid to Durant. Durant sued the company. It was held by the House of Lords that Durant could not succeed because the purported ratification was ineffective since Roberts had not disclosed the fact that he was acting for a principal. Only a principal whose existence had been disclosed could ratify.[420] The case is especially significant for Lord Macnaghten's observation: "Civil obligations are not created by or founded upon undisclosed intentions" which was regarded as too wide as

---

416 [1918] A.C. 563

417 *Lloyds Bank* Case *supra* n.415.

418 (1866) L.R. 2 C.P. 174 C.C.P. See also the Nigerian Cases, *Dario Caligara v. Giovanni Sartori & Co. Ltd.* [1961] 3 All N.L.R.; *Shonibare v. Ali Mansour* High Court of Lagos Suit No. LD 104/1961; *Dr. Urhobo v. Chief Tarka* High Court of Lagos [1970] 11 C.C.H.C.J. 262 and the English case of *Newborne v. Sensolid (GB) Ltd.* [1953] 1 All E.R. 708 C.A.

419 [1900 - 3] All E.R. Rep.40

420 For a contrary approach see *Dalgety & Co. v. Cluer* [1961] E.A. 178

it did not take into account the possible situation of an undisclosed principal. For this reason Lord Davey remarked that there is a distinction between an undisclosed agency existing as at the date of the contract and which can be proved and an undisclosed intention in the mind of one of the contracting party capable of being abandoned.[421] The *Maxted case* may be contrasted with *Re Tiedemann & Ledermann Freres*[422], where the position of the third party was considered to be important. In that case A sold wheat on behalf of the principal. Later the market rose and A then rebought the wheat and sold it at a profit to a third party (T). The later purchase and sale was made by A on his behalf but in his dealing with T he used the name of P for financial reasons. Later, P purported to ratify the contract. It was held that this was permissible. The case shows that the principal may ratify even if the agent intended to defraud him. In *Dalgety & Co. Ltd. v. Cluer*, [423] the appellants sold coconuts to a buyer in London on behalf of the respondents. The existence of the respondents was not disclosed to the buyers. They rejected the coconuts as not matching description and the appellants paid them damages under an arbitration agreement. The respondents refused to indemnify the appellants claiming that they had acted contrary to instructions. The Court decided in favour of the appellants. Windham C. J. thus observed:

> In this contract the appellant company appear as the vendor and there is no mention of the respondent or that the appellants are contracting as agents for anyone.

After discussion of various correspondence that took place between the appellants and respondents, the Chief Justice added:

> He (the respondent) thereby ratified the contract and acknowledged that the appellants were in fact entering into it as his agents.

A distinction should be drawn between an agent *purporting* to act for a principal and *intending* to act for him. It is possible for the former situation to occur without the latter situation. If an agent purports to act for the principal, then the latter can ratify. However, if the agent only *intends* to act for him, the principal can decline to ratify.[424]

(iii) The principal must have the capacity to Act

If an agent of a company does an act *ultra vires* the company, it cannot be ratified even by the unanimous vote of all the company's shareholders.[425]

The rule applies even if the company changes its objects so as to make the act *intra vires.* The company must have capacity when an unauthorised act was done and not just at the time of ratification. In Britain and Nigeria (where British Statutes of general application apply), Section 2 of the Infants Relief Act, 1874 makes unenforceable ratification by adults of contracts made by them in infancy because they do not have the capacity.

(iv) The act must be ratifiable

The act done by a purported agent must be capable of ratification. Thus an *ultra vires* act which is done on behalf of a company cannot be ratified. Thus in the *Ashbury case*[426] a company made a contract which was outside its objects in the memorandum of association. It was held

421 The position of an undisclosed principal is discussed *infra*.

422 [1899] 2 Q.B. 66

423 [1969] E.A. 178; Note, Thomas 1969 E.A.L.R. 259

424 *Keighley Maxsted case supra* n.419; *Abigall Folashade v. Alhaji Duroshola* [1961] 1 All N.L.R. 87 (Nigeria).

425 *Ashbury Railway Carriage & Iron Co. v. Riche* (1875) L.R. 7 H.L. 653; See also Bakibinga, *Company Law In Uganda* (1993), pp.49 - 50; Bakibinga, *Ahmadu Bello University Law Journal* Vol.1, pp.110 - 121 (1983) (Zaria, Nigeria).

426 *supra* n.425

that this contract could not be ratified even by the votes of all the shareholders, as it was a nullity in law. A forgery cannot also be ratified. In *Brook v. Hook*[427], an agent forged his principal's signature to a promissory note. It was held that the principal could not ratify the signature, although there is the view that a forgery can be adopted.[428] However Professor Treitel says that a forgery cannot be ratified because the agent is not purporting to act on the principal's behalf but on his own behalf.[429] An *Ultra vires* act and a forgery are *void ab initio*. In the Nigerian Case, *Urhobo v. Tarka*[430], it was held that if a pre-incorporation contract is purported to be made by the company which does not exist the contract is a nullity and neither the company when formed nor its promoter, whose signature is added can sue or be sued on the contract and the company cannot benefit under it. In *Newborne v. Sensolid (GB) Ltd.*[431] the contract was for sale to Sensolid of 200 cases of tinned ham. The contract was written on a printed form headed "Leopold Newborne (London) Ltd." The contract ended with the typewritten words:

> Yours faithfully, Leopold Newborne (London) Ltd.

The market fell and Sensolid refused to accept the cases. When Sensolid was sued on the contract, it claimed that on the date when the contract was made, *Leopold Newborne (London) Ltd.* had not been incorporated and that neither the company nor Newborne could personally enforce it. This was upheld by the English Court of Appeal. Goddard C. J. reasoned that the contract purported to be that of the company and not of Mr. Newborne. He was not selling his goods but those of the company. The only person who had any contract here was the company. Newborne's signature confirmed the company's signature. Since, though, the company was not in existence when the contract was signed, there was no contract. In *Banque Jacques Cartier v. La Banque D'Eparque de Montreal*[432] Lord Fitzgerald stated:

> ratification ... must be in relation to a transaction which may be valid in itself and not illegal and to which effect may be given as the party by his ... adoption of the transaction

The statement distinguishes "illegal acts" from those which "may be valid (voidable acts). Acts which are only voidable are ratifiable. Thus in *Danish Mercantile Co. & Others v. Beaumont & Anors*[433], the solicitor of a company started legal proceedings in the name of and on behalf of the company without proper authority. Later, the liquidator of the company (which was being wound up) purported to ratify the act. It was held that the ratification was valid. In *Alexander Ward & Co. Ltd. v. Samyang Navigation Co.*[434] a liquidator was held to be entitled to exercise the residual powers of the general meeting in the absence of the company's directors who were non-existent, to ratify the acts of individuals who brought the action on behalf of the respondent company.

The rule that ratification is retrospective to the time of the agent's contract is subject to the possibility that the agent may contract subject to the principal's acceptance thereof. Thus in *Warehouse & Forwarding Co. of East Africa Ltd. v. Jafferali & Sons Ltd.*[435], the appellant

---

427 (1871) L.R. 6 Ex.89

428 Hanbury, *The Principles of Agency*, p.102

429 Treitel, *Law of Contract, supra* p.348 (5th Edn. 1979); p.627 (8th Edn. 1991)

430 [1976] 11 C.C.H.C.J. (Lagos High Court). See also *Caligari v. Sartori & Co. Ltd.* [1961] 1 All N.L.R. 534

431 [1954] 1 Q.B. 45; [1955] 1 All E.R. 708

432 (1880) 13 App Cas. 111

433 [1951] 1 All E.R. 925

434 [1975] 2 All E.R. 424 H.L.

435 [1963] 3 All E.R. 571 PC (Kenya)

company, through its Nairobi manager, entered into negotiations for the respondent's godown. The appellant company explained that any agreement made was subject to ratification by the company's general manager. Dispute arose as to whether the lease was to run for one or three years. the appellants entered into possession of the property, but being unhappy about the length of the lease gave notice that they would vacate the premises six months after entering. The respondents sued for breach of contract. At the trial, the appellant's manager admitted that at some point in the negotiations, the general manager had confirmed the contract. Counsel for the appellant argued, though, that the original negotiations being conditional on the general manager's ratification, it was open to the appellants to revoke or repudiate their offer before the ratification was made. This was accepted by the Privy Council[436] which agreed that one of the appellant's letters complaining about the insistence of a three year lease amounted either to a revocation or a counter-offer. Therefore, there was nothing to ratify.[437]

(iv) The Principal must be aware of ratification related facts

In *De Bussche v. Alt*[438] Thesinger L. J. thus stated:[439]

> ... before the principal can properly be said to have ratified or adopted the act of his agent or waived his right of complaint in respect of such acts, it should be shown that he has had full knowledge of its nature and circumstance, in other words that he has had presented to his mind proper materials upon which to exercise his election.

In *Freeman v. Rosher*[440], L let premises to T. When T fell into arrears with his rent, L instructed A to levy distress. A wrongly seized and sold a shed which T used as a workshop. He then accounted to L. T sued in trespass. It was held that as L was not aware of the wrongful seizure, his acceptance of the money did not amount to ratification of the tort. Consequently, he was not liable. In contrast, in *Hilbery v.Halton*,[441] A bought a ship on behalf of P without authority. When he heard of this P said to A "You had better make a hulk of her". The ship belonged to T and A's purchase was unlawful. T sued P for conversion. it was held that P was liable. It follows that in tort, it is sufficient if the principal ratifying knows of the act of conversion; although he need not know that it is a conversion. In contrast, with a contractual situation, ratification is valid if the principal knows that the agent exceeded his authority of knowledge or terms and circumstances of the contract. Thus in *Savery v. King*[442], A entered into an invalid agreement. P, in ignorance of the invalidity purported to ratify or adopt the agreement. It was held that the principal's ratification was of no effect.

With regard to a criminal act, the knowledge of the principal must be of both the act and state of mind of the agent before he can be held liable except in offences of strict liability.

(vi) Principal must ratify in time

In order to be effective, ratification must be within the time limit, if any, prescribed by the parties or by the nature and circumstances of the particular case or within a reasonable time. In *Abigail Folashade v. Duroshola*,[443] it was held that a proper case of ratification is subject to the important qualification that ratification must be within a reasonable time after which an act

---

436 reversing the Court of Appeal for East Africa.

437 See also Tanganyika Contract Act, Ss.148 - 152; *Habib Devji v. Tarmohamed & Anor.* [1960] E.A. 1022.

438 (1878) 8 Ch.D. 286

439 *Ibid.* p.313

440 (1849) 18 L.J.Q.B.340 See also *Lewis v. Read* (1845) 13 N & W. 834

441 (1864) 2 H & C. 822

442 (1856) 5 H.L. Cas 627

443 [1961] 1 All N.L.R.87 (Nigeria)

cannot be ratified to prejudice the third party. It has also been held[444] that a contract must be ratified within a reasonable after acceptance by an authorised person. Such a contract cannot be ratified after the date fixed for its performance has passed. Furthermore, in *Dibbins v. Dibbins*[445], P, who was a partner, had an option to purchase the share of his fellow partner exercisable within three months of the latter's death. The other partner died and within 3 months A purported to exercise the option on behalf of P. This was not authorised. However, later after the 3 months period, P purported to ratify the exercise of the option. It was held that he could not do so since by then other persons had acquired a vested right in the property.

A contract cannot be ratified at time when the principal could not validly have made it. Thus a person cannot insure his property after it has been destroyed. If an agent without authority insures the principal's property, the latter cannot ratify the insurance after destruction of the property.[446] However, the policy of marine insurance can be ratified after destruction of the property insured.[447]

(vii) Effect of ratification

The effect of ratification is to put the principal, agent and third party in the same position in which they would have been if the agent's act had been authorised from the start. The agent's authority is said to relate back to the time of the unauthorised act. In *Bolton Partners v. Lambert*,[448a] A, without authority purported to buy a house for his principal from the defendant who later repudiated the contract. The principal then ratified. It was held that the defendant was bound by the contract. His repudiation was ineffective as the principal's ratification related back to the agent's unauthorised purchase. The rule in the *Bolton* case is subject to three qualifications. First, the doctrine of relating back to the time of the unauthorised act will not be invoked if the effect is to deprive the stranger to the contract of a right of property which had vested in him before ratification. Thus in *Bird v. Brown*[449], P sent goods to T. On hearing of T's insolvency, P's agent gave an unauthorised notice to the carrier to stop the goods *in transitu*. T's trustees in bankruptcy seized the goods. P purported to ratify the agent's notice. It was held that it was too late to ratify as property in the goods had vested in T's trustees.

Second, the rule in the *Bolton case* will not apply where the agent contracts "subject to ratification". In such a case, a third party can withdraw before ratification. Thus in *Watson v. Davies*,[450] on January 7, the chairman of a charity accepted an offer to sell property to it "subject to ratification" by its board of management. On January 14, the proposed vendor revoked the offer, but on the afternoon of the same day, the board ratified the chairman's action. The board sued for the specific performance of the contract. It was held that the action failed. Since the acceptance of the offer was "subject to ratification", the purported ratification only took effect from the time of the ratification and by that time the offer had been effectively withdrawn. In the words of Maugham J. :[451]

> An acceptance by an agent subject to ratification by his principal is legally a nullity until ratification, and is no more binding on the other party than an offer, which can, as in the present case be withdrawn before acceptance.

Third, the rule of relation back will not apply where the agent and the third party have by mutual consent cancelled the unauthorised transaction before the principal ratifies.[452]

---

444 *Metropolitan Asylums Board v. Kingham* (1890) 6 T.L.R. 217
445 [1896] 2 Ch.348
446 *Grover & Grover Ltd. v. Mathews* [1910] 2 K.B. 401
447 *Williams v. N. China Insurance Company* (1876) 1 C.P.D.757
448a (1889) 41 Ch.D. 295
449 (1850) Ex.486
450 [1931] 1 Ch. 455. See also *Warehouse & Forwarding Co. Case supra* n.435
451 *Ibid.* at p.548
452 *Walter v. James* (1871) L.R. Ex. 124

(f) Authority of necessity[453]

A person who acts to save property of another, gives some form of personal assistance or performs some obligation of another may as a matter of law have authority of necessity. The principle applies in the following situations.

(i) Acceptance of a bill of exchange for honour of drawer

If a bill is not accepted by a person on whom it is drawn, a stranger may, with the consent of the holder accept the bill for the honour of the drawer. If the stranger pays on this acceptance, he then becomes entitled to the rights of the holder to sue on the bill.[454]

(ii) Shipmasters

Where it is necessary to do so in order to continue a voyage, the master of a ship has authority to borrow on the ship owner's credit to pledge or mortgage the ship, cargo and freight or the cargo alone and to sell part of the cargo.[455]

(iii) Salvage

A person who goes to the aid of a ship in distress at sea and saves life is entitled to reward for his efforts. The amount of the reward is discretionary on the Court.

(iv) Land carriers

A land carrier may also have authority of necessity to sell.[456]

Four conditions must be satisfied before the agent's act can be binding on the principal. First, there must be a genuine emergency.[457] In *Praeger v. Blatspiel, Stamp & Heacock Ltd.*,[458] the plaintiff was a fur dealer in Bucharest. In 1915 and 1916, he instructed the defendants, who were fur merchants in London to buy some furs for him and send them to Bucharest. They bought the furs for him, but could not forward them to him because Rumania had been defeated and occupied by German troops. So in 1917 and 1918, they sold the furs. At the end of the war, the plaintiff brought an action against them claiming damages for conversion. The defendants said they had sold furs as agents of necessity. It was held that the action succeeded for the defendants were not agents of necessity for the sale of furs. They could have been placed in cold storage. Additionally the defendant did not act *bona fide*. Second, it must be commercially impossible to get the owner's instructions before the act is done.[459] This is now minimised because of telephone, telex and telegram facilities available in modern times. Third, the act must be done in good faith.[460] Fourth, the act must be done for the benefit of the owner and not merely the convenience of the agent.[461] In *Munro v. Wilmott*[462], with the defendant's permission, the plaintiff left his car in the defendant's yard. Some years later, the defendant wanted to have the car moved and after trying unsuccessfully to contact the plaintiff spent Eighty five pounds on making the car saleable and sold it. It was held that the defendant was liable for conversion and the damages were reduced by Eighty five pounds he spent.

It has been suggested[463] that the doctrine of necessity may also apply where one person preserves the health of another. Thus a person can sue for the value of necessaries supplied to a mental patient who has no capacity for rational thought. Section 4 of the Sale of Goods Act[464]

---

453 See also Wade, 19 *Vanderbilt L. Rev.*; Mathews [1981] *Camb L.J.* 340; O'Neill, 36 M.L.R. 638, 642; 37 M.L.R.480.

454 Bills of Exchange Act, Cap.76, Ss. 65 - 68

455 *Notara v. Henderson* (1872) L.R. 7 Q.B. 225

456 *Sims & Co. v. Midland Railway* [1913] 1 K.B. 103

457 *Sachs v. Miklos* [1948] 1 All E.R. 67; *Praeger case infra* n.458.

458 [1924] All E.R. Rep. 524

459 *Springer v. GWR* [1921] 1 K.B. 257

460 *Praeger case supra* n.458

461 *Sachs v. Miklos supra* n.457

462 [1948] 2 All E.R. 983

463 Treitel, *Law of Contract* (8th Edn. 1991), p.624

464 Cap.79

provides that "where necessaries have been sold and delivered... to a person who by reason of mental incapacity ... is incompetent to contract, he must pay a reasonable price therefor", A doctor who gives medical attention to an unconscious person might also recover a fee on the same ground.[465] Under the Road Traffic Act of the United Kingdom[466], a medical doctor who gives emergency treatment to a victim of a road accident is entitled to recover his fee.

The issue arises as to whether the doctrine of necessity should be extended beyond the four situations considered above. McCardie J in the *Praeger case*[467] thought that it should be extended because "an expanding society demands an expanding common law". However, in *Jebara v. Ottoman Bank*[468], Scrutton L.J. thought that the doctrine of necessity should only be applied where there is a subsisting or pre-existing principal - agent relationship at the time of the act in question. It should not apply where there is no pre-existing agency.

(v) Wife's agency of necessity

The law recognises a wife's agency of necessity (i) when she is deserted or justified in leaving her husband or (ii) had inadequate means of support. In those cases she can pledge her husband's credit for necessities.[469] The husband is not bound by his wife's contract where the goods and services are not regarded as necessaries. The husband can also avoid liability if he has forbidden his wife to pledge his credit.[470] Furthermore the husband will not be liable if it can be shown that the third party elected to treat the wife as principal other than an agent of her husband.[471] The creditor has the choice of suing the husband or the wife. Having made his choice but unsuccessfully, in enforcing the judgment, he cannot then sue the other party.[472]

Cohabitation without marriage is also a ground for allowing the woman to pledge the man's credit if the third party believes that the two are husband and wife.[473]

4. Relationship between principal and third party

The rights of the principal against a third party depend on the distinction between disclosed and undisclosed principals. A disclosed principal is one whose existence the third party is aware at the time of contracting. He is a named principal if the third party knows his name. He is an unnamed principal if a third party did not know his name. An unnamed principal is one whose existence the third party is unaware of at the time of contracting.

(i) Disclosed principal

The general rule is that disclosed principal can sue a third party.[474] In *Tot Ram v. Mistry Waryam Singh*[475], A was asked by his uncle (P) to obtain transport from T (third party) to take Y to Kampala. T knew that A negotiated the contract on behalf of P. Unfortunately, P later left the country and gave T a cheque that was later dishonoured. T sued A on the contract. It was held that A was not liable. T based his claim on Section 230(3) of the Indian Contract Act, then applicable in Uganda.[476] This section states the basic common law rule that A shall not be

---

465 *Cotram v. Wisdom* 83 Art. 601 104 SW 164 (1907); *Re Crisan's Estate* 362 Mich, 569, 102 N.W. 2 d 907 (1961)

466 Ss. 155, 156

467 *supra* n.458

468 [1927] 137 L.T. 101, 105

469 *Chaganlal P. Jani v. Ranchoddas Kalvanji & Anor* 8 Z.L.R.95 (Zanzibar)

470 *Debenham v. Mellon* (1850) 6 App. Cas 24

471 *Jewsbury v. Newbold* (1857) 26 L.J. Ex. 247

472 *Total Oil Products (East Africa) Ltd. v. Nuato Ltd.* 1967 (2) A.L.R. Comm. 346. See also *Nanyuki General Trading Stores v. Peterson* (1948) 15 E.A.C.A. 28.

473 *Blades v. Free* (1829) 9 B & C 167. See also Tanganyika Contract Act, S.139.

474 *Langton v. White* (1868) L.R.6 E.q.165

475 5 U.L.R. 76.

476 equivalent S.182(c) Tanganyika Contract Act Applicable in Tanzania

personally liable but gives three exceptions to the rule. The third exception applied and A should be liable. The Court explained that the true meaning of the exception was that it applied only where P cannot be sued at the time the contract was made. If a wider meaning was given then A would be liable in situations where P later died, or where P was a company that later ceased to exist. the Court added thus:

> It would be ludicrous ... if an agent having brought two parties together for their benefit where both were competent to contract and credit was given exclusively to his principal should become personally bound by the contract because at some later date it became legally or physically impossible to sue the principal.

Conversely, a third party is not discharged by settling with the agent unless the principal by his conduct induced the third party to do so or unless the agent had authority to receive payment.[477] Furthermore, a third party cannot set off against the principal any debt which the agent may owe to the third party.[478] This is because a custom which enables the agent to receive payment by such set off is unreasonable.

A foreign principal can also sue a third party.[479] In *Khonam v. Elizabeth Fife John*[480], in 1937, the defendant as attorney of Young entered into an agreement with the plaintiff for lease of certain premises in Lagos. The plaintiff tenant and Young were referred to in the agreement as owners of the premises. The plaintiff possessed the premises until 1938 when the defendant obtained judgment against him for possession. Young was living in England and the plaintiff sued the defendant for specific performance of the agreement. It was held that as the defendant entered into the agreement on behalf of a known and disclosed principal, she incurred no personal liability herself. This would be the case even if the principal was foreign. In *West African Umbrella Ltd. v. Royal Interocean Lines Ltd.*[481], the defendants were common carriers operating among other places between Japan and Lagos. The plaintiffs delivered 29 cases of umbrella clothing for purposes of conveying them from Japan to Lagos. The second defendants were agents of the first defendant for this purpose and this fact was known to all parties. The goods were short-delivered at Lagos. The plaintiffs claimed from the agents (second defendants) and the principal (first defendant) jointly and severally. It was held that the principle of the law is that where the agent's principal is foreign, it is presumptuous that the intention is to bind the agent and not the principal. The presumption does not give rise to an intention to bind the principal where this is clear from the contract itself or from the circumstances of the case. Arising from this, it is possible on construction of the contract to hold that the agent is in fact a party to it and does not merely drop out. In such a case, the third party can elect to sue the agent rather than the principal. In this instance the third party cannot later sue the principal where he fails to obtain damages from the agent. However, the situation whereby the agent is regarded as a party to the contract is unusual and the court will require fairly concrete evidence before holding the agent is liable. In *Karimjee Jivanjee & Co. v. Gulmohamed Fazaldin*[482], the plaintiff (third party) sold rails to the defendant (principal). The sale was negotiated by an agent. The principal argued that he had ordered the rails from the agent and there was no privity between the plaintiff and himself. The agent in fact presented a note drawn on himself as payment but this was dishonoured. The Court invited argument on the possibility that the

---

477 *Butwick v. Grant* [1924] 2 K.B. 483

478 *Pratt v. Willey* (1826) 2 C & P 350; *Fish v. Kempton* (1849) 7 C.B.687

479 *Teheran-Europe Co. ltd. v. S.T. Belton (Tractors) Ltd.* [1968] 2 Q.B. 545; [1968] 2 All E.R.886; *Alibhai, Adamjee Dar v. Thomsen & Eber & Sons* 16 K.L.R. (Kenya)

480 15 N.L.R. 10 (Nigeria)

481 CCHCJ/4/74, 391 (High Court of Lagos, Nigeria)

482 1 T.L.R.(R) 447

plaintiffs had elected to treat the agent as personally liable on the contract. Defence Counsel did not pursue this line of argument and the Court found on the facts that the contract was between the plaintiff and the defendants and that the former, by accepting the agent's note, had not elected thereby to surrender their rights as against the defendants. There was no evidence to show that the defendants had altered their position by reason of the promissory note given by the agent to the plaintiffs. The defendants were, therefore, liable for the price of the goods.

In *Alam Bajor Bros. v. Greek W.A. Lines & Anors,*[483] the second plaintiff and second defendant executed a contract of carriage of goods from Lagos to Valencia, Spain. Both parties signed the agreement as a "agents only". The first plaintiff and first defendant were referred to in the agreement as principals. It was common ground that the second plaintiff and second defendant acted throughout as agents. The goods arrived in Valencia without a clean bill of lading and dealing with the goods became difficult. the negotiations on how to remedy the situation between the plaintiffs and defendants failed. The plaintiffs sued the defendants for damages of Twenty-five Thousand Pounds for breach of contract of carriage. It was held that as a general rule no liability attaches to the agent who contracts on behalf of a disclosed principal whether or not the agent had the principal's express authority to make the contract. Personal liability may be imposed by the terms of the contract or by ordinary course of business. In this case the second plaintiff and second defendant acted on behalf of disclosed principals. Consequently, no liability attached to the second defendant and the right of action would be in favour of the second plaintiff. It has also been held[484] that an agent selling specific goods for a disclosed principal does not warrant the title of those goods, only that he knows no defect of in the principal's title.

(b) Undisclosed principal

An undisclosed principal can sue a third party.[485] This right is limited in three main respects.

(i) Where exercise of right inconsistent with terms of the contract

The right by an undisclosed principal to sue will not be exercisable if this is inconsistent with the terms of the contract. Thus in *Humble v. Hunter*[486] a person signed a charterparty as owner. It was held that this meant that he and he alone was the owner. In the circumstances an undisclosed principal could not intervene. However, in *Drughorn v. Transatlantic,*[487] was held that the fact that an agent signed a charterparty as "charterer" did not exclude his undisclosed principal's right to enforce the contract.

(ii) Personal Considerations

If a third party shows that he intended to deal with the agent and no one else an undisclosed principal cannot interfere. Thus in *Collins v. Associated Greyhound Racecourses Ltd.*[488], a person agreed to underwrite a new issue of shares to be made by a company that is to take up any shares for which the public did not apply. It was held that the contract relied on the business reputation and integrity of the underwriter. Consequently, his undisclosed principal was not permitted to enforce it. In *Grace v. Downs Supply Co.*[489], a person bought timber from a person who owed him money on terms that the debt should be set off against the price. It was held that he intended to deal with the seller and no one else. Consequently, the seller's undisclosed principal was not allowed to intervene. Furthermore, in *Nash v. Dix*[490] a committee of Roman Catholics wanted to

---

483 H.C. Lagos No. LD/697/69 Unreported (Nigeria)

484 *Imam v. Ahmadu Bello University* [1970] N.N.L.R.39 (Nigeria)

485 *Pople v. Evans* [1969] 2 Ch.255; *Cropton co. Inc. v. Salami Alhaji Atande* (1967) N.M.L.R. 383 (Nigeria).

486 (1842) 12 Q.B. 316

487 [1919] A.C.203

488 [1930] 1 Ch.1

489 [1927] 2 K.B. 28

490 (1898) 78 L.T. 445

buy a Chapel from the defendants and turn it into a place of Roman Catholic Worship. The defendants refused to deal with the Committee as they did not want the Chapel to be used for that purpose. The committee told the plaintiff to buy the Chapel and promised to pay him an extra One Hundred Pounds for it. The defendants sold the chapel to the plaintiff but repudiated the contract when they discovered that he intended to resell to the Committee. It was held that the defendants were bound for two reasons. First, the plaintiff was not an agent, but a person who had bought to resell. Second, the plaintiff had not been guilty of any misrepresentation. It has been observed[491] that the plaintiff would have failed if he *had* been the agent of the Committee because it was undisclosed and personal considerations were vital.

In *Said v. Butt*,[492] the plaintiff wanted to go to the first night of a play but knew the owners of the theatre would not sell him a ticket as he had in the past strongly criticised their conduct. He, therefore, sent a friend to the box-office to buy a ticket for him without disclosing his name. Later, when he turned up for the show, he was refused admission by the manager of the theatre. He sued the manager for inducing a breach of contract. It was held that there was no contract between the proprietors and the plaintiff since the proprietors reserved the right to sell first night tickets to specially selected persons the "personality" of the other contracting party was a material element. In contrast, in *Dyster v. Randall & Sons*,[493] the plaintiff wanted to buy land from the defendants, who , to his knowledge would not deal with him as they distrusted him. He, therefore, employed an agent to buy land in his name. He then claimed that he was entitled to intervene as an undisclosed principal. This was upheld by the Court, which observed that it would be futile to deny the plaintiff's right to sue since the agent could in any event have assigned the benefit of the contract to him. It was also felt that while "personal considerations" entered into the earlier two cases,[494] they did not affect this one. The case has been described[495] as unsatisfactory because in both *Said v. Butt* and *Nash v. Dix*, the agents could also have assigned the benefits of the contract to an undisclosed principal. Furthermore, how does one distinguish "religious grounds" as being personal and "distrust" against personal. It is suggested[496] that an undisclosed principal should not be allowed to intervene if he knows that the third party does not want to deal with him. If a principal directly concealed his identity as in *Said v. Butt,* the contract would be void for mistake and voidable for fraud. The principal should not be able to improve his position by employing an agent.

(iii) Third party defence

An undisclosed principal can only sue the third party subject to defences which the third party has against the agent. The rule is necessary where the third party claims he is dealing with the agent only. Consequently, if the third party owes the third party money, the third party can set off this money against anything he owes the principal.[497] An undisclosed principal is only bound by the third party's set-off where the agent has actual or apparent authority to contract as principal. Thus in *Cooke v. Eshelby*[498], A who was acting for an undisclosed principal, P, sold cotton to a third party (T). P sued T, who claimed to set-off a debt due from A to T on general account. Before the trial, T admitted that he dealt with A as broker without knowing whether

---

491 Treitel, *Law of Contract* (8th Ed,), p.632.

492 [1920] 3 K.B. 497

493 [1926] Ch.932

494 *Said v. Butt, supra* n.492; *Nash v. Dix supra* n.490

495 Treitel, *supra*, n.491, p.633.

496 *Ibid.*

497 *Cooke v. Eshelby* (1887) 12 App. Cas. 271; *Drakeford v. Piercey* (1866) 14 L.T. 403; *Chellarms v. Najih Abdalla* (1954) 14 W.A.C.A. 495; *Basma v. Gladys Muriel Weeks & Ors.* (1948) 12 W.A.C.A. 316; [1950] A.C. 441 P.C.; *Crompton Richmond Co. v. Salami Alhaji Atande* [1967] N.M.L.R. 383 (High Court of Lagos, Nigeria)

498 *Ibid.*

they were acting for the principal or themselves. The House of Lords held that the plea of set-off failed. In *Drakeford v. Piercy*[499], it was held that a plea of payment to an agent is insufficient unless the agent was a factor or had been authorised by the undisclosed principal to act as principal or to receive payment.

(iv) Liability of principal to third party

The general rule is that a principal whether disclosed or undisclosed is liable to a third party. The limitations on the right of the undisclosed principal to intervene are aimed at protecting the third party. Consequently, they do not apply where he third party sues the principal. However, an undisclosed principal is not liable if the true effect of the contract is that the agent shall alone be entitled under it. The effects of this are that a principal cannot set off against the third party any money owed to him by the agent.[500] If the principal gives the agent money to pay the third party and the agent fails to pay it over, the principal is still liable to the third party.[501] The principal is only discharged by payment to the agent if such payment is made against the third party's request[502] or if the third party expects payment from the agent and so induced the principal to settle with the agent.[503] In the Tanzanian Case, *Tanganyika Farmers Associations Ltd. v. Unyamwezi Development Corporation Ltd.*,[504] money was paid by the defendants to the plaintiff's agents who subsequently disappeared. The plaintiffs successfully claimed from the defendants. The Court of Appeal for East Africa approved the words of the trial judge thus:

> I find they (the agents) had no authority to receive payment on behalf of the plaintiffs. There is no evidence of it and no reason to assume it. Such authority is not necessary to the business of brokerage and was not necessary to this particular transaction. There is no evidence or precedent of any relevant customary authority ... there was no ostensible authority.

In *Acharya Travel Agencies (Uganda) Ltd. v. Arua Bus Syndicate,*[505] the third party supplied A with air tickets knowing that they were intended for P. P paid the money to A, but A disappeared. P was liable to the third party. P argued, however, that by debiting A's account the third party had shown that A was in a position to receive such payment. This was rejected. In Bennet J.'s words:

> I do not consider that the mere fact that the plaintiff debited Bhatt (A) with the price of the tickets in its ledger and sent the invoices to him, amounted to a representation that the plaintiff looked to Bhatt (A) alone for payment. There is no evidence that the defendant knew that the plaintiff had debited Bhatt's account with the price of the tickets and that it had sent the invoices to Bhatt, so that these two facts cannot amount to a representation that the credit was given exclusively to Bhatt. As already indicated, I do not consider that, having regard to the nature of the contract, the delay in applying to the defendant for payment amounted to a representation that the debt had been paid or entitled the defendant to infer that the plaintiff had abandoned its right of recourse to the defendant.

---

499 (1866) 14 L.T. 403

500 *Warring v. Favenck* (1807) 2 Camp 85

501 *Irvine v. Watson* (1880) 5 Q.B.D. 414. c.f. *Armstrong v. Stokes* (1872) L.R. 7 Q.B. 598.

502 *Smyth v. Anderson* (1849) 7 C.B. 21

503 *Wyatt v. Hertford* (1802) 3 East. 147 c.f. *Ebrahim Sherif v. Bousted Bros.* 1 Z.L.R. 178 (Zanzibar, Tanzania); Hodgin, *Law of Contract In East Africa* (1975), p.265 - 266. See also *Hussein Aly Dharamsi Hasmani v. National Bank of India Ltd.* 5 E.A.C.A. 99(T)

504 [1970] E.A. 620

505 [1966] E.A. 511; 1966(2) A.L.R. Comm 246

5. Relationship between third party and agent

(a) General rule

The general rule is that an agent is neither liable under[506] or entitled to enforce[507] a contract he makes on behalf of his principal.

(b) Exceptions

(i) Where agent contracts personally

An agent is liable if he in fact intended to undertake personal liability under the contract. Thus in *Basma.v. Weekes*[508], an agent who was described as a party to a written contract and who signed it without any qualification was held to be liable under it, even if the third party knew he was contracting as agent. However in *Mahony v. Kekule*[509] it was held that an agent who is descried as agent and signs as agent is not liable. Similarly where an agent is liable he is also entitled under the contract.[510]

(ii) Trade usage or custom

An agent may be personally liable or entitled if that is the usual course of business either between particular parties or in relation to a particular class of agents. For instance where "one attorney does work for another, it is common practice for him to give credit to that other and not to the client."[511] A local or trade custom can have the same effect.[512]

(iii) Principal undisclosed

An agent is both entitled and liable under the contract where the principal is undisclosed.[513] However, if the agent uses words of representation, he will not be liable even if he does not name the principal.[514]

(iv) Agent in fact principal

If an agent purports to be acting for an unnamed principal when he is in fact acting for himself he can enforce a contract for his benefit. In *Schmalz v. Avery*[515] a person was described in a charterparty as "agent for the freighters". He was held personally liable after it was proved that he was in fact the freighter. However, if he purports to act for a named principal, he can only enforce the contract after giving notice to the third party that he acted on his own behalf.[516] Even then, the agent may not be allowed to sue if this would prejudice the third party.[517]

(v) Where principal non existent

Where the agent contracts on behalf of a non-existent principal, he is himself personally liable. In *Kelner v. Baxter*,[518] the promoters of a company were held personally liable on a contract

---

506 *Robins v. Bridge* (1837) 3 M & W 114; *Ferguson v. Wilson* (1866) L.R. 2 Ch. App.77; *N & J Vlassopulos v. Ney Shipping Ltd.* [1977] Lloyds Rep. 478

507 *Lucas v. Beale* (1851) 10 C.B. 739; *Fairie v. Fenton* (1870) L.R. 5 Ex.169

508 [1950] A.C. 441; [1950] 2 All E.R. 146 PC (Nigeria)

509 (1854) 14 C.B. 490

510 *Brandt & Co. v. H.N. Morris & Co. Ltd.* [1917] 2 K.B. 784

511 *Scrace v. Whittington* (1823) 2 B & C. 11

512 *Fleet v. Murton* (1871) L.R. 7 Q.B. 126

513 *Sims v. Bond* (1833) 5 B & Ad 389, 393

514 *Universal Steam Navigation Co. v. James McKelvie & Co.* [1923] A.C. 492; *Benton v. Campbell, Parker & Co. Ltd.* [1925] 2 K.B. 410

515 (1851) 16 Q.B. 655

516 *Bickerton v. Burell* (1816) 5 M & S 383

517 *Fellowes v. Gwydyr* (1829) 1 Russ. & M.83

518 (1866) L.R. 2 C.P. 174 See c.f. *Phonogram Ltd. v. Lane* [1982] Q.B. 938

made by them on behalf of a company which had not yet been formed. In *Holman v. Pullin*[519] it was held that the Chairman of the *Turnbridge Wells Medical Association* could not sue on behalf of the Association before it existed as a legal person. It follows that an agent is not a contracting party merely because he purported to act for a non-existent principal, the question being one of intention in each case.[520]

(vi) Deeds

At common law, an agent who executed a deed was personally liable on it even though the deed is expressed to have been executed on behalf of his principal.[521] This rule appears to have been overruled in the United Kingdom by statute.[522]

(b)Third party election

A third party may elect to sue either the agent or the third party. However, this remains a question of fact depending on the circumstances. The issue of a writ against the principal does not necessarily mean that the agent cannot be sued, after the third party has previously threatened to sue the agent.[523]

(c) Under collateral contract

There may be a collateral contract between the agent and the third party distinct from the main contract between the principal and the third party. For instance, an auctioneer to whom goods are given for sale undertakes certain obligations towards the buyer, but these are not the same as those of the seller. The seller undertakes that he has a right to sell, but the auctioneer undertakes to give the buyer possession.[524] Consequently, the auctioneer is not liable for the seller's lack of title.[525] The collateral contract may confer rights, as well as impose liabilities on the agent. Thus an auctioneer can sue the buyer for the price of the things sold.[526]

(d) Implied warranty of authority

(i) Liability

If an agent purports to act for a principal when in fact he has no authority to do so he is liable for breach of warranty of authority. Thus in *Collen v. Wright*[527]A purported to act on P's behalf. He granted a lease of P's land to T (third party). A had no authority to do this and P was not bound by his acts. It was held that A's personal representatives were liable to T for A's breach of warranty of authority. In *Yonge v. Toynbee*,[528] a solicitor conducted litigation on behalf of a client who had gone mad. Following this, but before the solicitor heard of it, he took further steps in the action. It was held that the other party to the action could recover from the solicitor the costs incurred by him in consequence of the solicitor's continuing the litigation after his authority to do so had come to an end because of his client's madness. It was irrelevant that the solicitor had acted in good faith and with due diligence.

---

519 (1884) Cab. & El. 254

520 *Black v. Smallwood* [1966] A.L.R. 744; Baxt 30. Mod. L.R. 328; Adelaide L. Rev. 102; See also *Newborne v. Sensolid (G.B.) Ltd.* [1954] 1 Q.B.45.

521 *Appleton v. Binks* (1804) 5 East. 148

522 Powers of Attorney Act 1971, S.7(1) as amended by Law of Property (Miscellaneous Provisions) Act, 1989; Ss. 1(8) and 4 and Scheds. 1 and 2.

523 *Clarkson Brooker Ltd. v. Andjel* [1964] 2 Q.B. 775; [1964] 3 All E.R. 260; c.f. *The Scaplake* [1978] 2 Lloyd's Rep. 380

524 *Woolfe v. Horne* (1877) 2 Q.B.D. 355; *Wood v. Baxter* (1883) 49 L.T. 45

525 *Benton v. Campbell, Parker & Co.* [1925] 2 K.B. 410

526 *Coppin v. Walker* (1816) 7 Taunt 237

527 (1857) E & B. 647

528 [1910] 1 K.B. 215

In contrast, in *McDonnel v. Kimani*[529] P agreed to sell his farm to T. Before the transaction was completed, P left Kenya and appointed A, an Advocate, as his power of attorney. T was informed of this . P told A that if any lesser sum was offered for the farm then A must contact P for instructions. Contrary to this order, A negotiated a contract for a smaller sum than P had intended. P now refused to execute the formal deed. The Court held in favour of T and granted a decree of specific performance. Newbold, P explained that A was authorised to act as an agent in the negotiations and as the contract had been entered into in good faith the later limitations placed on A by P could not affect the contract in the absence of knowledge of the limitation by T. Spry J. A. drew a distinction between A acting as an advocate and A acting under a power of attorney. In the first category, he considered A would only bind P if he was acting on the express instructions of P. But acting under power of attorney was a different matter. Here he had power to conclude a contract and although he had exceeded his specific instructions his act still bound P.

(ii) Restrictions on liability

An agent is not, or may not be, liable for breach of implied warranty of authority in the following cases:

(i) Where lack of authority known to third party

An agent is not liable if the third party knew or must be taken to have known that the agent had no authority.[530] The agent may also not be liable where he and the third party had equal means of knowing that the agent had no authority. In *Smout v. Ilbery*[531] a wife ordered goods from the plaintiff as agent for the husband, who unknown to either party had died in China before the order was placed. It was held that the wife was not liable because the continuance of the life of the principal was a fact equally within the knowledge of both contracting parties. Professor Treitel has argued[532] that the case is not actually authority on breach of warranty of authority but on a claim for goods sold and delivered, that is, on the main contract. It is, therefore, not authority for an agent's breach of warranty.[533]

A related point is that in practical terms, the principal must make effort to inform those who might have dealings with the agent that the agent no longer has powers formerly exercised by him. It is common, in this respect, in Uganda to advertise in local newspapers that a particular person no longer has the power to negotiate on behalf of the principal. While express notice by the principal to the third party might not be necessary, the principal must still show that the matter came to the attention of the other party. Thus in *Rwenzori Construction Co. v. B.K. Musenze*,[534] the plaintiff company had supplied goods to the defendant to the value of Shs.36,844/= Out of that sum Shs.25,000/= had been paid but the defendants argued that they were not liable for the remainder as they had warned the plaintiff not to deal further with their former agent. This warning had been given to the father of the manager of the plaintiff company. It was held that this was not sufficient notice, actual or constructive and the principal was liable for the price outstanding. This applied even if the agent had contracted on his own behalf without intending to bind the principal.[535]

---

529 [1967] E.A. 702; 1967(3) A.L.R. Comm. 147

530 *Jones v. Hope* (1880) 3 T.L.R. 247; *McDonnel v. Kimani, Ibid.*

531 (1842) 10 M & W. 1

532 Treitel, *Law of Contract* (8th Ed.), p.641

533 See *Oliver v. Bank of England* [1901] 1 Ch. 652, 660

534 Civil Suit No. 101 of 1969 (Uganda)

535 following *Trueman v. Loder* (1840) 11 A & E 589

(ii) Representation of law
An agent is not liable where the representation of authority is one of law.[536] For instance, the construction of a document is a matter of law. Consequently, the agent is not liable for misrepresenting its meaning. Thus in *Rashdall v. Ford*,[537] a director of a company (which on a true construction of its memorandum of association had no borrowing powers) borrows on its behalf is not liable for breach of an implied warranty. He would be liable where the company has borrowing powers up to a given limit which he exceeds, this being a misrepresentation of fact.[538]

(iii) Where principal liable on main contract
An agent who has no actual authority is not liable for breach of warranty if the principal is liable to the third party on the ground of apparent or usual authority. Thus in *Rainbow v. Howkins*,[539] an auctioneer who had authority to sell a horse, subject to a reserve price sold it without reserve. It was held that he was not liable for breach of implied warranty as the buyer could have enforced the main contract as seller on the ground that the auctioneer had apparent authority to sell without reserve. Furthermore, an agent is not liable for breach of implied warranty if he did an unauthorised act which the principal later ratified.

6. Termination of Agency

Subject to certain limitations on the termination of the agency relationship, which shall be examined shortly, an agency may be terminated in two principal ways. First, by the act of the parties to the agency. Second, by operation of law.

(i) Act of the Parties
Since the agency relationship is normally created by an agreement between the principal and agent, it could similarly be determined by both of them agreeing to end the relationship. This is so even if there is an agreement that the relationship will last for a given period or indeed should be irrevocable. The agreement as to termination may be contained in the contract creating the agency. Thus in the Nigerian case of *Esso West African Inc. v. Ali*[540], an agency agreement provided for termination at the end of six months or thereafter by one month's notice. It was held that the agreement could be terminated by either party at the end of six months without notice. The court observed that in an agency contract any unilateral termination of the relationship by either party is wrongful unless it is in accordance with the contract. However, where the agency has not ended in accordance with the agreement, the other party to it would be entitled to reasonable notice of its termination.

(ii) Revocation by principal
Since normally an agency is created for the benefit of the principal, he is free at any time to revoke it or any authority granted to the agent. Such revocation may well constitute a breach of contract. The effect of this is that even if the revocation is effective the principal may be liable in damages to the agent or third party for breach of contract. In *Moritz Eber v. A Thomsen*[541], P employed A to sell goods on a commission basis for a period of five years. During that period P attempted to persuade A to accept a lower rate of commission and threatened to dismiss him if

---

536 *Saffron Welden v. Raynor* (1880) 14 Ch.D. 406

537 (1866) L.R. 2 Eq. 750

538 *Cherry v. Colonial Bank of Australasia* (1869) L.R. 3 P.C. 24; *Weeks v. Propert* (1873) L.R. 8 C.P. 427

539 [1904] 2 K.B. 322

540 [1968] N.M.L.R. 414 (High Court of Ibadan)

541 2 E.A.C.A. 34

he did not conform. A elected to treat P's behaviour as a repudiation of the original agreement and sued for damages. P's defence was that on an earlier occasion A had acted in such a way that P would have been entitled to dismiss him. It was held that once P condones A's behaviour he cannot at a later date use that as an excuse for breaking the contract. Consequently, in this case, A was entitled to damages.

The general principle as to liability for damages for breach of contract is subject to situations of irrevocable authority and the requirement of reasonable notice before termination. In *Alexander Logios v. A-G of Nigeria,*[542] it was held that although the principal has a right of revocation, a third party with whom the agent had dealt was entitled to assume that the agency was still subsisting since no step was taken to inform him that the agency had been revoked and warning him not to deal further with the agent on the principal's behalf.

The agent may be dismissed summarily if he is found to be guilty of any misconduct or breach of duty to his principal. No formality is required for revocation. Revocation is effective if the principal informs the agent or third party personally or if both of them learn independently of the event revoking the agent's authority. Revocation may be by word of mouth or by the principal intervening during the course of negotiation by the agent and informing the parties concerned.[543]

Where the agency was created by written authority for instance by a power of attorney, the principal's revocation should also be effected in the same way. This should be contrasted with the view that a deed may be revoked by word of mouth.[544] A revocation may be implied where the principal withdraws all necessary facilities originally provided to the agent for proper execution of the agency. Conversely, until the principal takes such action, the agent or third party is justified in assuming that the agency is still in existence.[545]

(iii) Renunciation by agent

Renunciation by an agent occurs where the agent personally terminates the agency relationship between him and the principal. Apart from situations of irrevocable authority, there is implied in all agency relationships a power to renounce his authority at any time before it ends.[546] Similar to revocation by the principal, renunciation of authority by the agent may be a breach of the agency contract and render him liable in damages to the principal. Additionally, reasonable notice of revocation must be given by the agent.[547] However, the agent may revoke his authority without notice where the principal is guilty of misconduct or breach of duty to the agent. Renunciation may be in writing by word of mouth or simply refusing to act in accordance with the agency. If the renunciation is wrongful, the agent may be liable in damages or forfeit his commission or remuneration. In cases of lawful renunciation, the agent is entitled to reasonable value of such services and a proportion of agreed commission or remuneration excepting damages sustained by the principal as a result of the renunciation.

---

542 (1938) 4 W.A.C.A.

543 *Alexander v. Davis & Co.* (1885) 2 T.L.R. 142

544 *The Margaret Mitchell Case* (1858) SW.582; 4 Jur. N.S. 1193

545 *The Oriental Bank Corpn. ex parte Guillemin* (1885) 28 Ch.D. 643.

546 *Lowe v. Rutherford McRae Ltd.* (1971) 14 D.L.R. (3d) 772 (Canada); *The Margaret Mitchell Case, supra* n.544.

547 *Ekuigbo v. Ibru Sea Food Ltd.* Suit No.3/36/1969 (High Court of Benin, Nigeria); *Harold Sodipo v. Daily Times of Nigeria* High Court of Lagos Suit No. LD 130 1969; *Esso Standard (Nig) Ltd. v. Adekunle* High Court of Ibadan Suit No. 1209/1968.

(b) Termination by operation of law

(i) By performance

Where the agent's authority was given for a specific purpose, his authority will terminate when that purpose is accomplished. For instance, the authority of a solicitor who is engaged to prosecute a particular case will cease when judgment is delivered in that case.[548] Similarly, the authority of an auctioneer engaged to sell specific property terminates after the sale of the property.[549] Furthermore, a broker who has sold goods for a sale for which he was employed is regarded as *functus officio*[550] Professor Fridman has argued[551] that is difficult to know when some agents have executed their authority as in the case of estate agents. Second, although the agent's express or implied authority may have been executed, it is possible that the agent may continue to act in a way which suggests to the third party that he still has authority. In such case the agency relationship is one of apparent authority *(supra)*. This apparent authority will only end in two ways. First, when it is turned into real authority by ratification and then termination by performance. Second when notice of the agent's lack of authority has reached third parties.

(ii) Effluxion of time

The agency will end when the period for which it was created expires. This will be so regardless of whether the task for which the agency was created has been carried out or not. Where no time is fixed by the parties to the agency, a reasonable time for the duration of such agency is implied and the authority will terminate at the end of such reasonable time. What is a reasonable time depends on the facts of the particular case and surrounding circumstances. This period may also be fixed by custom or usage of the particular trade, business or profession to which the agent belongs. In *Dickinson v. Lilwal*[552], general authority to sell certain goods was given to a broker. The custom of the particular trade in which the broker was employed provided that such an authority if not limited by express agreement, was to expire at the end of the day on which it was given. The broker made a contract on behalf of his principal two days after the day he was given his authority. It was held that the contract was not binding on the principal.

(iii) Frustration

If property, which is the subject-matter of the agency is destroyed, or otherwise ceases to exist, for instance where the principal sells business with which the agent is connected, the agency terminates automatically. In *Rhodes v. Forwood,* [553] the agent was employed under a contract to sell the principal's coal. After four years, the principal sold the colliery and went out of business. It was held that the principal was not liable to the agent for breach of contract. It was observed that there was nothing in the agency contract by which the principal bound himself to maintain the colliery. There was also no term as to the length of service. Lord Hatherley further stated that the agency was not necessarily determined when its subject-matter was gone or disappeared without *mala fides* (bad faith) on either side.

Regardless of the end of the agency, the agent may still be entitled to a commission or remuneration. Thus in *Turner v. Goldsmith,*[554] A was employed on a commission basis by P to sell Shirts. P's factory, at which shirts which were manufactured were accidentally burnt down. It was held that P was liable to pay A a reasonable sum representing what he would have been likely to earn by way of commission.

---

[548] *Butler v. Knight* (1867) L.R. 2 Ex. 109

[549] *Bell v. Balls* [1897] 1 Ch.D. 663

[550] *Blackburn v. Scholes* (1810) 2 Camp 341 per Lord Ellenborough

[551] Fridman *Law of Agency* p.309.

[552] (1815) 4 Camp 279.

[553] (1876) 1 App. Cas 256

[554] [1891] 1 Q.B. 544

(iv) Death of principal or agent

If either the principal or agent dies, the agency is determined.[555] This is because the agency relationship is confidential and personal. Consequently, the physical existence is very material. The effect of death is that the rights of the parties are frozen at the time of death. In *Pool v. Pool,*[556] it was held that if the principal died, the agent could not recover expenses incurred after the date of death even if he had no knowledge of the death of the principal. In *Campanari v. Woodburn*[557], A was appointed to sell a picture for P. He made several attempts but failed to sell it. Then P died. Unaware of P's death, A continued with efforts to sell the picture and eventually did so. It was held that P's personal representatives were not liable to pay A commission on sale. However, personal representatives are liable to pay the agent a reasonable sum for services he had performed. They can also be held liable to pay a commission if they ratify the agent's contract of sale.[558]

Where the agent dies, his personal representatives are not bound to execute his authority. Where the principal or agent is a company, the agency ends when the company is dissolved or ceases to exist.

(v) Insanity of the principal or agent

Except in cases of irrevocable authority, the insanity or other legal incapacity of the principal or agent will in ordinary circumstances terminate the agency. This is because the insane person cannot validly contract so as to appoint or act as agent.[559] However, the termination of the agency may not affect the liability of the principal or agent to third parties. Thus in *Drew v. Nunn*[560], a husband gave his wife authority to act on his behalf and held her out as his agent. Then he became insane. While he was insane the wife ordered goods from the plaintiff, who knew nothing of the husband's insanity. Later the husband recovered his sanity. It was held that he was liable to the plaintiff for the price of the goods. However, this approach appears to have been contradicted in *Yonge v. Toynbee*[561], where the English Court of Appeal held that where the principal became insane, the solicitors who were acting for him in litigation were personally liable to the other party for costs incurred in the proceedings. This was so even if they were unaware of the principal's insanity. This was because the solicitors warranted the authority which they did not have because of the principal's insanity. This reasoning contradicts *Drew v. Nunn*[562] where the agent in similar circumstances was held to continue to have authority although it was *apparent* rather than *real*. Both cases have been criticised[563] as being irreconcilable because they seem to indicate that *both* the principal *and* agent can be made liable to a third party who transacts business with the agent in ignorance of the principal's insanity. In *Re Parks, Canada Permanent Trust Co. v. Parks,*[564] the New Brunswick Supreme Court held thus:

> Unsoundness of mind ... is ... sufficient to determine a contract of agency between the principal and agent though the authority of the agent is not revoked with regard to the third party who has been dealing with the agent, unless such third party has knowledge of the mental incompetency of the principal.

---

555 *Blades v. Free* (1829) 9 B & C 167; Tanganyika Contract Act, S.153

556 (1889) 58 L.J.P. 67

557 (1854) 15 C.B. 400

558 *Foster v. Bates* (1843) 12 M & W 226

559 *Drew v. Nunn* (1879) 4 Q.B.D. 661

560 *Ibid.*

561 [1910] 1 K.B. 215. Se also Tanganyika contract Act, S.153

562 *supra* n.8

563 Powell, *Law of Agency* (2nd Ed.)

564 (1957) D.L.R. (2d) 155.

This supports the view that the agent should not be liable personally to a third party at least where the agent has acted in ignorance of the disability.

(vi) Bankruptcy of the principal or agent

Since agency is a personal relationship, when a person becomes bankrupt his rights vest in the trustee in bankruptcy. As a result the agency is affected in this way and ceases to have a personal touch. Where the principal is bankrupt the agency is terminated unless the agent's authority is irrevocable.[565]

(c) Termination of agency created by operation of law

(i) Agency of necessity

Since agency of necessity does not arise from express agreement, it is not terminated by either agreement of the parties or unilateral act. The relationship terminates only when the necessity which brought it into being has disappeared.[566]

(ii) Agency by cohabitation

This presumed agency arises from cohabitation between a husband and wife or man and woman who are not married. A woman's authority ceases when the couple cease to cohabit unless the man holds the woman out as having apparent authority to act on his behalf. A woman's authority may also terminate when notice is given to a tradesman that parties have ceased to cohabit.[567] The wife's authority ends in the following circumstances. First, if the marriage is terminated by a decree of divorce or declared void by decree of nullity. Second, if the parties no longer cohabit as a result of a decree of judicial separation. Third, if the spouses have separated by mutual consent without any agreement about payment of maintenance by the husband. Fourth, if the spouses have separated by mutual consent without agreement as to maintenance and the wife has means of support. Fifth, if the wife has left the deserted husband. Finally, if the husband dies. The wife's authority may also be terminated by the insanity of the husband, but the wife may be personally liable for breach of the implied warranty of authority.[568] However, if the husband recovers then he may be liable for goods supplied while he was insane.[569] Furthermore, if the husband gives his wife sufficient allowance then her authority to pledge his credit will no longer exist.[570] This also applies to a mistress.

(d) Restriction on termination

(i) Irrevocable authority/authority coupled with interest

Revocation will not be possible without the agent's consent where the agent is given authority to act on the principal's behalf but in respect of or for the protection of the agent's authority. The principle only applies where the purpose of the agency is to secure the agent for instance in respect of a debt, owed by the principal to the agent or where the purpose of the agency is to create a beneficial interest in favour of the agent. The principle does not apply where the sole purpose of the agency is to enable the agent to earn his commission by acting on the principal's behalf. In *Smart v. Saunders*,[571] a factor sent goods to sell on behalf of a principal. He made advances to the principal on security of goods. It was held that the authority was irrevocable. In

565 *Elliott v. Turquand* (1881) 7 App. Cas. 79; Tanganyika Contract Act. S.153

566 Fridman *Law of Agency* (4th Ed.) p.312

567 *Munro v. De Chemant* (1815) 4 Camp 215; *Ryan v. Sams* (1848) 12 Q.B. 460

568 *Yonge v. Toynbee, supra* n.561

569 *Drew v. Nunn, supra* n.559

570 *Morel Bros & Co. v. Earl of Westmoreland* [1903] A.C. 11; *Debenham v. Mellon* (1880) 6 App. Cas 24

571 *Smart v. Saunders* (1848) 5 CB 595

572 (1896) 75 L.T. 45

Re Hannan's Empress Gold Mining & Dev. Co. Ltd.[572], Phillips was a promoter of a company to which he was going to sell mining property. In February, 1896, he received from Carmichael an underwriting letter by which he agreed to subscribe for 1,000 shares in the company should the public not take them up. Carmichael was to be paid an underwriting commission for so doing. The company was incorporated on 24 March. On 30 March, Carmichael wrote to Phillips repudiating any authority contained in the underwriting letter to apply for shares on his behalf. On 2nd April, Phillips applied for the shares for Carmichael and the company allotted them to Carmichael. Carmichael applied to have his name removed from the register of shareholders. It was held by the English Court of Appeal that the authority given to Phillips to apply for shares for Carmichael was coupled with an interest. Its purpose was to enable Phillips to obtain a purchase price for the mine. Consequently, it was irrevocable and Carmichael's name could not be removed from the register.

In *Raleigh v. Atkinson*[573], P entrusted goods to A for sale. From time to time, A made advances to P and received authority to dispose of the goods at market value and to repay himself the advances out of the proceeds. It was held that his authority was coupled with an interest and was, therefore, irrevocable.

(ii) Accrued or vested interest

Where the agent incurs personal liability, the principal is bound to indemnify him in respect of the liability. Thus in *Read v. Anderson*[574], A was employed to make bets on behalf of P. He was authorised to pay if he lost. It was held that P could not revoke after this had happened, but was liable to indemnify A since A for the sake of character and business was bound to pay the amount that had been lost.

---

573 (1840) 6 M.W. 870

574 (1884) 13 Q.B.D. 779.

13
ASSIGNMENT[575*]

The benefit of a contract can be transferred to a third party by a process known as assignment. This is a transaction between the person entitled to the benefit of the contract (called the creditor or assignor) and the third party (called the assignee) as a result of which the assignee becomes entitled to sue the person liable under the contract (called the debtor). The debtor is not a party to the transaction and his consent is not necessary for its validity.

1. Assignment at common law

The Common law refused to give effect to assignments of "choses in action" that is rights which could only be enforced by bringing an action and not by taking possession of a physical thing. Examples of these are debts, shares, debentures, copyrights and insurance policies. The early lawyers found it difficult to comprehend the transfer of something intangible like a contractual right.[576] The rule was based on the fear that assignments of choses in action could lead to maintenance or unnecessary litigation.[577]

However, the common law enforced three types of transactions which in effect amounted to assignment.

(a) Novation[578]

Novation is a contract between debtor, creditor and a third party that the debt owed by the debtor shall from that point on be owed to a third party. This is not assignment because the consent of all three parties,[579] including that of the debtor, is necessary and because the original debt is not, strictly transferred. The third party's rights against the debtor are based on the new contract between him and the debtor.[580] Consequently, the third party will fail if no consideration moves from him for the debtor's promise to pay him.[581]

(b) Acknowledgment[582]

If a creditor asks his debtor to pay a third party and the debtor agrees to do so and notifies the third party of the agreement, then the third party is entitled to sue the debtor.[583] The issue arose as to whether such a transaction had to be supported by consideration from the third party. Originally, the view was that consideration was in general necessary but that it was not necessary where the debtor actually had in his hands (e.g. as banker) a fund belonging to the creditor.[584]

575* See also Marshall, *Assignment of Choses in Action;* Bailey, 47 L.Q.R. 248, 547.

576 Pollock and Maitland, *History of English Law*, Vol.II, p.226.

577 *Johnson v. Collings* (1880) 1 East 98; *Fitzroy v. Cave* [1905] 2 K.B. 364, 372; *Wilson v. Coupland* (1821) 5 B & Ald. 228, 232

578 Ames, *Lectures*, p.298

579 *The Aktion* [1987] 1 Lloyd's Rep. 283, 309

580 *Rasbora Ltd. v. J.C.L. Marine Ltd.* [1977] 1 Lloyd's Rep. 645

581 *Tatlock v. Harris* (1789) 3 T.R. 174, 180

582 Davis, 75 L.Q.R.220

583 *Wilson v. Coupland, supra* n.577

584 *Liversidge v. Broadbent* (1859) 4 H & N. 603, 612

Such a distinction has been disregarded in the relatively more recent case of *Shamia v. Joory*[585]. The defendant owed some One Thousand, Two Hundred Pounds to his agent Youssuf, who asked him to pay Five Hundred Pounds of this to the plaintiff, Youssuf's brother. The defendant agreed to pay and notified the plaintiff of this. It was held that the plaintiff could sue the defendant for the Five Hundred Pounds, though no consideration moved from him. If this decision is right[586] acknowledgment "is in one respect more advantageous than assignment since certain types of assignment have to be supported by consideration."[587] However, it is less advantageous than assignment since it requires the consent of the debtor.

(c) Power of attorney

A creditor gives a third party a power of attorney authorising him to sue for a debt in the creditor's name without liability to account to the creditor. This is not helpful, though to the assignee because the creditor can at any time revoke the power and this is automatically done at his death.[588]

2. Equitable assignments

Equity regarded choses in action as property.[589] which could be transferred.[590] Enforcement of such assignment of a chose-in-action depended on their nature which could be legal or equitable. A legal chose-in-action is one which could only be sued for in a common law court e.g. a contract debt. An equitable chose is one which could only be sued for in the Court of Chancery, e.g. interest in a trust fund.

(a) Legal choses

The issue arises as to why a person could only sue for a legal chose in common law Court. Four reasons have been given.[591] First, equity did not enforce purely legal debts. Second, a debtor may suffer if he were sued again for the same debt by the original debtor at common law. He would have to take separate proceedings in Chancery to make good his defence. Third, the assignor may retain some interest in the debt, e.g. he might only assign part of it. Consequently, it was desirable for the action to go before the Common Law Court so that the rights of all parties could be determined in one action. Fourth, the assignor might challenge the validity of the assignment. In such a case it was better for him to appear before a Common Law Court.

All these problems were solved by allowing the assignee to sue the debtor at common law in the name of the assignor. If the assignor was unco-operative, equity could compel him to do so. Now that the common law and equity are administered in the same courts, the first two reasons have been discarded. However the third and fourth reasons are still important and make it necessary to have all the parties before the Court, where there is a dispute.[592] However, the action against the debtor does not have to be brought in the name of the assignor.[593] He is merely joined as co-plaintiff if he co-operates with the assignee, and as co-defendant if he is not, for instance where he challenges the validity of the assignment. Nevertheless, the machinery for joining the assignor as

---

585 [1958] 1 Q.B. 448

586 For critique see Goff & Jones, *The Law of Restitution* (3rd Ed.) pp. 518 - 521

587 Treitel, *Law of Contract* (International Student Edition, 8th Ed., 1991), pp.577, 585 - 592.

588 *Ibid.* p.651

589 c.f. *Alloway v. Phillips* (Inspector of Taxes) [1980] 1 W.L.R. 888, 893

590 *Crouch v. Martin* (1707) 2 Vern 595

591 Treitel, *supra* n.587, p. 578

592 *The Aiolos* [1983] 2 Lloyd's Rep. 25, 33

593 *Weddel v. J. A. Pearce & Major* [1988] Ch. 26, 40

a party to the action may breakdown if the assignor ceases to exist e.g. where the assignor, being a company, is dissolved.[594] Where, however, the assignor is a natural person and has died, it appears possible for the assignee to sue, joining the assignor's legal personal representative.[595]

(b) Equitable choses

The assignee of an equitable chose could in his own name sue the trustee in the Court of Chancery.[596] Since the chose was equitable, the trustee was not exposed to the danger of a later action in the Common Law Court by the assignor. It was only necessary to make the assignor a party to the proceedings if he retained some interest in the property. If he wished to dispute the validity of the assignment, he could take separate proceedings for that purpose.[597]

3. Statutory assignments

Certain specific contracts such as life and marine insurance policies and bills of lading were made assignable by statute during the nineteenth century in Britain.[598]

A more general provision was made by the Judicature Act, 1873 which fused the Courts of common law and equity.[599] The effect of this was to render obsolete the reasons *(supra)* for the old method of enforcement of legal choses. In addition, an assignee could sue in any division of the high Court. Furthermore, a debtor who had been successfully sued by the assignee no longer had to engage in separate proceedings if sued again by the assignor: he could simply rely on his payment to the assignee as a defence against the second action. Consequently, it was no longer necessary to have the assignor before court unless he retained an interest in the subject matter or wished to dispute the validity of the assignment.

Section 25(6) of the Judicature Act,[600a] provides that an absolute assignment in writing under the hand of the assignor (not purporting to be by way of charge only) of any debt or other legal thing in action, of which express notice in writing has been given to the debtor or trustee, is effectual in law to pass the legal right to the debt or thing in action to the assignee. The effect of this is to enable the assignee to sue the debtor in his own name, and to sue alone, i.e. without joining the assignor as a party to the action. The subsection also makes provision for enabling the assignor to dispute the validity of the assignment; if he does so, the debtor can drop out of the proceedings and leave the dispute to be fought out between assignor and assignee.

(a) Absolute assignment

The assignee can only sue alone if the assignment is absolute; this excludes cases where the assignor retains an interest in the subject matter so that it is desirable to have him before the Court. Absolute assignments should, therefore, be contrasted with the following:

---

594 *M.H. Smith (Plant Hire) Ltd. v. D. L. Mainwaring (T/A Onshore) Ltd.* [1986] 2 Lloyd's Rep 244

595 Treitel, *supra* n.587, pp 578 - 579.

596 *Cator v. Croydon Canal Co.* (1841) 4 Y & C. Ex. 405, 593; *Donaldson v. Donaldson* (1854) Kay 711

597 *Bridge v. Bridge* (1852) 16 Beav. 315

598 Bills of Lading Act, 1855, S.1; Policies of Assurance Act 1867 (Life insurance); Marine Insurance Act 1868 (now 1906 Act, S.50(1))

599 For Uganda see the Judicature Statute,1996 S.16(2). See also *Ambalal & Co. v. Durgo Das Boury* 23 E.A.C.A. 68 per Briggs Ag. V.P. which suggests that the principles relating to absolute assignment as developed in England apply to Uganda.

600a Now of historical interest in view of Section 16(2), Judicature Statute 1996. See also *Uganda Motors Ltd. v. Wavah Holdings Ltd.* Civil Appeal No.19/91 (Supreme Court). But See n.24 *ibid.*

(i) Assignments by way of charge

In *Durham Bros. v. Robertson*[601], One Thousand and Eighty Pounds was due to a builder under a building contract. He borrowed money and assigned the One Thousand and Eighty Pounds to the lender as security for the loan, "until the money (lent) ... be repaid." It was held that this was an assignment by way of charge. This was because the builder did not assign the One Thousand and Eighty Pounds absolutely to the lender. He only charged that sum with repayment of money borrowed. However, an assignment may be absolute although it may be made by way of mortgage and does not transfer the subject matter absolutely. Thus in the *Tancred Case*,[602] a debt was assigned as security for a loan of money, with the proviso that if the assignor repaid the loan, the debt should be reassigned to him. This was held to be an absolute assignment.[603]

(ii) Assignments of part of a debt

An assignment of part of a debt (e.g. Shs.50,000/= out of the Shs.100,000/= which X owes me or half of what X owes me) is not absolute.[604] In such a case, a debtor who wants to pay may know perfectly well how much to pay to whom. To hold such assignment to be absolute might cause hardship to a debtor who wished to dispute the debt. To protect the debtor against numerous actions where the debt has been signed to many parties, it may be necessary to have all the interested parties before court. Similarly, an assignor of part of a debt cannot sue for the part he retains without joining the assignee as a party to the action.[605] This reasoning does not apply to an assignment of the *balance* of a debt. Suppose A owes B Shs.100,000/= and pays off Shs.25,000/= of the debt. An assignment of the remaining Shs.75,000/= would be absolute as it would be an assignment of B's remaining interest in the debt.[606]

(iii) Conditional ssignments

Section 25(6) of the Judicature Act, 1873 contrasts absolute assignments with assignments by way of charge. However, some judgments also distinguish between absolute and conditional assignments.[607] A conditional assignment is not absolute. For instance if A assigns rent due under a lease "to my daughter until she marries". It is necessary in this case for A to be party to an action brought by his daughter against the tenant for rent. If the daughter could sue without A, she might be able to prove that she was unmarried, and so entitled to the rent. However, this would not prevent A in a subsequent action against the tenant, from proving that the court in the first action had made a mistake in finding that the daughter was unmarried, so that the tenant would have to pay over again. What matters to the tenant is not whether the daughter is married but that the question should be decided, one way or the other, so as to bind both A and the daughter.[608]

(b) Debt or other thing in action

Section 25(6) of the Judicature Act 1873[609] refers to "debt" as a sum certain due under contract or

---

601 [1898] 1 Q.B. 765 c.f. *Tancred v. Delagoa Bay* (1889) 23 Q.B.D.239

602 *Ibid.*

603 For an explanation of the rationale for the distinction between the *Durham Bros* and the *Tancred* Cases see Treitel, *supra* n.587, p.580. See also in this respect *The Halcyon The Great* [1984] 1 Lloyd's Rep 283 *Bank of Liverpool v. Holland* [1926] 43 T.L.R. 29

604 *Foster v. Baker* [1910] 2 K.B. 636; *Re Steel Wing Co.* [1921] 1 Ch.349 *Williams v. Atlantic Assurance Co. Ltd.* [1933] 1 K.B. 81, 100.

605 *Walter & Sullivan Ltd. v. J. Murphy & Sons Ltd.* [1955] 2 Q.B. 584

606 *Harding v. Harding* (1886) 17 Q.B.D. 442.

607 *Durham Bros v. Robertson* [1898] 1 Q.B. 765, 773

608 c.f. *The Aiolos* [1983] 2 Lloyd's Rep 25, 33

609 See supra n.600a

otherwise.[610] The phrase "other legal thing in action" has been interpreted to mean any "debt or right which the common law looks on as not assignable by reason of its being a chose in action but which a Court of equity deals with as being assignable"[611] The phrase includes equitable choses in action,[612] though this point is of little practical importance since an assignment of an equitable chose is no more as effective under the statute than in equity. The phrase also includes a debt not yet due but accruing due[613] and the benefit of an obligation to do something other than to pay cash[614] or to forebear from doing something.[615] It does not include choses in action which can only be transferred by complying with some other statute. Thus shares in a company cannot be assigned by statutory assignment under Section 25(6), but only in the manner prescribed by the articles of association of the company.[616]

4. Requirements for valid assignment

(a) Formalities

As already seen (supra) statutory assignment must be in writing and signed by the assignor. Assignment which does not satisfy this requirement may take effect as an equitable assignment. For instance, while an oral assignment cannot take effect under the statute, it may be valid in equity.[617] Consequently, the statute merely provides an alternative method of assignment, it does not destroy the old method.

A disposition of an equitable interest must be in writing and signed by the assignor or his agent.[618] Consequently, an oral assignment of an equitable chose is void.[619]

Although writing is not necessary for an equitable assignment of a legal chose in action, the contract may provide that rights under it shall only be assigned by use of a certain form, such as writing. Consequently, an attempt to assign without using the stipulated form may be ineffective as an assignment, although it may amount to a contract to assign.[620]

(b) Intention to assign

It is necessary to establish an intention to assign. Thus in *William Brandt's Sons & Co. v. Dunlop Rubber Co.*[621] Lord Macnaghten stated thus: [622]

> An equitable assignment does not always take that form. It may be addressed to the debtor. It may be couched in the language of command. It may be a courteous request. It may assume the form of mere permission. The language is immaterial if the meaning is plain. All that is necessary is that the debtor should be given to understand that the debt has been made over by the creditor to some third person.

---

610 e.g. under Statute: *Dawson v. Great Northern & City Ry* [1905] 1 K.B. 260

611 *Torkington v. Magee* [1902] 2 K.B. 427, 430

612 *Re Pain* [1919] 1 Ch.38, 44

613 *Brice v. Bannister* (1878) 3 Q.B.D. 569, 574

614 *Torkington v. Magee supra* n.611

615 *Jacoby v. Whitmore* (1883) 49 L.T. 335

616 Companies Act Cap.85, S.75, Articles 22 - 27 Table A.

617 Treitel, *supra* n.12 pp. 585, 591

618 Contract Act Cap.75, S.4

619 *Oughtred v. I.R.C.* [1960] A.C. 206; c.f. *Grey v. I.R.C.* [1960] A.C. 1

620 Treitel, *supra* n.587, p.582

621 [1905] A.C. 454

622 *Ibid.* at p.462

It should be observed that simply because a creditor has asked a debtor to pay a third party does not mean that he has assigned the debt. Thus in *Exp Hall,*[623] a landlord authorised his tenant to pay rent to his bank to his credit. It was held that this was not an assignment but authority to the tenant to pay the bank. Such a mandate does not give the third party any rights against the debtor. Similarly, a person who draws a cheque on his bank in favour of a third person does not thereby assign part of his bank balance.[624]

(c) Communication to assignee

An assignment is not effective, unless it is communicated to the assignee [625] by the assignor, or someone with his authority;[626] unless it is made pursuant to a prior agreement between the assignor and assignee. While the reason for the requirement is not immediately obvious some person can have property transferred to him without his knowledge, subject to a right to repudiate when he learns of it,[627] the requirement may be regarded as evidence of intention to assign,[628] although such an intention could equally be proved by other evidence. The other explanation for requiring communication to the assignee is that it is equivalent of the delivery which is necessary to perfect a gift of a chattel made otherwise than by deed.[629] Finally, the requirement is based on the nature of assignment as a transaction between assignor and assignee.

(d) Notice to debtor

(i) Form of Notice

Notice of an equitable assignment may be oral.[630] However, if the chose assigned is equitable, oral notice is seldom effective between successive assignees.[631] Notice of a statutory assignment must be in writing.[632] It need not be given by the assignor, nor at the time of the assignment; it may be given by the assignee and is effective so long as it is brought before action is brought.[633] No particular form of words is necessary;[634] but the notice must clearly and unconditionally[635] tell the debtor to pay a third party *as assignee*, and not merely as agent for the creditor.[636] A notice which incorrectly states the date of the assignment or, it seems, the amount of the debt, is invalid.[637] However, a notice which says nothing at all about these particulars would appear to be valid so long as it describes the debt with sufficient certainty. A notice will be valid although it inaccurately states that another notice had been previously given.[638]

---

623 (1878) 10 Ch.D. 615

624 Bills of Exchange Act, Cap.76 S.53

625 *Alexander v. Steinhardt, Walker & Co.* [1903] 2 K.B.208 where posting was held to be sufficient communication, though doubted in *Timpson's Executors v. Yerbury* [1936] 1 K.B. 645, 657.

626 *Burn v. Carvalfio* (1839) 4 My & Cr. 690

627 *Standing v. Bowring* (1885) 31 Ch.D. 282

628 *Re Hamilton* (1921) 124 L.T. 737

629 Treitel, *supra* n.587, pp.584, 589.

630 *Ex. p. Agra Bank* (1868) L.R.3 Ch. App.555

631 Treitel, *supra* n.587, pp.584, 585

632 Judicature Act, 1873, S.25(6)

633 *Walker v. Bradford Old Bank* (1884) 12 Q.B.D. 511

634 *Smith v. Ss "Zigurds" Owners* [1934] A.C. 209

635 *The Balder London* [1980] 2 Lloyd's Rep 489, 495

636 *James Talcott Ltd. v. John Lewis & Co. Ltd.* [1940] 3 All E.R. 592

637 *Stanley v. English Fibres Industries Ltd.* (1889) 68 L.J.Q.B.839; *W.F. Harrison & Co. Ltd. v. Burke* [1956] 1 W.L.R. 419. Criticised: R.E.M. 72 L.Q.R.321

638 *Van Lynn Developments Ltd. v. Pelias Construction Ltd.* [1969] 1 Q.B. 607

A notice sent through the post takes effect when it is received by the debtor.[639] However, where there is a dispute between successive assignees, it is fair that the first to post should have priority over any other assignee who has not yet posted his notice (otherwise communicated to the debtor) when the first notice was posted.

(ii) Effects of the Notice

Notice may affect the relative rights of the assignor and assignee, of assignee and debtor, and a number of successive assignees.

Between assignor and assignee

The rights of these parties may depend on whether the assignment is statutory[640] and it can only have this character if notice is given. In the absence of notice, the assignment may take effect in equity.[641] It is significant that notice to the debtor is not necessary to perfect the rights of an equitable assignee against the assignor.[642]

Between assignee & assignor

Notice is necessary to perfect the title of an equitable assignee against the debtor,[643] because without such notice the debtor is entitled to assume that he remains liable to his original creditor (assignor) and that he will get a good discharge by paying the assignor.[644] Notice may also turn the assignment into a statutory assignment, in which case the debtor is liable to be sued by the assignee alone: he can no longer insist that the assignor be made a party to the action.

Between successive assignees

A chose in action may be successively assigned by an insolvent assignor to several persons for more than it is worth. It is then necessary to decide in which order the assignees are to be paid. The rule is that successive assignments taken in good faith rank in the order in which notice is given to the debtor. Consequently, a later assignee may gain priority over an earlier one by giving notice first.[645] Notice of the assignment of an equitable chose should be in writing, since oral notice of an assignment of such a chose does not give priority over later assignees in good faith for value.

5. Consideration

The issue arises as to whether an assignment must be supported by consideration between assignor and assignee. It is suggested[646] that this issue is restricted to the relative rights of assignor and assignee. Consequently, the debtor cannot refuse to pay the assignee on the ground that the assignment was gratuitous;[647] he is liable to pay the debt in any event and his only interest is to see that all possible claimants are before court so that he does not run the risk of having to pay twice over. It follows that once the possibility of prejudice to the debtor is removed by the joinder of all appropriate parties, it is only the assignor who can raise an issue as to the validity of the assignment on the ground that no consideration was given for it. In fact the only reason for this course of action is to enable the assignor to claim payment of the debt for himself.

---

639 *Holt v. Heatherfield Trust Ltd.* [1942] 2 K.B. 1, 6

640 Judicature Act, 1873, S.25(6)

641 *Holt v. Heatherfield Trust Ltd. supra* n.639

642 *Gorringe v. Irewell India Rubber Co. etc. Works* (1886) 34 Ch.D. 128 *Re Trytel* [1952] 2 T.L.R.32

643 *Warner Bros Records Inc. v. Rollgreen Ltd.* [1976] Q.B.430; [1975] 2 All E.R. 105

644 *Stocks v. Dobson* (1853) 4 D.M. & G. 11

645 *Dearle v. Hall* (1828) 3 Russ 1.

646 Treitel, *supra* n.587 p.586.

647 *Walker v. Bradford Old Bank* (1884) 12 Q.B.D. 511

A statutory assignment, whether of a legal or of an equitable chose in action, is effective, although it is made without consideration.[648]

With regard to equitable assignments, the requirement of consideration is restricted to uncompleted transactions,[649] although if a donor has done all that he needs to do to transfer the property, the gift is complete even though further steps to vest the property in the donee have to be taken by a third party.[650]

6. Rights which are not assignable

(a) Contracts expressed not to be assignable

A contract may expressly provide that the rights arising under it shall not be assigned. If assignment is nevertheless made, the assignee cannot enforce the rights under the contract.[651]

(b) Personal contracts

The benefit of a contract cannot be assigned if it is clear that the debtor is only willing to perform in favour of a particular creditor and if it is unjust to force the debtor to perform in favour of another. In such cases the personal nature of the contract prevents assignment. For instance an employer cannot assign the benefit of an employee's promise to serve.[652] Similarly, a publisher cannot assign the benefit of an author's contract to write a book if the author relied on the publisher's skill and judgment as a publisher.[653] Furthermore, the holder of a motor insurance policy cannot assign it since the insurer relies on the holder's skill and record as driver and on the principle of disclosure based on utmost good faith.[654]

Exceptionally the above principle may apply to contracts for the sale of goods where the buyer is relying on the peculiar business experience of the seller.[655]

(c) Mere rights of action

An assignment of a mere right of action such as a bare right to sue for breach of contract cannot be assigned because this could lead to maintenance or champerty.[656] The rule also applies to claims in tort,[657] although exceptionally a right of action can be assigned to an insurance company which has compensated the victim of the tort[658] based on the principle of subrogation. The principle also applies to a right to claim unliquidated damages following a breach of contract.[659]

Where there is difficulty in determining whether a right of action is assignable the criterion should be whether the assignment savours of maintenance or champerty.[660]

---

648 *Harding v. Harding* (1886) 17 Q.B.D.442; *Re Westerton* [1919] 2 Ch.104

649 *Harding's Case Ibid.* See also *Milroy v. Lord* (1862) 4 D.F. & J. 264

650 *Re Rose* [1952] Ch.499; *Re Rose* [1949] Ch.78. See also *Kekewich v. Manning* (1851) 1 D.M. & G. 176

651 *Helstan Securities Ltd. v. Hertfordshire C.C.* [1978] 3 All E.R. 262; Munday [1979] C.L.J.50; Alcock [1983] C.L.J. 328; *United Dominion Trust Ltd. v. Parkway Motors* [1955] 1 W.L.R. 719; [1955] 2 All E.R. 557

652 *Nokes v. Doncaster Amalgamated Collieries Ltd.* [1940] A.C. 1014

653 *Stevens v. Benning* (1854) 1 K & J 168; *Griffths v. Tower Publishing Co.* [1897] 1 Ch.21

654 *Peters v. G.A.F.L.A.C.* [1937] 4 All E.R. 628

655 *Cooper v. Micklefield Coal & Lime Co. Ltd.* (1912) 107 L.T. 457 (sale of coal) *Kemp v. Baerselman* [1906] 2 K.B. 604 (supply of eggs by a farmer to a company).

656 *Rees v. De Bernardy* [1896] 2 Ch. 437; *Laurent v. Sale & Co.* [1963] 1 W.L.R. 829

657 *Defries v. Milne* [1913] 1 Ch.98

658 *King v. Victoria Insurance Co.* [1896] A.C. 250; *Hobbs v. Marlowe* [1978] A.C. 16, 37; [1977] 2 All E.R. 241; *Rahemtulla v. Singh* 14 K.L.R. 91

659 *May v. Lane* [1894] 64 L.J.Q.B. 236 *Dodd v. Nandha* [1971] E.A. 58

660 Treitel, *supra* n.587, p.600.

(d) Public policy

(a) Public Officers

In law, an assignment of wages or salary is generally valid, so long as it does not deprive the employee of his sole means of support.[661] However, a public officer cannot assign his salary.[662] The rule is rationalised on two grounds. First it was thought that a public officer should not be deprived of the means to maintain the dignity of his office, although this argument now has little force except perhaps in the case of ambassadors. Second, it was thought that public officers must have the means to pay damages for wrongs committed by them or by their order; but this is no longer important since the injured party can now sue Government.[663] Arguably such assignments could lead to corruption among public officers although this is regarded as a remote contingency.[664]

(ii) Maintenance and payment to a Wife

Maintenance and other payments following matrimonial proceedings cannot be assigned since they would leave the wife destitute.[665]

(e) Mere expectancies

There can be no assignment of rights which do not yet exist or belong to the assignor. These are called expectancies or future property. An attempt to assign future property may operate as an agreement to assign which must be supported by consideration if it is to be binding.[666]

7 Assignment by operation of law

(a) Death

On the death of a contracting party, his rights generally pass to his personal representatives,[667] who can recover any sums due under the contract or damages for its breach.

However, contracts which involve personal considerations terminate on the death of the parties. An example is a contract of agency or one which involves reliance on the skill, judgment and confidence of another. This is true of a contract of employment.

(b) Bankruptcy

When a person becomes bankrupt his things in action forming part of his estate at the commencement of the bankruptcy are deemed to have been assigned to his trustee in bankruptcy.[668] Consequently, the trustee can recover debts due to a bankrupt and claim damages for breach of any contract with the bankrupt. If the contract is executory, the trustee is entitled to perform it and claim payment from the other party. However, certain "personal" rights do not pass to the trustee. These include a right to claim damages for injury to reputation,[669] a right to personal treatment[670] and where the contracting party - relies on the skill and judgment of the bankrupt.[671]

---

661 *King v. Michael Faroday & Partners Ltd.* [1939] 2 K.B. 753

662 *Liverpool Corporation v. Wright* (1859) 28 L.J. Ch. 868

663 Under the Government Proceedings Act, Cap.69

664 Treitel, *supra* n.587 p.601

665 *Watkins v. Watkins* [1896] P.222; Bromley & Lowe, *Family Law* (7th Ed.) p.657.

666 *Tailby v. Official Receiver* (1888) 13 App Cas 523; *Glegg v. Bromley* [1912] 3 K.B. 474

667 *Anguilla v. Estate & Trust Agencies* [1938] A.C. 624; Law Reform (Miscellaneous Provisions) Act Cap.74

668 Bankruptcy Act Cap.71, S.52(4)

669 *Wilson v. United Counties Bank* [1920] A.C. 102

670 *Beckham v. Drake* (1849) 2 H.L.C. 579, 627

671 *Knight v. Burgess* (1864) 33 L.J. Ch.727; *Oliphant v. Wadling* (1875) 1 Q.B.D. 145; *Ex.p. Shine* [1892] 1 Q.B. 522

A trustee in bankruptcy is in a less favourable position than an ordinary assignee in that he cannot gain priority over a previous assignee for value by being the first to give notice to the debtor.[672]

8. Negotiability

There are specific rules which apply to the assignment of certain written contracts called negotiable instruments. The most important of these are bills of exchange, cheques and promissory notes, which are regulated by the Bills of Exchange Act.[673]

A bill of exchange is a written order made by one person (the drawer) requiring another (the drawee) to pay a sum of money either to the drawer or to a third party or simply to bearer.[674] The request may be to pay money on demand or at some stated future time. If the drawee accepts the request he becomes liable as acceptor of the bill. A cheque is a bill of exchange drawn on banker payable on demand.[675] A promissory note is an unconditional promise in writing to pay a person a sum of money.[676] The categories of negotiable instruments are not closed, so that instruments can still become negotiable by mercantile custom i.e. by being so treated by businessmen.[677]

The transfer of a negotiable instrument differs from the assignment of an ordinary chose in action in the following ways.

(a) Transfer by delivery

A negotiable instrument may be transferred by mere delivery. A bill of exchange payable to bearer can be transferred by handing it to the transferee. If the bill of exchange is payable to A, he can transfer it by indorsing it i.e. by signing his name on it and then handing it to the transferee. Notice of transfer need not be given to the person liable on the instrument.

(b) Defects of title

While an ordinary assignee takes "subject to equities" (i.e. with all defects to the title) negotiable instruments are like cash. The transferee of a negotiable instrument takes it free from certain defects in title of the previous holders[678] and from defences available among them if he is a "holder in due course".[679] Such a holder is a person who has in good faith given value for the instrument provided that it is complete and regular on its face, not overdue and that it has not to his knowledge been dishonoured. Every holder is presumed to be a holder in due course,[680] unless the instrument is affected by duress, fraud or illegality.[681]

---

672 *Re Wallis* [1902] 1 K.B. 719. The rule is not affected by the Bankruptcy Act, Cap.71 S.52(4)

673 Cap 76 Laws of Uganda 1964 Edn.

674 *Ibid.* S.3

675 *Ibid.*, S.73

676 *Ibid.* S.83(1). A promissory note should be distinguished from an IOU, which is only evidence of a debt.

677 *Crouch v. Credit Foncier of England Ltd.* (1873) L.R.8 Q.B.374

678 Bills of Exchange Act, Cap.76, S.38(b)

679 *Ibid.*, S.29

680 *Ibid.*, S.30(2)

681 *Ibid.*

(c) Consideration

The holder of a bill of exchange is deemed to be a holder for value if consideration[682] has at any time[683] been given for the bill. Consequently, he can enforce it against (for example) the acceptor (bank) even if he himself has given no consideration for it. This rule should be distinguished from the additional rule that consideration is not necessary for the validity of a transfer of a negotiable instrument.[684] For instance if A draws a bill of exchange on B who accepts it. If A transfers the bill to C, neither A nor B can deny the validity of the transfer on the ground that it was gratuitous, and that C gave no consideration for the transfer. While lack of consideration consideration may enable the acceptor to resist an action on the bill, it does not entitle the transferor to deny the validity of the *transfer*.

---

682 An antecedent debt or liability is sufficient by way of exception to the rule that consideration must not be past: Bills of Exchange Act, Cap.76, S.27(1)(b)

683 *Ibid.* S.27(2)

684 *Easton v. Pratchett* (1835) 1 Cr M & R 798, 808

14
DISCHARGE OF CONTRACT

1. Discharge by agreement

A contract which has been entered into by agreement can be discharged by subsequent agreement between the affected parties. This can take basically two forms:

(a) Waiver/accord and satisfaction

A contract is discharged by the parties agreeing to waive their duties and obligations under the contract. This is possible when the contract is executory that is when it has not yet been performed. Where the contract has been executed, waiver is ineffectual. In such a case the agreement to discharge the contract must be either under seal or supported by fresh consideration. Where it is supported by fresh consideration, the transaction is known as accord and satisfaction. The effect of accord and satisfaction is that where one party to the contract is in breach of his obligations under the contract, liability for the breach is discharged by the parties making and performing a new agreement in the place of the earlier obligation. The agreement to be discharged from the old obligation is called the "accord", while the performance of the agreement is called "satisfaction" that is to say the fresh consideration.[1] It has been suggested in this respect that payment of a lesser sum of money owed under the contract cannot discharge the sum owed since the agreement to accept the lesser sum is naked and unsupported by consideration.[2]

It is notable that under the Common law, a contract had to be discharged in the same way in which it was formed. For instance, a contract under seal had also to be discharged by another contract under seal. The rule has been relaxed by allowing an oral contract to discharge a written contract or one under seal.[3]

(b) Substitutional contract

Parties may waive their rights or duties under the contract by substituting the original agreement with a new one. The effect of this is that the new contract ends all aspects of the old one.[4] For instance if A agrees to sell a second hand copy of a book to B, but before execution of the contract the parties agree that the copy to be sold should now be new. This is regarded as substitution of the original contract with a new one.

The subject-matter of the contract may remain, but the parties to the contract may be substituted. However, instead of substitution the contract is varied. In this regard a distinction should be drawn between simple substitution and variation. Where a contract is required by law to be in writing it should be varied by writing.[5] With substitution, a contract which is written may be substituted orally.

---

1 *British Russian Gazette Ltd. v. Associated Newspapers* [1933] 2 K.B.616, 643 - 644.

2 *D & C Builders Ltd. v. Rees* [1965] 3 All E.R. 837. See also *Foakes v. Beer* [1881 - 5] All E.R. 106.

3 *I.T. Palmer of Nigeria ltd. v. Julia Fonseca* [1946] 18 NLR 49

4 *Morris v. Baron* [1918] A.C. 1

5 Contract Act, Cap. 75, S.4

2. Discharge by performance

The most common way of discharging a contract is by both parties performing their duties or obligations under the contract. If only one of the parties performs his part, he alone is discharged. He will be entitled to sue the other party if that party fails to perform his part of the contract.

Generally performance under the contract must be complete, that is, it should be in accordance with the terms of the contract. Where it is incomplete or is not in accordance with the terms of the contract, then the party in breach may be sued for damages for breach of contract. For instance if X has contracted to buy three dozen eggs, from a grocer and the grocer delivers ten dozen eggs, this amounts to incomplete performance which entitles X to reject the whole consignment and to sue the grocer for breach of contract.[6] Furthermore, where X has contracted to do a particular job for a certain fee and only does part of it, he will only be entitled to be paid for the work done under the doctrine of *quantum meruit* in equity.

(a) Time for Performance

Pursuant to the requirement that a contract must be performed in accordance with its exact terms, a contract must be performed at the time and place agreed upon. Where no time has been agreed upon, then it must be completed within a reasonable time and this depends upon the circumstances of the particular case. Where a specific date or a specified time is mentioned, then "time is of the essence"[7a] of the contract and completion in accordance with the time or date is a fundamental condition of the contract.

In *Panesar v. Popat*[8], X ordered furniture from Y to be delivered on April 30th. the consignment was not ready by that date but X extended the date to May 10th. There was still no delivery and, therefore, X cancelled the order. Y nonetheless proceeded to deliver on May 12th. X refused to accept delivery. Y argued that even if time was of the essence, X had abandoned that condition by allowing an extension. The Court of Appeal held that X did not have to accept delivery and explained that in contracts where time is of the essence, but one party is in default for an unreasonable time, it is open to the other party to serve notice requiring completion within a reasonable time, and such notice, if in the circumstances, is reasonable in effect unilaterally makes or reintroduces time as the essence of the contract. This element of notice is particularly important where previously time has not been of essence. Without it, a party to the contract cannot abruptly terminate the contract.[9]

(b) Partial performance

Under the common law, a party who had only partly performed his duties under the contract could not recover the agreed fee. Thus in *Cutter v. Powell*,[10] the defendant agreed to pay Cutter, a seaman 30 guineas provided he continued and did his duty from Jamaica to Liverpool. The voyage started on 2nd August and the ship arrived in Liverpool on 9th October, but Cutter had died on 20th September, 19 days from Liverpool. The widow brought an action to recover on *quantum meruit* for work already done by her deceased husband. It was held that she could not succeed because under the contract, Cutter was only entitled to the agreed sum under the contract, if and when he had completely performed the whole of his duties as a second mate on the ship. The principle in this case has also been applied to building contracts. Thus in *Sumpter v. Hedges*,[11] the plaintiff, a builder agreed with the defendant to erect certain buildings on the

---

6 *Hart v. Mills* (1846) 15 L.J. Ex.200

7a See e.g. Sale of Goods Act, S.12

8 [1968] E.A. 17 applying *Nurdin Bandali v. Lombank Tanganyika Ltd.* [1963] E.A. at p.316 per Newbold J.A.

9 *Aida Nunes v. John Mbiyo Njonjo & Charles Kigwe* [1962] E.A. 88. See also Tanganyika Contract Act, S.55(2)

10 (1795) 6 T.R. 320

11 [1898] 1 Q.B.673

defendant's land for Five Hundred and Sixty five Pounds. The Plaintiff performed part of the work to the tune of Three Hundred and Thirty three Pounds and was paid part of the price. He then informed the defendant that owing to financial grounds, he could not continue with the work. The defendant then completed the buildings on his own using some materials left on the site by the Plaintiff. The Plaintiff sued for work done and materials provided. The Court found that the plaintiff had abandoned the contract and gave judgment for him only for the value of materials used by the defendant but nothing for work done.

(c) Exceptions to the rule in *Cutter v. Powell*

Where the contract allows for payments at various stages of work done, then the rule in *Cutter v. Powell* does not apply in the following circumstances.

(i) Divisible contracts

Where there is part performance of a divisible contract, the plaintiff may be entitled to recover for work already performed even if part of the contract remains to be done. While it may be difficult to determine when a contract is divisible or not this may be gathered from the intention of the parties.[12] For instance, supposing X sends his car to Y's garage for adjustments on (i) brakes, (ii) the windscreen, (iii) valves, (iv) parking lights, (v) interior renovation. Assuming also that each aspect of the work done has a fixed charge payable upon its being completed, if Y completes the work under (i) to (iv) but not (v), he will be entitled to payment for the work done.[13]

(ii) Acceptance of partial performance

Where partial performance has been accepted by the defendant the plaintiff can claim on *quantum meruit* for the work done.[14]

(iii) Non-completion due to fault of defendant

If the non-completion of the contracted work is due to the fault of the defendant, the plaintiff is entitled to recover on *quantum meruit* for work already done in addition to other remedies.[15]

(iv) Substantial performance

The plaintiff can recover a reasonable amount of money for work already done if he can plead the doctrine of substantial performance. Its effect is that a person who has substantially performed his promise even though not performing exactly what he promised to do will be entitled to sue under the contract. In awarding him the amount due to him, allowance is made for any defects in the work done. Thus if X contracts to build a house of a particular specification for Y and the house is so built except that a bolt is wrongly fitted on a door, X is entitled to recover the contractual price less the price of fitting the bolt on the door.[16]

Similarly, in *H. Dakin & Co. Ltd. v. Lee*[17], the contract was for repairs to a house. The work when completed did not conform with the contract in certain respects. It was held by the Court of Appeal that the plaintiff was entitled to the contract price subject to a counter claim or set-off for damages by the defendant for failure to accurately perform. Furthermore where the promisor or plaintiff has only broken the contract in such a way as not to entitle the promisee/defendant to treat him as having abandoned the contract, the promisor can sue on *quantum meruit* on the ground that the promisee has benefitted from the work done.[18]

---

12 Achike, *Nigerian Law of Contract* (1981) p.262

13 *V. O. Taiwo v. F.B.A. Princewell* [1961] All N.L.R. 240. See also *Ritchie v. Atkinson* (1808) 10 East 295; Hodgin, *Law of Contract In East Africa*, p.174.

14 *Sumpter v. Hedges* [1898] 1 Q.B. 673; *Munro v. Butt* (1858) 8 E & B 738

15 *Appleby v. Myers* (1867) L.R. 2 C.P. 251

16 *Hoeing v. Isaacs* [1952] 2 All E.R. 176

17 [1916] 1 K.B. 566

18 *Hoeing v. Isaac supra* n.15

These principles have been applied in the East African Case of *Melita & Co. Ltd. v. Baron Verhegen*[19] where X built a bungalow for Y, the price to be paid by instalments. On completion, Y withheld the balance due on the basis that there were some structural defects. The Court of Appeal; for Eastern Africa allowed the builder's claim on the ground that he had substantially completed the contract. Sir Newnham Worley Ag. P. specifically held that the case of *Dakin v. Lee*[20] and *Hoeing v. Isaac*[21] applied to East Africa despite earlier doubts about *Dakin v. Lee*[22].

(d) Tender of performance

This is an offer or attempted performance of the contract. There are two types of offers of performance. First, offer to perform a promise to do something. Second, offer to perform a promise to pay something.

Where the seller has promised to deliver goods to the buyer he fulfills a promise under the contract if he offers to make delivery. If the buyer refuses to accept delivery, the seller is discharged from his obligation and may sue the buyer for breach of contract. It has been suggested that tender of performance is equal to performance.[23] However as far as goods are concerned is subject to the Sale of Goods Act S.28, 30(4)

The tender must be made at a reasonable hour and in accordance with the terms of the contract. Otherwise it is invalid.

With regard to tender of payment, this is ineffective unless the money is actually produced or unless production is dispensed with by the creditor.[24] It is not enough for the debtor to offer to pay money by simply putting his hand in his pocket[25] as this does not amount to production of the money. The tendering of a part of a debt is ineffective.[26] Furthermore, the tender of a larger sum than the one owed and requiring change is also ineffective since it puts an unreasonable burden on the creditor.[27]

3. Discharge by breach

A breach of contract occurs, when a party to the contract, without lawful excuse (i) fails or refuses to perform the contract; (ii) performs defectively; (iii) incapacitates himself from performing the contract.

(a) Failure or refusal to perform the contract

(i) Promise to perform

It is necessary to ascertain whether the party who is alleged to be in breach has in fact promised to perform. This is gathered from the agreement between the parties. For instance if A promises B Shs.100,000/= if he will walk to Mukono, B has not promised anything. Consequently, B does not commit a breach if he does not walk or if after starting the walk he fails to complete the walk.

(ii) Whether performance is due

A party is not in breach before the time to perform is due. Where the agreement is subject to a

---

19 21 E.A.C.A. 153

20 *supra* n.16

21 *supra* n.15

22 *Eshelby Federated European Bank Ltd.* [1932] 1 K.B. 254 per Greer L. J.

23 *Startup v. Macdonald* (1843) 6 Man & G 593

24 *Farquharson v. Pearl Insurance Co. Ltd.* [1937] 3 All E.R. 124

25 *Finch v. Brook* (1834) 1 Bing N.C. 253

26 *Dixon v. Clark* (1847) 5 C.B. 365

27 *Betterbee v. Davis* (1811) 3 Camp 70. *Ajoke v. A. Y. Oba & Ors* (1958) W.R.N.L.R. 208 (Nigeria)

condition precedent, then failure to perform does not amount to a breach if the condition has not occurred.

(iii) Promise to perform without reciprocal promise

A contract may contain a promise by one party but fail to indicate what has been promised in return by the other. Thus in *Churchword v. R,*[28] a contractor agreed with the Admiralty that he would for eleven years carry from Dover to Calais such mail as he should from time to time be asked to carry by the Admiralty or Post Master General. He was not given any mail to carry and claimed damages. His claim failed on the ground that the agreement did not place an obligation on the Admiralty to employ him. It only obliged him to employ him to carry mail if the Admiralty asked him to do so.

Problems sometimes arise in connection with employment contracts. The main issue is whether an employer is bound to give an employee work. It is felt that an employer is only bound to pay wages.[29] However, if the object of the contract is to enable an employee to gain or retain his skill or to keep his name before he public, then his employer must give him work.[30]

(iv) Failure to substantially perform

There may be a breach of contract if a party thereto in *substance* fails or refuses to perform. Consequently "working to rule" or slow performance aimed at disrupting an employer's business may amount to a breach of the contract of employment.[31] Furthermore, if performance is of the type agreed but it differs only in point of time, quantity or quality it is regarded as defective performance.

(b) Incapacitating oneself if party to contract

A party to the contract breaks the contract if he incapacitates himself. For instance, a contract to sell something is broken if the item is sold to another person.[32] In *Omnium D'Enterprises v. Satherland,*[33] a ship which had been chartered was sold by the owner, "free from any charter engagement." It was held that the owner was in breach of contract to the charterparty. However, a person is not incapacitated from performing a contract under which he is obliged to pay money, simply because he becomes insolvent.[34] His trustee in bankruptcy can enforce it.[35]

There is no breach of contract if the non-performance of the contract is justified by lawful excuse. For instance, if goods are sold cash on delivery and the buyer fails to pay or tender the price, the seller is excused from non-delivery. Furthermore, non-performance may be excused if it is caused by a supervening extraneous event, such as where the subject matter of the contract has been destroyed or there is a crop failure.[36] Additionally the illness of an employee may excuse performance under an employment contract, if he is thereby prevented from going to work. The contract may also provide circumstances for non-performance.

A distinction also exists between breach and lawful termination. This is significant where a contract indicates circumstances in which a contract may be lawfully terminated. In this instance, it may be difficult to know whether a contract has been lawfully terminated or broken. Thus in *Bridge v. Campbell Discount Co. Ltd.*[37] a hire purchase agreement gave the hirer the right to

---

28 (1865) L. R. 1 Q.B. 173

29 *Turner v. Sawdon* [1901] 2 K.B. 653

30 *Herbert Clayton v. Oliver* [1930] A.C. 209. N.B. the right to work is recognised in *Langston v. A.U.E.W.* [1974] 1 W.L.R. 185

31 *Secretary of State v. A.S.L.E.F.* (No.2) [1972] 2 Q.B. 455

32 *Lovelock v. Franklyn* (1846) 8 Q.B. 371

33 [1919] 1 K.B. 618

34 *Re Agra Bank* (1867) L.R. 5 Eq.160

35 *Ex.P. Chambers* (1873) L.R. 8 Ch. App. 289

36 *Howell v. Coupland* (1876) 1 Q.B.D. 258

37 [1962] A.C. 600; [1962] 1 All E.R. 385

terminate it by notice. He wrote to the owners thus: "owing to unforeseen circumstances, I am very sorry I will not be able to pay anymore payments. Will you please let me know when and where I will have to return the car. I am sorry regarding this but I have no alternative. It was held by the House of Lords by a majority that the hirer had not terminated but had broken the contract. The reason was that if he knew that he was exercising the right of termination, why did he apologise twice humbly?

An issue arises as to whether a strike by workers amounts to a breach of contract. In *Rookes v. Barnard*[38] it was held that there is a breach of contract if the contract contains a "no strike" clause. An employee will also be in breach of contract if he stops work without giving the notice required by the terms of the contract.

(c) Effects of breach

The breach of a contract entitles the injured party to (i) claim damages; (ii) claim the agreed sum (iii) specific performance of the contract; (iv) an injunction. However a distinction is normally made between breach of a condition and a warranty in the contract.[39] A condition is a major term of the contract, the breach of which permits discharge of the contract, while a warranty is a minor term that attracts only an award of damages. A breach which goes to the root of the contract or is fundamental affects its commercial viability and discharges the contract.[40]

A breach of condition may be treated merely as a breach of warranty where the injured party elects to affirm the contract or is compelled because he has already derived substantial benefits from it.[41] In such a situation, the condition becomes a "warranty ex post facto"[42]

(d) Repudiation before performance of contract

If a party to the contract declares his intention not to perform the contract before its time for performance is due, this is known as repudiation of the contract or anticipatory breach.[43] In this instance the innocent party may elect to sue at once or wait until the time of performance is due and sue then. If he decides on the latter, the guilty party may "reform" and complete his part of the contract. It may even be that something occurs to prevent the original innocent party from completing his own obligations. Thus in *Avery v. Bowden,*[44] the defendant was to load cargo into a ship chartered by the plaintiff. The defendant refused and the plaintiff continued to demand performance rather than to treat this as anticipatory breach. In the meantime war broke out in the area and the contract was thereby frustrated. It was held that as the last day for loading as per the contract had not passed, the plaintiff had no cause of action.

Furthermore, the innocent party who decides to wait for the breach at the time performance is due must show that he is able and willing to perform his part of the contract. Thus in *Aldina v. Globe Mercantile Corp. Ltd.,*[45] the plaintiff agreed to deliver seventy eight tons of sisal to the defendant. He delivered twenty five tons and the defendant refused to accept any more. The plaintiff chose to treat the contract as still existing up to the contractual date of delivery. The

---

38 [1964] A.C. 1204; [1964] 1 All E.R. 367; Hoffman, 81 LQR 116.

39 See *supra* Chap.6. See also Hodgin, *Law of Contract In East Africa* pp.188 - 191; *Kampala General Agency (1942) Ltd. v. Mody's (E.A) Ltd.* [1963] E.A.549 *Hong Kong Fir Shipping Co. Ltd. v. Kawasaki Kisen Kisha Ltd.* [1962] 2 Q.B. 26 [1962] 1 All E.R. 474

40 *supra* Chap.6

41 Sale of Goods Act, Cap.79 S.13(3)

42 *Wallis v. Pratt* [1911] A.C. 394; *Mohammed Anwar v. Marjaria & Ors* Civil Appeal No.5 of 1973; Hodgin *supra* n.39, pp.189 - 190.

43 *Universal Cargo Carriers Corp. v. Citati* [1957] 2 Q.B. 401, 438 [1957] 2 All E.R. 70; *Brodley v. Newsom* [1919] A.C. 16,153

44 (1855) 5 E & B 714

45 [1968] E.A. 114

Court of Appeal dismissed his claim for damages for loss of profit on the undelivered tonnage on the ground that he had not shown his ability to perform his own obligations. The *Aldina* Case was distinguished by the Court of Appeal in *Containers Ltd. v. Kencon*[46]. In this Case, the appellant company contracted to sell 7,200 gross of rat traps to be delivered at the rate of 600 gross, a month over a period of two years. The respondents (buyers) accepted half of the first month's delivery but refused to accept any more. The appellants did not treat this as a breach but continued to offer delivery. Three months later they sold some of the traps to other buyers. The appellants sued for breach and the respondents cross-appealed on the grounds that the appellants' behaviour did not amount to tender of performance and therefore they themselves were in breach. Concerning the cross-appeal, the Court observed that although legally there was no tender of performance this was because of the respondents' "direct and general refusal" to accept anymore traps, although the appellants had offered to deliver and were in a position to do so. They were, therefore, "willing and able to perform the contract." In the *Aldina case,* however, the party concerned had not even obtained an option to purchase the sisal he was to supply. He had failed to satisfy the Court that he was willing and able to supply the goods in question. In the present case, the respondents behaviour amounted to waiver of tender and the cross-appeal failed.

The main appeal shows the type of problem explained under *Avery v. Bowden.*[47] The respondents had been appointed distributors of rat traps and this was considered by the court to be a fundamental term of the contract. On the initial refusal to accept delivery, the appellants had chosen to treat the contract as still alive and to offer further delivery. However, when they chose to sell elsewhere, that act constituted a breach of the agreement on their part disentitling them from their claim for damages.[48]

Where the party decides to treat the other party's behaviour as anticipatory breach he may apply to Court for specific performance so that the Court may compel the guilty party to perform. It is not a defence to plead that the cause of action does not arise until the final date for performance is due. Thus in *Hasham v. Zenab Yo Chandu Mansi,*[49] the defendant agreed to sell certain premises to the plaintiff. However, before he final date of completion, the defendant repudiated his side of the bargain. The plaintiff sued for specific performance. The Court of Appeal upheld the claim and applied the principle in *Hochester v. De La Tour,*[50] where the defendant agreed to employ the plaintiff as a courier for three months from June 1st. Prior to that date, the defendant repudiated the contract. It was held that the plaintiff was entitled to claim damages at once. He did not have to wait for June 1st before commencing the action. The Court also applied the statement by Cockburn C. J. in *Frost v. Knight*[51] thus:

> It is, therefore, quite right to hold that such an announcement [of repudiation] amounts to violation of the contract in *omnibus*, and that upon it the promise if so minded, may at once treat it as a breach of the entire contract and bring his action accordingly.

Except where there is express repudiation, care should be exercised in deciding whether a particular act or statement amounts to implicit repudiation. An investigation of the nature of the contract and the surrounding circumstances at the time of the supposed repudiation is, for this purpose, required. Thus in *Rashid Moledina & Co. (Mombasa) Ltd. v. Hoima Ginners,*[52] X

---

47 *supra* n.43

48 per Mustafa J. A. applying *Frost v. Knight* (1872) L.R. 7 Ex.111 at p.112 and Vol.8 *Halsbury's Laws of England*, 3rd Edn., p.203 para 344

49 [1957] E.A. 38; [1960] E.A. 7. See also Note (1958) *Journal of African Law*, 55

50 (1853) 2 E & B. 628

51 *supra* n.48

52 [1957] 2 Q.B. 401, 436 per Devlin J. See also Tanganyika Contract Act., S.39

agreed to sell quantities of coffee to Y on certain dates. Coffee, however, was in short supply and X tried to come to an arrangement with Y but failed. X then was unable to make delivery to other parties and Y claimed that this amounted to repudiation of their contract. The Court decided that the surrounding circumstances were such that repudiation could be inferred.

A final issue is what would happen if a party gives notice to the other party of his intention to break the contract and the innocent party rather than accept such notice and sue for damages in fact continues with his part of the bargain? While in such circumstances the innocent party would be expected to mitigate his losses,[53] a decision of the British House of Lords has adopted the opposite view albeit by a majority. Thus in *White & Carter (Councils) Ltd. v. McGregor*[54] the Council had contracted to carry advertisements of the other parties product on their waste litter bins. The contract was to last for a three year period. The day the contract was made and before the Council had incurred any expense, the other wrote cancelling the contract. The Council, however, chose to ignore this and proceeded to carry the advertisements for the full three year period and then sued for the cost. The House of Lords by a majority of 3:2 overruled the Scottish Court of Session and allowed the Council's claim. While the case has been criticised on the ground that it enhances inflation of damages due to the injured party contrary to the principle of mitigation of damages, it has been supported[55] on the ground that the injured party may have entered into commitments with third parties which he must honour as a matter of business and also where discontinuing performance would prejudice him by for instance leading to injury to his reputation for which damages (if recoverable at all) could not be accurately assessed or where part of the loss which the injured party would actually suffer is legally irrecoverable because it is remote.

Nevertheless it has been suggested[56] that the Courts in East Africa should not follow this decision and in the interests of equity should follow the *American Restatement On Contract* which states[57]

> After an anticipatory breach is known to the injured party, just as in the case of other kinds of breach, the damages that will be awarded are limited by the rule as to avoidable harm. He is not permitted, merely because the breach is anticipatory to enhance his damages by *unreasonably continuing his performance* or unreasonably omitting action that would prevent harm.(Emphasis supplied)

The comment should be read together with paragraph 336(1) of the *Restatement* which provides:[58]

> Damages are not recoverable for harm that the plaintiff should have foreseen and could have avoided by reasonable effort without undue rest, expense or humiliation.

In the American Case, *Eaton Factors Co. v. Bartlett*,[59] the plaintiffs had received orders from the defendants to advertise their wares on plastic telephone covers. Prior to any work being carried out, the defendants cancelled their order. It was held that the plaintiffs were under a duty to mitigate the damages.

---

53 Hodgin, *Law of Contract In East Africa, supra* p.196

54 [1962] A.C. 613; [1961] 3 All E.R. 1178. For a critique see Cheshire & Fifoot *Law of Contract supra* pp.617 - 618; Goodhart 78 L.Q.R. 263, Nienaber [1962] Camb. L.J. 213. Supported by Treitel, *Law of Contract* (8th Edn. 1991) pp.899 - 900.

55 Treitel, *ibid.* p.899

56 Hodgin, *supra n.39*, pp.196 - 197

57 Comment C to para 338. This is said to be in line with Lord Reid's dissenting judgment in the *White & Carter* Case

58 The provision is in line with Common Law Rules on mitigation of loss: *Southern Highlands Tobacco Union Ltd. v. McQueen* [1960] E.A. 490 discussed *infra* Chapter 15.

59 24 Conn. Supp.40; 186 A 2d 166; Hodgin, *supra* n.39, p.197

4. Discharge by frustration

The essence of the doctrine of frustration is that parties to a contract are excused from further performance of their obligation if some unexpected event occurs during the currency of the contract without the fault of either party. This is especially so if further performance is impossible, illegal or makes the contract radically different from what was originally undertaken. The doctrine does not apply where (i) the parties have expressly provided for the contingency which has occurred; (ii) the frustrating event was self-induced or foreseen; (iii) performance has simply become onerous or less profitable than originally anticipated.

It is intended to briefly consider events which may amount to frustration before dealing with situations which do not give rise to frustration.

(a) Where performance of the contract is illegal

A contract may be discharged by a supervening prohibition if the prohibition would have made the contract illegal had it been in force when the contract was made.[60] In this regard, the Court considers the relative interests of the parties as well as the interests of the public in seeing that the law is observed and public interest may outweigh the importance of achieving a fair distribution of loss.

A good example of supervening illegality is where as a result of a war-time prohibition against trading with the enemy a contract becomes illegal. Thus in the *Fibrosa Case*,[61] the contract for sale and delivery of machinery to be shipped at Gdynia was frustrated when that port was occupied by the enemy during the Second World War. Although it might have been physically possible to get the goods to the destination, the contract was discharged because of the strong public interest in ensuring that no aid should be given to the enemy economy in time of war. The same principle applies where the goods are to be imported from an enemy country: the contract is frustrated even though the enemy source is not specified in the contract but only contemplated by the parties.[62] This English Law approach may be contrasted with the result in the East African Case, *Twentsche Overseas Trading Co. Ltd. v. Uganda Sugar Factory Ltd.*[63] In that case, X agreed to buy from Y three miles of railway line in keeping with "Krupp" specifications. Y intended to obtain the rails from Germany, although this was not mentioned in the agreement. Owing to the outbreak of the second World War it became impossible to buy the rails from that country. Y argued that the contract was frustrated. The Privy Council rejected that argument. Lord Wright explained that:

> ... a carefully drawn specification has defined precisely what are the goods called for by the contract. That specification contains no term intended to define what is to be the source of the goods... In a case like this the contract is not frustrated because only one of the many ways of performing it has become illegal and impossible.

There are other prohibitions which could frustrate a contract. Thus in the *Denny Mott Case,*[64] a contract for the sale of timber was frustrated by a war-time prohibition against dealing in goods of the contract description. In the Nigerian Case of *Uzomah v. Uzomah*[65] a contract to build on a designated site was held to be frustrated when Lagos Executive Development Board acting under its statutory powers prohibited erection of any building in the locality. Contracts can also be prohibited by export or import restrictions on the movement of capital[66] or by licensing requirements.

---

[60] Treitel, *supra* n.54, p.786

[61] [1943] A.C. 32

[62] *Re Badische Co.* [1921] 2 Ch.331

[63] 12 E.A.C.A. 1; Hodgin *supra* n.53, pp.179 - 180

[64] [1944] A.C. 265

[65] [1965 - 66] M.N.L.R. 88

(b) Destruction of subject matter

In *Taylor v. Caldwell*,[67] the defendants let a certain musical hall to the plaintiffs. Before the dates of the proposed concerts, the hall was accidentally destroyed by fire. It was held that the contract was frustrated. A similar situation arose in *Ryde v. Bushell & Harvey*[68]. The plaintiff leased his farm to the defendant and one of the conditions was that a certain acreage of coffee was to be planted. The plaintiffs brought an action for breach of that covenant. The defendants argued that because of the heavy rains they had not been able to complete their obligations. However, the East African Court of Appeal held that on the facts this plea of Act of God could not stand since this was not an Act of God "whose occurrence was due exclusively to natural causes of so extraordinary a nature that it could not reasonably have been foreseen and the results of which occurrence could not have been avoided by any action which could have been taken by the person who seeks to avoid liability".[69]

In *Krell v. Henry*[70], the plaintiff agreed to let a room to the defendant for the purpose of viewing a procession. The Procession was cancelled. It was held that the purpose of hiring the room had been frustrated and the defendant was discharged from paying. Although there had been no specific mention of the purpose in the agreement, the Court was of the view that without the Procession the foundation of the contract disappeared. In contrast, in *Herne Bay Steamboat Co. v. Hutton*[71], the defendants hired the plaintiff's boat for the purpose of viewing the naval review and for a day's cruise around the fleet. The naval review was cancelled and the defendants alleged that the contract was frustrated. The Court decided against them on the ground that while part of the contract had disappeared not all of it had disappeared and what was left was capable of performance.

(c) Death or incapacity

Contracts with a "personal" element such as contracts of employment, apprenticeship or agency, are discharged by the death of either party.[72] A commercial contract may also depend on the personal skill of one of the parties in which case the death of the party possessing the skill (though not of the other) can discharge the contract.[73] The same rules apply where a party becomes permanently incapacitated from performing the contract. This would be case where a contract to write a book is frustrated by the supervening insanity of the author.[74] Similarly a contract for dancing lessons would be frustrated if the student becomes seriously injured as to be unable to dance.[75]

(d) Unavailability

A contract may be frustrated if a thing or person essential for the purpose of its performance, though not ceasing to exist or suffering permanent incapacity becomes unavailable for that purpose. Thus charterparties have been frustrated where the ship was seized, detained[76] or requisitioned[77]

---

66 *Libyan Arab Foreign Bank v. Bankers Trust Co.* [1989] Q.B.728, 749 although there was no frustration in that Case.
67 (1863) 3 B & S 826
68 [1967] E.A. 817
69 per Newbold, P.
70 [1903] 2 K.B. 740
71 [1903] 2 K.B. 683 decided by the same judges as in *Krell v. Henry ibid.*
72 *supra* Chap.13 on contracts which are not assignable.
73 *Ibid.*
74 *Jackson v. Union Marine Insurance Co. Ltd.* (1874) L.R. 10 C.P. 125, 145
75 *Condor v. The Barron Knights Ltd.* [1966] 1 W.L.R. 87
76 *The Evia* (No.2) [1983] 1 A.C. 736; [1982] 3 All E.R. 350 *The Adelfa* [1988] 2 Lloyd's Rep.466

and where cargo was unavailable because of a strike at the port of loading;[78] a contract of sale of goods has been frustrated where the goods were requisitioned;[79] a contract to operate and share the profits of an oilfield has been frustrated where the interests of both parties were expropriated by the government of the country in which the oilfield was situated;[80] and contracts for personal services have been frustrated where one of the parties fell ill[81] or was interned or conscripted.[82]

In the Ugandan case of *Victoria Industries v. Ramanbhai Bros,*[83] a Ugandan company agreed to ship maize via Lake Victoria to Mwanza. While part of the shipment was being loaded, E. A. Railways refused to accept shipment. It was held that the railway's behaviour frustrated the contract as there was no feasible or alternative route. In arriving at its decision the Court followed the Court of Appeal decision in *Tskirogolou & Co. Ltd. v. Noblee & Thorl G. M. B. H.,*[84] which was later overruled by the House of Lords.[85] In that case, groundnuts were sold and were to be shipped from the Sudan to Germany. The obvious route was through the Suez canal. Owing to the invasion of Egypt by Israel, the Canal was blocked and the sellers argued that the contract was thereby frustrated. This argument was rejected by the House of Lords which refused to imply a term that the voyage had to be via Suez. It was held that the contract could still be performed by going round the Cape of Good Hope. The extra expense could not be regarded as a frustrating event.

The case shows the Courts' reluctance to extend the doctrine too far. Courts in East Africa are now faced with the problem of whether to follow the *Victoria Industries Case* or the House of Lords decision in *Tsakirologou.* It has been suggested[86] that if the implied term theory is accepted, a more liberal approach would be that the parties intended that the most economic route should be used as the *Victoria Industries Case* would suggest. On this basis it would be realistic to allow the parties to renegotiate the terms of their contract.[87]

In *Samson Engola v. Nabitalo,*[88] a hiring contract of a car between the parties was held to be frustrated by the seizure of the car by soldiers at gun point from the hirer.

(e) Governmental or statutory intervention

Where government rules, regulations or enactments prevent one party from fulfilling his obligations under the contract, the contract is thereby frustrated. Many English decisions stem from the outbreak of war and legislation arising therefrom prohibiting trade with the enemy. The *Twentsche Overseas Trading Case*[89] was an attempt to excuse an East African contract on that basis. Definitely if the contract had specified Germany as the country of manufacture of the contracted goods, it would have been frustrated on ground of statutory prohibition.[90] In the early Zanzibar decision, *Davis & Keating v. Jessa Bhaloo,*[91] X contracted to sell goods to Y that were to be delivered at Zanzibar on a German Ship. The outbreak of the 1914 - 1918 war

77 *Bank Line Ltd. v. Arthur Capel & Co.* [1919] A.C. 435

78 *The Nema* [1982] A.C. 724; [1981] 2 All E.R. 1030

79 *Re Shipton, Anderson & Co.* [1915] 3 K.B. 676

80 *B.P. Exploration (Libya) Ltd. v. Hunt* [1983] 2 A.C. 352; [1982] 1 All E.R. 925

81 *Hart v. A.R. Marshall & Sons (Bulwell) Ltd.* [1977] 1 W.L.R. 1067; [1978] 2 All E.R. 413

82 *Morgan v. Manser* [1948] 1 K.B. 184; [1947] 2 All E.R. 666

83 [1961] E.A. 11

84 [1960] 2 All E.R. 160

85 [1962] A.C. 93; [1961] 2 All E.R. 179

86 Hodgin, *supra* n.13, p.180

87 It is now common practice to include a "Suez Canal clause" in an attempt to provide for financial difficulties of the type which arose in the *Tsakirologou* Case.

88 [1988 - 1990] H.C.B. 169

89 *Supra n.63*

90 See Trading With Enemy Act Cap.324

91 (1868 - 1918) Z.L.R. 517; Hodgin, *supra* n.53, p.182

caused the ship to divert from Zanzibar and the goods were never delivered. Y sued X for breach and X successfully defended himself under section 56 of the Indian Contract Act.[92]

In the *Victoria Industries* Case,[93] Uganda Government banned the export of maize to Tanganyika shortly after the railways refused to accept more shipment. However, this aspect was not adverted to in the judgment.

In the Court of Appeal decision, *Maclaine Watson & Co. Ltd. v. Shah*[94], the buyer agreed to buy five tons of rice at Mombasa, apparently with the intention of selling within East Africa. The government refused to issue an import licence. The buyer argued that the contract was frustrated. The Court disagreed. It observed that he could still take delivery at Mombasa and then resell out of Kenya by reshipping the goods since the Government ban did not prevent this.

Finally the contract (if any) under which a person holds a public office is discharged if the office is abolished by statute.[95]

(f) Self-induced frustration

The Courts, as we have seen, do not readily infer frustration. Where there is an event which has destroyed the basis on which the contract was made, the party relying on the frustration must conclusively prove the occurrence of that event. Once this is done, it is then for the other party to show that the event was due to neglect or negligence of the party claiming frustration. Thus in *Howard and Co. (Africa) Ltd. v. Burton*[96], the plaintiffs had agreed to supply the defendants with mid-day meals for their labourers. The labourers, however, objected to the meals and the fact that deductions were made from their wages to cover part of the cost. The defendants allowed the men to choose and the result was that the number of meals dropped from 2,500 to almost nil. The plaintiff sued for breach of contract and the defendants pleaded frustration. The Court allowed the plaintiff's action on the ground that it was the defendant's positive act of allowing labourers to choose that led to the decline in numbers and the subsequent failure on their part to take delivery of the agreed quantities. Similarly in *Karachi Gas Co. Ltd. v. Issaq,*[97] X agreed to sell pipes to Y. The agreement required X to obtain a Kenyan export licence. Y failed to obtain his licence and claimed that the contract was frustrated due to the government's refusal to grant such a licence. The court held that Y failed to show that he had taken necessary steps to perform his obligations. His failure was due to his own inadequacies and the defence of frustration failed. Furthermore, in *Neon & Norlo Sigus (Kenya) Ltd. v. Alarkhia & Ors.*[98], the plaintiffs were to hire out neon signs to the defendants. The defendants intended to display the signs on premises that they did not own but the contract made it a condition that the defendants's task was to obtain the landlord's permission. The plaintiffs constructed the signs but the defendants failed to obtain permission to erect them. Upon being sued, the defendants unsuccessfully claimed that the contract was frustrated. It was held that the procurement of permission amounted to a condition or an essential stipulation the non-fulfillment of which amounted to breach of the agreement.

In the more recent Ugandan case of *Himaco v. Republic Motors*[99], the plaintiff paid against a proforma invoice for a fully registered motor vehicle. He made numerous demands to the defendant for the delivery of the vehicle over a period of 20 months, but without success. The plaintiff then sued the defendant who pleaded that it was a term of the contract that the transaction

---

92 *Pari materia* to S.56 Tanganyika Contract Act

93 *supra* n.83

94 23 E.A.C.A.366

95 *Reilly v. R.* [1934] A.C. 176

96 [1964] E.A. 540

97 [1965] E.A. 42 (C.A.(K))

98 [1970] E.A. 82 applying the *Karachi Case ibid.*

99 H.C.C.S. No.597/89, [1992] II K.A.L.R. 78 Tinyinondi Ag. J.

was dependent on the availability of foreign exchange, from the Bank of Uganda for the importation of the motor vehicle. Furthermore that it was agreed that if the said foreign exchange was unavailable, the defendant would refund the money. It was finally averred that the plaintiff was informed of the unavailability of the foreign exchange and advised to collect its refund but declined to do so. It was held[100] that the plea of frustration based on unavailability of foreign currency failed on the ground that the defendant did not take any sufficient steps to obtain the necessary foreign currency. Tinyinondi Ag. J. thus stated:[101]

> The defendant could not receive the plaintiff's money and sit back for about twenty months, and when confronted, claim that it had started the machinery of chasing foreign exchange after that long period and hope to convince anyone.

Arising from the above case, it is evident that when frustration is pleaded, care must be taken to ensure that it is not merely an attempt to hide an earlier breach on the part of the person attempting to rely on the doctrine. Thus in *Alibhai Gulam v. Mohamed Yusuf,*[102] the defendant agreed to lease certain shops to the plaintiff. He failed to do this. Six months later, a Rent Restriction Ordinance prevented this type of transaction. The defendant then pleaded frustration. The Court rejected this defence on the ground that the breach of contract arose long before the supervening frustrating legislation and its retrospective effect did not affect the defendant's liability up to the period of supervening frustration.

(g) Special features affecting land

It was previously thought[103] that leases of land could not be frustrated. However, in the more recent House of Lords case, *National Carriers Ltd. v. Panalpina (Northern) Ltd.*[104], it has been held that the doctrine of frustration could apply to leases of land. The rationale of the decision was that no type of contract should as *a matter of law* be excluded from the doctrine. The Court did not disapprove of earlier decisions to the extent that they held that the leases in question *were not* frustrated. It was, in those cases held that the leases were not discharged by the destruction of the premises by enemy action,[105] by requisitioning of the premises;[106] by war-time legislation which prevented the tenant from residing on the premises[107] or from developing the land;[108] or by the death of the tenant of furnished rooms.[109]

However the doctrine of frustration is likely to apply where the lease is a short-term one for a particular purpose: e.g. where a holiday cottage which has been rented for a month is burnt down without the fault of either party. Similarly the contracts in cases like *Taylor v. Caldwell and Krell v. Henry (supra)* could be frustrated, even if the transactions were expressed as leases and not (as they actually were) as licences.

The doctrine of frustration also applies to contracts for the sale of land,[110] although its operation in relation to such contracts is somewhat restricted.

Land is commonly bought for the sake of the house or other buildings on it; but the contract

---

100 following *Alex Bwambale v. Spear Motors* HCCS 690/88; *Munyanganizi v. Spear Motors Ltd.* HCCS 468/83 (unreported)

101 [1992] II KALR at p.88

102 13 E.A.C.A.25

103 E.g. *Cricklewood Property & Investment Trust Ltd. v. Leighton's Investment Ltd.* [1945] A.C. 22; [1945] 1 All E. R. 252

104 [1981] A.C. 675; [1981] 1 All E.R. 161

105 *Redmond v. Dainton* [1920] 2 K.B. 256; *Denman v. Brise* [1949] 1 K.B. 22; *Cusak-Smith v. London Corp.* [1956] 1 W.L.R. 1368

106 *Whitehall Court Ltd. v. Ettlinger* [1920] 1 K.B. 680; *Matthey v. Curling* [1922] 2 A.C. 180; *Swift v. Macbean* [1942] 1 K.B.375

107 *London & Northern Estates Ltd. v. Schlesinger* [1916] 1 K.B. 20

108 *Criklewood* Case *supra* n.103

109 *Youngmin v. Heath* [1974] 1 W.L.R. 135

110 *Amalgamated Investment & Property Co. Ltd. v. John Walker & Co.* [1977] 1 W.L.R. 164

is not frustrated if those buildings are destroyed or seriously damaged or destroyed between contract and completion. The premises are, moreover, at the buyer's risk, so that he must pay the full price even though the premises are damaged or destroyed between those dates.[111] This rule promoted certainty by making it unnecessary to ask whether partial damage was sufficiently serious to bring about frustration; and the hardship which the rule would cause was mitigated by the fact that the purchaser had the benefit of the vendor's insurance.[112] However, as he could not be sure of the adequacy of this insurance he would normally take out his own insurance as soon as contracts were exchanged. In view of the resultant windfall to insurers in the form of receipt of double premiums, the rule is commonly varied by contract: for example, by provisions leaving the risk with the seller till completion, and giving the right to rescind the contract *either* to the purchaser if the property becomes unusable for its purpose at the date of the contract, *or* to the vendor if the property has been destroyed and cannot get planning permission to rebuild it.[113]

(h) Effects of frustration

Frustration determines a contract automatically at the time of the frustrating event[114] irrespective of the behaviour or views of the parties on the matter,[115] although their attitudes may be taken into account.[116] The effect of automatic determination is that unlike the position of breach where the victim may choose to treat the contract as discharged, the parties have no choice in the case of frustration.[117]

Two results arose from the rule that frustration determines the contract at the time of the frustrating event. First, rights which accrued before frustration remain enforceable. Second, rights not yet accrued at the time of frustration remain unenforceable. These rules sometimes cause hardship which has been mitigated by statute. Thus by the Law Reform (Frustrated Contracts) Act, 1943 of the United Kingdom which applies to Uganda[118] both parties are released from further obligations under the contract once the frustrating event occurs. Any money paid out can be recovered from the party to whom it was paid, that person not necessarily being a party to the contract. However, if the party to whom the money was paid or to whom it was owed had incurred expenses, before the date of discharge, in furtherance of the performance of the contract, then the Court may at its discretion allow payment to be made or retained up to the amount of the expenses incurred.[119]

The statutory approach expressly deals with the problem which arose in the *Fibrosa* Case.[120] In that Case, the contract was for sale and delivery of machinery. The contract price was Four Thousand, Eight Hundred Pounds for which One Thousand, Six Hundred Pounds was payable in advance. The purchaser paid One Thousand Pounds towards the advance payment. The contract was frustrated due to the war. The purchaser asked for the return of One Thousand Pounds already paid but the manufacturers refused on the ground that they had done considerable work on the machinery. The purchaser sued in quasi-contract for the refund of One Thousand Pounds. The House of Lords held[121] that he was entitled to recover the money because there had been a

---

111 *Paine v. Meller* (1801) 6 Ves. 349

112 See e.g. Law of Property Act 1925, S.47 (U.K.)

113 See e.g. British Law Society's Standard Conditions of Sale (1990) Conditions 5.1.1. to 5.1.4.

114 *Hirji Mulji v. Cheong S. S. Co. Ltd.* [1926] A.C. 497, 507; *B.P. Exploration (Libya) Ltd. v. Hunt* [1979] 1 W.L.R. 783, 809 (affirmed [1983] A.C. 352; [1982] 1 All E.R. 925)

115 *Hirji Mulji* Case, *Ibid.* p.509

116 *Bank Line Ltd. v. Arthur Capel & Co.* [1919] A.C. 435, 460; *The Wenjiang* (No.2) 2 Lloyd's Rep. 400, 408

117 *Shepherd Ltd. v. Jerrom* [1987] Q.B. 301, 327

118 Contract Act Cap.75

119 See further *B.P. Exploration Co. Case supra* n.114

120 [1943] A.C. 32 [1942] 2 All E.R. 122

total failure of consideration. The Court explained that[122] in quasi-contract, unlike contract, consideration meant actual benefit and not just a promise. To the extent that the decision was restricted to situations of total failure of consideration, it did not go far enough and was open to two criticisms.[123] First, once the plaintiff gets a benefit, however small, he cannot any longer recover because there would then be no total failure of consideration.[124] Second, the defendant who has done some work or spent money in execution of the contract gets nothing for his work or expenses so long as the benefit of his work or expenses has not actually passed to the plaintiff. The total loss would fall on the defendant or payee in the event of frustration.

---

121 Overruling *Chandler v. Webster* [1904] 1 K.B. 493 C.A. (E)

122 per Lord Simon [1943] A.C. 32 at p.48

123 Treitel, *Law of Contract, supra* pp.809 - 810

124 See also *Whincup v. Hughes* (1871) L.R. 6 C.P. 78

15
REMEDIES FOR BREACH OF CONTRACT

Where a contract is breached or broken five courses of action are open to the injured party. These are (i) refusal to further perform the contract; (ii) a right to bring an action for damages; (iii) a right to sue on *quantum meruit*; (iv) a right to sue for specific performance; (v) a right to sue for an injunction.

1. Refusal of further performance

If one of the parties has broken the contract, the other party may treat the contract as rescinded and refuse to further perform it. Rescission has the effect of restoring the parties to the position they were in before the contract. Consequently, if the injured party has received any benefits under the contract, he must return them to the other party unless the contract otherwise provides.[125] Where the breach is one of warranty, the injured party is obliged to perform the contract but will only be entitled to an award of damages.

2. Damages

The general rule is that whenever there is a breach of contract by one party, the other is entitled to bring an action for damages. If it is shown that he has actually suffered no loss from the breach, he will only be entitled to *nominal damages* that is damages which simply recognise he has suffered a legal infringement of his right. This view is based on the proposition that damages are only awarded to compensate the plaintiff. Therefore, damages are based on the loss to the plaintiff and not the gain to the defendant. Thus in *Teacher v. Calder*[126], a financier broke a contract to invest Fifteen Thousand Pounds in the business of a timber merchant. Instead, he invested the sum in a distillery. It was held that the timber merchant's damages were based on a loss to his business and not on the much larger profits which the financier got from the distillery. Similarly, an employee who leaves in breach of contract to take up a better job is not liable to account for the extra pay but only to compensate the employer for any loss he has actually suffered.

(a) Loss

Loss includes harm to the person or property of the plaintiff or any other injury to his economic position. Punitive damages are not generally awarded in a contractual action, although they are normal in certain tortious cases.[127] Their purpose is not to compensate but to express the Court's disapproval of the defendant's conduct.

The basic object of damages for breach of contract is to put the plaintiff "so far as money can do it ... in the same situation ... as if the contract had been performed".[128] The plaintiff is

---

125 *Dies v. British & International Mining Corp* [1939] 1 K.B. 724. See also Chapter 8 *supra*.

126 (1899) 1 F.(H.L.) 39

127 *Addis v. Gramophone Co.* [1909] A.C. 488 (Contract); *Obongo v. Kisumu Municipal Council* [1971] E.A. 91 (tort)

128 *Robinson v. Harman* (1848) 1 Ex. 850, 855

entitled to be compensated for the loss of his bargain based on the principle, *restituo in integrum*. The burden of proving the loss suffered is on the plaintiff.[129] In *Kaloli Sempa v. Latif's Garage Ltd.*,[130] the plaintiff had taken a car on hire purchase terms from X. The car was later re-possessed for alleged nonpayment of the instalments. The plaintiff successfully proved that X had fled the Country and he was unable to make payment. He demanded the return of the car and special damages to recover the loss of profits he would have made when using the car to sell second hand clothing in outlying markets of Kampala. The Court ordered the return of the car or its value but refused the claim for special damages on the basis that the plaintiff had alleged but not proved such loss. Furthermore in *Nalumba v. Uganda Wildlife Development Ltd.*,[131] the plaintiff had been employed as an apprentice hunter under a contract that provided for medical treatment and personal accident insurance equal to five times the plaintiff's annual salary. In fact the defendants never took out this insurance and when the plaintiff injured his knee he sued to recover from the employers Two Thousand, Seven Hundred and Fifty Pounds representing five times his salary. The Court dismissed the claim for that amount and awarded nominal damages of Shs.40/=. Fuad J. explained that the clause could not be construed in such a way as to make payment of Two Thousand, Seven Hundred and Fifty Pounds automatic upon the occurrence of any type of injury. The plaintiff could only expect payment up to that figure. No evidence was led to show the extent of the injury and in those circumstances only nominal damages were available. The Court, could, however, take a lenient approach on the issue of the necessity to plead special damages if these are clear from the pleadings.[132]

(b) Remoteness of damages

Damages must be such as are reasonably foreseeable when the contract was made as likely to result from the breach of contract. The purpose of the rule is that damages are only recoverable if they are caused by a proximate cause but not by an event which is too remote. The rules governing the award of damages were laid down in *Hadley v. Baxendale.*[133] In that Case a mill belonging to X had a broken shaft. X delivered the shaft to Y, a carrier, to take to a manufacturer and copy it to make a new one. Y delayed the delivery of the shaft beyond a reasonable time. As a result the mill was idle for a longer period than necessary. X did not make known to Y that delay would result in loss of profits. It was held that Y was not liable for the loss of profits during the period of delay. The loss of profits for nondelivery or delayed delivery may be recovered when the party in breach could reasonably have contemplated that it was unlikely or that there was serious possibility that such loss will be incurred. In this vein Alderson B in delivering the judgment of the Court of Exchequer thus formulated the rule:[134]

> Where two parties have made a contract which one of them has broken, the damages which the other party ought to receive in respect of such breach of contract should be such as may fairly and reasonably be considered either arising naturally i.e. according to the usual course of things, from such breach of contract itself, or such as may reasonably be supposed to have been in contemplation of both parties, at the time they made the contract, as the probable result of the breach of it.

---

129 *Mukisa Biscuit Manufacturing Co. Ltd. v. West End Distributors Ltd.* (No.2) [1970] E.A. 469, 474 per Spry V - P. See also *Frank Rwakijanju Case infra.* n.130

130 H.C.C.S. 642 of 1965 (Uganda). See also *Frank Rwakijanju v. Prince Patrick Kaboyo* [1992] IV K.A.L.R. 132

131 1966 (2) A.L.R. Comm 210 (Uganda)

132 *Caltex (Africa) Ltd. v. Kassam* [1965] E.A. 35 at p.40 per Newbold Ag. V.P.; *Salum v. Twentsche Overseas Trading Company Ltd.* 1967(3) A.L.R. Comm 108.

133 (1854) 9 Ex. 341; see also *Wayne Tank & Pump Co. Ltd. v. Employers Liability* [1974] Q.B. 57

134 *Ibid.* at p.354; See also Tanganyika Contract Act, S.73(1)

The rules have been further illustrated in subsequent cases. In *Victoria Laundry v. Newman Industries*[135], V bought from N a boiler for use in his laundry. Delivery was to be made on 5th June, but was not made until November 8. V claimed (i) loss of the profit the laundry would have made had the boiler been delivered in time; (ii) loss of profit from profitable dyeing contracts. It was held that the laundry profits could be recovered as N must have contemplated their loss if there was delay. However, the loss on the dyeing contracts could not be recovered since they could not have been contemplated. In the *Heron II*[136], the appellant was a shipowner who had contracted to carry the respondent's sugar from Constanza to Basrah. The Ship deviated from the route and arrived at Basrah nine days later than it would normally have done. During that time the price of sugar had dropped whereby the respondent received Four Thousand and Eleven Pounds less than he would have got if they arrived on time. The British House of Lords held that the appellants were liable for the loss. In contrast to the approach in the *Victoria Laundry* Case where emphasis was placed on whether the defendant should have foreseen the result, in this case it was emphasized that both parties should have reasonably contemplated at the time the contract was made that such could result from the breach. Furthermore, it is not sufficient that the defendant knew of special conditions attaching to the contract to make him liable for the ensuing damage. It has to be shown that he had agreed to accept the contract with the extra condition attached. Thus in *Woodruff v. Dupont,*[137] the defendant hired the plaintiff, a professional hunter, to organise a hunting safari for him. A deposit was paid but the client then cancelled the contract. The plaintiff claimed for loss of goodwill and publicity. The claim was dismissed as being not reasonably foreseeable. The deposit paid was considered to be sufficient compensation. The evidence showed that the plaintiff had hired an extra two hunters at his cost, entirely to enhance the success of the safari and therefore the success that would go with such success. The defendant knew of the plaintiff's hopes of publicity but this did not mean that he was willing to shoulder the extra financial burden.

In the unreported Tanzanian Case of *Hamisi Sinabato v. Gladness Haduri*[138], the defendant purported to sell a piece of land to the plaintiff for Shs.6,000/=. After the plaintiff had built house foundations on the plot, it was discovered that the defendant had no title to the property at the time of the sale. The plaintiff claimed damages representing not only the purchase price but also the money spent on the foundations. The Court allowed the claim and Hamyln J. thus stated:

> Where as a result of representations of a party, the other party to the contract is led to expend further sums, and where it turns out that such representations are false to the knowledge of the party making them that party is liable for additional damages which were in the contemplation of the two parties at the time of making the contract.

(c) Assessment of damages

The basic rule is that the injured party should be placed in the same financial position as if the contract had been performed. The measure of damages is the value of the performance to the plaintiff. In a contract of Sale of goods, the measure of damages when there is an available market for the goods is the difference between the market-price at the date of the breach and the contract price. Where the market price is equal to the contract price, the plaintiff will be in the same financial position as if the contract had been performed. In this instance, the plaintiff

---

135 [1949] 2 K.B. 528

136 *Konfos v. Czarnikow Ltd.* [1969] 1 A.C. 350; Pickering 31 MLR 203

137 [1964] E.A. 404

138 (1969) Civ. App. 66 - D - 67

will only be entitled to nominal damages. In *H. W. Guggenheim Ltd. v. K. K. and V. K. Rajguru*[139], the plaintiff agreed to export bicycle spokes to the defendant in Uganda. The defendant tried to revoke the contract on the grounds that the delivery was late. The Court rejected this claim and therefore had to assess damages on behalf of the plaintiff on the grounds of non-acceptance. Such a situation is regulated by the Sale of Goods Act which provides thus:[140]

> Where there is an available market for the goods in question the measure of damages is *prima facie* to be ascertained by the difference between the contract price and the market or current price at the time or times when the goods ought to have been accepted or, if no time was fixed for acceptance, then at the time of refusal to deliver.

The Court, however, conceded that it would be difficult to find an easy and ready market to absorb this particular commodity. In such circumstances the Court decided to make an estimate of the probable loss and awarded 50% of the contract price. The matter was also considered by the Court of Appeal for Eastern Africa in *Devshi Samat Shah v. Budhram Mohanlal*,[141] where the court took into account the profit margin which the innocent seller would have made. The contract was for the sale of thirty tons of nuts at Shs.675 per ton. Thirteen tons were delivered when the market prices dropped drastically and the buyer therefore refused to accept the remaining deliveries. The seller treated this as a repudiation of the contract and claimed damages. The Court distinguished two sets of possibilities. First, if the subject-matter of the sale has yet to be produced, manufactured or repudiated when the repudiation occurs, damages will be the profit margin on that sale. Second, where the goods have been produced, manufactured or obtained, then the seller has incurred expenses in reaching this stage in addition to the loss of profit. In such a situation, he would be entitled to all the damage sustained, subject of course to him offsetting as much of the damage as possible by selling in an available market. In the present case, such market was not available and the seller having done all that a reasonable man in those circumstances could have done, was entitled to his expenditure in addition to the profit he would have made.

These cases deal with breach by the buyer and the need for the seller to find an alternative market and damages being calculated on that possibility being realised or not, together with his profit margin. Alternatively, if the party in breach is the seller by failing to deliver the buyer should try to buy on the open market and his damages will be the difference between the original contract price and the one he finally pays.

The date for fixing the market value of the goods is the date when the goods should have been delivered or if that was not fixed then the date of the refusal to deliver. Where the buyer pays less on the open market then he has suffered no damage. However, he will be entitled to a sum that represents "business inconvenience"[142]

Generally, damages in contract do not take into account injury to feelings.[143] However there is local decision to the contrary. Thus in *Chande v. East African Airways Corp.*,[144] the plaintiffs were a wedding party, who included the bride and bridegroom, booked return air tickets from Dar-es-Salaam to Bombay. The tickets were made out for Dar-es-Salaam, Zanzibar, Tanga, Mombasa, Nairobi and Bombay. The intention, as explained to the travel agency, was that at the smaller airports reception parties would be waiting. These instructions were passed onto the defendants and tickets issued accordingly. The outward journey passed normally. At Nairobi airport on the

139 7 U.L.R. 55

140 Cap. 79. S.51(3)

141 18 E.A.C.A. 79

142 See discussion *infra*

143 For English exceptions see Treitel, *op.cit.* pp.876 - 878

144 [1964] E.A. 78 following *Cook v. Spanish Holiday Tour (London) Ltd.* (1959) 103 S. J. 873

homeward journey, the plaintiffs were told that there were only three available seats on the morning flight. An afternoon flight was offered but rejected on the grounds that the reception parties would meet the morning flight. In the end the plaintiffs chartered two small planes and sued the defendants for breach of contract. The Court noted that the attitudes and behaviour of some of the defendants staff may well have shown "a regrettable lack of frankness and possibly deliberate mendacity", but such matters were not to be taken into account when assessing contractual damages. However, the plaintiffs had suffered considerable disappointment in having their plans upset.

(d) Mitigation of loss

.The injured party under a contract which is breached, is under a duty to minimise the damage that is to mitigate his loss. In *British Westinghouse Electric & Manufacturing Co. v. Underground Railway*,[145] Lord Haldane stated the principle as follows:[146]

> The fundamental basis is compensation for pecuniary loss naturally flowing from the breach; but this first principle is qualified by a second, which imposes on the plaintiff the duty of taking all reasonable steps to mitigate the loss consequent on the breach and debars him from claiming any part of the damage which is due in part to his neglect to take such steps.

The rationale for the rule is that the injured part should not recover more than he would have suffered if he had acted reasonably because any further damages do not reasonably follow from the defendant's breach.

In *Mussa Hassan v. Hurt & Another,*[147] the appellants contracted to buy all the milk produced by the respondents for one year. The contract contained special provisions in the event of breach of contract. The appellants rejected the milk arguing that it did not conform with the agreed quality. The respondents proved that it was fit for human consumption when delivered and they therefore sued for breach of contract claiming the sum mentioned in the contract as liquidated damages. The appellants argued that even if they were in breach, the respondents should have attempted to sell the remaining milk on the open market rather than convert it to ghee and casein, which fetched a lower price. The Court of Appeal for East Africa rejected this interpretation of mitigation and explained that it was up to the appellants to show that the respondents had acted unreasonably in their efforts to mitigate their loss, which they failed to do. While admitting that the respondents might have been wiser to sell the milk at a slightly lower price rather than convert it as they did in the circumstances, their conduct was not unreasonable.

Issues of mitigation have also arisen in cases of wrongful dismissal of an employee. In *Brace v. Calder*,[148] B was employed by a partnership which consisted of four (4) members for a period of two years. After 6 months, the partnership was dissolved through the retirement of two of the partners. Thereafter, the business was carried on by the remaining partners. The continuing partners were willing to continue B's employment on the same terms. It was held that although the dissolution of the partnership operated as a wrongful dismissal of B, he was only entitled to nominal damages as he had suffered no loss. The principle in this Case is that an employee who has been wrongfully dismissed is under a duty to minimise the loss to himself by finding employment.

---

145 [1912] A.C. 673

146 *Ibid.* p.689 See also *Payzu Ltd. v. Saunders* [1919] 2 K.B. 581, 589

147 [1964] E.A. 201; 1964(2) A.L.R. Comm 94

148 [1895] 2 Q.B. 253

In *Southern Highlands Tobacco Union Ltd. v. David McQueen*,[149] the plaintiff was employed by the defendant company as their general manager on a four year contract at Two Thousand Pounds per annum. The contract was silent about dismissal procedures and the High Court decided that none could be implied. While the plaintiff was completing his earlier contract with the company, he was given notice of termination of his employment thereby cancelling the four year contract. He sued for Eight Thousand Pounds plus housing allowances leave pay and travel money. The High Court awarded Ten Thousand, Four Hundred and Twelve Pounds and the company appealed. The main issue was the *quantum* of damages. It was argued firstly, that no deduction had been made to reflect the possibility that the employee might obtain alternative employment and had done nothing to find work. Secondly was the tax liability of the award. The Court of Appeal dismissed the appeal on the grounds that the respondent had tried to secure employment without success on account of his age of fifty-eight. However in *Leuben Lugendo v. Bukedi District Administration*,[150] a muluka (parish) chief was wrongfully dismissed from his post. In his claim for damages, Russel J. pointed out that a dismissed employee was not entitled to "sit and twiddle his thumbs" and expect to receive his monthly salary. He had to convince the Court that he had made a determined effort to find suitable employment. On the evidence the chief appeared to have made no"genuine or diligent effort" to minimise his loss. Despite this, he was awarded six months pay.

The issue arises as to the effect of an employee who has been dismissed getting a position later at a higher pay, on an award for damages. Furthermore, should the Court take into account sums that may have been earned by a terminated employee through part-time employment? In *Givon Battista Liberti v. Kassam Jivraj*,[151] the plaintiff was unemployed for 16 months before finally securing a job which paid considerably more than the one from which he had been dismissed. The judge noted that while accepting that the plaintiff may have remained unemployed for 16 months "he must have been able to earn something during that time in work of a temporary nature if he had wanted to. The judge then awarded him 16 months' pay at Shs.1,000 and then deducted Shs.400 a month based on a suggestion by the plaintiff. On the issue of whether new employment should offset the damages for the time unemployed, it was decided negatively on the ground that all future employment had an element of uncertainty attached and in addition the extra pay most probably reflects greater duties and responsibilities. Consequently, there was no justification in making the new salary set off the defendant's liabilities to the plaintiff.

Mitigation may also involve the innocent party accepting certain alternative proposals from the person in breach. Thus in *The Iron & Steel Wares Ltd. v. G. W. Martyt & Co.*,[152] the plaintiffs contracted to buy bicycle forks from the defendants. What was delivered did not fit the frames. The plaintiffs attempted to reject the consignment as unmerchantable but the Court held that the particular remedy was lost on the grounds that they had already collected insurance money because of the faulty delivery and in addition they had not informed the sellers within a reasonable time of the defect. The claim for loss of profit on future sub-sales was also dismissed because the defendants had no notice of the sub-sales. The defendants however had offered to replace the faulty parts which the plaintiff refused to accept. It was held that the plaintiffs ought to have mitigated their loss by accepting the defendant's offer to supply fresh forks. Having refused to accept this offer, they were only entitled to recover damages for such loss as they would have suffered had they accepted the defendant's offer. The Court then considered the state of the market and decided that it was the seller's market and, therefore, no real financial loss had been

149 [1960] E.A. 490 (Tanzania)

150 H.C.C.S. 456 of 1965 (Uganda)

151 24(2) K.L.R. 4

152 7 U.L.R. 146

suffered, damages were only granted for "business inconvenience" which the plaintiffs suffered and for any period of credit which they had lost.

(e) Liquidated damages and penalties

Parties to a contract may agree in the contract that in the case of breach thereof, damages shall be a fixed sum of money to be calculated in a particular way. These are known as liquidated damages. Damages are unliquidated when they have not been assessed by agreement between the parties. Where the parties have agreed to liquidated damages, then when there is a breach, the injured party only recovers those damages and no more. In *Cellulose Acetate Silk Co. v. Widnes Foundry (1925) Ltd.*,[153] W agreed to build a plant for C on a certain date and also agreed to pay Twenty Pounds for every week they took beyond that date. They were 30 weeks late and C claimed Five Thousand, Eight Hundred and fifty Pounds representing their actual loss from the delay. It was held that W had agreed to pay Twenty Pounds a week for delay and were not liable for more.

Liquidated damages will not be awarded if they are not a genuine estimate of loss. If they are excessive, they are regarded as a penalty. The essence of a penalty is normally to compel a party to perform the contract. For instance in a hire purchase agreement, if there is a provision that the hirer cannot terminate the agreement until he has paid 75% of the hire purchase price, this is a penalty which cannot be recovered since it is excessive. Where the rate is lower i.e. 50%, this may not be regarded as a penalty.[154] Where the Court finds that a contractual clause is in effect a penalty, it may decline to enforce it and instead award damages based on actual loss proved.[155] The description of a clause as either "liquidated" or "penalty" will not bind the Court as to its essence. Thus in *Dunlop Pneumatic Tyre Co. Ltd. v. New Garage and Motor Co. Ltd.*,[156] the tyre company supplied the garage with tyres on condition that the garage did not tamper or alter the markings of the tyres; did not sell below a certain price; did not sell to persons on a suspended list and did not exhibit or export tyres without consent. If the garage were in breach of any of these conditions, they were to pay Five Pounds per tyre used in the breach by way of "liquidated damages". The House of Lords held that the Five Pounds figure was to be regarded as liquidated damages. Lord Dunedin formulated four rules of construction of a liquidated damage clause thus:[157]

(a) It will be held to be a penalty if the sum stipulated for is extravagant and unconscionable in amount in comparison with the greatest loss that could conceivably be proved to have followed from the breach.

(b) It will be held to be a penalty if the breach consists only in not paying a sum of money, and the sum stipulated is a greater sum which ought to have been paid.

(c) Where a single lump sum is made payable ... on the recurrence of one or more or all of several events, some of which may occasion serious and other but trifling damage, there is a presumption that it is a penalty clause. Consequently, a sum will not be regarded as penal if it is expressly proportioned to the seriousness of the breach e.g. if a lease provides for payment of One Hundred Pounds *per acre*[158] for land not restored to its former condition, or if a contractor agrees to pay Five Hundred Pounds *per week* for delay.[159]

---

153 *Cellulose Acetate Silk Co. v. Widnes Foundry* [1933] A.C. 20

154 *London Trust Ltd. v. Hurrell* [1955] 1 W.L.R. 391; *Robophone Facilities Ltd. v. Blank* [1966] 1 W.L.R. 428. See also Kenya Hire Purchase Act 1968, S.12(1)

155 *Guaranty Discount Co. Ltd. v. Ward* [1961] E.A. 285 per Gould J. A. (C.A.)

156 [1915] A.C. 79. See also *Mistry Popat Mulji v. Lewis Paton and Co.* 8 Z.L.R. 230 (Zanzibar)

157 *Ibid.* pp.87 - 88

158 *Elphinstone v. Monkland Iron & Coal Co.* (1886) 11 App Cas. 332; *Mistry Popat Case supra* n.156

159 *Clydebank Engineering Case* [1905] A.C.6. The clause will not operate where the contract is totally abandoned (since otherwise the payments would go on for ever)

(d) It is not obstacle to the sum stipulated being a genuine preestimate of damage that the consequences of breach are such as to make precise preestimation an impossibility. This is illustrated by the facts of the *Dunlop Pneumatic Tyre Case.*

The Courts are normally faced with "depreciation clauses" in hire purchase contracts which violate the rules on liquidated damages considered in this section. Thus in *Guaranty Discount Co. v. Ward,*[160] W had taken a car on hire purchase terms from the company, paid a deposit of Shs.3,000 and agreed to pay Shs.580 a month for 17 months. He defaulted on the first two payments and the car was repossessed. The company claimed for the payment due up to the date of repossession and the cost of repossession were not objected to. The issue was in relation to a claim of Shs.7,081 "agreed depreciation" under a clause in the agreement which read:

> the hirer shall be liable to pay the owners: (c) by way of agreed depreciation of the goods, the difference between three quarters of the total hire purchase price payable under this agreement and the total sum already paid.

The Court of Appeal in agreeing with the Supreme Court held that such a clause was a penalty and remitted the case back to that Court to assess what reasonable compensation, if any, should be awarded.

A problem may arise where a hirer exercises his option to terminate the hiring under a hire purchase agreement, but is then faced with "depreciation clause" which is disproportionate to the Case suffered by the owner. In *Associated Distributors Ltd v. Hall,* [161] it was held that the hirer is liable to pay the sum on the grounds that as he had not broken the contract the rules governing penalties do not apply. The decision was doubted but not overruled by the House of Lords in *Bridge v. Campbell Discount Co. Ltd.*[162] However in *Export Credits Guarantee Department v. Universal Oil Products Co.*[163], the House of Lords in fact held that the penalty rules only apply where the money is payable on an event which is a breach of contract as between the plaintiff and the defendant. The Courts, nevertheless try to avoid the rule in *Hall* and *Export Credits* cases by interpreting whenever possible, the hirer's conduct not as amounting to voluntary termination but as breach. In that event penalty clauses come into operation.[164] It is suggested[165] that a solution would be to control the damages by clearly worded hire purchase legislation. This has been attempted by the Tanzania and Kenya Hire Purchase Acts,[166] which provide that if the hirer under a hire purchase agreement terminates it prior to final payment by returning the goods to the owner, he is liable to "pay the amount, if any, by which one half of the hire purchase price exceeds the sums paid and the sums which were due in respect of the hire purchase price immediately before the termination or such lesser amount as may be specified in the agreement". This approach is unsatisfactory, since it is possible for one-half of the hire purchase price together with the value of the car on the open market to exceed the original price of the car.[167] The owner would, consequently, be better off after the termination and hirer would have paid a sum exceeding due compensation. The English Hire Purchase Act, 1965 has recognised this possibility and allows the Court to award a smaller sum if it thinks that such sum more truly reflects the loss suffered by the owner.[168] Consequently a hirer may allege that under the East African Acts, one half payment still amounts to a penalty and ask the Court to award a lesser sum[169]. Needless to add, where the

160 Supra n.155
161 [1938] 2 K.B. 83
162 [1962] A.C. 600; [1962] 1 All E.R. 385; Wedderburn [1961] C.L.J. 156; Fridman 24 Mod. L. R. 507; 26 Mod. L.R. 198
163 [1983] 2 All E.R. 205; [1983] 1 W.L.R. 339
164 *Amusan & Thomas v. Bentworth Finance (Nigeria) Ltd.* 1965 A.L.R. Comm. 601
165 Hodgin, *Law of Contract In East Africa* (1975), p.214
166 Act No.22 of 1966 (Tanzania); Act 42 of 1968 (Kenya), S.12(1)
167 Hodgin, *supra* n.165 p.214
168 S.28(2). See also Hodgin, "The Need for Hire Purchase Reform In Uganda" Vol.1 No.4 *Uganda Law Focus 220*

Acts do not apply[170], the common law rules on penalty and preestimate clauses, discussed above would apply.[171]

(f) Taxation of damages

The value of the plaintiff's loss may be affected by the incidence of taxation. Thus in *B.T.C. v. Gourley*,[172] the plaintiff was injured by the negligence of the defendant's servants, and claimed damages for loss of earnings. It was estimated that, but for the accident, the plaintiff would have earned Thirty Seven Thousand Pounds. Had he actually earned this sum, it would have been taxed and Six Thousand Pounds would have been left to him. But had he been awarded damages of Thirty Seven Thousand Pounds, he would have kept the whole amount, since damages for loss of earnings resulting from personal injury are not taxable. The House of Lords held that the proper measure of damages was Six Thousand Pounds reflecting the plaintiff's actual loss. Although this was a tortious action, it is suggested[173] that the same principle is applicable to contractual liability e.g. in assessing damages for wrongful dismissal.[174] The rule is premised on the reasoning that the plaintiff ought not to make a profit out of the tort or breach of contract by getting tax-free damages to compensate for loss of a benefit which would have been taxable. It applies in two situations. First, the damages must be compensation for loss of a taxable income or gain, and not simply for loss of a capital asset. In this respect, the rule would not apply if a buyer of goods claimed the amount by which their market value exceeded the contract price since these damages are meant to compensate him for failure to obtain a capital asset (out of which he might make a profit or a loss)[175]. Second, the damages themselves must be taxable. In *Diamond v. Campbell Jones,*[176] a dealer in real estate lost profits of Eight Thousand, Five Hundred Pounds through the defendant's breach of contract to sell him a house. The argument that damages should be reduced because of tax liability was rejected because the actual damages were taxable in the dealer's hands. In *Southern Highlands Tobacco Union Ltd. v. David McQueen*[177], the defendant argued that tax deduction should have been made from the award of Ten Thousand, Four Hundred and twelve Pounds. The Court referred to Section 3(1)(a) and 5(2)(c) of the East African Income Tax Management Act[178] which made "any amount received as compensation for termination of any contract of employment or service" chargeable to tax and decided that he damages were taxable in the hands of the plaintiff and should not be deducted before the defendant's payment of damages.[179]

Where a particular type of breach is not covered by legislation Ugandan Courts have applied the rules in the *Gourley* Case.[180] Thus in *Bwavu Mpologoma Growers Co-operative Union Ltd. v. Gasston & Barbour,*[181] the defendants committed a copyright infringement of the plaintiff's engineering plans whereby the plaintiff lost Two Thousand Pounds profits. The Court of Appeal held that the profits would have been liable to tax and therefore the plaintiff should not receive

---

169 Hodgin, *supra* n.165, p.214

170 by the hire purchase agreement exceeding the financial limits of the Acts: Shs.60,000/= (Tanzania); Shs.80,000/= (Kenya).

171 c.f. *Dr. Syenda Sakeb & Ors. v. Jamil Din & Ors.* Civil Suit No.387 of 1971 (Uganda).

172 [1956] A.C. 185; [1955] 3 All E.R. 796

173 Treitel, *op.cit* p.946

174 See *Beach v. Reed Corrugated Cases Ltd.* [1956] 1 W.L.R. 807;*Re Houghton Main Colliery* [1956] 1 W.L.R. 1219; *Phipps v. Orthodox Unit Trusts Ltd.* [1958] 1 Q.B. 314

175 c.f. *Lim Foo Yong Ltd. v. Collector of Land Revenue* [1963] 1 W.L.R. 295

176 [1961] Ch. 22; [1960] 1 All E.R. 583

177 *Supra* n.149 and text thereof

178 Cap 24 Laws of the East African Community then applicable. For the equivalent provision in Uganda, see Income Tax Actm 1997, Ss, 5, 20

179 See also *Shah v. Abdulla* [1964] E.A. 742

180 *Supra* n.172

181 [1960] E.A. 490; Note *Journal of African Law* 198 (1959)

more than he would have done if there had been no infringement. The result is that the tax, as assessed by the Court - who are not particularly well equipped for the task - is deducted from the defendant's payment of damages. This deduction does not, however, go to the tax authorities. Windham J. A. explained the operation of the common law rule:

> The rule (in *Gourley*) may be briefly stated thus: In assessing such damages a court ought to award a sum approximately to the plaintiff's net loss of profits that is to say the net profits that he would have made after deducting the approximate amount of tax (if any) that he would have had to pay on it, unless the damages that are being awarded will themselves be subject to taxation in the plaintiff's hands after he has received them. The later part of the rule is, of course, necessary in order to prevent the plaintiff from in effect being taxed twice over, once by the judge's approximate deduction and later by the tax authorities precise taxation.

The rule in *Gourley's* Case has been criticised. It is said to involve a paradox: for revenue purposes damages for loss of earnings are treated as compensation for loss of a capital asset, since otherwise they would be taxable; while in assessing damages they are treated as compensation for loss of income, since otherwise the plaintiff's tax liability would be irrelevant.[182] Other criticisms[183] relate to the practical effect of the rule. It is said to enable the defendant to take advantage of wholly extraneous circumstances, e.g. that the plaintiff has a large private income; that it makes the assessment of damages highly speculative; and that it may make it cheaper to break a contract than to perform it.

In 1958 the rule in *Gourley's* Case was referred to the British Law Reform Committee.[184] Three views were proffered. First, the plaintiff should recover his gross loss and not have to pay tax on damages. However, this is unfair since the plaintiff is allowed to make a profit out of a wrong. Second, the plaintiff should recover his loss but should have to pay tax on the damages.[185] The objection to this view is that the assessment of the tax payable necessarily involves speculation[186] while speculative damages can be accepted, speculative taxation should be resisted.[187] Third, the majority felt that the rule in *Gourley's* Case is the most satisfactory solution to the problem, as it gives effect to the principle that damages are meant to compensate the plaintiff for his actual loss. This is regarded as the best view.[188]

3. Equitable remedies

(a) Quantum meruit

Where there is a breach of contract, the injured party, instead of suing for damages may claim payment for what he has done under the contract. The right to payment does not arise out of the original contract but is based on an implied promise by the other party arising from the acceptance of an executed consideration. This is known as *quantum meruit*. Two basic situations of *quantum meruit* may be identified.

(i) Where one party abandons or refuses to perform contract

Where a party to the contract is prevented from completing his obligations under the contract he may claim under *quantum meruit*. Thus in the leading case of *Planche v. Colburn*,[189] P was

182 Jolowicz, [1959] Camb. L. J. 85
183 Treitel, *op.cit.* p.847
184 7th Report (1958) Cmnd. 501
185 as was the case in *McQueen* Case *Supra* n.149
186 e.g. as to the allowance which the plaintiff could, over the years, have claimed, and as to rates of tax
187 Treitel, *op.cit.* p.847
188 *Ibid.*
189 (1813) 3 Bing 14; [1824 - 1834] All E.R. Rep. 94. See also *Lodder v. Slowey* [1904] A.C. 442.

engaged by C to write a book to be published by instalments in a weekly magazine. After a few numbers had appeared, the magazine was abandoned. It was held that P could recover on *quantum meruit* for the work he had done under the contract. A claim under *quantum meruit* is not possible where the party claiming is responsible for the breach of contract, unless the innocent party impliedly accepts the work so far done and derives some benefit from it.[190]

(ii) Where work has been done under void contract

Where one party has derived benefits under a void contract, a claim based on *quantum meruit* is possible. Thus in *Craven-Ellis v. Canons Ltd.*,[191] C was employed as a Managing Director by the company under a written contract. The contract was not binding on the company because the directors who made it were not qualified and could not, therefore, bind the company. C rendered services to the company and sued for remuneration. The Court of Appeal held that the agreement was void and a claim based on the contract must fail. However, since services had in fact been rendered whereby the company benefited, the alternative claim on the *quantum meruit* could succeed. Greer L. J. emphasised the *quasi* contractual nature of this claim thus:[192]

> The obligation to pay reasonable remuneration for the work done when there is no binding contract between the parties is imposed by a rule of law, and not by an inference of fact arising from the acceptance of services or goods. It is one of the cases referred to in books on contract as obligations arising *quasi ex contractu*

However, this principle may be displaced where the terms of the agreement gives rise to a conflict between the claimant's own financial interest and his fiduciary duty to the company as one of its directors.[193]

A claim on *quantum meruit* is also possible where the contract between the parties is silent on the precise sums to be paid. Thus in *Silvestra Gidudu Bulafu v. Mayobo - Mulambuli G.C.S. Ltd.*,[194] the plaintiff had a written contract to construct a building for the defendant. The plaintiff also claimed that there was an oral agreement that he should clear and level the site. It was held that as the work was done and needed to be done before the construction could start, the plaintiff should receive Shs.1,800 as reasonable remuneration for the work done.

(b) Specific performance[195]

(i) Scope

In place of or in addition to an award of damages, to the injured party, a decree of specific performance may be granted to him by the Court. Specific performance means the actual carrying out or execution by the parties of their contract. In *Beswick v. Beswick,*[196] Peter, a local merchant entered into a written contract with his nephew, John, whereby Peter sold his business to John. The contract provided that after the death of Peter,the nephew should pay the widow (who was not a party to the agreement) an annuity of Five Pounds per week. Peter died and the nephew refused to pay her. It was held that the widow was entitled to the amount as administratrix of Peter's estate. However, she could not enforce the obligation under the contract in her personal capacity as she was not a party to the contract.

---

190 *Sumpter v. Hedges* [1898] 1 Q.B. 673

191 [1936] 2 K.B. 403; [1936] 3 All E.R. 1066; Denning L.Q.R. 54 (1939)

192 *Ibid.* 2 K.B., 412

193 *Guiness plc v. Saunders* [1990] 2 A.C. 663; Beatson & Prentice 106 L.Q.R. 365

194 Civil Appeal M.M.59 of 1969 (Uganda). Hodgin, *op.cit.* p.229

195 See also Spry, *Specific performance* (6th Ed.); Jones & Goodhart, *Specific Performance*

196 [1968] A.C. 58; [1967] 2 All E.R. 1197

The remedy of specific performance is a discretionary one and will not be granted in five main instances. These are, where (i) damages are an adequate remedy;[197] (ii) the Court cannot supervise the execution of the contract e.g. a building or construction contract;[198] (iii) the contract is for personal services;[199] (iv) one of the parties is a minor;[200] the contract is to lend money. The remedy is common in contracts relating to land[201] or to take debentures in a company. In cases of sale of goods, the remedy can only be granted in the case of specific or ascertained goods[202] and in practice is not ordered unless the goods are unique and cannot easily be obtained on the open market.[203] Although a Court does not normally order specific performance of a contract for personal services, it may order such a contract to be entered into.[204]

(ii) Limitations on specific performance

Although the remedy of specific performance is discretionary, such discretion is only exercised in accordance with fixed and settled rules.

(i) Clean hands

Specific performance will not be granted in favour of a plaintiff who has not come to equity with clean hands and clear conscience.[205] Consequently, where there is evidence of fraud, mistake, misrepresentation or illegality[206] on the part of the plaintiff the Court will not degree the remedy. In *Birsingh v. Paramar*,[207] the appellant agreed to sell land to the respondent. The appellant defaulted and the buyer successfully sued for specific performance. On appeal, the appellant argued that the respondent had not shown himself ready and willing to perform the agreement in that he had not paid the deposit and could not be believed and therefore he had not come to Court with clean hands. The Court of Appeal dismissed the appellant's claim on the grounds that non-payment of the deposit in this particular case was not sufficient to disentitle the buyer from a remedy. The buyer had always been ready and willing to pay.

(ii) Laches or Delay

The equitable remedy of specific performance will not be decreed where the plaintiff has unreasonably delayed his request for relief and that delay affects the position of the defendant. In *Mzee Bin Ali v. Allibhay Narbhoy,*[208] the remedy was refused "on the ground that he (the plaintiff) had slept on his rights."

(iii) Hardship

The remedy being equitable, it will not be granted if it will cause hardship to the defendant or to an innocent third party.[209] In the Sudanese Case of *Mohammed Nasar Abdalla v. Ibrahim Abdalla el Garai*[210], the Court refused to order specific performance in a contract for the sale of land because the defendant was suffering from mental disorder and the plaintiff in all probability

---

197 *Hulton v. Watling* [1948] Ch.26; *Re Scott & Alverer's Contract* [1895] 2 Ch.603, 615

198 *Wolverhampton Corp. v. Eammons* [1901] 1 K.B. 515;*A-G v. Block* [1959] E.A. 180

199 *Rigby v. Connol* (1880) 14 Ch.D. 482; *De Francesco v. Barnum* (1890) 45 Ch.D.430; *Re Industrial Court Uganda* 1967(1) A.L.R. 119

200 *Flight v. Bolland* (1828) 4 Russ 298, E.R. 817; *Lumley v. Ravenscroft* [1895] 1 Q.B.D. 683.

201 *Fakoya v. St. Paul's Church, Shagamu* 1966(1) A.L.R. Comm. 461

202 Sale of Goods Act, Cap.79, S.52

203 *Cohen v. Roche* [1927] 1 K.B. 169, 181; *Behnke v. Bede shipping Co.* [1927] 1 K.B. 649, 661; *Sulaimani Mukasa v. Archmotors (Uganda) Ltd.* H.C.C.S. 169 of 1969; *Khalid v. Athanas Bros (Aden) Ltd.* [1968] E.A. 31; *Mawogola Farmers & Growers Ltd. v. Kayanja (No.2)* [1971] E.A. 272.

204 *C. H. Giles & Co. Ltd. v. Morris* [1972] 1 W.L.R. 307

205 *Forthergill v. Phillips* (1871) 6 Ch.App. 770, 778 per Lord Hatherley

206 *Motibhai Manji v. Khursid Begum* [1957] E.A.101; *Lamare v. Dixon* (1873) L.R. 6 H.L. 414

207 [1971] E.A. 209; *Shirmbai Bandali Jivan v. Moledina* 8 Z.L.R. 319

208 1 K.L.R. 58 (Kenya)

209 Spry, *op.cit. supra* n.195, p.183

210 1969 Sudan L.J.R. 116

knew of this. In *Taylor v. Arthur*,[211] the West African Court of Appeal refused the decree of specific performance on the ground that the legal title to the land, the subject-matter of the contract had passed to a *bona fide* purchaser for value without notice of the contract and that it would be most inequitable that there should be a possibility of his being evicted.[212] However, where there is evidence that the third party was aware of the contract at the time of purchase, specific performance will be decreed.[213] In general, the mere fact that the defendant will suffer hardship if specific performance is granted is not *perse* sufficient ground for refusing the decree. The exercise of the equitable discretion is premised on balancing the hardships: that which the plaintiff will suffer as against that which the defendant will suffer if the relief is denied or granted.[214]

The remedy of specific performance may be granted before the due date for performance of the contract. Thus in *Hasham v. Zenab*[215], a contract for the sale of two acres of land was agreed between the parties, the transaction to be completed within 6 months. Within minutes of signing the contract, the defendant tore it up on the basis that it did not reflect her intentions. The plaintiff sued for specific performance before the end of the six months period. The Privy Council upheld the decision of the Court of Appeal for Eastern Africa and granted the decree of specific performance effective from the due date agreed by the parties.

(c) Injunction

(i) Scope

An injunction is an order of the Court restraining a person from or ordering him to do a particular act. Normally the remedy is granted to enforce a negative stipulation in the contract where damages would not be an adequate remedy. The order is mandatory or positive where it compels a party to do an act; it is prohibitory or restrictive where it prohibits the doing of the act.

Even where there is no express negative stipulation, the court may infer one. Thus in *Metropolitan Electric Supply Co. v. Ginder*,[216] G agreed to take the whole of electric energy required by his premises from the plaintiffs. It was held that this was, in substance, an agreement not to take energy from any other person and could be enforced by injunction. In a contract for personal services a clear negative stipulation will be enforced by injunction in a suitable case. Thus in *Lumley v. Wagner*,[217] W agreed to sing at L's theatre and nowhere else. She did in fact sing elsewhere. It was held that she could be restrained by injunction from singing elsewhere or for a third party, Z. This case was followed in the Zanzibar Case, *Charlesworth v. MacDonald*.[218] Both parties were medical practitioners and M had responded to an advertisement by C for a medical assistant to help with his practice in Zanzibar. After some prolonged negotiations a contract was signed containing the phrase "the ordinary clause against practising must be drawn up". The contract was to last for three years. However, after one year, M left the practice to set up on his own account. No "ordinary clause" had been drawn up. C sued for an injunction to prevent M from practising as a doctor in Zanzibar.[219] The Court granted the injunction for the remainder of the three years. In so doing it drew a distinction between negative and positive stipulations. Furthermore in the Uganda Case of *Lalji Maranji v. Laxman Kanji*[220], the plaintiff advanced

---

211 (1947) 12 W.A.C.A. 174

212 See also *Safiatu Savage - John v. Daudu Jobe* (1944) 10 W.A.C.A. 144; *Tetteyfio v. Aguku* (1955) 14 W.A.C.A. 723

213 *Ajoke v. Oba* [1962] 1 All N.L.R. 73 (Nigeria)

214 *Hamby v. Northage* (1579) Cary 77; 21 E.R. 41

215 [1957] E.A. 38; [1960] E.A. 7; [1960] A.C. 316 REM 76 L.Q.R. 200

216 [1901] 2 Ch. 799

217 (1852) 1 De G.M. & G. 604

218 [1868 - 1918] Z.L.R. 81. See also *Charlesworth v. Illingworth* [1868 - 1918] Z.L.R. 70

219 See Chapter 10 for discussion of contracts in restraint of trade.

money to the defendant to buy a lorry. The agreement was that the defendant should then transport the plaintiff's cotton and in that way work off the amount of the loan. It was also provided that he should not use the lorry for any other purpose while the plaintiff had cotton to transport. The defendant did use the lorry for other purposes before the loan had been repaid. The Court granted the injunction, whose effect was to compel the defendant to work for the plaintiff. This is felt to be unconscionable and in other jurisdictions the unconscionable clause could be struck out and not enforced by the Court.[221]

(ii) Limits on injunction

Similar to the remedy of specific performance,[222] the remedy of injunction being equitable, will not be granted where (i) the plaintiff's hands are not clean; (ii) it will cause hardship; (iii) the plaintiff has delayed in seeking it. Furthermore, it is granted only in respect of legally enforceable rights[223] and a clearly defined and ascertainable right[224] or where there is sufficient interest in the subject-matter by the plaintiff.[225] The remedy is also only decreed if it can be effectively enforced.[226] An injunction will also not be granted in favour of a volunteer that is in contractual terms one who is not a party to the contract or has not provided consideration thereto.[227]

4. Limitation of action

The Limitation Act[228] limits the period of time within which an action in contract must be started or brought. With a simple contract the limitation period runs for six years from the date the cause of action accrues. This period also covers actions to enforce a recognizance, which is an acknowledgment in court that the promisor is bound to effect a certain payment unless a specified condition such as an appearance in court on a later day of payment of bail is made and also actions to enforce awards made by the Court.

Nevertheless, there are exceptions[229] to the six year period of limitation. These arise from instances where the plaintiff is put at a disadvantage by a personal disability, fraud, mistake or ignorance of a material fact.[230]

---

220 3 U.L.R. 159, applying the *Lumley Case, supra* n.217; see also *Warner Bros v. Nelson* [1937] 1 K.B. 309

221 See Uniform Commercial Code S.2 - 302 (U.S.A.) See further Dawson, 45 Michigan L. Rev. 253; Hodgin, *Law of Contract in East Africa* (1975) pp.227 - 8.

222 See *supra* notes 195 - 215 and text thereof

223 *Day v. Brownrigg* (1878) 10 Ch.D. 294

224 *Cother v. Midland Railway Co.* (1848) 2 P.H. 470; 41 E.R. 1025

225 *Maxwell v. Hogg* (1867) 2 Ch. App. 307, 317

226 *Eleko v. Baddeley* (1925) 6 N.L.R. 65

227 *Akenzua v. Benin Divisional Council* (1959) W.R.N.L.R. 1 (Nigeria)

228 Cap. 70 Laws of Uganda (1964 Edn.)

229 *Ibid.* Ss.22 - 31

230 *Mara Rita Godinho v. Jashbhai Patel* [1962] EA.242

INDEX

www.ingramcontent.com/pod-product-compliance
Lightning Source LLC
LaVergne TN
LVHW080045210926
848481LV00011B/3284
* 9 7 8 9 9 7 0 0 2 2 4 5 8 *